Stephen Bonsal,

Leon Dennen,

Henry Pozzi:

BALKAN READER

*First-hand reports by Western correspondents
and diplomats for over a century*

Edited by

Andrew L. Simon

Library of Congress Card Number: 00-110527

ISBN: 1-931313-00-8

Distributed by Ingram Book Company

Printed by Lightning Source, La Vergne, TN

Published by Simon Publications, P.O. Box 321, Safety Harbor, FL

Contents

Introduction 1

The Authors 5

Bulgaria

Stephen Bonsal; 1890: 11

Leon Dennen; 1945: 64

Yugoslavia

Stephen Bonsal; 1890: 105

Stephen Bonsal; 1920: 147

John F. Montgomery; 1947: 177

Henry Pozzi; 1935: 193

Ultimatum to Serbia: 224

Leon Dennen; 1945: 229

Romania

Stephen Bonsal; 1920: 253

Harry Hill Bandholtz; 1919: 261

Leon Dennen; 1945: 268

Macedonia and Albania

Stephen Bonsal; 1890:   283

Henry Pozzi; 1935:   315

Appendix

Repington; 1923:   333

Introduction

About 100 years ago, the Senator from Minnesota, Cushman Davis inquired from Stephen Bonsal, foreign correspondent of the *New York Herald*: "Why do not the people of Macedonia and of the Balkans generally, leave off killing one another, burning down each others' houses, and do what is right?"

"Unfortunately", Bonsal replied, "they are convinced that they are doing what is right. The blows they strike they believe are struck in the most righteous of causes. If they could only be inoculated with the virus of modern skepticism and leave off doing right so fervently, there might come about an era of peace in the Balkans—and certainly the population would increase. As full warrant and justification of their merciless warfare, the Christians point to Jushua the Conqueror of the land of Canaan, the Turks to Mahomet. The war of extermination is in large measure inspired by their spiritual advisers, and the luckless contestants find full warrant for it in Scriptures which they accept as Holy Writ."

As proven by the recent atrocities in the former Yugoslavia, little has changed in the temperament and in the inclination toward vengeful violence in the Balkans during the past century. It is also a regrettable fact, that Westerners in general, and Americans in particular, have no better clues about Balkan matters than their ancestors had one-hundred years ago.

This book is an attempt to describe the roots of the ethnic conflicts among the Balkan peoples through the unbiased eyes of experienced and knowledgeable Western observers. The authors of these 'on the spot' reports are foreign correspondents of American newspapers and British and American diplomats familiar with the region. The single exception is Henry Pozzi — erstwhile secret agent — foreign correspondent of the respected French newspaper, *Le Temps*. Their experiences range in time from the late 1880s to the end of World War II in 1945. By coincidence, their visits to the Balkans coincide with some major cataclysms in the region: Bonsal soon after the Russo-Turkish war and the Treaty of San Stefano, Bandholtz, Pozzi, Montgomery and Repington after WW1 and Dennen at the end of WW2.

Their books, published between 1932 and 1947, are similar in one aspect: They are long out of print.

Most of these books were written on a much broader scope than what is included here. Only those chapters were selected from these books that deal directly with the authors' personal experiences in the Balkans. One exception is Dennen's description of the Warsaw uprising and the Soviet non-response, which is a necessary and telling prelude to what was to happen in the Balkan countries at the time of the Soviet occupation.

The combination of these reports and reminiscences, spread over time and space, fit together well. They provide a series of historical snapshots, and give an overall glimpse of the background of the multitude of problems that changed but little in this period. This is not intended to be a history book. Rather, it is 'history in the raw'. On the spot recollections, conversations with participants of events that often became fossilized facts — true or false — that later appear in history books.

There is no scarcity in history books on the Balkan countries. A number of scholarly books were written on the topics beginning with Emile de Laveleye's *The Balkan Peninsula* (1887), Ferdinand Schevill's *The History of the Balkan Peninsula, from the Earliest Times to the Present* (1933) to the recent *Columbia History of Eastern Europe in the Twentieth Century* (1992). They all provide a great background on the region's history. Some of the writers even visited the region before they set out to write. Roy Trevor's *My Balkan Tour: An Account of Some Journeying and Adventures in the Near East, together with a descriptive and historical account of Bosnia & Herzegovina, Dalmatia, Croatia and the Kingdom of Montenegro* (1911) and William Sloane's *The Balkans: a Laboratory of History* (1914) which was written after the Columbia University professor visited the area on three occasions between 1903 and 1910. But some books written in a time of conflicts may be strongly biased, such as Pierre Renouvin's *The Immediate Origins of the War* (1928), and P. B. Stoyan's *Spotlights on the Balkans*,(1940). Even Richard Holbrook's *To End a War* (1998) may well end up in this category.

The habitual unbiased and pedantic style of Western historians is not well equipped to describe the history of the Balkans. How does one explain the endless series of fratricidal political murders and genocidal blood-baths in a homogenized and pasteurized manner to readers who can not conceptualize blood-feuds beyond the tales about the McCoys and the Hatfields? In stark contrast, just across the cultural/political divide, in Hungary's thousand-year history no more than a handful of murdered statesmen maybe brought up: Laszlo Hunyadi, George Martinuzzi, Miklos Zrinyi, Stephen Tisza, and, of course the Archduke killed by a Serb.

It may not be a *politically correct* statement, but by their prior experience in history the people of the Balkans — Romanians, Albanians, Macedonians, Montenegins, Bulgars, Serbs, Greeks, Dalmatians and the rest are different from their Western counterparts. They had to learn to live as the Turks' "Christian dogs" and became accustomed to the doubtful morality that came with it. Treachery, duplicity and perfidy are survival skills. So it is not surprising that, for instance, it was said about a British diplomat posted in Bulgaria in 1921: "He doesn't think much of the various folks in this part of the world ... They usually lie, and always lie about each other".

The people of the Balkans have plenty of reasons to be different. For 500 years they were subjected to cruel ethnic and religious oppression by the Ottomans. During these centuries they were excluded from the Western experience of Renaissance, Reformation and Enlightenment. They are still mired in their calcified Orthodox Christian religion that sanctifies xenophobia in place of brotherly love. Their historical experiences with the Western countries give them no reason to trust. Ever since the Battle of Mohács in 1526, when their immediate neighbor, Hungary, has became a Habsburg dominion, France, for instance, was in frequent alliance with the Turks. Consequently, fortified by the French alliance, the Moslems have done their best to keep their Christian subjects enchained. At the end of the Turko-Russian War, when the Balkan's people had a chance to gain their freedom in 1878 by the San Stefano Treaty, the British saved the day for Turkey few months later by the patently unjust Peace of Berlin. France's blind support of the grandiose Serb dreams alter WW 1 caused the subjugation of Croats, Bosnians, Kosovars and others. Their sufferings, that culminated in the 1990s, still go on. At the end of WW2, British and French policy handed the region to the Communists, causing untold misery. The people of the Balkans have plenty of reasons to distrust the West.

After reading these stories, one may ask: Will they ever live in peace? Can they? It much depends on the Western nations. Will they give them a chance to prosper? Or will they be forgotten and left to their own devices? What the future brings we do not know. One thing is certain: The nations of the Balkans will not *celebrate diversity* for many years to come.

The Authors

The backgrounds of the authors are described below. The precise titles and publication data of their works from which the quotations are made are given where they appear in the following chapters.

Stephen Bonsal Jr. (1865 - 1951), the son of Stephen and Frances (Leigh) Bonsal, was born in Baltimore, Maryland, and died in Georgetown D.C.. His Quaker ancestors came from England with William Pitt. He married Henrietta Fairfax Morris, daughter of novelist Gouverneur Morris; they had four children.

Bonsal had a colorful career as a foreign correspondent of major New York newspapers, as a writer and as a diplomat. Several of his books contained his interpretation of the events leading up to the writing of the Treaties of Paris after World War I. Other events covered by Bonsal as a reporter included the Macedonian Uprising of 1890, while he was a foreign correspondent of the New York *Herald* stationed in Vienna. For 21 months, he served as the Herald's Balkan correspondent after his Vienna assignment. Later, as a foreign correspondent of the *New York Times,* he covered the Chino-Japanese War of 1895, and the Spanish American War of 1898. With the exception of Persia, he has visited every country of the world.

Bonsal's government assignments included Secretary of Legation and Chargé d'Affaires in Madrid, Tokyo, and Seoul from 1893 to 1897, Commissioner of Public Utilities in the Philippines in 1914, and American representative of the Congress of Oppressed Nationalities in Paris, in 1918. During World War I, Bonsal served as a colonel in the American Expeditionary Forces, directing of the forerunner of "psychological warfare": Propaganda efforts to weaken the resolve of the soldiers of the Central Powers. He knew President Wilson's assistant, Col. Edward House from before the war, and at the beginning of the Armistice negotiations, the Colonel had asked that he be assigned to him. After first serving as an expert on the Balkans, he was soon assigned to maintain liaison with the representative delegations of all but the major nations. In retrospect there hardly seems to have been an international event of the late 19th and earlier 20th century that

Bonsal did not witness either as a reporter or a member of a government mission.

After World War I, Bonsal was urged to publish his diaries. Countering his objection that this might be indiscreet on the part of a professional writer who had been given access to confidential information, President Wilson told him, "You can't be too indiscreet for me. I give you full absolution in advance." He held out against their friends pleas to publish his notes until it became clear to his informed mind that the world is about to repeat the same mistakes that led to the tragedy of Versailles. Many of the important figures as Clemenceau, Lloyd George, Balfour, Smuts, and Masaryk were more than mere names to Bonsal, they were acquaintances or warm personal friends. He had a genius for self-effacement, or, using Colonel House's term: "low visibility". His diary, written up day by day, include not only actual notes taken during meetings, but also the personal and human side of the interchanges. To preserve their integrity, Bonsal made no attempts to cover up mistaken judgements or even to improve the records literary style. They are original source documents of genuine historical importance.

His important literary contributions to the analysis of international affairs include: *Morocco as It is: With an Account of Sir Charles Euan Smith's Recent Mission to Fez*, (1893), *The Real Condition of Cuba* (1897), *Fight of Santiago* (1899), *The American Mediterranean* (1912), *Edward Fitzgerald Beale, a Pioneer in the Path of Empire, 1822 – 1903* (1912), *Heyday in a Vanished Land*, (1937), *Unfinished Business, Paris Versailles 1919 –* for this he got a Pulitzer Price in 1944; *When the French were Here: A Narrative of the Sojourn of the French Forces in America, and their Contribution to the Yorktown Campaign* (1945), *Suitors and Suppliants – the Little Nations at Versailles* (1946), *The Cause of Liberty: The Story of the American Revolution* (1947).

Harry Hill Bandholtz (1864 – 1925) had a distinguished career in the United States Army. Born in Columbine, Michigan, he graduated at West Point in 1890. His name first appears in the annals of the American Military Police when he was appointed as Deputy Chief of the 6th Cavalry Constabulary, based in the Philippines. On June 30, 1907 Colonel Bandholtz was promoted to be the Chief of Constabulary with the rank of Brigadier General, still stationed in the Philippines. This assignment ended on September 1, 1913.

On September 27, 1918, Bandholtz was appointed Provost Marshal General with the American Expeditionary Forces in France. On August 1919 he was relieved of duty by orders of General Pershing and assigned to the Assistant Secretary of State, American Commission to Negotiate Peace – at the Hotel Crillon in Paris – for duty. Subsequently, he was sent as the American Member of the Inter-Allied Military Commission to Budapest with the assignment to enforce the orders of the Supreme Council to Romania to withdraw from Hungary.

After his departure from Budapest in early March, 1920, a Hungarian paper wrote: "The members of the American Military Mission and their chief, General Bandholtz, are soon leaving our capital, probably about the fifteenth of February. The affairs of the Mission are now being handed over to the American High Commissioner. The Magyars will always remember General Bandholtz with the feelings of deepest gratitude, as there is such a lot we must be thankful for to him and to the Mission. In the days of our profound sorrow, during the occupation of our country by the Roumanians, it was he who stood up for our righteous cause, and we don't know of any instance when he did not defend us. General Bandholtz persuaded the Roumanians to evacuate Transdanubia and the territories between the Danube and the Tisza, and it is owing to him that the Roumanians did not pillage our museums. The General personally sealed the entrance of our National Museum. Also we owe it to the energetic intervention of the Mission, that the Roumanians' endless efforts to liberate arrested Communists were frustrated. was General Bandholtz who initiated the American actions of benevolence and hereby dried a sea of tears on the Hungarian faces."

General Bandholtz has left Europe on August 3, 1919. After his diplomatic assignment, Bandholtz attempted to establish a permanent Military Police Corps in the U.S. Army. Despite Pershing's support, the Act failed in Congress. He retired from the Army in 1923 as a Major General. After his death, his wife, Inez Claire Bandholtz has given his detailed diaries to Fritz-Konrad Krüger, a professor of History and Political Science at Wittenberg College in Ohio, who has prepared it for publication. The book, entitled *An Undiplomatic Diary* was first published by Columbia University Press in 1932[1].

John Flournoy Montgomery (1878 - 1954) was appointed in 1933 to his ministerial post, "U. S. Envoy Extraordinary and Plenipotentiary to Hungary" by President Roosevelt to find out what precisely was going on in that tinder-box region of Europe. He lived in Hungary for eight years, knew and liked Hungarians of every political persuasion, class and interest – and his unusually well-informed book, *Hungary – the Unwilling Satellite* is of the utmost importance to all who are interested in foreign relations, modern history and the politics of our time. Inserted as an Appendix, he included an apparently unrelated topic to the subject of his book: *The Secret Contacts Between King Alexander of Yugoslavia and Mussolini*, which he has obtained from an anonymous source.

Leon Dennen (1907 - 1974) was born in New York City. As a child he lived in Russia, Poland, and other European countries. He is a graduate of a Gymnasium in Russia-Poland, attended the College of the City of New York. and has had considerable other university work both here and abroad. Because of his diversified background, he spoke Russian, Polish, German, Yiddish, and Hebrew fluently and had a knowledge of the Balkan Slavic languages.

In 1945, Dennen was a contributing editor of the *New Leader* and director of public relations in charge of foreign affairs for the League of Human Rights (American Federation of Labor). He was the author of a book entitled *Where the Ghetto Ends* and has also translated David Dallin's *Soviet Russia's Foreign Policy*.

While co-operating with the labor and anti-Nazi underground movement in the Balkans, Leon Dennen gathered the material for this book, *Trouble Zone*. He has written extensively on European affairs for the *American Mercury, Annals of the American Academy of Political and Social Science*, the *Nation*, and *New Europe*.

Henry Pozzi (1879 - 1946) was of an old French Protestant family. His mother was English, a direct descendant of Hamden. For nearly thirty

1   It is on the market today.

years, Pozzi was a member of the French and English intelligence services in the Balkans and Central Europe. For ten years following that, he worked as a foreign correspondent of the Paris newspaper, *Le Temps*. In1935 he published an English translation of his book, *Black Hand over Europe*, the original French title being *La Guerre Revient*. In that, he claimed to have first hand information about Serbia planning to start WW1 months before the Sarajevo assassination. In his book he demonstrated how the Yugoslav state was created to promote Serbian domination over her surrounding neighbors, and revealed the existence of the secret ultra-nationalist organizations of the Serbs.

Charles à Court Repington was born into the British aristocracy. Educated at Eton, served as a Lieutenant-Colonel in the British Army, sometime intelligence operative, British diplomat Repington was a keen observer of European politics during the early part of the twentieth century. After WW1, Repington's *Vestigia: Reminiscences of Peace and War* (Boston: Houghton- Mifflin, 1919) and his monumental two volume book *The First World War, 1914 - 1918: Personal Experiences* (London: Constable & Co. 1920; Boston: Houghton - Mifflin, 1921) made him a celebrated author throughout the world. In 1921 he traveled extensively throughout Europe, visiting most major capital cities. He met with kings and prime ministers, diplomats and political leaders in most European countries. His diary, written during these visits and published under the title *After the War*, (Boston: Houghton-Mifflin, 1922) records his personal experiences, impressions and his conversations with many influential persons. In his Preface he outlined his reasons for writing the book:

"When the Peace Treaties, with one exception, were ratified and in full operation, I felt the need of a wander-year in order to acquaint myself with the new personalities and new ideas which the great war-storm had thrown up to the surface of affairs in continental Europe. It was useless to content oneself with archaic notions when all was changed, if one wished to keep abreast with the times, and there was no better way to discover what was happening than to go and see for oneself."

"A mission suggested to me by Viscount Burnham enabled me to carry out my wish under favourable conditions. To him, and to many other good friends at home and abroad, my thanks are due for their confidence, their hospitality, and their assistance. Later in the year the opportunity was presented of attending the Washington Conference for the Limitation of Armaments. I offer this diary as a small contribution to the knowledge of people and events in the world of to-day in the hope that it may aid my readers to judge for themselves the proper direction of foreign policy in the future."

Repington's unconditional support by the British diplomatic establishment in all European capitals suggests that he was more than a traveling writer of history books or a mere correspondent of the *Daily Telegraph*. He had a level of access to political and governmental leaders that suggests a roving British ambassador, rather than that of a well known and respected author. Commander of the Order of Sts. Michael & George—a title usually given to British diplomats—Commander of the Belgian Order of Leopold, Officer of the French Legion of Honour suggests a respected diplomatic background. Without doubt, he was an insider at the British Foreign Office. He spent a great effort in each country to assess the potentials of trade with Britain. According to his diary, he often reported to the British Foreign Office during his travels. His remarks and comments clearly demonstrate his deep insight into Europe's future political problems.

Only Chapter VII is included in this excerpt [pages 154 through 175]. It describes Repington's visit to Budapest between April 15 and 21, 1921. It is included here in the Appendix to illustrate the enormous difference in social and political life—even after a devastating war and huge losses of territory—across the cultural divide, between the Balkan countries on one side and Central Europe on the other.

Bulgaria

Stephen Bonsal; 1890:

Excerpts from *Heyday in a Vanished World – Adventures of a Foreign Correspondent at the Turn of the Century*; New York: W. W. Norton & Co. Inc. 1937.

[In the previous chapter, Bonsal described his experiences in Vienna, where he worked as the correspondent of the New York Herald. The owner of paper, James Gordon Bennett, otherwise known as the Commodore[1], has dismissed all his European correspondents, but on the next day, he rehired Bonsal. This conversation is described below. – Ed.]

"That's good," he [the Commodore] brightened. "Well, I have made plans for YOU that is, if you are footloose."

I assured him that I was superlatively footloose, and then the Commodore went on. "I have not lost interest in European conditions, but I think our system of stable correspondents and a constant flow of cables and letters from the capitals has not worked out very well, so I am going to try another scheme, and if you are willing I shall begin with you. I would like you to leave tonight on the Orient Express, and take charge of the Balkans. If you pass by the cashier's window, you will find I have instructed him to let you have what money you need. Charley Christianson (this was a young Scandinavian, long a cabin boy on the *Namouna*, who had now become Bennett's factotum) will secure your tickets and reservations and leave them at your hotel."

"Instructions?" I asked.

---

1   Bennett spent most of his time on his oceangoing yacht, the Namouna. His lofty naval title was accorded by the New York Yacht Club.

"Well, I shall expect you to take charge of the Balkans and be on hand whenever and wherever anything happens. I advise you to go now directly to Sofia. Wire me to the secret code address when you arrive. There is a promising rumpus going on, as you know, in Macedonia, and in Bulgaria Prince Ferdinand may be kidnaped, as was his predecessor, any moment. When things quiet down, of course you can come back to Vienna where your good friend Taafe[2] will take care of you and when you go on to Constantinople I will send you a letter to Tashin Pasha, he is the Sultan's right-hand-man, and can be useful. Of course you have complete liberty of movement. You can swing back and forth as you please between Vienna and the Bosphorus, that is your beat. But if and when Hell breaks loose in that territory well, I shall expect you to be on the spot."

I assured him I would do my best and that I was duly flattered by his confidence, and I was being dismissed when the Commodore had another thought. "Do you correspond with Billy Reick?" he inquired.

"No," I answered. "He is my very good friend, so we never write."

Reick was Bennett's head man in New York, his managing editor in fact, though very wisely he never assumed the honorific title.

"Well, don't write Reick or any of the other men. Envelop your mission in mystery. Only turn up when the fireworks begin."

I had a good laugh going down the stairs... I had heard of Mr. Bennett's extraordinary jealousy of the New York office, and how he loved to mystify and even deceive those who worked there. Even in the years when he had agents scattered pretty generally throughout the world, he would never let New York have a complete list. What he enjoyed more than anything else, perhaps, was to have the searchlight of world interest focus, let us say for a moment, upon Madagascar and get a despairing cry from New York about the impossibility of securing news from that distant point and then be able

---

2   Earlier, he was Prime Minister of Austria, who gave Bonsal an exclusive interview that caused quite a stir. - Ed.

to reply, "I knew of course what was coming; I have had my man in Tamatave waiting these three months. You will have five thousand words about it at least for the late edition."

Often, but not always, the Commodore exhibited a wonderful prescience in these matters and a foreknowledge of things that were to come. And when he had rescued Reick from real or feigned despair, he would preen his feathers and pat himself on the back in the most amusing and boyish manner. But sometimes the big events that he had anticipated did not come off, and then his agent in some faraway, somnolent place drifted into the discard of the forgotten men. Henry M. Stanley[3], the greatest of the Commodore's correspondents, once told me a story, that at the time struck me as amusing, of a *Herald* man, a colleague of his, who was forgotten in Persia, and being without funds to return home, joined a caravan of Mecca pilgrims who fed him well because he acted the part of a holy, howling dervish to perfection. Later on I was to be forgotten too in many strange lands, but for the moment I basked in the great man's favor and it was very pleasant.

As I passed through Vienna on my way to the fabulous Balkans I stopped off for a few hours and gave another banquet to which my friends had been summoned by wire. Lady Hamilton was there and Ilka Palmay and "Rudi" Kinsky and Countess O'Sullivan, the name by which Charlotte Wolters, the great tragedienne, was disguised in private life. She called down blessings from heaven upon her *edles Indianer Kind...*

10. IN THE BALKANS

When they were committed to my charge in the summary manner I have indicated, I knew very little about the Balkans range, and, despite the flood of news that has been poured forth from that region in the last thirty years, some of my readers may still be in the same plight. Of course I knew the catchwords, and during my stay in Vienna I had forwarded much informa-

3   Of the Dr. Livingstone fame.

tion from these distressed lands, but it was, I fear, mostly based on the flashes of the agency which we called, and not without reason, the Agence Volcanique, though that was not its name. But, of course, I did not have the remotest idea of what the Balkans and the Balkan peoples, with whom I was to be confronted, looked like. I was soon to learn by harsh personal contact, and in the course of the next two years I crossed and recrossed the length and breadth of the peninsula half a dozen times, and I was to become more familiar with its outstanding features, geographical as well as political, than with those of my native land.

While, of course, geographers are by no means in perfect agreement, these are the generally accepted metes and bounds of the peninsula. Its northern boundary extends from the Kilia mouth of the Danube (where it enters the Black Sea) to the Adriatic near Fiume. On the east it is bounded by the Black Sea, the Sea of Marmora and the Aegean, on the south by the Mediterranean, the Ionian Sea and the Adriatic; and the whole looks rather like an inverted pyramid, with the great river courses, the Danube, the Save, and the Kalpa, romping through it. Apart from the valleys of the Danube and the Maritza, the region is very mountainous, and this fact is important. I wish I could recall the name of the geographer, also a philosopher, who stated that the character of the inhabitants depends upon the rugosity of the land they occupy. Mountain peoples, he insists, have a rugose or belligerent character. This man understood and in a sentence explained the Balkan peoples.

The great chain of the Rhodope Mountains traverses the center of the peninsula, shooting out spurs both towards the Aegean and the Black Seas. Further west rise the lofty Shar Dagh and the mountains of Montenegro and Albania. Owing to this distribution of the mountain chain, the rivers flow generally in a southeasterly direction, but the Maritza and the Vardar turn to the south and enter the Aegean.

The summers are exceedingly hot and the winters, although short, are intensely cold. Little wonder that the Latin poets, including Ovid who was exiled to Thrace, complained of the northeast winds that blow so frequently. But October and November, before the great winds begin to blow, are wonderful months indeed.

The population at this time (1889) was about twenty-one million, mixed as to race, confusing and antagonistic as to customs, and irreconcilably divided by religious dissensions. The Turks numbered barely two million, and they were decreasing, while the Slavonic population was increasing rapidly. Among the ethnic fragments were the or Tzintzars, or Arumani[4] as they call themselves, who according to tradition were left behind when the Romans abandoned Dacia. The Albanians, generally thought to be a remnant of the primitive Illyrian population, were and are still seated along the Adriatic littoral from the southern frontier of Montenegro to the northern boundary of Greece; for obvious political reasons these peoples were greatly encouraged in their racial aspirations by the Turks. The Greeks, who according to the wise pundits of the Berlin Congress (1878) controlled the whole country, I found in the minority almost everywhere. Seafaring men and traders as a general thing, they clung to the coast or to the towns and commercial centers. The Jews, while they composed at least half of the population of Salonica, were very sparsely scattered throughout the country districts, and the gypsies in small groups were to be found practically everywhere.

I shall not endeavor to go into details as to the many Slavic tribes; as will appear later, this is an impossible task, but there were certainly ten million of them divided into many discordant groups. The Armenians also were quite numerous in the commercial centers, but they were shortly to be greatly reduced by the massacres of 1896. Including about half the Albanians and the converted Pomaks, of whom more later, the Moslem population must have numbered about three million. Since at this time, as now, all religious and political questions were intimately connected, I shall only endeavor to assort them as it becomes necessary later on. The church feuds of the Greek Patriarch and of the Bulgar Exarch were quite as disturbing to the peace of the peninsula as were those of the temporal Powers. The Armenians, unfortunately, had two patriarchs, representing an unhappy schism, and the Roman Catholic Church had many followers in Dalmatia and Croatia, and among the Gheg tribes of Albania, and in the Greek Islands off the coast. To make confusion worse confounded, in Macedonia and in sev-

---

4   The 'tradition' of Roman heritage did not stand up to scientific analysis. -Ed.

eral other districts were to be found not a few members of the Uniate Church, accepting dogma from Rome but with Greek Orthodox rites.

As to language, the peninsula was a veritable Tower of Babel. The Bulgarian, as a written language, was just emerging from the monastic retreats where it had taken refuge and been preserved during the Dark Ages. Turkish and Greek were, of course, the only languages officially recognized. The Albanian speech, handed down possibly from the ancient Illyrians, was just discovered and is still the most fascinating study of philologists, to whom we shall leave it.

Before the coming of the Slavonic tribes in the fourth century, the Roman Empire was in more or less complete control of all the lands south of the Danube. Driven back by the onset of these migratory tribes, the Thracians and the Albanians took refuge in the mountains, while the Greeks were pushed to the seacoast and the near-lying islands. The Bulgars only came in numbers towards the end of the seventh century, and under the great Tsar Simeon they ruled from the Adriatic to the Black Sea, and to this period hark back the dreams of a Greater Bulgaria that have been the cause of so much bloodshed in our day. After Ivan Assen II (1230), the Bulgarian Empire declined, and then came the period of Serbian dominance under Stefan Dushan, who extended his power over the greater part of the peninsula. But shortly after his death in 1391 his empire, too, disintegrated. His day of power and of glory is, of course, the foundation of the Greater Serbia idea.

Then came the conquering Ottoman Turks under Mahomet II, 1460 or thereabouts. Their empire increased in power and extent under Suleiman the Magnificent (as a particular favor, I was once shown his wonderful war tent in Stamboul), but after the defeat before Vienna, their power also declined (1683). Characteristic of the decaying power of the Turks was the formation of practically independent *pashaliks* within the realm. Later, in 1829, Greece became independent; Serbia, nominally a tributary principality, in 1830. But the great changes in the political complexion of the peninsula came as the result of the Russo-Turkish war in 1878 and the arrangements that were made at San Stefano and modified by the Congress of Berlin. Bosnia and Herzegovina came under the wing of the Dual Monarchy, Roumania was recognized as a kingdom in 1881, Serbia in 1882, and Bulgaria, as a principality with the Sultan a nominal suzerain.

Practically this was the Balkan situation as I entered upon it. Of course even an eye as unskilled as mine can see many gaps in this picture, but it should convey an idea of the racial, political and religious antagonisms which made of the Balkans the cockpit of Europe, from which the World War at long last emerged. It should, however, be noted that even in these discordant days a voice for conciliation was heard. Under Ristich, the Serbian statesman, as early as 1877, attempts were made to confederate the Balkan peoples, but then, as later, they failed, and in view of the increased animosities that now prevail and divide this unhappy region of the world, anything like reconciliation would seem impossible in the near future.

On reaching Sofia, I found the "City of Wisdom," the head center and the source of canards which amused or affrighted the world, and depressed or exhilarated the stock and grain markets.

The heat was intolerable, about 100 degrees Fahrenheit in the shade, but the atmosphere of the political world was still more torrid. Stransky and Salabashoff had resigned from the ministry rather than sign the death warrant of Panitza; but Stambouloff had prevailed with the Prince, and the hero of the Serbian War was shot, tethered to a tree like a traitor, on the windy plain without the city. Prince Ferdinand had gone to Carlsbad, Stambouloff was known vaguely to be somewhere on the shores of the Black Sea, the remaining ministers were recruiting their health at the various thermal springs scattered through the Balkans, and Bulgaria apparently was ruling itself.

The town was thronged with the correspondents of world newspapers, and a confusion of tongues reigned in the cafés. The ex-ministers – and their name was legion – worked through the early morning at the great Bulgarian dictionary, which was the only means of livelihood for politicians out of office, slept through the noonday heat, and in the evening assembled in the Cafe Panachoff to read the *Times* and *Le Temps* by the aid of pocket dictionaries, and concluded the evening with checkers and tric-trac, the while as uncommunicative as schools of fish. Army officers, looking very fresh and cool in their white duck uniforms, sat about in the public garden, sipping successively glasses of grenadine, slivovitz, raki, and mastique, and telling in undertones how grandly Kosta Panitza had led the Macedonian "brigade of bandits" to the storming of Pirot, which they captured at the point of the yataghan. In the cool of the evening the newspaper "specials" could be seen giving their Barb ponies gentle "breathers" on the plain beneath snow-crested Mount Witosh, preparing for the hour when the news that the world was awaiting would come, that Stambouloff was assassinated, that Ferdinand had abdicated, that the independence of the principality had been declared, or that the Russians were crossing the Danube – awaiting the great news that would send them out like a flight of hawks through the night on a mad race for the wire which encircles the world, and which could only be entrusted safely with a dispatch at Pirot, a hundred miles away, across the Serbian frontier.

Every morning there came a surprise which sent the "special" to his stables, and every evening some bitter disappointment which sent him to bed or to the baccarat tables. Strange signs and symbols appeared on the political horizon, but the great event hung fire. The little stunted willow where Panitza had been shot began to play an important if objective role in politics. One morning it displayed a banner with a touching tribute to the worth of the patriot or traitor who had died so bravely in its shadow. There followed on the next day another banner bearing a threat and a menace to the life of the Prince. The official and diplomatic world was aghast to see waving from the willow this black ominous banner with the regicidal device, *Tirani zai tooka ste luidi grabot ne Fernanda*. ("Tyrant! know here will be the grave of Ferdinand.") Then it was decided to cut down the tree which bore such anti-dynastic fruit, but when the soldiers reached the plain with axes, the willow had disappeared.

The arrival of a Georgian prince and an ex-chamberlain of the Great White Tsar furnished an amusing interlude in the succession of more serious scares. With singularly tenacious filial piety, the Prince had come, he claimed, to visit the tombs of his ancestors who were sleeping in a cairn near Sofia. Their resting-place had been neglected by his forefathers for more than a thousand years, yet he had come to put it in some repair, and to plant a few rose bushes. But the Prefect of Police packed him off to the frontier, sandwiched between gendarmes, without as much as a short delay for breakfast.

News came through strange channels in Bulgaria. As we slept in the hotel, proclamations with mourning bands would flutter in through the transom in the most mysterious manner, and not rarely the "special" would find neatly tucked away in his boots outside the door the prophecy of a coming pronunciamento. In opera, at least, the Barber of Seville was a remarkable gossip and agent of rumor; in real life his colleague of Sofia was an inveterate disseminator of news. He was at once the stumbling block and the mainstay of the "special." His news was rarely "ready for the wire," but at the same time his information could not be dispensed with. A sign in a dozen tongues in Mustapha's shop told that a "silent shave," without conversation, cost ten piastres; but the gossipy shave – which Mustapha advised - with a cigarette and *les dessous* of the latest political move, what Mustapha heard from Yildiz Kiosk, from Belgrade, Moscow, or the Minister-President, the creamy Turkish coffee, with which the canard was washed down, and the salaam with which the rather inhuman treatment of your chin was gracefully rounded off, cost thirty piastres, and was cheap at the price.

Once at midnight I left Sofia, to cross the Balkans and find M. Stambouloff in the vague somewhere in which, according to the Foreign Office, he was awaiting the course of events, and especially the upshot of the interview between the Tsar and the German Emperor, which was soon to take place at Peterhof. I had purchased half a dozen scraggy and sorry-looking ponies that, however, were reputed to climb mountains like goats, and procured a guide who knew the Balkans well.

By daybreak we reached the mountains and later the Petrus *han*, or inn, famous for its bad food and wide sweeping view. Though I came with letters-patent from the Foreign Office, which Mihail, my guide, displayed with great pride to everybody we met and would naturally have been taken for a friend of Stambouloff's government, the sturdy proprietor of the *han* replied to my question, as to what sentiment of the people toward Russia really was, as follows:

"*Gospodin Amerikanitz* (Mr. American), we have not forgotten our brave brothers who took away the heathen fez, and gave us the Christian kalpak to wear. When we pray, we pray for the soul of the Tsar Liberator. Gospodin Amerikanitz, we love and revere Russia." During my subsequent journeyings through Bulgaria, I never heard anything which made me change my belief that the voice of the sturdy little keeper of the Petrus *han* was the voice of the great silent majority of Bulgarians. As we trotted along the road which, until we reached Klissourah, was the historic highway between Belgrade and Stamboul, I noticed that the few huts that we saw were generally a mile away from the road, and that the doors were so low one must enter crawling on hands and knees. Mihail explained, with a grin of gratification, that this state of things was only a memory and a reminder of the unhappy days of Turkish domination, that the hovels were hidden away as much as possible from sight of the road in order that the peasants might escape the requisition for *mouna*, or provisions, of the passing Pasha, and that the doors were cut so low that the Effendi might not enter the houses and carry off whatever chanced to please his looting fancy.

I did not know whether Mihail was a good guide, but his Bulgarian was limpid, and every now and then through the remnants of the Russian that Stepniak had imparted to me the previous year in London I grasped his meaning. In his earlier days Prince Alexander had sent him to Vienna to learn the veterinary art. In this he had not progressed very far but he had acquired a few words, key words they proved to be, of Viennese, and these helped to clear up several difficult situations later on. Everything looked all right as we left Sofia, but in the morning I was surprised and not a little exasperated to find that the tails of my ponies, the only good points they had, were gone. They had disappeared during the night, and as with daylight the horseflies renewed their cruel activities, all the poor animals could do was to swish at them with their pitifully shortened stumps.

I never was more angry in my life, and not at all pacified by Mihail's statement, which seemed so completely satisfactory to him, that he was engaged to be married and that his bride was awaiting him at our next halt! I am afraid I treated Mihail very roughly, and his protest after the fracas to the effect that I was entirely ignorant of Bulgarian customs was undoubtedly true. Finally he was successful in conveying to me the idea that when a man in Bulgaria became engaged the proper way to proclaim his good fortune to the world was to cut off the tails of his horses and present them to the lady of his choice to be entwined with her own coarse long hair. My statement that, after all, the ponies belonged to me did not carry conviction, and for the next three days the unfortunate animals suffered terribly from the onslaught of ravenous bluebottle flies, against which they had been robbed of their natural means of defense. Of course I made him tie the tails back, but they were switched off and at last, as on so many subsequent occasions, I had to submit and conform to the custom of the country.

On the evening of the second day we reached Klissourah, and Mihail dashed off after his sweetheart, brandishing in the air what remained of his booty of pony hair. The ostler of the *han*, after having conveyed in pantomine the information that I was at liberty to utilize his head as a foot-stool if it should so please me, greeted the ponies with an effusive kiss, and inquired if they had been "good boys." My pony replied with an affirmative whinny, whereupon the delighted ostler grasped him firmly by the ears, and pulled with all his might, until the joints of the ears cracked. This operation is popularly supposed in the Balkans to bring surcease to a pony's headache resulting from his pounding along the rough roads, and certainly they are very fond of it, and insist upon its being gone through with at every post station.

That evening the notables of Klissourah assembled on the green beside the han. It was a holiday. The pretty but dull-looking girls danced the *hora*, a Grecian dance, which has, however, become acclimated throughout the Balkan countries. It is rather a rhythmic march, *a quatre temps*, than a dance. The arms of the dancers, who are drawn up in a single or double line, cross and rest around the neighbor's waist. Between the dances a minstrel, who was popularly supposed to have lived several centuries, twanged away on the one-stringed monotonous *gusle* the epics of the country celebrating the champions of Bulgarian liberty, from the days of Tsar Simeon down to the Battenberg Prince who, as the epic ran in about the thousandth stanza, "stooped to tie the latchet of his Bulgarski brogans on the battlefield of Slivnitza, so little did he fear the Serbskis."

In the course of the evening I was initiated by the village gossips into the mysteries of Mihail's love affair which, as it reveals a novel custom, never departed from in the Balkans of that day, seems worthy to be told. He was in love with Rayka, a girl who was not pretty, but endowed with great ca-pacity for work. She had made many journeys with gangs of working peo-ple from Klissourah into Roumania, and was supposed to have amassed a dot amounting to nearly twenty pounds Turkish, which she had buried away in the ground. She loved Mihail, and what his sentiments were the barefaced robbery of my ponies' tails plainly revealed. Still, the ceremony could not come off, because Rayka had an elder sister who did not as yet have the right to wear a head-covering which only comes to the Bulgarian girl with matrimony, and no well-brought-up girl would marry, her elder sister being still a spinster. I was presented to the elder sister, and was surprised to find her very beautiful; her hair was long and black as the raven's wing; her eyes soft, melting, and she was altogether charming. I immediately advised Mihail not to delay the ceremony any longer, but to conform to the custom of the country and marry the simply adorable elder sister. This he absolutely refused to do, saying that Magda was very idle, had not accumulated a dot, but spent her time dancing and listening to the weird morbid music of the Tsiganes, as they played in the quarter of the village allotted to them. So Mihail is doubtless a bachelor still. Romantic love does not flourish in the Balkans, as I found out later on.

The next day, diverging from the Belgrade road, we bore off to the east, along bridlepaths and sheep tracks, toward the Danube. The heat was terrific, and the sad fate of the Roumski traveler, who in these high mountain lands, with the rarefied atmosphere and the intolerable heat, generally loses his front teeth, owing to the relaxing of the gums, haunted me. I remember very little of these last two days, except that we seemed to be swimming in boiling oil, and that dreams of great tankards of rich, brown Bavarian beer came to torture me. Of one thing I was quite certain, that when next I crossed these mountains it would be in winter. What was freezing to death in comparison to roasting alive? ... I became rational in the evening of the second day, as the frantic ponies dashed into the waters of the Danube, icy with the floods from the Tyrolean and Styrian Alps, and after a swim I made my apologies to Mihail for much harsh treatment. He was not rancorous, but carefully tapped my teeth, and thought they would not fall out, though very loose.

I came up with the mysterious Prime Minister, who seemed to be hiding, even from his own people, at Sistova, where in 1878, in their advance upon Turkey, the Russians had crossed the Danube. He was a short thick-set man of sturdy build, with a dark olive complexion, and most uncouth in his manners. But his whole appearance breathed vitality. He was a doer, and not a word-monger. From under his heavy beetle brows there looked out with suspicion upon his surroundings as penetrating a pair of eyes as I have ever beheld. I spent many instructive mornings with him, and he spoke with what at first appeared to be engaging frankness on every subject under the sun. He admitted that he was ruling the country backed by a small but active minority of his people against the will of a majority which would have been overpowering had it not been, as he observed with contempt, "so lethargic."

He frankly admitted that under his rule every article of the Constitution had become a dead letter, but he justified this by stating that the Constitution had been bestowed upon the Bulgarians by the Tsar for the purpose of sowing discord and general political dissatisfaction among his countrymen, until finally, like a ripe peach, the principality would fall into the lap of Mother Russia and be incorporated as a crown land in the Muscovite Empire. Like many other Balkan statesmen, Stambouloff had served a stage in journalism. Representing a Sofia paper, he had followed the Russian army for a few weeks during the war and had witnessed many interesting incidents in front of Plevna and during the delay at Shipka pass. Here he had received an indelible impression of the corruption in the non-combatant services of the Russian army, the incompetence of many officers in high command, and the pathetic ignorance of the rank and file.

"Two years before the war began," he explained time and again, "I thought that Russia could whip a world in arms. After what I saw in the bogs of the valley and on the bloodstained heights of Shipka, I came to the conclusion that, without the Roumanian contingent and the Macedonian volunteers, the Great White Tsar would have been stopped at Plevna. The conclusion was forced upon me that Bulgaria would have to stand on her own feet, and that is why I am now trying to walk alone." In confidence he admitted that he had no illusions either as to the value or the motive, nor yet the permanence, of the friendship which the Austrians and the English were displaying. "They are seeking their own selfish political ends. I do not blame them; I am doing the same thing; but I shall thwart their purpose, in mine I shall succeed."

I confess I was a little surprised when the semi-barbarian Stambouloff went on to speak of his sovereign, Prince Ferdinand, the grandson of Louis-Philippe, descended from a long line of mighty kings, in much the same tone that a millionaire merchant might refer to one of his clerks who was diligent in small things, and for the moment useful, but who could be easily replaced. There was not a suggestion of personal loyalty to the young Prince who, at his urgent request, and after many others had refused, had embarked on the Bulgarian adventure. The only thing he seemed to dwell upon with satisfaction was the fact that, thanks to the generosity of Princess Clementine, his devoted mother, Ferdinand was spending a great deal of money in the principality, and he congratulated himself and his people on the fact that, come what might, much of this would remain.

We spent our mornings talking politics, and during the heat of the day, which was still very great, we enjoyed siestas. In the early evening we would go for a swim in the Danube. Soldiers would row us out into midstream and then, favored by the current, we would swim down the river, often as far as Giurgevo on the Roumanian shore, always followed by a police galley and under the protection of a score of rifles. The Prime Minister swam like a seal. It was his only form of exercise. In winter, he told me, he hibernated and never took a step he could avoid or a bath.

It was perhaps natural, in view of his antecedents and upbringing, that Stefan Stambouloff was such an uncouth individual. In his seventeenth year he ran away from a seminary in Odessa, where he was being educated for the priesthood, and since then it was his boast that he had never opened a book. Embarking at this early age upon a life of adventure, he had become the lucky survivor, not the hero many asserted, of plots and counterplots against the Turkish suzerain as well as the Christian overlords. He was at this time one of the very few that were left of the band of adventurers and patriots, for both categories were as usual represented in the movement, who in 1875 started the uprising against the Crescent which provoked the atrocities committed by the highland Pomaks and the bashi-bazouks, brought about the Russo-Turkish war and in the end resulted in the freedom of Christian Bulgaria from Ottoman rule.

This band of brothers, as Stambouloff called them, to whom Katkoff and the Moscow Pan-Slavs furnished the sinews of war, was greatly reduced in numbers now. Some, the best of them I fear, fell as volunteers in the Russian army. A few, it is true, still survived, though broken in health and spirit by the *bastinado*, a Turkish form of punishment which Stambouloff had not abolished. Some of these, like Petko Karaveloff and Peter Stanchoff, had been rewarded by long imprisonment in the Black Mosque. Others had been executed for treason (to Stambouloff) and without trial, like Kosta Panitza, though in his breast there were lodged many bullets received in fighting for the Fatherland.

Stambouloff was only thirty-seven when I met him, and he complained quite bitterly of his loneliness. "All who began with me have fallen," he said in a voice which did not ring quite true. And when I returned to Sofia and looked up the meager records that were available, I was not surprised to read the name of Stambouloff on the death warrants of many of his comrades of the early days. Certainly, if a smiling countenance and an unwrinkled brow is a reliable criterion, the dictator enjoyed at this time the blessing of a quiet conscience. Certainly he had an iron constitution and a digestion – well, I am completely at a loss for an analogy. I saw him devour repasts that would have staggered an ox and put a ravenous wolf on a diet for weeks. His sturdy health and enduring strength were, I have no doubt, the natural result of the years of hardship and exposure he had spent with the shepherds in the bleak fastnesses of the Balkans, always on the move with the Turkish *zaptieh* ever at his heels, with but a sheepskin between him and the weather, a sheepskin that was his cloak by day and his couch by night.

If I ever reached a full understanding of Bulgarian aspirations, or of the extraordinary man who at the time, and for five years longer, presided over the destinies of this long submerged and voiceless people, I have to thank a visit I paid two months later to the ancient crowning city of the Bulgarian Tsars, to Tirnovo on the Yantra. Again Stambouloff had disappeared from the face of the earth and a cabled instruction from the Commodore sent me from the relative comfort of Sofia in search of him once more.

After some fruitless wanderings and many uncomfortable days and nights, I came up with the vagrant Prime Minister secluded in the house of one of his closest political associates within a stone's throw of the Church of the Forty Holy Martyrs, the Westminster Abbey and a sacred place of pilgrimage for all Bulgarians, whether born in the principality or outside its boundaries, in Thrace or Macedonia. But for this ancient shrine, the town of Tirnovo of this day might aptly be described as a pig-wallow and a very common pig-wallow at that. But in this church over which so many hordes of conquerors have passed are still to be seen the inscriptions which for many, with the force of Holy Writ, lay down the metes and bounds of the ancient empire upon which so many base their dream of a Greater Bulgaria in the future.

After we had discussed the topics of the day, the Bulgarian Prime Minister came with me to the shrine and, with the aid of local antiquarians, we read the testament carved on stone of the great Autocrat which the Bulgarians still regard as the covenant of their far-reaching claims and aspirations. It runs:

"In the year 1230, I, John Asen II, Tsar and Autocrat of the Bulgarians, the son of the old Asen, obedient to God in Christ, have built this most worthy church from its foundations and completely decked it with paintings in honor of the Forty Holy Martyrs by whose help in the twelfth year of my reign, when the church had just been painted, I set out to the war in Roumania and smote the Greek army and took captive the Tsar Theodore Comnenus with all his nobles."

"And all lands have I conquered from Adrianople to Durazzo – the Greek, the Albanian and the Serbian lands. Only the towns around Constantinople and that city itself did the Franks hold; but these too bowed themselves beneath the hand of my sovereignty, for they had no other Tsar but me. And I prolonged their days according to my will as God had so ordained. For without Him no word prevails and no work is accomplished. To Him be Honor and Glory forever. Amen."

"What a truly great man he was," commented Stambouloff, and his dark and rather dull features brightened with the glow of patriotic enthusiasm. "Today I am working to the end that some Bulgarian, some son of our soil, may come into his patrimony and rule over all our brothers just as did the Tsar John – eternal glory be to his name."

Little wonder then that in the years to come Prince Ferdinand, at once a Bourbon and a Coburg, feared Stambouloff. In the eyes of the Bulgarian leader this princeling with his Franco-German background was but a stop-gap, filling for a season the throne that belonged to a son of the blood-drenched soil. (And why not to Stefan Stambouloff?) Men being what they are when driven by ambition, is there any wonder that Prince Ferdinand some years later accepted the brutal assassination of his ambitious lieutenant with Christian fortitude and resignation or even, as some thought, with levity?

When the news was flashed around the world of Stambouloff's murder in 1895, I did not rejoice, but I certainly shed no tears. He had lived by the sword and he died by the knife. At the moment I was passing through Paris on my way to the Far East from Spain, where for three years the Pyrenees had shielded me from most of the Balkan rumors, and there, at the corner of the Café de la Paix nearest to the Place, as I strolled along I saw a woman and at the same moment she saw me; the woman whom I had set down in my mind, when the first news of the assassination reached me, as the murderess of Stambouloff, not indeed with her own hands, but surely it was she who had nerved the arm that struck him down and then cut him to pieces. Her smile broke into laughter as she caught sight of me, not with joy at our chance meeting, I cannot claim it was that, but because of what she called "the good news," "the comfortable news" from the Balkans, which she immediately began to retail with many bloody details that had been overlooked in the press dispatches.

"Ah! Stefan Stefanovitch, you must return to our country and dance the *ryllo* on his grave, as I will when things quiet down." I protested that my return to the Balkans in the immediate future was unlikely, that I was bound for Japan, and that in any event I did not propose to dance on his grave.

"You are a good friend, but a poor hater, Stefan Stefanovitch. Think how the *sapages* dogged your footsteps and how Petkoff, the dictator's jackal, in his newspaper called upon the patriots to put you out of the way. The people can show their true feelings now, and when you return they will bless – they will adore you."

There is high authority for saying that revenge is sweet, but in this instance, as I can testify, it was also beautifying and rejuvenating. The woman who now sat at this corner of the universe preening her feathers was absolutely transfigured; and those who passed by beheld an unmistakably happy and contented human being. For some five years, in and out of Bulgaria, she had preached and plotted destruction to the little dictator, and undoubtedly she had been behind several of the attempts that had been made on his life; but always there had been a slip and Stambouloff had escaped, his lieutenants had fallen, but he had survived. With every failure a mark of disappointment and of suffering had been added to her deeply-lined face, but now all these wrinkles and furrows had been smoothed away. Joyous contentment sparkled from her eyes, the worn, bedraggled woman had grown quite beautiful and her constant smile was fascinating. Perhaps I should conceal this bloody recipe from the knowledge of beauty parlors, lest the quota of murders be greatly increased!

I delayed my return to Bulgaria too long. Nine years had elapsed before once again I put in my appearance in Sofia; and many things had been forgotten, among them even the dynamic woman whom I had last seen in the hour of her greatest happiness sipping a liqueur in a corner seat at the Café de La Paix. She too was dead, quite as dead as Stambouloff, her unmourned victim. By persistent inquiries I at last learned that she also had fallen by the sword – in one of those guerilla skirmishes in Macedonia, where neither age nor sex, nor anything else, was respected by the blood-crazed combatants.

The following lines which I wrote the Commodore at the time of my first visit, and which rather carelessly he published, will help to explain the situation in Sofia, at least as I saw it, on my return from the Danube excursion.

"The seeker after truth here at the very outset is confronted with the fact that while the men and women who play important roles in the Bulgarian capital are very few – say at a generous estimate half a hundred – they are divided into half a dozen cliques and of these it is impossible to know more than one at one and the same time."

"Here you cannot avail yourself of the foreigner's pleasant privilege in most European capitals of being on polite and even friendly terms with members of all parties at once. You, too, for the nonce must be a partisan. If you bow to Radoslavoff in the Tergoska Street you cannot shake hands with Petko Karaveloff when you meet him in that arid waste which is known officially as the Public Garden. If you salute Madame Panitza you cannot take tea with Madame Karaveloff which would be a pity, and if you are even suspected of having the most incidental contact or conversation with a Zankovist, your career at the palace is closed."

"So the seeker after the truth has no choice. He must dissemble. Only after having loudly proclaimed his loyalty and learning all the ins and outs of palace politics can he allow himself to be converted seriatim by the leaders of the hostile groups until finally he descends to the camp of the Zankovists who are supposed to receive the sinews of war and their guidance from St. Petersburg."

"Then the seeker should desist or better still leave Bulgaria, or the *Swoboda* (the government gazette) will denounce him as a Russian spy and stout-limbed *sapages*, political heelers who carry long sticks and use them ruthlessly, will dog his footsteps and then come forward to swear that he endeavored by means of the traditional ruble notes to shake their allegiance to the throne. And then the *Narodny Prava* will publish his photograph under the caption 'another traitor unmasked' and demand his expulsion from the sacred soil. But if he dissembles there will be interesting and even amusing moments in his sojourn and most certainly he will be rewarded by an invitation to lunch at the palace and there, from the silver service, a reminder and a legacy of Prince Ferdinand's ill-starred predecessor, the Hessian lions will frown at him."

This publication was far from helpful to me personally but it did outline the things that were to happen with a correctness which some of my other peeps into the future fell short of. Certainly the *sapages* dogged my footsteps, the doors of the Black Mosque often seemed about to open for me, decrees of expulsion were drawn up – but I must not anticipate. Before it became apparent that I had become set in the ways of error all the parties sought my favor and even the forlorn Prince in his palace assured me that there was always a place for me at his table.

I should and will admit that the dictator whom I now began to dislike cordially not seldom was subjected to experiences which serve to explain, if they by no means justify, the way in which he discarded the restraints and even the amenities of political life, at least as they are recognized in the civilized countries. His footsteps were constantly dogged by assassins and, though years were to elapse before they hacked him to pieces in the streets of Sofia, it is certain that attempts upon his life were most frequent. Indeed only a few weeks after our visit to the Tirnova shrine the Minister of the Interior who bore a striking resemblance to the Prime Minister was shot down and killed as he came out of Stambouloff's office. As an indication of the savagery prevailing at the time I may say that it was generally stated in the capital that this man owed his portfolio to this resemblance which was indeed remarkable, and soon signs appeared on many of the government offices with the announcement, "I want a man who looks like me to share my responsibilities – and the bullets that are aimed at me. Stefan Stambouloff."

In mid-summer, from the standpoint of the "special," a most unholy calm spread over the stormy Balkans; even the commercial skirmishes subsided and hardly a sibilant word came from the conspirators who wished to restore Prince Alexander or in any event to remove Prince Ferdinand, and something like a truce was apparently (but only apparently!) arranged between the component parts of that ethnic salad which was and is Macedonia. But there was to be no peace – suddenly the slumbering religious antagonisms entered upon an acute phase and these require a few words of explanation.

[Continued in the chapter on Macedonia and Kosovo]

13. COURT LIFE IN BULGARIA

I was in Varna on the Black Sea, not then the Newport of the region it has since become, but a backwater from which in those days your best escape was as a deck passenger on a Russian tramp bound for Constantinople. I was not only physically marooned but in a mental quandary. My responsibility for revolutionary outbreaks and all other news developments in the Balkans was weighing more heavily than usual upon me. There was little difficulty in detecting the symptoms of approaching trouble, but alas! while unmistakable at this moment they were widely scattered. As a result it was most difficult to say (and yet that was my job and I had to say it every day) where the next world-peace-menacing explosion would occur. Would it detonate in that great swamp land of the Dobruja on the Danube, now in control of the intruding Roumanians, or under that pile of rocks and dynamite which is Albania frowning down on the Adriatic from its banditti-ridden crags?

Well, worse luck! the chances seemed to be about fifty-fifty. The Austrians following the will o' the wisp of the *drang nach Osten* were at their stuff in the home of Scanderbeg and – Well, I have forgotten his name but a claimant Bulgaro-phone patriot, who had his day of renown, was calling upon the web-footed inhabitants of the Dobruja to cast out the descendants of Trajan and join their fortunes with their brethren of the Principality. It was indeed a dilemma. Which horn should I grasp? Only one thing was certain, grim-visaged war might break out here, and worse luck it might break out there! The decision could no longer be delayed when a happy solution presented itself in the form of a wire from the Commodore. He ordered me to report to him personally in Paris, as soon as possible and, he added, pregnant phrase! "Bring your heavy luggage.

Nothing loath I was there in five days, as fast as the Orient Express I picked up in Sofia could carry me. And then, as on not a few previous occasions, the Commodore opened up a question with which I had often harassed him as though the subject was quite new to me and indeed that he had initiated it. In a confidential manner he imparted to me all the information in regard to the Senussi Brotherhood of the Sahara with which I had pestered him twelve months before. But I must be fair; he made many additions to my report and so added greatly to my slender store of knowledge. Perhaps I should only claim that I had spurred him on to further research by drawing on the innumerable sources of information which he enjoyed.

"I think the situation in the Balkans will remain stagnant for some months to come," he said, "and as that will not suit you, or for that matter, me, I have decided to transfer you temporarily to a more active and I hope a more profitable field of activity. I want you to visit the Senussi Mahdi, the veiled Prophet of the Sahara. I want you to get behind the veil with which his activities are cloaked. In my judgment his shrine in Djerboum may shortly become the greatest new news-center in the world. Today the Mahdi is in close touch with five hundred million Africans and probably with two hundred million Asiatics. This is a news-center that has never been tapped, and I want you to tap it. His missionary agents are swarming all over the Mohammedan world; what are they preaching? While there are many rumors as to their activities, I want you to find out exactly what they are up to; that is your job. Pick up all the Arabic you can, and I hope you will be ready to start in about six weeks. Probably I shall land you from the yacht at Bengazi on the Tripolitan coast....

[Bonsal spent several weeks in Paris preparing for his trip to the Sahara. Then the Commodore learned that the Mahdi is on the move and cannot be reached. He canceled the trip and said to Bonsal:]

...In the meantime I have every reason to think that there is going to be a blow-up in the Balkans." Lowering his voice he continued, "I think Ferdinand will be kidnaped as was Alexander and perhaps he will be handled more roughly than was the Battenberg. Make for Sofia as quickly as you can. I shall be pleased if you catch the express tonight. Keep the carriage as long as you need it and send me a wire when you arrive and lots of good luck," and he was gone. My packing and the other details of departure did not take up much time. Two hours later I was on the Orient Express hastening back once more to the cockpit of southeastern Europe.

I traveled to Sofia now as fast as the Express would carry me. I did not venture to leave the train in Vienna even for a minute, for fear of being left behind. I read very carefully the account of the Zankovist plot to kidnap Prince Ferdinand which Christianson[5] had turned over to me at the station, and then carefully destroyed it. The kidnaping was to be pulled off on the following Sabbath and as I reached the Bulgarian capital on Thursday, I was in plenty of time for the fireworks. I called at the Palace and wrote my name in the book. As I came away I noticed that the Princess Clementine was looking out of the window at the dreary scene which, in those days at least, and to my eyes always, Sofia unfolded. She seemed very pensive and for a moment I was tempted to warn the poor lady who, seeking popularity with the Bulgars, was spending, or as it seemed to us, wasting, such huge sums in her son's opera bouffe principality. But it was not my secret.

I was surprised in the course of the next twenty-four hours to meet almost all of the correspondents who, like myself, were responsible for this dynamic news center. Their presence seemed to substantiate the rumor that had brought me back to the Balkans, but made it quite plain that whatever happened I should not have an exclusive story. All the correspondents were visibly embarrassed as they ran across their colleagues and competitors at the club or in the Café Panachoff, and made labored explanations of their presence. Beaman of the *Standard* had come from Constantinople where things were deadly quiet, he reported. His purpose, he avowed, was to kill a black wolf that had been seen on the slopes of Witosh. Starshenski, the sportsman of the Austrian legation, was on its tracks but he hoped 'to get ahead of Starshenski as he had, he added in his blustering way, so often before. Bouchier of the London *Times* came from Athens. He was exceedingly hard of hearing, and this failing had aided him to ignore a number of revolts and many more discreditable things for which he was later rewarded by having his picture on one of the Bulgarian postage stamps.

5   Charley Christianson, Bennett's assistant.

The *Times* was further represented by Sir Donald Mackenzie Wallace, who at this juncture arrived most unexpectedly from London. That was a surprise to all of us and a disagreeable one for Bouchier. Wallace was a diplomat, and he made it quite plain his visit had nothing to do with current politics. He averred he had come to seek out original documents for his long-planned history of the Bulgarian people, from Tsar Simeon to Prince Ferdinand. It was to run to seven volumes and as he was approaching sixty he felt that the time had come for him to get on with it.

On the Sabbath, the critical day, we were all bidden to luncheon at the Palace. It was a stag affair, the Princess-Mother remaining in her own apartment, a prey, doubtless, to many fears. Most of the reasons I have presented as to why my colleagues had come in a bunch as it were, and so unexpectedly, were extracted by the cross-examination to which the Prince subjected us one and all as we appeared. "And you?" he inquired, and, unblushingly, I answered that I was simply making a routine round of my beat which, as he knew, extended from Vienna to the Bosphorus. We had a pleasant luncheon and when it was over the Prince led the way out on to a balcony where, protected by glass from the rude winds of November and embowered in flowers, we had a charming view of the snow-tipped heights of Mount Witosh. Then he handed us Giubec cigarettes (and there are none better) and began his cross-questioning again. His eyes fastened upon us with a searching expression and then suddenly he burst out into an uncontrollable fit of laughter. I, as the youngest and certainly the least court-broken of the company, insisted that he share the joke with us; and then, growing serious, he said, "Of course, I believe it has happened casually, just as you say it did. But I must admit that when I heard that you had all arrived here, coming from the various points of the compass and within twenty-four hours, I said to myself, 'The vultures are gathering; soon Ferdinand of Coburg will be carrion. " While I made a deprecating gesture, I felt guilty and tried to hide it by laughing heartily and so did most of the other men, but not so decidedly not so Mackenzie Wallace. After all, he belonged to quite a different category. He was a newspaper correspondent recently knighted because for years he had shaped world news so that it would be most useful and helpful to the British government. He flushed deeply and bridled. It was some weeks before the witty if unscrupulous Ferdinand made his peace with him.

I have not given anything like an intimate picture of Prince Ferdinand. My reticence is due to the fact that up to now I had seen very little of him. He was frequently taking the cure in Carlsbad or visiting his Hungarian estates, and when he did return to Bulgaria I was often away in Macedonia or in Serbia or some other trouble zone in my large and turbulent area. He rather plumed himself on the fact that he had been in America, and he had an amusing way of mixing up the empire of Brazil, which he knew, with our republic, which most certainly he did not know. He had visited Rio during the reign of Dom Pedro as the guest of his kinsman, the Comte d'Eu, who was the prince consort of the learned Pedro's daughter. At this time Prince Ferdinand was unmarried and led an exceedingly lonely life, which probably accounted for the fact that he set such store by our visits. There were only two foreigners in his household, M. de Bourbalon, a courtly Savoyard of a family that had served the Prince's forefathers for generations; and Baron Lobner, a smart cavalry officer, who in his day had "witched" Vienna with his horsemanship and was now engaged in the difficult task of teaching the Bulgarian cavalry the Austrian seat in the saddle.

The Prince was not unprepossessing in appearance. At this time his Bourbon nose, upon which so many caricatures have been hung in later years, was neither abnormal in size nor unpleasing in its effect. His eyes were light blue, a little too light and washed-out, but they did reveal the great intelligence which he possessed. In his cavalry boots he stood a little over six feet, and he had the easy graceful carriage of every Austrian cavalry officer I had ever met. His voice was unpleasant. He had a nasal twang and, in spite of his many French ancestors, vocally at least the German strain dominated. This was a great misfortune and a heavy handicap, as the Bulgarians at this time had a very healthy hatred of everything German or "Swab." The Prince was exceedingly friendly to all the correspondents; and, while he evidently preferred ornithology to political situations as a topic of conversation at the luncheon table, he was often quite amusing.

In the more private conversations which I frequently enjoyed with him, at this time and later, the Prince was at pains to explain the ill luck which had so often attended his family engaged in the kingly *métier* both in Europe and America, and he made it quite plain that he proposed to avoid the pitfalls into which they had fallen. Many a sermon he preached about Dom Pedro the Second, for so long Emperor of Brazil. "He had only himself to blame for his deposition and later his exile. The poor man was a savant," the

Prince was wont to say. "He devoted himself to the history of the dead past and to speculations as to the future of science. He was surrounded by antiquarians conversant with what happened in the Middle Ages, and with star-gazers whose speculations as to what the world would look like in the twenty-second century fascinated him. But he ignored absolutely the living world. The statesmen and the editors who were shaping the destinies of his people he did not consult; indeed, he did not even know them by name, and he paid the penalty. For this he forfeited his throne and lost his crown." These criticisms were to the point, and well taken I am assured, by those who knew Brazil in the critical years. But, while he was able to avoid the pitfalls that he knew of, Prince Ferdinand fell into others; and, as a last resort in 1918, rather ingloriously, he fled the principality which had become, under his tireless fostering care, a kingdom.

The career of the Prince, afterwards king of Bulgaria, and now, after the days of *sturm und drang* are over, an aged exile in the little town of Coburg where he potters about collecting coins and birds' eggs, is rather startling to those who believe, if any such survive, in the divine right of kings. After the kidnaping of his predecessor, Prince Alexander, and his subsequent abdication, owing to the opposition of the Tsar to his return to power, the Bulgarian throne went begging, as was natural in the untoward circumstances, and the situation of the country grew daily more critical. The Regents to whom the administration was confided were having great difficulty in carrying out their duties in the face of the unfriendly attitude of the Tsar, as represented by General Kaulbars. Stambouloff ruled the Regents and he in quick succession offered the uneasy throne to Prince Waldemar of Denmark, brother of Alexandra, Princess of Wales, and of the Empress of Russia, and then to King Charles of Roumania. They, one after the other, declined the honor and then the Turks, a humorous gesture doubtless, put forward a Prince of Mingrelia[6], but this nomination did not prosper.

It was at this juncture that the Regents who were entirely controlled by Stambouloff sent three delegates to inspect the royal cadets of Europe in a search for an eligible ruler. One of these delegates, M. Stoileff, who after-

6   Prince Dadian.

wards became Prime Minister, told me later many amusing details of this adventure. Apparently they had been rebuffed in many quarters and, preparatory to returning to Sofia by the Orient Express the next day, were spending the evening at Ronarchers, at the time a famous night café and music hall in Vienna. Their quest had been a failure and the vacant throne still stared them in the face. The princelings who were willing to go to Bulgaria, to secure what Bismarck called in his famous talk with the Battenberg prince "an interesting souvenir for their old age," were not eligible. And those who were, did not want to go.

Everybody in the night café knew the Bulgarian trio. They had been the subject of many cartoons in the comic papers, so Stoileff was not greatly surprised when a man who was a complete stranger to him and whose name he never knew came over and sat himself down at their table. "You gentlemen are looking for a prince," he said. "Why don't you take Prince Long Nose over there? We could get along without him – splendidly." Prince Long Nose, who sat at an adjacent table, was no other than Prince Ferdinand of Coburg, then a lieutenant in a Hussar regiment. It was notorious that he had no inclination for soldiering and that he spent his time stuffing birds and collecting rare coins. He lived at the chateau of Ebenthal near Vienna where his widowed mother, a daughter of Louis Philippe, resided. The unknown man and the Bulgarian delegates clinked glasses and soon separated, but the suggestion stuck.

The next morning Stoileff made inquiries and learned that the Princess Clementine was exceedingly ambitious for her children, and also very wealthy. After the failure of the Comte d'Eu to realize her dream of empire in South America, the hopes and aspirations of the ambitious woman centered upon her young son. The more he thought about the matter the more Stoileff became convinced that a promising lead had been given him. He told me that he immediately wired Stambouloff and that the Regent came incognito to the Austrian capital to look the princeling over. This statement has been disputed, but I believe it is in accordance with the facts.

The people who hated and feared Stambouloff, and they were many, said that the reasons why the choice of the Regents finally rested upon Ferdinand were selfish rather than patriotic. It is certain that at this time Ferdinand had none of the popular and even endearing qualities which his unfortunate predecessor, Alexander, had possessed to a remarkable degree.

Despite the French blood that flowed in his veins, Ferdinand was very German in appearance, and the Bulgarians hated all Germans, especially the blond ones and those who have, as Ferdinand had, a high, almost falsetto, voice in which nasal tones dominated. He had, of course, traveled far and wide in Europe and had enjoyed and availed himself of unusual educational advantages, but he had never been in southeastern Europe and was wholly ignorant of the languages and the customs of the people over whom he was to rule. It may not be true but, by those who knew the ambitious man best, it has always been believed that Stambouloff with his eyes open brought to the throne a young man whom he expected would remain unpopular and consequently but a puppet in his strong, masterful hands. It is true that Ferdinand always remained unpopular among his adopted people, but it is equally true that he soon showed an aptitude for Balkan diplomacy and that in many a tangled intrigue he bested his bullying Prime Minister.

Ferdinand accepted the offered throne conditionally upon his being elected by the Grand Sobranje or extraordinary legislative assembly and upon the approval of the Powers. Russia, however, ignored the selection and so from the start Ferdinand was subjected to a diplomatic boycott. Indeed, it was only in 1908, twenty-one years after his accession, that the position he had made for himself was generally recognized. In May 1894, Ferdinand summoned up the courage to dismiss Stambouloff. He had forgiven his many high crimes and his misdemeanors, but as he was an obstacle to recognition by Russia, the liberating nation the Prime Minister had fought so bitterly and so unfairly, the Prince finally kicked him out. Then Stambouloff, in an access of fury which even his friends deplored, unbosomed his secret thoughts and uncorked all the vials of wrath to a German journalist. It was a terrible story and what was untrue was unimportant. The Prince instituted legal proceedings for defamation of character and would not permit Stambouloff to visit a German spa which the state of his health made advisable. And yet the libel suit, for some reason, never came to trial. A few weeks later, in July, while returning from dinner at the Union Club, Stambouloff was set upon by three assassins. He defended himself manfully, but in the end was well-nigh cut to pieces with the curved yataghans the assassins carried. And three days later the ex-Premier, the maker of much that was good and much that was bad in modern Bulgaria, died.

It was, of course, most unfortunate for me that my dispatches from Sofia, and, indeed, whatever news I was able to get out of Bulgaria, should have been reproduced in the *Temp* and other Paris papers with a promptness which even I, with the high opinion I had of their worth, thought remarkable. The editor of the *Swoboda*, the Stambouloff organ, initiated a newspaper crusade against me on this charge, but he overplayed his hand and a few of the open-minded publicists rallied to my support, in conversation at least, if not in their papers. The editor of the *Swoboda* even went to the extreme of saying that I was a Russian by birth and that the exceedingly bad Russian that I spoke was an elaborate and clumsy camouflage!

While I became *persona non grata* at court later, under amusing circumstances which I shall relate, Prince Ferdinand at this time often asked me to the Palace and seemed to endure what were generally considered my "attacks" on his Prime Minister with fortitude, and at times I thought, with pleasure. Once he asked me how it happened that *Le Nord*, admittedly a Russian-subsidized organ, published in Brussels, reproduced my articles a very few hours after they had appeared in the *Herald*, and he advised me to have this stopped if I could; but the thing was, of course, impossible and I never attempted it. While, as the Stambouloff papers charged, Mr. Bennett was on terms of intimacy with leading Russians and with members of the Imperial family, it is only fair to say that when he sent me to Bulgaria, he neither then nor later gave me the slightest intimation (much less pro-Russian instructions) as to how he viewed the situation. So I found it not difficult to explain to the Prince that, as I was apparently trying to send out the only impartial news that came from Bulgaria, it was natural that such papers as were seeking the truth should reproduce it by arrangement with my editor, or simply pirate it.

About this time the difficulties of my position were increased by an incident that most certainly was not of my contriving. On my return from a Macedonian foray[7] I found that Petko Karaveloff, a former Prime Minister whom I knew and admired, was being held in prison although no charges were advanced against him. Stambouloff hated him because he was a man of culture and breeding and also because he was one of the few men in public life upon whom the groups hostile to the little dictator might possibly

7   Described the the chapter on Macedonia and Albania

unite. In my absence, Karaveloff had been lodged in the Black Mosque, a noisome dungeon, as I was well aware, because I had visited it to interrogate my former guide, Tryko, who was being held there on charges which had nothing to do with his relations with me.

When it became apparent that Karaveloff, who was old and very feeble, would not be brought to trial, but was to be held in the filthy prison until he died, I began to move in his behalf. Madame Karaveloff told me that she had reason to believe that her unfortunate husband was subjected to the *bastinado* at least once a week. Having asked permission to visit the prison, and having been curtly refused, I published the facts that were known to me and also the rumors as to the treatment of the unfortunate statesman which, as I cabled, Stambouloff made it impossible for me either to verify or to deny.

This aroused the Vienna papers and de Burian, who during the World War served as one of the last foreign ministers of Austria-Hungary (at the time he was Consul-General in Bulgaria) became interested and insisted that I see the prisoner. As I stumbled into the filthy place I finally made out the emaciated forms of three or four hundred wretched vermin-ridden men crouching on the floor of the mosque. The only light there was came from a hole in the minarets.

When my soldier escort asked for Karaveloff the prisoners pointed to the topmost rung of the ladder that led up into the minaret and here I found the former Prime Minister reading by the feeble light, and with the aid of a dictionary, The *American Commonwealth*, the classic which, although only published a few months before, had already, and most literally, reached "darkest Bulgaria." Karaveloff admitted that he had been roughly handled, that in all probability he would soon be brought before a firing squad, but he denied he had been *bastinadoed*. Many thought this denial was inspired by fear, but I cabled what he said and two weeks later he was liberated and sent into exile.

After the death of Stambouloff this charming old man became Prime Minister again. Lord Bryce enjoyed the picture I drew of the unfortunate statesman who was given by the convicts the right to always sit on the topmost rung of the ladder, the only one where you could see to read, with the understanding that he would pass on to his comrades in misfortune the story of the bright and happy land beyond the seas. And indeed the story is told at great length in the official biography of Lord Bryce by Mr. H. A. L. Fisher.

As I have said, the *Swoboda* people overplayed such cards as they had to use against me and, as far as I was concerned, things were quieting down, although Stambouloff, as was his nature, remained relentless, when an incident occurred which in government circles at least reduced the belief in my impartiality to the vanishing point. On this unlucky day for me I was riding with some friends along the foothills of Mount Witosh when a heavily bearded, and from the newspaper accounts of the incident, an important-looking man arrived at the station on the international train, coming from "Europe" as we exiles in the Balkans were accustomed to call all those countries west of Serbia. He drove directly from the station to my hotel and expressed regret and unfortunately some surprise that I was not in. He wrote on his card on which was inscribed the name "Tatistcheff, (his given name I have forgotten) Privy Councilor to the Emperor of Russia, St. Petersburg," and in French he scribbled, "It is most important that I should see you." Being told by the porter that I would probably be back at the luncheon hour, Tatistcheff went into the café for a drink and was immediately surrounded by military police and a bevy of the plain clothes "stick men" who were always dogging my footsteps. At first Tatistcheff demanded to be taken before the Russian Consul; but, as all relations with Russia had been cut off for a year and there was no consul present, this would have been most difficult for the police to do. With little ceremony they bundled him into a conveyance, and surrounded by half a dozen mounted men he was escorted back to the railway station. A few minutes later I reached the hotel and, hearing what had happened, I, in my turn, hastened to the station as fast as one of the three horse phaetons that then abounded in Sofia could carry me.

The station was heavily guarded by troops and at first I was refused entrance. When I finally got into the waiting room, Tatistcheff was in the midst of the guards and, while he was not manacled, one of the plainclothes men was swinging a chain and clinking what seemed to be handcuffs in a menacing manner. As he saw the effort I made to get within speaking distance, the prisoner smiled wearily and waved his hand. A few minutes later the slow train to Constantinople lumbered in. To it was attached a prison caboose with iron barred windows through which the stranger waved a sad farewell. I never saw or heard from him again, nor did I ever secure any light upon the incident. I never again heard Tatistcheff's name pronounced until, on the eve of the Great War, Emperor Nicholas in one of his last desperate efforts to avert hostilities, cabled to Emperor William, "Delay all you can; I am sending Tatistcheff to you with special instructions." This may have been the same man and it may not have been, Tatistcheff being rather a common name in Russia, and one borne by many bureaucrats of high rank as well as by court officials. One, during the Great War, became Finance Minister and another was faithful to the end and was murdered together with the Tsar and the Imperial family at Ekaterinburg.

After this unfortunate incident it became increasingly difficult for me to get my dispatches out of the country or, as a matter of fact, to receive any news from Europe. The cables were closed to me and all my letters that were openly posted were intercepted and suppressed. Not a single copy of the *Herald* reached me for weeks and even the *Temps* in the issues where my telegrams or letters were reproduced did not get past the censorship. Two of the messengers I had hired from time to time to carry my articles across the border to the nearest Serbian telegraph station were in the Black Mosque prison and I could do little to help them, except supply food, because they were held on trumped-up charges that had, ostensibly at least, nothing to do with their relations with me. In the circumstances, I did not feel justified in employing other messengers and, as we had no official representatives in Bulgaria (at the time the existence of the Principality was not recognized by the State Department and travel there was not covered by our passports), I had no justification for an appeal to Washington. O'Connor, the British diplomatic agent, did what he thought it was proper for him to do, but the first step he took was unfortunate. He had met the Commodore in London, and so he wrote him a personal letter to the effect that my life was in danger and that it was advisable to send me to another post. No one, not even Stambouloff, wanted to get me out of Bulgaria more than O'Connor, but he tackled the business in the wrong way. His perhaps kindly-meant letter provoked a curt note from the Commodore which read, "I am surprised you do not know that I never withdraw my men when under fire."

For some weeks now I maintained clandestine communications with friendly informants, who could not afford to come out into the open and be seen with a correspondent who had been placed under the official taboo, by a very simple device. The Hotel Panachoff where I lived was a public place, and as open to all as the railway station or the square before the Sobranje building. At some hour of the day or night every inhabitant of the capital of the Peasant State passed through it. So, upon going to bed, I would, following the American custom, place a pair of boots outside my door. Of course, as I admitted when rallied on the subject, I knew there were no bootblacks in Sofia but it was a practice, a habit, of which I could not break myself. In the dark hours of the night ghostly figures would hasten stealthily through the dimly lighted corridors and slip into my boots invaluable information in a disguised handwriting but with a key word to inspire me with confidence. But, alas! one morning my letter-box-boots were gone and no trace of them was ever discovered, and I abandoned the system without a moment's hesitation. In the Balkans news was valuable, of course, but boots were invaluable as they could not be replaced.

Cut off from routine communications I sometimes slipped down to Constantinople and sometimes up to Belgrade to find out what was going on and to orient myself. But this was doubly dangerous and I soon abandoned the plan. In my absence some important news event might break and also, despite the fact that the border control was exceedingly stupid, and rather easily circumvented, I might on my return from one of these jaunts be refused entrance into Bulgaria. I escaped from the dilemma in which I was then placed, and broke the blockade against me, by an expedient so simple that it seems almost incredible, and yet it worked like a charm. I went down to the station when the international trains were expected, which happened every other day. Many other exiles in Sofia had this habit and they came merely to felicitate the fortunate people who were on their way to Europe or to Turkey. When the train arrived I would slip into the mail car box a letter which was not very important, as I knew it would be immediately fished out and destroyed. Then, with a Tauchnitz or some other volume of light reading under my arm in which was concealed a letter or a cable marked, "Receiver to pay," I would walk through the train and when I came to a decidedly European-looking passenger I would greet him effusively as one would an old acquaintance. In a loud voice I would say, "I m delighted I was able to find the volume you said you wanted," then in a lower tone I would explain the situation. With but one exception, a stodgy suspicious German who said, "Dot ist nicht der volume I wanted," all my chance acquaintances were game and all the letters or cables I sent in this haphazard way got through to Paris with little delay.

I was very friendly with the train men and they often smoothed my path. One and all, they loathed Stambouloff and, indeed, most of them detested all Bulgarians, so at times I would find that they had, even before I appeared on the scene, prepared some passenger for the role he was selected to play. The police remained on the platform and apparently were quite content to secure and suppress the letter I would mail so ostentatiously. Finally it seemed advisable to give Sofia, for a few weeks, at least, the absent treatment and, if possible, to escape from constant police surveillance which, increasingly harassing, was getting on my nerves. I also, somewhat to my surprise I confess, received from Mr. Bennett his approval of this step.So one night, with my good friend S. . . . , a Polish landowner who served as Secretary of the Austro-Hungarian Legation, although he was one of the many Poles who hated the Dual Monarchy intensely, I left the Union Club with pack horses and ponies laden with proveder and ammunition, ostensibly, and even ostentatiously, bound for the pursuit of bears in the fastnesses of Mount Witosh. Three days later, having caught one of the slouchy local trains at a way station, I was in Philippopolis, greatly pleased at my translation to the rest and quiet and the charm of this romantic town.

At this distant day Philippopolis was as different from dreary and dusty Sofia as night is from day. Still a Turkish community with its uphill and down dale streets and its wonderful gardens musical with bubbling springs and living waters, it was not only charming and above all invigorating in itself, but it was also the starting point for many delightful excursions which live in my memory as the most pleasant of my Balkan experiences. The town sits astride the brawling Maritza which, despite the admonition of the song which all Bulgarians sing from the cradle to the grave ("Be quiet, Maritza!"),will not be still.[8] Perhaps it is the song of the great days, before the Ottoman Turks came this way, that will not be hushed; when here in Trimontium, as the town was called from the three high hillocks on which it is built, the Roman Pro-Consuls planned their forays into the lands of the barbarians.

8   In my day there were current as many versions of this folk song as there were singing
     cavalcades coursing through the Balkan passes. It has now become the national
     anthem of the Bulgars and the official version runs "Make silver music, boisterous
     Stream," etc. Certain it is that we shall hear of the Maritza in the years to come. S.B.

One of these rocky crags rising above the plain and river to the height of six or seven hundred feet still bears the Turkish name of Dschambas-Tepe. This was the preferred residential quarter and along its dark and narrow streets, particularly on the north side, rose the picturesque residences of well-to-do Turks and Greeks, all painted in as many colors as Joseph's coat. Here and there one caught a glimpse of the little summer pavilions behind the main buildings where the Turk took his ease (as far as that is possible for a true believer who must live under the Cross) in neglected gardens embowered in flowers and fragrant with the blossoms of fruit trees. Hanging over the narrow streets, where two mounted men could pass only with difficulty, were verandahs of beautifully carved woodwork. The sliding shutters were perforated with peep-holes and the flashing eyes that often were pressed upon them seemed to justify any dream, however extravagant, of harem beauty.

From the south side of this mountain crag rising out of the center of the town was a wonderful view of the Rhodopian Mountains, with their peaks not seldom capped with snow. From my first sight of them this prospect fascinated me. There lived Akmet Agha and his pure-blooded Bulgarian henchmen. They, after going over to Islam at an opportune moment, figure in Balkan history as the oppressors of the Bulgarians of the plains who, while they have remained steadfast to the teachings of St. Cyril and St. Method, have, through the lawless lust of their overlords, received a considerable admixture of Turkish blood and show it.

I lodged in a little inn kept by a Greek which, though not picturesque, like the great Turkish caravansary next door with its ten massive leaden cupolas, was fairly clean. My good friend, Slaveikoff, a graduate of Robert College, the American educational foundation near Constantinople which then (as now) was doing so much for the advancement of Balkan youth, owned a summer house and fruit farm a few miles out on the Dermendere road, and here in his garden bright with flowers and aromatic with tempting fruits I dreamed many hours away. As in duty bound, I explained to the Slaveikoffs, father and son, how disastrous I had proved to my friends and even to some of my chance acquaintances in Sofia, but they asserted this did not bother them. They had, apparently quite frankly, if somewhat passively, opposed Stambouloff for many years and, for reasons which they could not understand, he had not gone after them in his usual ruthless manner; in fact, he had left them severely alone, the father to write poems which recalled the heroic days of the Bulgarian people and the son to tend his fruit trees.

With young Slaveikoff, who proved a charming companion, I rode to Shipka Pass where for long months the Russians were stopped by the entrenched Turks, and where so many were left in their shallow graves. When you review their history throughout the bloody years from Plevna to Gallipoli, the conclusion is forced upon you that as trench soldiers the Turks are second to none. Then we went on to Kazanlik some twelve hundred feet above the scorched and sultry plains, a charming place where invigorating breezes are ever stirring through the pines. I delighted in these surroundings and I was prepared to share the enthusiasm of Field-Marshal Von Moltke when I visited him in Silesia a few months later and the silent soldier recalled his Roumelian memories in terms that were almost lyrical. I was glad to tell him that the whole countryside which he loved was still shaded by the great nut trees, and that the air was still redolent with the perfume of hundreds of rose farms. And indeed rose farms they are, rather than gardens, some of them running to fifty or sixty acres and I must add, regretfully, the rose bushes are planted in great furrows like corn or potatoes! As was the case with the Spaniards in Andalusia, after the Moors were expelled, I noticed that the Bulgarians had taken on much of the folklore of their predecessors in this happy valley. Certainly they were of the opinion that there were no roses in the world until Mahomet made his remarkable flight to heaven. When he came back from Paradise the peasants who dwell in this great flower garden say that the Prophet brought with him a few rose slips hidden under his prayer rug.

"And how do they account for the great variety of colors that abound in the fields?" I inquired. "Well, the white roses were watered," they explained to Slaveikoff, "by the sweat drops that fell from the forehead of Mahomet. The yellow roses were colored by the lather that fell from his horse."[9] "And the red roses?" I asked. "Well, they were colored and invigorated by the perspiration of the Archangel Gabriel who on this occasion acted as the

9   We also heard the tradition that on this remarkable journey the Prophet rode his famous white donkey, Albornek. But, incorrigibly romantic, Slaveikoff rejected this version.

Prophet's guide. If you do not believe this, read your Koran." As I looked
about me and feasted my eyes upon the acres of red roses, it was clear to me
that on this arduous night journey it was the Archangel Gabriel who
sweated the most.

After enjoying this ride through the vale of Kazanlik in an atmosphere fragrant with attar of rose, with my eyes fascinated by the great fields of the
Damascene flower, extending before me to the horizon, a sense of duty
hitherto ignored compelled me to visit the mountain villages where the
Bulgarian atrocities were committed; above all, to go to Batak, where thirteen years before many thousand unarmed men and helpless women and
children were murdered in cold blood. The name of the hamlet still con-
noted horror, even in Philippopolis, which narrowly escaped being included in the mass murders; men shivered when Batak was mentioned.
Slaveikoff could not go with me, but after some difficulty I secured an
agreeable guide, a small tradesman in the Roumelian town who soon, however, developed into a poet and a ballad singer, qualities which served to
brighten the toilsome two days journey to the beautiful village where one
of the most ghastly scenes in the history of horrors was enacted.

My companion was a Stoyanoff, I think, although I am not sure. I can see
him now as he rode ahead of me on the mountain trail, singing the story of
his long- downtrodden race and putting into verse his hatred of the Moslem
invader. His face and his voice I shall always remember, but his name I fear
I have forgotten as I have the names of so many who have helped and
guided me on many journeys in my vagrant career. Our capacity to forget is
really given a wonderful illustration in these mountain villages. Who could
have thought that thirty-nine years after the massacres, and twenty-four
years after my visit, when the atrocities were still a living memory to some,
these villagers should march shoulder to shoulder with the Turks and so
help to delay the triumph of civilization in the Great War by at least a year!
The only answer to this question, I suppose, is the negative one – that man
is an incomprehensible animal!

I had in my pocket a transcript of MacGahan's letters, the correspondent of
the *New York Herald* and the London *Daily News* who, aided by Eugene
Schuyler of our legation in Constantinople and harassed by Sir Henry
Elliot, the British Minister, (who under his instructions from Disraeli and
Salisbury was, as they later put it,"backing the wrong horse"), had visited

the villages while they still smouldered and sought out in their mountain caves the few villagers who had escaped.

On the long journey I had ample time to recall what Stanley and also Fox of the *Herald* had told me of their most distinguished contemporary, MacGahan. At twenty-six he was apparently a lawyer without clients, but he had the gift of tongues and Mr. Bennett had the good fortune to secure his services during the Franco-Prussian War. The speed and the brilliance of his dispatches, as Forbes admitted to me later, gave the "old-line" correspondents a cruel shock. In 1873 he was in revolutionary Cuba with Jim O'Kelley. He rode through Mambi land and made a gallant attempt to save the men of the *Virginius* from execution. The next two years he was campaigning in Central Asia. He was with the Russians throughout the Turcoman wars and when Skobelev saw that the young American could not be kept out of Khiva he took him into his official family. There followed ten months with Don Carlos in the mountains of Spain and when the rising collapsed he was captured and sentenced to death, for this was a war in which no quarter was given and war correspondents were not recognized. His execution was fortunately stayed by the energetic representations of our minister in Madrid, who was no other than General "Dan" Sickles, a fighter on his own account at Gettysburg who later became the one-legged First Nighter, and a very familiar figure to the theater-goers of New York in the Nineties. After this close squeak MacGahan in 1875 took part in the Arctic expedition of the *Pandora* under Captain Allen Young. Then fortunately for the Bulgarians his steps were turned to southeastern Europe. Hearing of the atrocities he, though his life was openly threatened by the Turkish authorities, rode to the scene of the mass murders and told in simple but forceful language the terrible story to an, at first, incredulous world.[10] MacGahan was denounced in unmeasured terms by the Turcophile press of London, with the mighty *Standard* leading the pack. He was reviled as a

10   As the Russians crossed the Danube and marched south to liberate Bulgaria MacGahan joined them. He was present at the battles in front of Plevna and saw the horrors of the Shipka Pass. With the conquering Russians he reached San Stefano and a few days before the treaty of peace was signed he died of typhus fever in that wretched village. In eight years what adventures! What experiences! What a loss to American journalism his untimely death! S.B.

sensationalist or, at best, an ignorant young American who lent a willing ear to what the cynical Disraeli had called the "babble of the coffee houses."

I thought at the time of my visit to the scene of the atrocities that such callous indifference to the conscience of civilization and such a complete abandonment of all humane principles under the spur of a fancied political or financial advantage would be impossible in America, but ten years later I found that I was mistaken. In 1897, when "Butcher" Weyler had herded the non-combatant inhabitants of Cuba, in revolution, into the concentration camps where within four months three hundred thousand of them were doomed to death by starvation or disease, the *New York Evening Post* (which had long before fallen from the pinnacle in American journalism on which it had been placed by Whittier and Godwin) struck the same contemptible note. The planned extermination of a liberty-loving people at our very doors, its editors maintained, was none of our business and, besides, the true situation in the camps had been grossly exaggerated where it was not entirely false. It has always comforted me to think that the editors who were responsible for this attitude, and plumed themselves upon it, were both of foreign birth, and that their paper failed, as did the London *Standard,* in these disgraceful campaigns.

I read MacGahan's affecting narrative as we toiled up the steep goat track, more often than not dismounted, that led to Batak. I read the winged words which Gladstone addressed to the English Parliament and his clarion call to the slumbering churches as I followed in the path MacGahan had gone on his dangerous quest just thirteen years before. When he entered Batak the dogs were still gorging themselves with human flesh and the mountain village stank like a charnel-house. When I came the air was pure and sweet, the church where so many died was rebuilt, but before it stood a mound of skulls to remind the living of their martyred dead. MacGahan speaks of a distraught woman who met him upon entering the ruined hamlet. Curiously enough, the same poor creature, or a sister in misfortune, greeted me upon my arrival and dogged our footsteps throughout my stay. Her cheeks were dry, she had no tears to shed, but always as she followed us she crooned a dirge which, with the help of Stoyanoff, I translated into the following doggerel:

> "I had shelter, now I have none,
> I had a man, now I'm alone,
> I had three sons, now I have none,
> I had five children, now I have one,
> She wears the Turkish veil,
> And serves the Pasha his slave."

It was pleasant to learn that here in this, by us, forgotten hamlet the names of the men who had truthfully reported the story of their sufferings and tried to save other Christian villages from a similar fate were not forgotten. Even miles away from Batak scores came out to meet me and brought wreaths of wild flowers to the countrymen of their benefactors. One little girl took me by the hand and led me to the pyramid of skulls in her village. One of these, almost split in twain, she pointed out as the skull of her grandfather. When I forced upon her some of the flowers with which I was overburdened, she made of them a wreath and, placing it on the weatherbeaten, fleshless skull, sank upon her knees in prayer. There can be little doubt that the people of Batak and of several of the adjacent villages were planning an uprising to take place in June or July of this year; and that, emboldened by the promises of help that were made by the leaders of the movement against Turkish domination, all of whom apparently remained at a safe distance in Bucharest, some hot heads among them fired upon minor Turkish officials and announced that for the last time they had paid taxes to the Turks. This was a sufficient pretext for the Sultan, Abdul Aziz (and not Abdul Hamid as generally stated), to let loose his Bashi-bazouks[11] and to invite the mountain Pomaks to flesh their swords in the bodies of their Christian brethren.

When I entered the little church at Batak, thirteen years almost to a day after the massacre, it was but little changed from the day of MacGahan's visit five weeks after the atrocities had been committed. True, the mangled and disemboweled bodies that lay around when he came on the scene were gone, but on a great wooden platform in the middle of the church about a hundred skulls were arranged in pyramidal form. Some had been perforated by bullets, others slashed by *yataghans*. Each skull had preserved its

---

11   Irregular, local troops serving the Turks.

identity, as it were. Those who accompanied us told us the name of this and that victim of Turkish fury and many placed flowers in the gaping clefts that revealed where the deadly wound had been inflicted.

An interesting character was the mayor of the village who, as soon as he heard of our arrival, insisted upon being our guide through the tragic scenes of which he was one of the few, the very few, survivors. He told me that he alone remained of the thirty-two souls that his family numbered at dawn on May 7, 1876. Shortly after sunrise the Agha and about a hundred of his men appeared on the outskirts of the village and demanded that the inhabitants give up their arms. This was an extraordinary request and filled the minds of the villagers with gloomy forebodings. While on several occasions during the long years of Turkish supremacy such a demand had been made, it was never enforced to the letter because the local Turkish officials recognized the necessity of having some rudimentary weapons for self-defense in a district that invited the lawless from many quarters. The Agha swore vengeance; but, for the time being, withdrew. This gave some of the villagers the opportunity to seek hiding places in the forests and to bury some of their most cherished possessions, sacred relics, church services, and family valuables in caves. But the great majority hastened to the church and to a rather substantial school house and prepared to defend their lives as best they could. Before noon the Agha was back, this time with five hundred well-armed men, and without further delay opened fire. As it was a shotgun battle against men with rifles, the result was a foregone conclusion. On the morning of the third day the villagers had lost half their number, and having nothing to eat or drink, they entered into a parley.

The mayor who took part in the negotiations claimed that the Agha swore the most solemn oaths, in both Christian and Moslem form, that if the besieged villagers would but give up their arms no harm should come to them. Once they were disarmed, however, the Pomaks demanded ransom money and to be led to the secret hiding places of their treasures. A few of the villagers again seized what weapons they could lay hands on and, again taking refuge in the church, resumed the fight against fearful odds. Early in the second fight the mayor had been wounded and fell. Several dead men fell across him, and he could not extricate himself from the weight of their bodies. After some hours, with what ammunition they had exhausted, and also all hope of relief by the arrival of their own people or the coming of Turkish regulars from Philippopolis gone, the villagers entered into another parley with the murderous crew. Again they were promised their lives if they submitted, and again the Agha broke faith. As the survivors of the struggle, dazed and starving, came out of the darkened church they were cut down. The place was soon so cluttered up with corpses that at last the Agha ordered his men to lead their prisoners down to the little river and there on the bank they were beheaded. While a much higher figure is given in the Bulgarian accounts, I think it is conservative to say that on that fatal day five thousand men, women, and children perished in and around Batak. Toward sunset the Pomaks set fire to the church and, with the strength of despair, the man who was later to become mayor, and act as my guide, extricated himself from the corpses that had fallen across him and favored by darkness, crawling on hands and knees, made his way to a cave where several other villagers had taken refuge. There his wounds were dressed. Of the many thousands who died it was the boast of the Agha that he himself "executed" as he preferred to say, four hundred with his own sharp cutting knife.

There was at the time, at least, much uncertainty as to the relations between the Agha and the Turkish authorities of the day; and I cannot claim to have made clear where the responsibilities lie by my subsequent visit to the Pomak chieftain in his mountain fastness of Tomrush. One thing, however, is certain; for these mass murders Abdul Hamid who afterwards was given, and certainly deserved, the name of the "great Assassin" was not to blame. As a matter of fact, he did not ascend the throne until many months later and at the time they were planned, and ruthlessly executed, he was living under the restraint and in the dignified retirement from active affairs which during this period the rulers of Turkey generally imposed upon all kinsmen who were thought eligible to replace them in the case of a successful uprising.

It is not quite clear that even the Sultan of that day, Abdul Aziz, gave the orders for the destruction of the Christian villages, but he certainly rewarded those who carried them out. Chefket Pasha, who was in command of the Turkish forces in Roumelia, who presided over the burning of so many of the mountain hamlets and, without batting an eye, saw the slaughter of their inhabitants, while not present in person at the massacres in and around Batak, was a few weeks later given promotion and for the remainder of his days enjoyed high favor at the Imperial court.

Of course, the orders under which the Agha carried out his devilish work never saw the light of day and in all probability were never written. At the first signs of unrest, he was given command of the local Bashi-bazouks or irregulars in accordance with the custom of the War Office of placing responsibility for maintaining law and order upon the most powerful headman in the vicinity. Probably he was never told in so many words to murder ten thousand men, women, and children in Roumelia. What he did was doubtless his interpretation of the general orders that were given him to maintain the supremacy of the Crescent. Certainly later, when the Agha and his mountaineers saw red and advanced toward Philippopolis with the avowed purpose of burning the Roumelian capital and, of course, putting all its non-believing inhabitants to the sword, Chefket Pasha placed his regulars between the threatened town and the irregulars who were now running amok through the valley of the Maritza. On the other hand, it cannot be denied that the title of Pasha was given the Agha a few weeks after the massacres, and that he was rewarded for his fanatical loyalty with several high decorations. If anything could be amusing in regard to this dark episode, it would be the following incident. Faced by the remonstrance of the "Concert of Europe," which the Turkish government knew so well how to disconcert, the Sultan agreed to appoint a committee to investigate the outrages which had been committed, as he asserted, "by a few irregulars who had gotten out of hand," and the Agha was selected to head the committee! While the "Concert of Europe" was digesting this affront the Russians declared war and crossed the Danube.

And so began the Russo-Turkish War, the most righteous war of the century. It cost Russia a million men and the Concert of Europe remained passive until the bloody struggle was over. Then, incredible as it may seem, the Concert, under the leadership of England and Disraeli, intervened, robbed the victors of the fruits of their victory, and insisted upon millions of liberated Christians being restored to their former servitude under Turkish supremacy. Doubtless this just war would never have been undertaken but for the visit that was made to the scene of the massacres by MacGahan, the correspondent, and Eugene Schuyler, the secretary of the American Legation in Constantinople who accompanied him. Schuyler made his official report to Horace Maynard, our very able minister to Turkey at the time, and he, being more of a man than a diplomat, saw to it that the narrative was not put to sleep in archives. Together these two Americans followed the bloody trail of the Turks through the hills and the valleys of Roumelia and it was

MacGahan's narrative, that he put on the wire in Bucharest on August 22, 1876, that inspired Mr. Gladstone's eloquent appeals to Christendom.

The truth about the massacres leaves Disraeli and Lord Salisbury in a very unenviable light before the bar of history, and it is only fair to say that their accredited representative in Turkey, the ambassador Elliot, was a very weak man, with, however, a keen appreciation of what his Foreign Office and his political leaders wished him to see and above all what to overlook. The massacres began on May 1st and continued for about ten days. No news reached Constantinople for a fortnight. The first fragmentary information came through official Turkish sources and this gave the Sublime Porte full opportunity to shape it, and full advantage was taken by the Turks to use Elliot as a cushion to minimize the terrible disclosures that could be delayed but not suppressed. From him came the reports that justified Disraeli in prating about the "gross exaggerations of the press," and the not over-subtle suggestion that the charges were largely Russian propaganda designed to justify the long-feared advance of the Tsar upon Constantinople. In any event, these reports satisfied Lord Salisbury with the result that, as he afterwards cynically admitted, he "put the English money on the wrong horse" and so thousands died who might have been saved and the well-deserved reputation of the English people as a bulwark of civilization in barbarous lands suffered an indelible stain.

I came back from my visit to Batak, and the other nearby scenes of racial and religious ferocity, determined that when there was a lull in what we correspondents called the higher politics of the Balkans I would visit the Agha in his mountain fastness and see how it had fared with the man who in that day was regarded as the outstanding mass murderer of modern times. Obviously my purpose was not easy of accomplishment, and the few to whom I dared broach the subject were most discouraging. And then as was so often the case I was called back to Belgrade where both Russian and Austrian intrigue had become more than usually rampant. The regime of the "tarnished generals" who composed the regency was tottering, and the ex-King Milan[12] and the ex-Queen Nathalie were washing their dirty linen

12 Obrenovich

in public, apparently indifferent to the effect this would have upon the fortunes of their son, the little Alexander.

And so it was that three months elapsed before I was able to return to Roumelia and once again enter upon the negotiations which my darling project entailed. Fortunately I was now able to interest the elder Slaveikoff, the father of my friendly guide, in my plan. He tried to dissuade me but when his arguments failed he turned to and was of the greatest assistance. Slaveikoff was a poet of more than local renown; indeed he was often spoken of as the Victor Hugo of Bulgaria. I was not in a position to judge if his reputation was well-founded, but he was an interesting old gentleman with an immense amount of leisure and quite unconsciously, I think, he whetted my desire to visit the Pomaks who, after having provoked the Russo-Turkish War, had retired into the obscurity, and incidentally into the security, of their mountain villages. Slaveikoff regarded the followers of the Agha as scoundrels of the deepest dye, traitors to their race and their faith, but with all that he made them quite fascinating.

At the time when the Ottoman Turks spread over the peninsula these mountain people, like the great Bosnian *begs*, saved their property and doubtless their lives by changing their religion. As I was later to learn, the life-saving slogan of those turbulent days "where the sword is, there is also the Faith" was accepted and honored with the closest observance by almost all of them down to our day.

Of course the Bosnian *begs* or landowners despite their backsliding, were squeezed a-plenty by the reigning pashas but the dwellers in the Rhodopian highlands were hard to get at and they were quite willing to pay for the more favorable treatment they received by services. The name Pomak with which they were baptized by the conquerors means, I understand, "helper or auxiliary soldier," and in payment of their devotion in many a foray into the Christian lands they acquired much booty and valuable privileges to which they clung tenaciously. Indeed under Sultan Mahomet the Fourth, a famous Nimrod who loved to hunt the bear in their wild country, they enjoyed rights and concessions which amounted to complete independence. They paid no taxes and lived under the rule of their own *beys* who were chosen from among the outstanding mountain men, and the Pasha of the Adrianople district always had the good sense to recognize this man as his *kaimakam* or prefect for the mountain region.

Gradually, according to Slaveikoff, the headship of the mountain clan remained with the members of one family. Hassan Agha, the hero of many legendary exploits, died with his boots on in 1860 and he was succeeded by his son, Akmet Agha, a man of great local fame and also of world-wide infamy and detestation of which, when I visited him some weeks later in his eyrie nest, I found he was entirely ignorant. Akmet had been quite successful in maintaining the independence of his people from the encroachments of both his Christian and his Moslem neighbors, and as a symbol of his sovereign rights he maintained an ambassador in Philippopolis. This extraordinary envoy was not lodged in a luxurious embassy and, as I later gathered, no funds for entertainment were at his disposal. Rain or shine, poorly garbed, he was to be found lounging on the front steps of the Ottoman Bank. Here the foreign affairs of the mountain satrapy were transacted before all men. Here as nowhere else in Europe at the time "open covenants" were "openly arrived at." Here men who would venture up in the highlands to buy skins or timber presented themselves for examination and scrutiny and here, when at last I decided upon the pilgrimage to the Great Assassin, I paid two pounds Turkish to have a traveling visa painted on my passport.

One afternoon while still in Philippopolis and only just getting on my legs again after another sharp attack of Vardar malaria, I fell in with a band of Pomaks who were coming into the Roumelian town, though at this time they were bent on trade and barter and not upon war. It was quite a caravan coming slowly down the rocky road that led into the city. Their horses, very diminutive creatures they were, but evidently sturdy, and the donkeys and oxen they convoyed were laden with timber and buckets of tar, and with skins they were planning to sell in the market. The men were tall and handsome, wore the *fez* or turban and, unlike the Bulgarians, most of them had beards. The fortune of war had gone against the mountain men but there was nothing obsequious in their bearing. They still took more than their fair share of the road and I noticed that the Bulgars only made slighting remarks about them when the Pomaks were out of hearing. These evidences of trade and commercial exchanges convinced me that the stories I had heard of the isolation of Pomak land had been exaggerated, to say the least. (I also learned that the Agha, whose lands had been handed back to the Sultan as a slight indemnity for his loss of the more fertile province of Eastern Roumelia by the Congress of Berlin, still tried to maintain the appearance of an independent sovereign although under the suzerainty of the Sultan.)

Then and there I determined to make the pilgrimage, and some days later I started on my journey. It might prove hazardous as Slaveikoff maintained, but on the other hand the mountain air would help me to get fit again. While sorely tempted, the younger Slaveikoff could not come with me, but he supplied a substitute and without this man the venture would have been a fiasco. He was a Spanish Jew, one of the thousands who had taken root in the Balkans after their expulsion by the Catholic kings and who, in my day at least, controlled all horse and mule transport throughout Roumelia.

While engaged in working out the time-taking arrangements for my visit to the Agha an incident occurred which would seem to indicate that I was not always such an alert newsgatherer as I have sought to make my readers believe. According to mythology even Jove nodded at times, and I can at least plead an extenuating circumstance. When caught napping I was in the throes of one of the attacks of the Vardar malaria which as a matter of fact continued to recur for several years.

One morning I was waited on in my inn by a strange, weird-looking man who, while he spoke English fluently, belonged to a race and a church that is most unpopular in Mohammedan countries. I shall not be more precise as to nationality and religion because while the Turks made strenuous efforts during the World War to exterminate these people quite a few scattered remnants still survive. My visitor told me that he and a group of his co-religionists were about to hold a meeting to discuss a very topical subject which was "The State of the World and What We Should Do to Improve it." He said he wanted me to be present, and as this was right up my alley I said I would be pleased to come. He seemed delighted and went away assuring me that shortly before the appointed hour he would call and lead me to the secret meeting-place.

The following day my visitor arrived and I had to receive him in my bedroom. I had had several chills and was dizzy from the quantity of quinine I had taken and I made it quite clear, indeed it was self-evident, that I could not attend the meeting.

"There is only one thing to be done," said my visitor. "We cannot go on without your advice and counsel so we shall assemble about midnight here in your bedroom. There are only five of us and as three of our number are staying in the caravansary adjoining your inn we can come in quite unobserved."

I acquiesced, and about midnight they were grouped about my bed. Two spoke excellent English and they started the proceedings. Their talk was discursive but I shall put the gist of the matter, as I digested it, rather briefly. For years they had been appealing to the conscience of the civilized world to put an end to the wrongs they suffered in the Turkish Empire. "But we have appealed in vain. Our prayers have gone unheeded. And now we have reached an important decision we mean to take what was promised us at the Congress of Berlin."

I began to take notice. Ten eyes burning like coals were fixed upon me. In the darkness of the chamber, a darkness that was intensified by the faint flickering light of two candles, they were grouped about me like so many predatory animals of the jungle.

"We have decided – to strike," said the spokesman. "No longer will we be cajoled into silence while we are being killed off one by one."

My suggestions that they should petition the Pasha, send a protest to the Sultan, setting forth the details of their harsh treatment, and file copies with the embassies, were waved aside courteously but firmly.

"No – we are going to strike the Turk where he will feel it – in his pocket. We are going to destroy the great commercial city upon which he levies tribute and grows rich – "

I never was more wide awake than at this moment as the plan came to me in sibilant whispers; I saw that fever or no fever I would have to think fast.

"We have decided to destroy the city of Salonica. We shall reduce it to ashes next week. The world will take notice, and even the Sublime Porte. The tobacco trade will be interrupted and the revenues will stop. As we know your paper supports the oppressed and the disinherited of the world we want you to come with us and see that we get fair play. In any event you can explain why we were driven to this step –".

I protested, as they could readily see, I was in no condition to go anywhere. But I insisted that I would not go with them even had I been in robust health. I explained what seemed to me the folly of their proposed action. To begin with, more than half the property and the wealth of Salonica was in the hands of the Spanish Jews, their companions in misfortune, their fellow-sufferers under Turkish oppression. They would be the greatest losers by such a conflagration as was proposed. Above all, while I admitted that the sympathy of the civilized world had not been very helpful, they would be poor indeed if they lost it and I concluded with the bromide of the day that political agitation should never depart from due processes of law.

The group listened patiently and the questions they put after my discourse was over were well considered and reasonable. When shortly before dawn they took their departure I thought that I had convinced them of the error of the plan and brought them back to a campaign within the limits of the law.

"You must keep within the bounds of legitimate political agitation," I insisted as they bowed themselves out and I sank back exhausted on my pillow.

I never saw my strange visitors again but a week later I heard from them and was compelled to revalue the effect of my oratory. Salonica was swept by a terrible conflagration, two thousand houses were reduced to ashes, tens of thousands became homeless although fortunately only a few of the bedridden and aged were roasted alive. It was found that combustibles had been placed in many quarters and the fire was undoubtedly of incendiary origin. Scores of suspects were arrested, not a few Armenians, Macedonians and Serbs. All representatives of the disaffected nationalities and minorities were lined up and shot while scores were sent to the convict stations in Tripoli where death came to them more slowly but no less surely. As it was quite clear to me that I had not handled this situation very intelligently, either as a newspaper correspondent or in any other capacity, I have never referred to it until the present writing...

At last all difficulties had apparently been brushed away. Manuel Abeles had even paraded before me the horses with which the journey was to be attempted and I had approved of them. They were far from pleasing to the eye but they looked capable of making the mountain climb. Then suddenly, although I protested that he was paying me too much honor, the Ambassador of the Pomak King announced that he would accompany me on my mission. He would, he insisted, introduce me and vouch for me. I was getting along very well with Abeles and the archaic Spanish which his forbears had brought from Andalusia to the Balkans in the fifteenth century, and I feared, not without reason, that the injection of the Ambassador's Turco-Bulgarian would prove perplexing – and it certainly did.

I advanced a number of arguments, most convincing ones I thought, why the Ambassador should remain on the steps of the Ottoman Bank and there before all men attend to his important duties. But as Slaveikoff suspected from the very beginning, there was more to this move than at first met the eye. He learned that the Ambassador's appointments were in arrears and assumed that he wished to take this matter up with the King of the Rhodopians at the moment when the arrival of a representative of a rising power from across the great water would be pleasing to his vanity. The debate lasted for several days but in the end the stubborn diplomat prevailed and I thanked him for his courtesy when it became apparent that unless he accompanied us our permit to travel to Tomrushlu would be canceled. And then the Ambassador, man of infinite resource that he was, had another idea which Slaveikoff thought was inspired by a desire to strengthen his financial situation even before we left Philippopolis. As I ignored several hints, although they were quite broad, he finally came out with, "What presents do you propose bringing to my Lord?" I told him that this was not the custom in our world but I did toy with the idea, and thinking that I was a more promising prospect than I later proved to be the Ambassador led me to a shop where in a back room a very beautiful gold-hilted and bejeweled *yataghan* was produced. The Ambassador and the happy owner of this weapon seemed to be on the best of terms, and after an amusing parley the owner said that, while it could not be bought by lesser mortal for any price, in view of the fact that the Agha greatly desired to add it to his armory he would let me have it for the insignificant price of ten thousand *piasters*!

At this I hung back, I made it quite plain that such a present was not contemplated in my instructions from the American people. These would justify an exchange of compliments and good wishes but a present of such magnificence might, by the exercise of Oriental imagination, immediately put me in the category of tribute-bearers. And to this position I clung, even when the price asked for the gold-hilted *yataghan* was reduced fifty per cent.

At long last we got under way and, wrangling in many languages, we toiled for several hours across the fertile Maritza plain toward the purple mountains the view of which had always fascinated me. As we came out of the city we halted for a moment at the simple memorial of the victorious war of 1878 which cost Russia so many men. I asked the Ambassador what it commemorated and he said he had not the remotest idea. He was not strong on history, but straight Bulgar though he was, he held his own with Manuel Abeles the Sephardin Jew when it came to discussing the value of hides and timber in *kopecks* or any other coin.

Our horses proved to be much better than they looked, and in a few hours we reached the little town of Belovo which is half-Pomak and half-Bulgarian. Here and all along the road I had an excellent opportunity of seeing that generations of servitude and oppression are not to be wiped away in a day or a year by a victory however brilliant or thorough. The Christians hereabouts still bore the physical marks of slavery. They were just beginning to walk upright and hold themselves as free men. The doors of their hovels, as I had noted in other districts, were always turned away from the road and so low you would think that the dwellers therein would have to enter on hands and knees. When I asked an explanation of this Manuel said, "The Turkish *Effendi* makes free with other people's property but he does not like to stoop."

We passed the night at a village famous for its medicinal springs, and the next morning started out through a great forest toward Tomrush, still the lair of Akmet Agha, the tiger of the Rhodopian hills. We passed through several villages of tiled roofed houses with limpid streams of water coursing down the streets. Everywhere elderly Turks were seated on well-worn carpets before their doors, sipping coffee and puffing at their long-stemmed pipes. Now and again we would meet a little caravan of Pomaks bringing timber down to the markets on the back of slow-moving oxen. Now and again we would see them shoeing their oxen with leather shoepads, a by no means easy job. All the oxen we fell in with seemed to have a decided preference for going barefoot.

A little before noon on the third day of our uphill journey we began to descend, and from now on our path was picketed by scouts who watched the intruders with unfriendly mien. They clutched at their guns and fingered their *yataghans* in a way that convinced me that but for the Ambassador the way would have been closed to us. Suddenly the valley narrowed and we were in Tomrush. I confess that the first view of the eagle's nest, the mountain eyrie of which I had heard so much, was disappointing. It was simply a wide place in a narrow trail. . . . And we certainly did not take the Lord of the Mountain by surprise; several runners had gone ahead announcing the strange visitor and when after a last steep and narrow ascent had been negotiated we came to the wide place in the road, there in front of a low stone-roofed house, by the side of a great ravine resounding with the rushing waters of a mountain stream, seated upon the stump of a tree, the Agha was awaiting us. Grouped behind him were four or five men with ancient muskets and belts bristling with *yataghans*. They were smoking long cigarettes and looked quite nonchalant. And well they might, as I had ventured into the mountain lion's den quite unarmed save for a swagger stick.

I had anticipated that the interview would not go off very smoothly. My brace of interpreters was not mutually helpful. Throughout the journey they had wrangled incessantly and their explanations often left me in great perplexity. It was natural that our conversation should limp a little, but I confess I was not prepared for the initial bombshell which put a quietus upon it for a minute or two. The Agha rose as I dismounted and drew near him, brought his right hand to his heart, then to his forehead in a gracious salute, and pointing to a vacant tree stump beside him resumed his seat.

Without awaiting any prompting from me, the Ambassador after a low bow opened up the conversation. It ran on for several minutes before I was taken into the inner circle. He was evidently explaining something and the Agha was receiving it with frank incredulity.

"Well! Well!" I exclaimed, in growing impatience.

"I have introduced you as the Envoy from America," at last the Ambassador explained. "Self-appointed," I insisted, and he nodded quick assent to my amendment. "But the Lord Agha says he has never heard of America. He says he has heard of Frankistan and has also received envoys from Nemski lands (the German countries) but never has he heard of America."

When I recovered my aplomb, of course, I sailed right in and explained that America was many times as big as the little countries with which he seemed to be familiar, that its inhabitants were more numerous than the leaves on the forest trees and that it was reached by sailing across a great expanse of water that was several times as broad as the Maritza River was long. I got off what seemed to me a fairly impressive spread-eagle speech, but I am not at all sure it carried conviction. When I concluded the Agha said a few words and these were, according to the Ambassador, "It may be so, Allah is great and the world is big. Of course I do not know all the lands of black infidelity!"

This rather nettled the self-appointed envoy from the land the Agha was inclined to ignore, and so I went ahead without gloves, which I would not have presumed to do if perfectly cordial diplomatic relations had been established. I flattered myself that hereafter the Lord of the Mountain would have a pretty good idea of the great country that had swum so unceremoniously into his ken, and then I changed the subject. We were well past the middle of December and I noticed over the doorways of many of the houses little green trees and I asked if they advertised the wine that was sold within. This suggestion was denied with some heat and then came the explanation that filled me with amazement. The Mohammedan Pomaks were preparing to celebrate the Feast of the Nativity, in other words our Christmas!

"How can that be possible!" I exclaimed, "when you and your people ... withdrew from our Church centuries ago."

"We honor all good men. We respect all strong men," came the answer.

I was quite reckless now so I said, "Tell me about the day when you entered the war under the Crescent and drew your sword upon your Bulgar brothers." With evident reluctance, the Ambassador passed this on.

"Brothers," repeated the Agha and then he spat out, "Dog-brothers."

"It happened in this way," he went on with perfect unconcern. "Our Sovereign Lord in Stamboul sent word that the dog-brothers of the plains and the valleys were waylaying his soldiers and he directed us to go down to their villages and quiet them."

"And you quieted them, ten thousand of them, men, women and children," I said bitterly. Now I knew I had burnt my bridges, but why should I dissemble when it was quite clear that the Lord of the Mountain would not enter into relations with a country he was confident did not exist?

"Yes, men, women and children," he answered softly. "The men were soldiers, the children were growing up, the women were the mothers of future soldiers. Yes, we killed them all. Where I was none escaped. Our Sovereign Lord was pleased. What happened would not have happened had not the One God approved."

I then, after a breathing spell, asked the Ambassador to draw the Agha out on the question as to which there has been so much dispute.

Whether the people of Batak had been slaughtered after a promise had been given that their lives would be spared if they surrendered their arms; but here the good man refused. "These things happen in war – always," he affirmed. "There was and always is in battle much confusion. It is an unpleasant subject let us not pursue it further. The Agha is a very old man and doubtless he has forgotten much." And I agreed that this was the wisest course to follow.

Coffee, cakes, and long cigarettes were now brought by the heavily-armed serving men who had hovered about during our talk. It was soon apparent that the Agha was toothless but munching on his hard gums he seemed to enjoy the light refection. Then he and the Ambassador began to talk about the trade in timber and the barter of skins and tar, the realities of life for which, as with other countries in ages past, the Mission in Philoppcpolis was maintained.

Soon I left them to their serious affairs and wandered about the village trying not to look crestfallen. But it was difficult, a strange role indeed was mine, that of ambassador from a country the receiving monarch had never heard of. Night fell, throwing a concealing mantle over my discomfiture, and suddenly it became bitterly cold. We were given comfortable, though by no means luxurious, quarters in an empty house. Nothing was said about supper, but fortunately some fragments of the provisions for the journey remained. I slept like a log on a skin-covered divan and at crack of dawn we, that is Abeles and myself, mounted our ponies and began the descent into the once blood-drenched valley. As we passed his house I caught my last glimpse of the man who enjoyed an unenviable fame in the land he had never heard of. He, too, lay on a skin-covered divan just outside his door. Two little boys with fly-swatters crouched beside him. On their hams the bodyguards formed a protective circle and apparently the Great Assassin was sleeping the sleep of the just. Nearby, crouching on his heels, like patience on an uneasy monument, the Ambassador awaited the awakening of the Lord of the Mountains. From his glum expression it was clear that the matter of his arrears in salary had not been satisfactorily arranged.

Leon Dennen; 1945:

Excerpts from *TROUBLE ZONE - Brewing Point of World War III?*; New York - Chicago: Ziff Davis Publishing Co., 1945.

INTRODUCTION

1.

During the months just before and following the break in German-Turkish diplomatic relations I was in Istanbul (Constantinople), age-old key to the Middle East and traditional watchtower of the Balkans. From the city of the Golden Horn I watched the collapse of the Nazi armies in southeastern Europe, the liberation of the Balkans by our allies, and their subsequent re-enslavement by their liberators.

I left New York City for Istanbul in March 1944 on a rescue mission for an American relief agency. My assignment was to help men and women of the anti-Nazi underground and resistance movements whose lives were in danger because of their active opposition to Hitler. These included Gentiles and Jews, labor people and journalists, scholars and artists. I was asked to undertake this mission because of my knowledge of European languages, familiarity with the countries of eastern and southeastern Europe where I had lived as a child and in later years as a newspaperman, and also because for many months prior to my departure I had been intimately associated with exiled leaders of European labor and through them with a number of anti-Nazi underground organizations.

The American agency on whose behalf I went abroad had a notable record in aiding anti-Nazis and anti-fascists in various parts of Europe. With the formation of the War Refugee Board and the prospect of generous co-operation by our State Department, new opportunities presented themselves to broaden the scope of its work. We had no illusions, of course. We knew how little we could do to relieve the suffering to which our allies of the underground were being subjected in the Nazi-occupied areas. Nevertheless, we all felt that if even a few of these people were rescued, or helped in some other way, our effort would be well invested.

Some day it will be possible to tell my story in full. Unfortunately democratic views and convictions are still a handicap rather than an asset even in the *"liberated"* countries of eastern and southeastern Europe; leaders of democracy are still being persecuted this time by their liberators. Under the circumstances, much of my experience must for the moment remain untold, to safeguard men with whom and for whom I worked.

I had a favorable opportunity, however, to observe at first hand the dramatic political events which rocked eastern Europe, the Balkans, and the Middle East during the summer, fall, and winter of 1944. In so far as they came within my purview, these events form the subject matter of this book.

I want to admit at the outset that I am not "objective" – if objectivity means a detached and automatic acceptance of handouts by the various propaganda agencies, each of which has its own ax to grind. Life in the Balkans today is entirely too grim for such spurious objectivity. The stakes for mankind are too large for any such neutrality of the spirit. I was and remain a partisan of the men and women who continue to struggle for their democratic faith and reject *ersatz* freedom.

Propaganda has become a fine art in our epoch. The nation with the most efficient and best subsidized public relations apparatus has the best chance to conceal and distort the truth, to impose its own version of the truth. It can mold public opinion through willing agents and unwilling dupes. The objective historian of tomorrow will have to probe deeply and diligently into the mountains of contradictory evidence to find the essential facts about our tragic era. And it is altogether likely that many a public-relations fable of the moment will go down as fact in the history books.

But propaganda is a dangerous substitute for truth. Humanity at large, and we Americans in particular, will pay dearly for illusions, self-deceptions, and a fear of confronting unpleasant truths squarely. The problem in post-war Europe, especially in the chaotic Balkans, is far more complex than some of our wishful thinking writers and commentators would have us believe.

Political events move fast these days. Much will have been altered by the time these words see print. Yet the basic problem will remain the same as long as democratic institutions are not restored and subjected peoples are not liberated genuinely and unconditionally. It is the over-all problem of freedom and self-determination without benefit of external threats and pressures.

2.

Personal danger did not evoke in me those emotions prescribed in the literature of war. I crossed the Atlantic and the Mediterranean in a Liberty ship. While our convoy of a hundred ships was being subjected to a combined air and submarine attack, I merely thought: "I hope they miss us. I hope this madness is over soon." The stirring feelings and words appropriate to such an occasion were nowhere in sight. But when it was all over I did think long about the amazing contribution to victory being made by the men of our merchant marine. They face the hazards of war like any soldier in combat, often against far heavier odds. While bombs, depth charges, and torpedoes were bursting all over and around us, and eight hundred guns were blazing away at seen and unseen enemies, the crews went about their business as coolly as surgeons during an operation.

In the midst of the din, noise, and terror the First Mate of the *William Meredith*, who had already been torpedoed twice and spent thirty days roaming the seas in a lifeboat, struck a pose like Winston Churchill. Imitating the British Prime Minister, he declaimed: "We have licked the menace of the submarine!" And the only comment of the First Assistant Engineer was: "Damn the torpedoes full speed ahead!" A gay little Irishman from Brooklyn, our First Assistant Engineer, explained that his only reason for not wanting to die was that he had a "witch" at home and five brats to feed.

As I write this, only a year has elapsed since that trip on the Liberty ship. My experiences and reactions of this crossing are already dim and all but forgotten. But etched in my mind as sharply as if it were yesterday I remember another scene. I stood on the shore of the Sea of Marmara awaiting the arrival of the *Mefkure*, a small Turkish motorboat, which was to have brought several hundred Jewish refugees from the Rumanian port of Constanta. It was already dark and the sea was getting rough. We feared that the tiny ship, packed to capacity with children and survivors of Nazi extermination camps in Poland, could not withstand a storm in the Black Sea. Gloomily we were discussing possible reasons for its delay when word reached us that the boat had been sunk by three German gunboats. Only five persons had been rescued, two of them women: Hilda Vumbrandt, a twenty-year-old student of the University of Bucharest, and Veronika Fulop, an eighteen-year-old Hungarian Jewess in the ninth month of pregnancy who, by a miracle, survived together with her husband.

Three hundred men, women, and children, after years of slavery, were at last within sight of blessed freedom, but perished before they could grasp it! There was more tragedy in it, it seemed to me, than in anything conceived by imaginative literature. This one atrocity, I felt, summed up the horror of our brutalitarian age. Here is the story of the *Mefkure* as Veronika Fulop told it to me:

The sea was calm and the weather was fine when we left Constanta. We knew that there was something wrong. All lawyers, doctors, engineers, and professors who had been assigned to different boats were ordered by the Nazi officials to transfer to the *Mefkure*. This was an unusual procedure. The first few hours after we left port things went smoothly, but we wondered uneasily why we were being followed by a number of armed boats. At two o'clock in the morning a flare suddenly lit up our boat. This was followed by a number of shells. Dark shadows were lurking a short distance from our boat.

The first two missiles fell into the sea, but the third, fourth and fifth hit the *Mefkure* and set it on fire. The men, women and children never had a chance. They were trapped in the burning hell, Some of us jumped into the water. The Nazis opened machine gun fire on us.

While the trapped people were burning and drowning, the Nazis jeered: "Look at the Jews swimming to Palestine."

"Was there much panic during the attack?" I asked her.

"No," she replied, "only the children cried. The older people stood in the burning hell awaiting death in silence. Hitler has taught us how to die without making too much noise."

3.

When I arrived in Istanbul in June, Greece, Bulgaria, Rumania, Poland, Albania, and most of Yugoslavia were still occupied by the Nazis. I quickly established contact with the underground leaders. Some of them had already escaped to Turkey. It was my mission to help others escape. I talked at length with many proven lifelong friends of freedom who were still in the thickest of the struggle.

Two months later, following the Turkish-German break, I stood with many others in front of Istanbul's imposing German Embassy when Franz von Papen, Hitler's Ambassador to Turkey, bade farewell to the city of his intrigues. He was departing for the Turkish-Bulgarian border, leaving behind him a host of frightened Gestapo agents and satellite diplomats.

Yesterday Hitler's "devil in top hat" celebrated the victories of the Nazi hordes in the fabulous Park Oteli; the "Heil Hitler" of his drunken henchmen resounded over the Bosporus and the Marmara far into the night. Today he was suddenly old and spiritless. His face was drawn, he looked frightened and broken. Assuming once more perhaps for the last time in his sinister career his old pose of the pious man thwarted, von Papen wept. But the bystanders only cheered. They saw in the broken old man the symbol of the doom of the *Herrenvolk*.

Turks and refugees from Poland, Czechoslovakia, Germany, Austria, Bulgaria, Yugoslavia, Rumania, and Hungary, who for several years had been helping the Allies and had, as a result, lived in constant dread of the mighty

Gestapo, now emerged into the open. They were determined to continue the fight until the final liberation of Europe. After many months of suffering in darkness they at last saw a glimmer of hope. Their sacrifices seemed rewarded and their courage was unbounded. Without exception, they looked toward a social, economic, and political order which, in its essential values and freedoms, would be modeled after America and Britain. It was for this they were fighting and risking everything. The prospect, for democratic federations of the eastern and southeastern European states was good indeed, if only the convictions of such men would find expression.

But their jubilation did not last long. Their hopes soon crashed against the realities of power politics. They faced betrayed hopes and broken promises on the part of the British; a reign of terror on the part of the Russians.

The people of eastern and southeastern Europe, I am able to attest, feel that they have been betrayed by the Allies. The Poles, Bulgars, Serbs, and Rumanians believed the promises made by Washington, London, and Moscow. They took the Atlantic Charter seriously and looked forward to enjoying its stipulated freedoms once the Nazi yoke was thrown off. They counted, as a matter of course, on honest Allied assistance in establishing truly liberal and democratic governments after the overthrow of the Nazi regimes.

They were rudely awakened out of this dream by one blow after another. The uprising of the heroic Polish underground in Warsaw, led by General Bor (T. Komorowski), coincided with the German-Turkish break and made it seem as if deliverance was really at hand. Only democratic leaders of the underground could understand to the full the self-sacrificial courage represented by that war of ill-armed men against all-powerful German forces of occupation. When the Poles were abandoned to their fate – ruthless extermination – by the Allies, the shock of bewilderment and disillusionment in southeastern Europe was indescribable.

A Turkish citizen who had lived in Warsaw for twenty years, operating a coffee shop, left the Polish capital only a few hours before the uprising started. Arriving in Istanbul a few days later, he gave an interview to the press. His close-up account and other information circulating among the refugees in Turkey are worth setting down, in view of the subsequent charges and counter-charges. Everything that we heard confirmed the fact that the Germans were cracking and that only a little help from the outside would have sufficed to turn the scales in favor of the insurgents.

At the beginning of July 1944 the German terror in Warsaw was greatly intensified. Daily, hundreds of people were arrested and sent to unknown destinations, or murdered in the cellars of Gestapo headquarters on Alleja Szuch in the city. The executions were no longer public; the Germans were beginning to show signs of panic. One now seldom saw Germans walking in the streets after dark. Most of them were confined in the streets around AlIeja Ujazdowa and Plac Teatralny where the Foreign Ministry was located. In effect it was a ghetto for Germans right in the heart of Warsaw!

The Polish underground answered terror with terror. More and more German officers and men were found dead in the streets. On July 15 the Germans began to evacuate all factories, plants, and offices. But to the utter astonishment of the Polish population, there was no bombing of the railroad stations, though the Russians by this time were in Otwock, only ten miles from Warsaw. There was considerable movement of German troops. Panzer divisions were hastily evacuating the vicinity of Warsaw. A rumor spread that the Nazis, before departing, intended to raze Warsaw completely. On July 22 the Nazi police left Warsaw and were replaced by *Sicherheits Dienst Upteilungen*, brought in from the city of Lwow. These detachments consisted mostly of Russians, former prisoners of war, from the Ukraine, Azerbaijan, and Soviet Georgia. The Turks whose café they patronized heard them boast of the fact that before coming to Warsaw they used to shoot seven thousand Jews daily.

The Polish population, the underground movement, and the Home Army expected the Red Army to move into the city at any moment. *To prevent the escape of German troops and the destruction of Warsaw General Bor gave the order for the uprising to begin.*

The rest is recent history, clear enough despite deliberate attempts to smear the facts beyond recognition. The Russian forces stopped on the very threshold of Warsaw. Not only did they call off the expected advance into the capital but they even ceased to harass the Germans. Soviet planes, which had operated against the enemy until then, disappeared as if by magic as if to give the Nazis a better chance to destroy the underground insurgents. For six weeks the Soviet authorities even refused to allow American bombers to use Russian shuttle-bases to assist the desperate Home Army of Poland.

Suddenly Moscow discovered that the heroic uprising was "premature" and "unprepared" as if that justified failure to help allies battling against the common enemy! The Moscow-made Lublin Government (at that time still called the Lublin Committee) obligingly followed the same line of accusations against the men who were being killed wholesale by the Germans. More than that, to justify the Kremlin's extraordinary charges the Lublin puppets launched a smear campaign – against the embattled patriots, with General Bor himself as the main target.

The underground leader, who had in the meantime been designated Commander-in-Chief of the Polish Forces at home and abroad by the Polish Government in London, was accused of failure to make contact with the Red Army Command. Actually there is overwhelming evidence that Moscow rebuffed all efforts of the fighting Poles to make such contact. Common sense indicates that as a matter of mere survival the insurgents would have wished Red co-operation; and certainly the London Government clamored for help.

While the entire world was paying a tribute of admiration to the heroism of the poorly armed people of Warsaw and their sixty-three day struggle against the German Army, Lublin "Prime Minister" Edward Osubka-Morawski proclaimed General Bor a criminal and a traitor. Thus the Polish patriot joined the distinguished array of democrats and anti-Nazi fighters - General Draja Mihailovich in Yugoslavia, Nikola Mushanoff in Bulgaria, and Iuliu Maniu in Rumania – who were similarly branded "traitors" and "war criminals" by Moscow and its Communist-dominated puppet regimes.

Democratic feelings in southeastern Europe were outraged. The reaction among anti-Nazi refugees in Turkey left no doubt of this.

4.

The most fantastic thing I encountered upon my return to the United States was the taboo imposed upon frank and honest discussion of Russia's role in the war and the coming peace. A kind of intellectual terror pervades our literary and political life. It is not only respectable but even "liberal" to criticize American and British policy, but to cast the slightest doubt on Russian policy is to leave yourself open to denunciation as a "fascist," a "reactionary," and even a "war criminal." In the Balkans, right in the lion's den, democratic men and women hope, suffer, and fight for lasting peace, for a free world, and for human decency in the face of overwhelming odds... Why this moral cowardice and intellectual bankruptcy in the United States, the most powerful and respected nation on earth?

Concealment of the unsavory facts about Russia's foreign policies, at the same time that we are outspoken in criticism of Great Britain, will certainly not help us to achieve the aim for which the youth of America and our Allies have been fighting and dying on the battlefields of Europe and Asia. We were indignant at Britain's veto of the inclusion of Count Carlo Sforza in the Italian Government. We criticized – superficially and unjustly, I think – Churchill's counterattack against the totalitarian forces in Greece. Why the taboo on criticism of Russia's imperialist policies in the Balkans, Poland, the Middle East, and other parts of Europe?

I shall have many harsh words to say about Prime Minister Churchill who, in his overpowering desire to preserve the British Empire, has sold democracy short in Yugoslavia, Palestine, and Poland. But I am wary of those who seek to drive a wedge between the American and British people. I am convinced that we must ward off all attempts to play Americans against the British.

A policy of frankness and forthrightness on our part toward our Soviet ally is instantly branded "anti-Russian" by the Communist and pro-Soviet press. It is nothing of the sort. America cannot afford to be anti-Russian. But neither can America afford to be anti-democracy. That we will fairly, constructively, and positively support democratic forces is what an overwhelming majority of the people throughout Europe hope for desperately. The realization of that hope would be long-term insurance not only for the democracies but for Russia. It is the world's best bet that the peace which comes will have in it a minimum of the germs of another war and a reasonable promise of orderly political, economic, and social progress.

It is difficult to write dispassionately of the suffering of the small countries in whose midst I lived. Nowhere is the democratic hope in greater need of support from the great democracies than in eastern and southeastern Europe. In common with millions of other Americans I am convinced that unless the United States, Soviet Russia, and Great Britain, in co-operation with China, France, Poland, Greece, Yugoslavia, and the other small nations, are willing and able to work out a common policy for the rehabilitation of the world and the restoration of true democracy, then the Yalta Conference, the San Francisco United Nations Conference on International Organization, the Atlantic Charter, and all plans for the future stability and the peace of the world will go up in the smoke of a third World War.

A common policy, however, cannot be worked out in a vacuum. Unless we are aware of the designs and plans of our allies in this war unless, in short, we know and boldly face the truth we shall have won the war but lost the peace.

CHAPTER ONE

RIVALRY IN THE EASTERN MEDITERRANEAN

At the very time Roosevelt, Stalin, and Churchill were meeting in the former Winter Palace of the Czars at Yalta to settle the fate of the postwar world, another international conference was convening at Cairo. On February 14, 1945, representatives of the Arab states in the Middle East gathered in Egypt's capital for the avowed purpose of working out a plan for Arab unity and eventually to set up an Arab League.

The general jubilation over the Crimea Charter, which ostensibly held out to a war-weary world a promise of democracy, security, and international co-operation, obscured the significance of Cairo. The Big Three, having disposed of Yugoslavia and Poland, made a perfunctory reference to the Balkans in their declaration: "There was also a general review of other Balkan questions." But the Middle East was not even mentioned. All the same it became obvious that the eastern Mediterranean ghost haunted the Yalta proceedings. On his way home the late President Roosevelt met once again with the British Prime Minister aboard an American cruiser in Egypt's Mediterranean harbor of Alexandria. Then, each of them separately consulted with a galaxy of Middle Eastern potentates, including King Farouk of Egypt, King Abdul Aziz Ibn Saud of Saudi Arabia, and Haile Selassie of Ethiopia. Churchill also met with the President of Syria, Shukri al-Kuwatli.

For a brief moment the curtain of censorship was lifted on the troubled eastern Mediterranean area where the ultimate collaboration of Great Britain, Soviet Russia, and the United States will be subjected to its severest test. It is in the countries clustered about the eastern Mediterranean in the Balkans and the Middle East that the great spiritual and political drama of the postwar world is now being enacted in an atmosphere of boundless cynicism and greed. From the Vistula to the Bosporus and thence to the Red Sea and ancient Nile, rivalries among the great powers threaten to complete the enslavement of the small nations commenced by Germany.

Exponents of "spheres of influence" and power politics never grow weary of telling us that the small "Balkanized" states are a quarrelsome lot who always entangle the "peaceful" great powers in their local wars. The truth is just the reverse – the big powers have used these small countries and their ancient conflicts as pawns in their own games.

A conglomeration of cultures, nationalities, and religions Serbs, Croats, Bulgarians, Macedonians, Greeks, Albanians, Rumanians, Turks, Hercegovinians, Montenegrins, and Bosnians the Balkan states have always fought doggedly for their freedom. Their folklore is replete with legends recounting the exploits of great hero-liberators. It is true that since their release from Ottoman rule they have been the "tinder box" of Europe. Failure to adjust their perennial territorial claims and the alliance of the Balkan states against the Turks in the tragic war of 1912 have left a residue of smoldering resentment on that unhappy peninsula which, on the slightest provocation, might flare up into a full-fledged war.

In addition to political tensions there have been religious conflicts. The Greek Orthodox Church which predominated in the Balkans has always been at loggerheads with the Uniat Catholics, Roman Catholics, and Moslems inhabiting those countries. These nationalistic and religious struggles have been augmented during the second World War by atrocities committed by Bulgarian occupation troops against the Greeks, Serbs, and Albanians, and the murder of defenseless Serbs by the Croat quisling group of *Ustashi*.

Nevertheless, history and events of which I was myself a witness do not confirm the cynical assertion of the exponents of power politics that the small nations breed wars. Within the past two centuries there have been few wars in the Balkans that were not deliberately started and supported by competing great powers or coalitions of powers. Indeed, the history of Balkan humanity is primarily the saga of the tiller of the soil who, with rifle or knife in one hand and plow in the other, had to struggle incessantly against foreign domination. Now that he has been "liberated" from the Nazis, power politics is once again finding full play in the Balkans.

The Balkans correspond, largely, with the area of the Danubian Basin. With the Yugoslav coast and with Albania, Greece, and Turkey, however, they are of vital economic and strategic importance in the eastern Mediterranean. This is the primary reason for their centuries-old tragedy. What we are witnessing today in this traditional crossroads of East and West is essentially a repetition of the conflicts which ninety years ago resulted, symbolically enough, in the Crimean War. Once again the Balkan peninsula and the Middle East have become the political battleground of mighty powers.

The Czarist statesman once said: *"The stronger Russia is in Central Asia, the weaker is England in India, and the more will she be conciliatory in Europe."* Just how this formula influenced Roosevelt and especially Churchill in their haste to assure "democracy" to Poland and Yugoslavia by consigning their outstanding exponents of democracy to the scrap heap will no doubt be the subject for deep probing by future historians. For the moment one thing seems obvious: the Crimean War between Britain and Russia, to paraphrase Georges Clemenceau, has not ended; it has merely changed its form. In the 1850's the word "jingoism" was born in the London music halls, and good Englishmen sang:

"We don't want to fight, but, by jingo, if we do,
We've got the ships, we've got the men, we've got the money too.
We've fought the Bear before and we'll do the same again,
The Russians shan't have Constantinople".

There is, of course, a profound difference in the present jockeying for power between Great Britain and Soviet Russia. In 1854, when England joined Sultan Abdul Medjid in his war against the Czar, she was fighting for an expanding empire. Today[13] Britain's basic aim is the preservation of her empire. Now as then, however, the British fear another great power perched on the shores of any sea communicating with the Eastern Mediterranean near the Empire's life line at the Suez Canal. This involves Egypt, Iran, Turkey and the Dardanelle Straits, Yugoslavia and Albania on the Adriatic, Bulgaria and Rumania on the Black Sea, and little Macedonia the much-disputed province on the Aegean Sea which, in December 1944, was one of the causes of widespread civil war and bloodshed in Greece.

Somewhere between Great Britain and Soviet Russia the United States, too, is now charting an uneven and deeply confused course in the Balkan and Middle Eastern countries. For the present, however, the rivalry is primarily between London and Moscow. Soviet Russia, like its Czarist predecessor, seeks first the control of the Balkans from the Adriatic to the Aegean and eventually control of the entire Middle East. Great Britain, weakened by World War II, is desperately seeking to hold on to the Empire's life line.[14]

Tito's attempt acting for Soviet Russia to seize Trieste in May 1945 by force of arms and present the Anglo-Americans with a *fait accompli* was but another in a series of incidents among the Allies in the Balkans. I am not at the moment concerned with the justice of the Yugoslav's claims.

13   Leon Dennen wrote this book in 1945.

14   In this connection it is interesting to note that just as the Greek Communists fought with arms to deliver the disputed territory of Macedonia to Bulgaria, so the Italian Communists demand that Italy yield Trieste and Fiume to Tito's Yugoslavia. An article in the Communist newspaper L'Unita, writes Herbert L. Matthews in the New York Times of February 8, 1945, "threw the whole delicate question of Trieste on the table with a startling bang, for it aligned Italy's most powerful single party, with its important connections with Moscow, with Marshal Tito. It is also significant as representing a change in what has been the consistently nationalistic policy of the Italian Communist Party."

There is no doubt that the Istrian Peninsula back of the coastal strip is inhabited by a majority of Slovenes and properly belongs to Yugoslavia. But Trieste and Fiume are predominantly Italian and were inhabited by a majority of Italians even before Rome took possession of them in 1918.

If international law is to rule the postwar world, only a plebiscite conducted under neutral auspices can determine the wish of the people of Trieste. Why, then, has Tito braved incurring the displeasure of his British supporters by employing arbitrary force? Why the haste?

To begin with, Trieste is the nearest large port having an excellent dock system to the vital bauxite deposits in northern Yugoslavia.[15] Even more important is the fact that this city, with close to a quarter of a million inhabitants, is vital in any scheme to control the eastern Mediterranean and the British sea route to India. Moreover, it is also the approach to, and the outlet from, the Danubian countries, and is only some two hundred and fifty miles from Vienna by a circuitous railway route. "With Trieste under Russia's dominance the economic and political influence of the USSR would be enormously augmented; in the hands of an Italy well inclined toward the British influence it could be a toe-hold on these portions of southeastern Europe which Britain once controlled economically and appears to have lost."[16]

For the moment a temporary solution to the dispute has been reached. Tito has agreed to withdraw most of his troops from the Adriatic-Austrian communication zone, pending a peace conference which will ultimately settle the disposal of this area.

Present Soviet aims, as a matter of fact, go far beyond Czarist ambitions. Russia has long since discarded Lenin's advocacy of independence and sovereignty for the "oppressed colonial peoples," which prompted Soviet Russia's dramatic withdrawal from the Middle East in the 1920's.

15   Until 1918, Trieste was the primary port of the Austro-Hungarian Empire, handling the bulk of the international commerce of a population exceeding 52 million. (Ed.)

16   New Leader, June 9, 1945.

At first limited to internal politics, the Kremlin's neo-Communist policies of intense nationalism have since spread to the foreign field. This change, as the London *Economist* recently pointed out, is not merely ideological. For one thing, it represents a sharp departure from the Soviet's earlier policy of autarchy. Russia is now ready to abandon autarchy at least to the extent of claiming a lien on the world's oil reserves. This retreat from economic isolationism may not be very rapid or immediate but the direction has already been set. There is no doubt that henceforth Soviet influence in the Middle East will have an economic as well as a political basis. Russia's industrial areas, embracing the Central Asiatic and Trans-Caucasian Republics, will be the nearest if not the most efficient workshops of the Middle East.

Beyond Anglo-Russian economic and political rivalries, however, there lurks the old problem of India. "Bolshevism," an old Balkan Communist leader told me last year in Cairo, "regards India as the weakest link in the British imperial structure – a key to the dissolution of the Empire."

Moscow has long been convinced that the British Empire is tottering and unlikely to survive for long another serious crisis. The Soviets count strongly on nationalist friction in India, in the Dominions and, incidentally, upon Anglo-American rivalry. At the moment the Big Three were announcing "international co-operation" at Yalta, Charles Waterhouse, Parliamentary Secretary of the British Board of Trade, indicated that Britain will adhere to her imperial preference policy in the postwar trading era, basing her international trade upon the policy of first consideration for the British Commonwealth. "Asserting that Britain would willingly enter into trade agreements with the United States and Russia," a dispatch from London said, Mr. Waterhouse added "that both countries must understand that Britain would not follow any subservient policy in concluding such agreements."[17]

While present British policy in the Middle East follows the traditional imperialist pattern and American policy is still in a nebulous stage, Russia's

17   New York Times, Feb. 13, 1945.

presents a strange amalgam of new "revolutionary" slogans and methods combined with old aims. Her long-range plans were perhaps best expressed by the Czarist General Kuropatkin in 1900:

"When we shall rule over the Bosporus [Turkey] and the entrance into the Mediterranean, we shall be able to tackle the Egyptian question with energy and to make the Suez Canal an international thoroughfare. When we have gained this entry into the Indian Ocean, we can constantly threaten India. Russia's competition on the world market will intimidate the highly developed countries of Europe and America... On railroads spanning Russia from the Baltic to the Great Ocean, we will extend our tentacles toward the Bosporus, the Indian Ocean and the Atlantic. Russia will be a permanent danger with her inexhaustible riches to the industries of all ranking powers".[18] When I was in Cairo there was talk that Russia had acquired a block or Suez Canal stock which would give her an equal vote with the British Government at shareholders' meetings.

In the past Russian plans in this area were counter-balanced by rival drives of Germany, Austria-Hungary, France, Italy, and England. Today England alone, for the present at least, remains facing the Red Army.

3.

In the struggle for domination of the Balkans and the Middle East "revolutionary" Russia has many assets which neither the United States nor Great Britain possesses.

Unlike the British and French, the Soviet Government has no political liabilities in the Middle East. Unlike the Americans, it has no history of oil imperialism to live down. In a word, Moscow's political record in the Near East is "clean." The Arabs remember the support they received from local Communist groups in the twenties and thirties. In Palestine, Arab Communists still quote Stalin's view, as expressed in 1913 in his pamphlet on "Na-

---

18   G. R. Treviranus, *Revolutions in Russia* (New York: Harper & Bros., 1944" p. 59.

tionalities," to the effect that "Zionism is the movement of the reactionary Jewish bourgeoisie and its hangers-on."

It is significant that both the predominantly Moslem Syrians and the predominantly Christian Lebanese requested the Russians to enter into diplomatic relations with them, a request which the Soviet Government acceded to at once. The Lebanese request specifically referred to Russia's generous treatment of all nationalities, and to the Soviet role as the "revolutionary champion" of the oppressed nations.[19] Moscow has also established diplomatic relations with Egypt, Ethiopia, and Iraq. While I was in Cairo negotiations were going on between the Soviet Union and King Ibn Saud of Saudi Arabia for the resumption of relations.

Soviet Russia has also given evidence that it knows how to exploit the nationalist sentiments and religious beliefs of the Christian and Moslem populations of the Middle East and the Balkans.

For many decades the Slav nationalities of the Balkans were used by the Czars as instruments in their expansionist policies in the eastern Mediterranean. After the Revolution, Czarist Pan-Slavism, too, was abandoned by Russia. The present Soviet revival of the Pan-Slavic slogan, however, has little in common with Dostoevski's Slavophilism, his plea in 1877 that Constantinople the ancient Byzantium should for intellectual and sentimental reasons remain the pivot of Russian foreign policy, it is in direct line, rather, with the Pan-Slavism of the Petersburg historian, Professor Mitrosanov, who, during World War I, in an open letter to Hans Delbrueck, his Berlin colleague and former teacher, said:

"From the Russian standpoint, the Balkan question is not a *guerre de luxe* nor the adventurous dream of Slavophiles. Its solution is unmistakably an economic and political necessity. . . Two-thirds of our exports go out of the southern ports and through the Turkish Straits (Bosporus and Dardanelles). If this outlet were blocked, Russian commerce would stagnate, and the economic consequences of this blockade would be unforeseeable. This was

19   The Economist, London, Oct. 21, 1944.

amply demonstrated in the last Turkish-Italian war in Tripolitania [in 1912]. Only the possession of the Bosporus and the Dardanelles by Russia can put an end to this intolerable situation, because the existence of Russia as a world power must not be left to chance and foreign discretion. On the other hand, Russia can hardly be completely indifferent to the fate of the South Slavs on the Balkan peninsula. First, the small Balkan states provide rear cover for the Straits, and, second, too much Russian blood and gold have been expended over the course of centuries to produce Balkan heroes."

To drop the whole thing now would be moral and political suicide for any Russian government.... And to repeat: The drive toward the south [*Drang nach Sueden*] is a historical, political and economic necessity for Russia. Any nation that opposes this drive becomes an enemy nation *ipso facto*.[20]

The vision of Pan-Slavism which involves the creation of a vast bloc from the Baltic to the Bosporus, has potentialities which even the German plan of *Mitteleuropa* never possessed. For one thing, there are more Slavs than there are Germans. As Peter Jordan points out in his plea for a Central Union of Europe, the power at the command of whoever might control this Pan-Slav Empire would be mightier than that of any other ruler in modern history.[21]

The re-establishment in Russia of the Greek Orthodox Church points in the same direction. The great liberal Russian historian, Paul Miliukov, wrote more than three decades ago that "Russia, Slavic from head to toe, imagines that she has been endowed with a mission to transform the Balkans into a Slav – a Russian to all intents and purposes – Empire. When in towns and villages of the Balkan peninsula one encounters shady characters who make the sign of the cross at every corner and display holy ikons, it is at once obvious that they are Russian agents and that violence is ahead..."[22]

20   Cited by Ernst Jackh, The Rising Crescent (New York: Farrar & Rinehart, 1944), p. 111.

21   Peter Jordan, Central Union of Europe (New York: Robert M. McBride & Co., 1944), p. 38.

22   Paul N. Miliukov, Balkanshi Krizis [Balkan Crisis], published in St. Petersburg in 1909.

During the first two decades of Bolshevism the Greek Orthodox Church which undoubtedly had been a widely abused instrument of Czarist oppression and corruption, practically ceased to exist in Russia. Symbolically, one of the most revered shrines in Orthodox Russia, at the entrance to Moscow's Red Square, was torn down and on a wall only a few yards away Muscovites read the inscription in bold letters: RELIGION IS THE OPIATE OF THE PEOPLE. Church lands were confiscated and priests were deprived of their citizenship. But as Russia prepared for war, particularly after 1939, official Soviet policy toward the church changed radically. The value of reconciliation with the church was recognized by the Kremlin as it became obvious that Hitler intended to use persecution of religion in the USSR as a propaganda weapon against Bolshevism.

The Soviet Government anticipated him by tapering off its persecution of the church and discontinuing all anti-religious propaganda. This rehabilitation of religion fitted well into the campaign to revive the glory of Russia's past as a means of mobilizing elements in the population who were unmoved by slogans of Communism and Sovietism. It helped, too, in the creation of this new Pan-Slavism in the Balkans where "Holy Russia" has far more appeal than "Red Russia."

Wherever Greek Orthodoxy is widely dominant, the Soviets have moved in as protectors of the faith. For instance, they have taken over the rehabilitation of all Greek Orthodox monasteries and convents in the Levant. After being closed for twenty-five years, the Orthodox Church attached to the old Russian Embassy in Istanbul was reopened with much heraldry. The Russian monasteries and churches in Palestine, once the pride of the Czars but for the past two decades abandoned by revolutionary Russia, have blossomed forth again; the aged monks and priests, once the obedient servants of the Little Father in St. Petersburg, are today pouring out their blessings and hosannas on the head of the Little Father in the Kremlin.

The visit of Nikolai Novikov, Soviet Minister to Egypt, to the monasteries and convents of Am Karim, Jerusalem, Hebron, Jericho, Mount Carmel, and Safed, is by now a *cause celèbre* in the cafes of the Middle East. At Safed, Novikov was introduced to "an old nun whose watery eyes had seen the glory and affluence of her church under the Czars, had known the dark days of the revolution and the lean years of Soviet atheism when the flow of the kopecks ceased and the church's properties rotted with despair."[23]

But now the Soviet Minister, well-dressed and with an air of affluence, had appeared as the miraculous protector of Greek Orthodoxy. Surely the forces of the Anti-Christ have been banished and the Almighty has heard the pleas of his suffering children! Novikov brought money to the institution and pledged to guard over its welfare.

"'When are you returning to Moscow?' the old nun asked, holding Novikov's hands in both her own.

"'Tomorrow, little mother,' Novikov replied.

"'And when you are gone, who will protect me?' worried the nun.

"'Father Stalin and myself, Novikov reassured her. 'If you are in trouble, send me a telegram and I will return.'"[24]

At about the same time, Greek Orthodox Patriarchs and Metropolitans of the Levant were invited to Moscow for the first time since the Revolution, to attend the first general Episcopal Assembly of the Russian Orthodox Church and the crowning of a new Patriarch. The opening of this Assembly in January 1945 was a memorable occasion, reminiscent of Czarist glory. Hundreds of spectators and bearded ecclesiastics from all over the world thronged the beautiful Church of Resurrection.

In a mixed atmosphere of ancient clerical gowns and caps and symbols of modern times, including floodlights and movie cameras, the newly-elected Patriarch, Metropolitan Alexei of Novgorod and Leningrad, opened the conclave with a prayer for the health and long life of all guests. He greeted the Patriarch of Serbia "who is still languishing in German enslavement" and the "highly honored Benjamin of America who inspires the hearts of our brothers in such a distant country as the United States." Nor did he forget to put in a good word for Stalin:

23   Frank Gervasi, "Russia vs. Britain in the Mediterranean," Collier's, Feb. 17, 1945.

24   Ibid.

"The church prays for the speediest victory of the USSR and the Allied countries over the enemy and the success of the Red Army, which is led and inspired by the great leader, Marshal Joseph Vissarionovich Stalin."

No sooner was Alexei installed as the new Patriarch than he issued a simultaneous attack on the "growth of irreligion" and on the Catholic Church. The Vatican was berated ostensibly because the Holy See was "trying to absolve Germany of the responsibility incumbent upon her for all her war crimes and to ask mercy for the Hitlerites." The Vatican quickly responded with an intimation that the Soviets were planning to make all the Orthodox Churches into political instruments of "international Communism and, above all, to widen the centuries-old schism between Rome and the Orthodox world."

"The Church of Rome in Poland, Czechoslovakia, and the Balkans," Professor Igino Giordani stated in a sharply worded editorial in the *Quotidiano*, organ of the Italian Catholic Action Party, "represents freedom of spirit. It represents an obstacle to dictatorship. Hence it must be fought. Moscow intends to make use of 'her church for gigantic imperialist aims."[25]

The controversy, essentially of a political rather than a religious character, reached its climax when the Vatican City newspaper, *Osservatore Romano*, found it necessary to refute a statement made on the Moscow radio. This Vatican organ makes denials only on important issues, so that its action is significant as an index of the growing tensions. Its editorial said:

"The Moscow radio in the Italian language affirmed on the afternoon of February 16 that, "The Vatican is not contented with the results of the Crimea Conference because it was not invited to participate in the Conference itself." We are authorized to declare that the Holy See never had even the least thought of participating in that Conference. Therefore, in this case also, it is a question of pure and simple calumny."

25   Feb. 12, 1945.

The same Moscow radio has attributed to the Holy See the fact that the Italian Government has sent an ambassador to the Spanish Government. Likewise, with regard to this insinuation, we are in a position to label as equally false the charge that the Holy See has intervened in any manner whatever in this matter.[26]

In the meantime, since his coronation, Patriarch Alexei, like a good and disciplined Soviet functionary, has been working overtime, blessing everything and everybody that has received the approval of the Little Father in the Kremlin.

"Brothers and Christians of the whole world," reads an appeal of the Bishops of the Russian Orthodox Church published in *Izvestia* on February 6, "it is now clear whose arms the Lord Jesus Christ blessed and whose arms He did not bless.... We believe that the one and only Ruler of Heaven and Earth who quieted the wind of the Sea of Galilee will soon quiet the world storm..."

Eleven days later, on February 17, Patriarch Alexei of Moscow and all the Russias "blessed the Crimea Conference," declaring that the decisions reached "by our great Stalin and the leaders of Allied Governments" had laid a solid foundation of world peace.

Preoccupied though His Beatitude the Patriarch has been with ministering to the spiritual needs of his flock, he found sufficient time in June 1945 to visit his co-religionists in Jerusalem, Alexandria, Cairo, Damascus, Beirut, etc. At the same time the Government of Lebanon announced that it had granted Moscow permission to erect a college in Beirut analogous to the famous American Robert College but which will serve "poorer sections of the community."

As a postscript to the whole religious farce-drama now being enacted in Moscow, which as the seat of the Communist International has for over two decades done all within her power to uproot religious beliefs in Russia and

---

26   New York Times, Feb. 18, 1945.

other countries, we have the "pastoral message" published by the same *Izvestia*, condemning "the growth of irreligion, the neglect of church ritual, the venality of certain priests, the diminution of church marriages, baptisms, and confessions."

This "message" also received front-page display in the New York Communist *Daily Worker* of February 6 whose editor, Earl Browder, once wrote that "... the social function of religion and religious institutions is to act as an opiate to keep the lower classes passive, to make them accept the bad conditions under which they have to live in the hope of a reward after death."[27]

CHAPTER THREE

DEMOCRACY IS SUPPRESSED IN BULGARIA

1.

The Bulgar has been aptly described as the "bad boy" of the Balkans. Twice within three decades Slavic Bulgaria, despite her sentimental attachment for Slavic Russia, has fought on the side of the Germans and always for the same reason: for a brief period in the nineteenth century Bulgaria came within an inch of becoming an "empire." Bulgarian politicians have never forgotten that.

There is a suburb near Istanbul, stretched out along the sapphire-colored Sea of Marmara, called Yeshelkoy by the Turks. In history books the peaceful village is known as San Stefano. Here one stormy night in 1878 the Czar of Russia sought to bury the Ottoman Empire the "Sick Man of Europe" and to consolidate his influence in the Balkans. Then, as now, Bulgaria was merely a pawn in power politics. By the abortive treaty of San Stefano

27   Earl Browder, Communism in the United States (New York: International Publishers, 1935) p. 334.

Czarist Russia hoped to establish a Greater Bulgaria which would include the whole of Macedonia to the frontiers of Albania and the territory between the Danube and the Aegean Sea. But the days of Bulgaria's glory were few and numbered. In the same year, only three months later, Bismarck and Disraeli engineered the Treaty of Berlin which revised the Treaty of San Stefano, and Bulgaria lost her acquisitions.

Once again Czarist Russia's ambitions in the Mediterranean had been thwarted by her imperialist competitors in the west. But the struggle went on unrelentingly, exploding finally in the Balkan wars of 1912-1913.

Since then Bulgaria has been a special trouble zone within the troubled Balkans, subject periodically to the influence of Italy, Germany, and Russia. On February 9, 1934, Turkey, Rumania, Greece, and Yugoslavia signed in Athens a pact of mutual understanding. Bulgaria refused to adhere to it. Although many attempts were made to persuade her to join her four neighbors, Bulgaria persistently refused to consider any multilateral agreement that involved renunciation of her territorial claims on portions of Rumania, Yugoslavia, and Greece.

The short-lived glory of San Stefano is still plaguing the Bulgarian Pan-Slavists. But this is only true of the urban bureaucracy and the military clique. Bulgaria is essentially a peasant country with over eighty per cent of the population engaged in, or dependent on, agriculture. Sturdy, hard-working, and at an extremely low economic level, the Bulgarian peasant, like tillers of the soil everywhere, is a confirmed individualist and natural-born democrat, with a fair-minded sense for the individual person's rights. The largest and most progressive political organization in the country is the Agrarian Party which was founded by Alexander Stambolisky, one of the greatest Balkan democrats and peasant leaders. For the past several decades, too, a city intelligentsia, led by men like Nikola Mushanoff, began to exercise greater influence upon political affairs in Bulgaria through the Democratic, Socialist, Communist, and other parties. These parties finally succeeded in breaking the stranglehold of the late King Boris' camarilla upon the country and to drive the Germans out of Bulgaria.

2.

When Bulgaria declared war on Germany in September 1944, the Bulgars were the happiest of all the hundreds of anti-Nazi refugees in Istanbul. Many of them were my friends. They thought they were seeing the dawn of real democracy for their country. They had been driven from their homeland for anti-fascist, pro-democratic activity, but now at last they could cross the Turkish frontier into Bulgaria and undertake openly the building of a free nation in their country.

Bulgaria had been at war with the United States and Great Britain for nearly three years. But she had been at peace, and even on friendly terms, with Russia. Moscow had approved Bulgaria's neutrality, so far as the Russo-German war was concerned, when it was announced by the middle-of-the-road Government of Premier Ivan Bagrianoff just prior to its overthrow. The Bulgarians had agreed to the opening of Soviet consulates in the Black Sea ports of Varna and Burgas, though these had been under German control.

When Bulgaria was ready to drop out of the war, Russia as a neutral consequently was not formally concerned with the process. Negotiations for an armistice were, as a matter of course, carried on between a Bulgarian peace mission and representatives of Britain and the United States. Russia was kept informed and appeared to be satisfied.

But the negotiations, first in Ankara, then in Cairo, dragged on mysteriously week after week despite the fact that the Bulgarians had come to offer unconditional surrender. I was sitting in Istanbul's famous Abdullah restaurant when a Bulgarian acquaintance of mine rushed in and announced, "It is all settled."

"What is settled?" I asked.

"The armistice... We are practically out of the war. Soon we shall be allies."

For three weary years this Bulgarian had lived and prayed for this day. Like all Bulgarian democrats, he had suffered horribly during the German occupation of his country. He was arrested four times, spent a month in isolation, a month in a concentration camp, and six months in internment. The Bulgarian fascist radio, Obedinnena Bulgaria, attacked him daily as a pro-Allied propagandist. Finally, through underground channels, he learned that the Nazis were going to deport him to a death camp in Poland and he managed to escape. His wife was arrested but escaped to Istanbul where I saw her soon after her arrival. The man was left behind. For seven months he lived illegally in Bulgaria until an opportunity presented itself for him to get to Svilengrad on the Bulgarian-Turkish border and thence to join his wife.

From the moment of his arrival in Istanbul, my friend worked feverishly to get Bulgaria out of the war. "I can t understand you Americans," he would tell me in despair. "Bulgaria is ready to capitulate. Now is the moment."

Now, for the first time in months he saw a glimmer of hope.

"What about Thrace and Macedonia?" I asked.

"That, too, has been settled. Our troops are already evacuating Thrace and Macedonia."

Thrace and Macedonia were the bones of contention. This stretch of un-happy territory on the Aegean Sea, which includes the port of Salonika, had been for decades the cause of friction among Czarist Russia, the Ottoman Empire, and Great Britain. Each used the small Balkan states as spring-boards. Yugoslavia and Greece today claim part of Macedonia. Bulgaria claims all of it. When Bulgaria declared war on us, the Germans gave her all of Macedonia as a reward. But now the problem seemed settled: Mace-donia would go to our Greek ally.

On August 28, 1944 Radio Moscow announced that the Germans were withdrawing from Bulgaria. The withdrawal, the Russians said, "would be completed in a few days. Disarming of German troops that are crossing the Bulgarian-Rumanian border is going on."

Two days later the Bulgarian Mission, headed by Stoicho Mushanoff, Pres-ident of the Bulgarian *Sobranje* (parliament), and Colonel Zheleskoff, for-mer Bulgarian Military Attaché in Ankara, departed for Cairo to complete the negotiations and sign an armistice. The British negotiators were the late Lord Moyne and his political adviser, C. E. Steel, while the Americans were represented by Harold Shantz, Chargé d'Affaires of the American Embassy in Greece and Yugoslavia, and his Second Secretary, Walworth

Barbour. Lincoln MacVeigh, our Ambassador to the Balkan countries, it was announced, was "unavoidably delayed" in Washington. By September 1 an agreement was reached in Cairo. The Bulgarian Army was to be demobilized after evacuating all territory in Greece and Yugoslavia; boundary settlements were to be reserved until a later date; the Government was to remain neutral and without change. A copy of these terms was immediately forwarded to Russia.

A final meeting of the negotiators was actually in session when the news was flashed from Sofia that the Government of Ivan Bagrianoff, which had been formed with Soviet approval, had been forced to resign in order to avoid war with Soviet Russia.[28] The negotiations at Cairo came to an abrupt end. Whatever Bulgaria's fate, it was plainly no part of Russia's policy to allow it to be worked out under Anglo-American auspices.

But the Bulgars still hoped for freedom. They immediately set up a new government which was a democratic triumph. It was headed by two veterans of the Bulgarian democratic movement: Constantin Muravieff as Premier, and Nikola Mushanoff as Minister without Portfolio.

Muravieff, at seventy, was the leader of the Agrarian Party. In 1923 he had been Minister of War in the government headed by the great Alexander Stambolisky. Mushanoff, at eighty, was the patron saint of Bulgarian democracy. During the Nazi occupation he was one of the spiritual leaders of the democratic resistance movement, not only in Bulgaria but throughout the Balkans. The Muravieff-Mushanoff Cabinet included many other veteran democrats.

Their government came to power on September 2. On the same day it took forthright action to prove the honesty of its democratic intentions. Amnesty was decreed for all anti-Nazi political prisoners; the forcible disbanding of pro-fascist organizations was begun; all anti-Jewish laws were revoked; the Nazi-dictated anti-Comintern Pact was annulled, and the withdrawal of Bulgarian troops from Macedonia and other territories overrun by the Na-

28   See "Balkan News and Propaganda," Sept. 2, 1944, OWI bulletin published in Istanbul.

zis was speeded. There was pride and confidence in the heart of every free-
dom-loving Bulgarian when, on the night of September 4, old Nikola
Mushanoff stepped to the radio and told his people and the world that democracy, in his land, had had a rebirth:

"The first task of this government is to give to the country a sane and united
authority as a basis for a true democratic government... The government
will treat with equal care all Bulgarian citizens without differentiation as to
religion and origin... It has decided to restore the constitutional liberties
and justice to Bulgarian citizens. ...It approves what has been done to the
present to put an end to the state of war with America and Great Britain...
with whom Bulgaria has already started negotiations for an armistice and
will take necessary steps to accelerate these negotiations... The withdrawal
of Bulgarian occupation forces continues. Soon it will be completed."[29]

The next day, September 5, 1944, the Soviets declared war on Bulgaria!

A few hours later I heard over the radio a broadcast describing Molotov's
interview with foreign journalists. Since I know Russian well I was able to
record every word of the interview. The correspondent of the United Press,
according to the broadcast, asked the Soviet Foreign Commissar whether
the British and American governments had previous knowledge of Russia's
intention to declare war on Bulgaria. The Soviet Foreign Commissar replied: "The note I gave to the Bulgarian Minister, Stamenoff, was also re-
mitted to the American and British Ambassadors."

The following day the British Broadcasting Company, commenting upon
this interview reported: "Molotov replied that the British and American
Ambassadors to Moscow were informed of the situation before the remit-
tance of the note."

"Is this Allied self-deception," a Polish diplomat in whose company I had
listened to the British broadcast asked me, "or just ignorance?"

29   Ibid., Sept. 5, 1944.

As their excuse for the declaration of war, the Soviets charged that the Muravieff-Mushanoff government had not moved fast enough, in its four days in power, from "neutrality" to an outright declaration of war on Germany. Yet the sponsor and chief support of Bulgaria's policy of neutrality had been Russia itself. Moreover, no other nation freed of the Germans had acted with such vigor to rid itself of the Nazi taint. Most startling of all, the very government which the Soviets attacked for its "neutrality" had voted, before that attack, for an outright declaration of war on the Nazis. The Soviet Chargé d'Affaires in Sofia, Yakovlev, had been notified of this Bulgarian decision prior to the Russian declaration of war.

The Soviet pretext for declaring war and invading the small neighbor, precisely when Bulgaria had achieved a democratic and vigorously anti-Nazi government, is so palpably trumped up that only political illiterates could have been expected to accept it literally. Yet so strong is the pro-Soviet propaganda influence that many well-meaning American correspondents and radio commentators proceeded to repeat without qualification the extraordinary Soviet version.

Even a normally well-informed newspaperman like Raymond Daniell reported from London that the Government of Muravieff fell because of a "muddle-headed attempt to avoid war with Germany by a policy of strict neutrality" which had "involved his country in a three day war with both Russia and Germany."[30] That this version is absolutely false was subsequently admitted by the Russians themselves in their official press. In October 1944 Dmitri Ganeff, a member of the Central Committee of the Bulgarian Workers (Communist) Party wrote in the Moscow *Pravda* a half-page account of "The Situation in Bulgaria." Among other things Mr. Ganeff stated: "During the six days that it was in power the Government [of Muravieff] ... announced a formal break with Germany and two days later declared war on Germany."[31]

30   New York Times, Feb. 4, 1945.

31   Pravda, Oct. 9, 1944.

Every informed Bulgarian knew, of course, that it was not because of "neutrality" that Russia, after having kept at peace with Bulgaria for three war years, had suddenly attacked. It was obvious to them that Russia's sudden war was declared in order to dictate unilateral peace terms to Bulgaria, to push out the British and Americans, and to thwart the establishment of a government aligned too closely with the United States and Great Britain. If such a government were to take root, Bulgaria would be – for the Soviets – a pro-British, pro-American sore spot at the very heart of the Balkans; it would become a formidable barrier to the Soviet plans for Balkan and east Mediterranean domination and even to the Kremlin's ambitions in the Middle East and India.

"What we most feared," a Bulgarian labor leader told me, "has now happened. This is not only a death blow to Bulgarian democracy. This is a death blow to the prestige of democracy in this part of the world."

Six hours after Russia's declaration of war, the Bulgarian government sued for peace. Peace came ninety hours later when the Soviet Marshal Feodor Tolbukhin, with his Third Ukrainian Army, arrived at the gates of Sofia.

In Svilengrad on the Turkish-Bulgarian border, where two weeks previously the Nazi swastika had flown, the Russian red flag with the hammer and sickle went up; the border building which had housed the Nazi Gestapo was at once occupied by its Russian counterpart, the NKVD (formerly GPU).

When the Russians entered Sofia they were greeted joyously by the population. Armed civilian partisans, *Shumkari*, came down from the mountains, singing Communist songs. Together with the citizens of Sofia they formed a large popular demonstration which reached its culminating point in front of the Kiveta Sofia square – spontaneously renamed Red Square – where the Russian legation was located. Red flags were displayed on private houses and government buildings of the Bulgarian capital.

But the joy was spoiled soon enough by indubitable signs that the Russians intended to act as masters of this newly conquered region. Under the guise of purging real pro-Nazis and alleged collaborationists, the new regime began to round up men and women whose democratic record was beyond doubt. The new state of affairs was heralded in broadcasts from Moscow to

Bulgaria by a speaker who used the name of the legendary Bulgarian hero and poet, Hristo Boteff. The voice behind these broadcasts was that of George Dimitroff, world head of the "dissolved" Communist International, and a Bulgarian by birth.

The Muravieff-Mushanoff Government, Dimitroff told the Bulgarian "patriots," was an "usurpatory" regime. It had been overthrown by "the will of the people and the mighty Red Army." He applauded the violence which had broken out in the Red Army's wake: "The workers, peasants, and patriots have begun to act," he said. "Factory workers and miners are striking. In Sofia, the tramway workers have declared a strike. In Plovdiv, patriot revolutionaries have acted decisively to establish the Fatherland Front."

Two days later the Moscow radio exultantly boomed forth again: "In forty-eight hours the Council of Regents has been abolished. All members of the former governments have been arrested. A majority of the members of the *Sobranje* are under arrest. Their newspapers have been suppressed." Under Communist pressure the newly-formed Union of Journalists forsook its democratic platform and decided "to establish at once liaison with our colleagues of the Soviet Press."

The democratic revolution of Mushanoff had been orderly and bloodless. Now, taking their cue from Moscow, the Communists began to act. The technique of this coup d'état has been described in detail in the Soviet *Pravda* by a Bulgarian Communist leader:

"On September 6 a strike of streetcar workers broke out in Sofia. They were followed by the workers of Sofia's railroad yards. On the same day mass demonstrations were arranged. These were guarded by armed detachments of the Fatherland Front... On the 7th a Partisan detachment made its way into Pernik, the coal mining district. The miners declared a strike which was supported by a party of the military garrison stationed there. On September 8 the tobacco workers of Plovdiv, joined by others, went out on strike... . The National Committee of the Fatherland Front, according to a plan worked out on the night of September 8-9, decided to deliver the decisive blow. With the aid of tank detachments and other Partisan forces which had been brought to Sofia, the Ministries of War, Interior, Post and Telegraph, as well as all radio stations and other vital points in the capital were occupied. In the morning the people attacked the police station and disarmed the police. Thus ... with united forces ... the government of the Fatherland Front was established."[32]

Nikola Mushanoff, Constantin Muravieff, and hundreds of other well-known Bulgarian democrats were arrested.

Behind the facade of the Fatherland Front, Marshal Tolbukhin formed a new government. The Soviets installed in the two most important posts those of Premier and Minister of War respectively two of the Balkans most implacable foes of democracy: Colonel Kimon Gheorghieff and Colonel Damian Veltcheff. Let us see who they are.

3.

In 1923 the Bulgarian Premier, Alexander Stambolisky, was assassinated by a *junta* led by Professor Alexander Tsankoff and Colonels Kimon Gheorghieff and Damian Veltcheff. It was a *coup d'état* which inaugurated in Bulgaria a reign of political chaos and bloodshed.

The assassins of the democratic peasant leader were undisguised reactionaries.

Democratic forces in Bulgaria were at that time strong enough to oppose their coup and eventually defeat it. In 1934, however, the Military League and the *Zveno* group, the fascist party of Bulgaria, led by the same Colonels Gheorghieff and Veltcheff, overthrew the Democratic Entente Government, jailed or executed all the liberal and democratic opposition elements, dissolved the *Sobranje*, and instituted a reign of terror which eventually paved the way for Bulgaria's entry into the war on the side of Germany.

– Professor Tsankoff, the third member of the 1923 anti-democratic *junta*, subsequently went to Germany to head a quisling "National Government." The Germans referred to him as "a friend of the German nation and an advocate of close and sincere co-operation between Germany and Bulgaria."

32   Pravda, Oct. 9, 1944.

95

His two partners, Colonels Gheorghieff and Veltcheff, now became the heads of the Russian-sponsored Fatherland Front Government of Bulgaria. At this writing they still hold their Moscow-made leadership. Incredible as it may sound to those unaware of what is happening in the Balkans, Russia had displaced a democratic Bulgaria with a regime headed by notorious pro-fascists!

On September 18, the "Voice of America," our propaganda broadcast to the Balkans, referred to a speech made by the new Minister without Portfolio, Nicholas Petkoff, in which he declared that the National Bulgarian Government would follow the principles of Alexander Stambolisky. The American comment was:

"This program is received with approval in America because it defends the interests of the popular masses and is in harmony with the principles of democracy for which the United Nations are fighting."

Our broadcast merely neglected to point out that the new regime was headed by Stambolisky's murderers. All the friends and followers of Stambolisky, indeed, were by this time in prison or concentration camps. Colonel Veltcheff, an old hand in crushing opposition, decreed a general mobilization for all men from the ages of sixteen to fifty, including the armed *Shumkari* who had come down from the mountains. Thus, with one stroke, he eliminated all dissident elements which might have challenged his power.

On September 13 Dimo Kazassoff, the new Bulgarian Minister of Propaganda, stated over the radio that the "bloody, destructive, horrible monster-revolution actually turned out to be a calm, orderly form of revolution which was greeted by the people with joy, with loud enthusiasm, with songs and cheers... Armed citizens mixed with the population and the soldiers, shots were fired in the air but there were no victims or wounded. Despite previous mistreatment of the patriots, the houses of the rich were not pillaged. But," added Mr. Kazassoff, "justice will be severe with those who are guilty."[33]

On September 25, upon my return to Istanbul from a trip to the Aegean Coast, I received a telephone call from Sofia. "The Foreign Minister, Petko Stainoff," my informant told me, "found it necessary today to deny again that the Red Army and armed Communists are committing acts of robbery and pillage." He read me the denial. "False information," said Mr. Stainoff, "has been given out by malevolent circles on the conduct of the brave fighters of the Red Army with a view of provoking misunderstanding. Official verification has been confirmed that everywhere the Red Army conducts itself with appropriate dignity and self-abnegation."

"Read this statement," my informant said, "and tell 'B' not to come to Sofia. The climate is bad for his health." "B" referred to a prominent Bulgarian democrat. Before my informant could tell me any more, our conversation was cut off.

In the meantime the Bulgarian peace mission which had negotiated with Britain and America, was stranded in Cairo. At a press conference in Washington, ex-Secretary of State Cordell Hull, was asked whether the mission had left for Bulgaria or Moscow. The Secretary replied that he did not know, but said that *it apparently had gone somewhere.*

Russian-sponsored Pan-Slavism was beginning to pay dividends. The first condition of the Anglo-Americans for the conclusion of an armistice with Bulgaria was that the latter withdraw at once from Thrace and Macedonia. Under the Muravieff-Mushanoff regime the evacuation by Bulgaria of these territories had actually been started. Now, prostrate and beaten Bulgaria was beginning to sing a different tune.

Events moved rapidly. On September 29 Propaganda Minister Dimo Kazassoff announced that a new provisional regime in western Thrace and eastern Macedonia had been formed in agreement with the Greek Communist organization, EAM. Until the Allies reached a decision on the final regime in these territories, he said, the Bulgarian Army would remain there as the principal armed force under the command of Marshal Joseph Tito, who assumed operational command over them on September 17.

33   Recorded by OWI and published in "Balkan News and Propaganda," Sept. 14, 1944.

The following day it became known in Ankara that Bulgaria and Russia had agreed to joint military occupation of Thrace for the duration. According to this agreement between Soviet Marshal Tolbukhin and the Gheorghieff-Veltcheff Government, rival Greek and Bulgarian claims to Thrace would be deferred for postwar arbitration.

British apprehension over the situation in Bulgaria was clearly expressed by the BBC in its broadcast on September 15 which strongly attacked the Bulgarian Premier, Kimon Gheorghieff, for his opposition to the evacuation of Greek Macedonia. It characterized Gheorghieff as the man who had been at the head of a dictatorial government in 1934 and now had as his collaborator the notorious Colonel Veltcheff.

In Washington, on October 2, Secretary Hull gave "as one possible reason" for the delay of the Allies in concluding an armistice with Bulgaria the latter's reluctance to withdraw her troops from Greece. Following Churchill's visit to Moscow in October 1944 the Soviet-sponsored Bulgarian Government finally announced that it accepted preliminary Allied terms to *evacuate Thrace and Macedonia within fifteen days*. On October 28 the armistice was finally signed in Moscow by representatives of the United States, Great Britain, and Russia, but Bulgarian troops never withdrew from Thrace and Macedonia.

Some months later Premier Gheorghieff visited Yugoslavia where he conferred with the Communist chief of Yugoslavia, Marshal Tito, on a Bulgar-Yugoslav federation to be sponsored by Moscow. The movement for a union between Bulgaria and Yugoslavia, to be sure, began shortly after the close of World War I. But the Macedonian problem always stood in the way of its realization. The Bulgarians were never reconciled to the Treaty of Neuilly which assigned part of Macedonia to Yugoslavia. Now Moscow has resolved this dispute. A Bulgar-Yugoslav confederation would permit Bulgaria to have Macedonia in her sphere while recognizing the "autonomous" status of this province.

The truth is, of course, that Gheorghieff and Veltcheff, whose Pan-Slavism coincided with Russia's plans, were merely serving as fronts. The real powers in the country were Miss Tsola Dragoytcheva, a forty-six-year-old Communist fanatic, and the Comintern agent, Anton Yugoff. As Secretary of the National Committee of the Fatherland – the committee that engineered the anti-Muravieff coup d'état – Dragoytcheva wielded unlimited power. Yugoff, as Minister of the Interior, was given full control of the newly-formed militia the only police force in Bulgaria which is directly under Russian control. Then George Dimitroff himself arrived in Sofia and assumed the Presidency of the Fatherland Front.

"Developments in the Balkans," says a London *Times* dispatch from Istanbul on May 22, 1944, "point to the existence of a plan carefully preconceived and systematically applied to establish a Communist regime, or one like it, in every country in the peninsula... The first step is to get hold of such key positions as the Ministries of Justice and the Interior with the control of the police and gendarmerie. The second is to exterminate political opponents and to break up kindred parties that might become rivals... Thus in spite of official appearances, Bulgarian public life today is under complete Communist sway."

An American correspondent, Joseph M. Levy of the *New York Times* succeeded in visiting Bulgaria. After he returned to Turkey and could write freely, he sent a number of dispatches which reflected the state of terror under which Bulgarian democrats were living and dying. "A virtual reign of terror," he reported, "prevails in Bulgaria, in which ordinary civil rights are almost nonexistent. Such elementary democratic principles as free speech and free press criticism are taboo. The writer, having just returned from a six-week stay in Bulgaria, is convinced that the vast majority of the people in that country are bitterly disillusioned over the present situation. They ardently are hoping for early Allied action to establish a democratic regime. The Bulgarian people are confused and hurt, but are clamoring for democracy."

4.

I was still in Turkey when our Mission of OSS (Office of Strategic Services) officers returned to Istanbul after it had been expelled from Bulgaria. The incident itself was unimportant, and Mr. Hull attributed it at that time to "a local misunderstanding." But it was symptomatic of the breakdown of the much-discussed Allied "unity."

Immediately following the demise of the Bagrianoff Government, some twenty Americans and Britons, led by the chief of British Military Intelligence, Colonel Gibson, went to Bulgania, where they were received with friendship by the pro-Allied Government of Muravieff. But by September 25 the Red Army was already in full control. The first act of the Soviet secret police was to expel the "unofficial" Anglo-American Mission. The Russians acted boldly and promptly: within twenty-four hours they escorted our officers to the Turkish border. The reason given by the Red Army spokes man was that Moscow had not officially accredited the Anglo-American Mission; that, technically, Bulgaria was still at war with the United States and Great Britain; and, finally, that the British and Americans had no business in Bulgaria anyway. Subsequently our Mission was permitted to return to Sofia, only to be expelled a second time on some new pretext.

In the meantime Major General John Alden Crane, chief of the United States Armistice Mission in Bulgaria, and Maynard B. Barnes, our Minister there, found it increasingly difficult to carry out their duties. They were constantly spied on and their movements were narrowly restricted. Both the British and United States Armistice Missions experienced enormous difficulties in obtaining Russian permission for planes bringing in supplies or personnel to land at the Sofia airport. American and British officers who were assigned to serve with the Armistice Missions had to wait for weeks before the Russians would grant them entry permits. Allied correspondents were not allowed to enter Bulgaria without the direct approval of Moscow.[34]

American prestige suffered immensely from this hostile attitude by the Russians. This is true not only in Bulgaria but throughout the Balkans and the Middle East. The Bulgars, like the Yugoslavs and Rumanians, saw the Russian armies riding in American cars, American jeeps, American trucks.

34   "The State Department is vigorously supporting applications from American newspaper correspondents who desire admission to liberated Balkan countries," stated a Washington dispatch to the New York Herald Tribune of February 5, 1945. Acting Secretary of State, Joseph C. Grew, emphasized, however, "that policies regulating entry into Russian-occupied regions are determined at Moscow. The Soviet government, he explained, elected to consider each application separately, a policy which is considered among correspondents to entail elements of protracted delay."

Then, when they noted how the Russians treated their American Ally they were puzzled. The people of the Balkans, particularly the Bulgars and the Serbs, admire the United States and have the highest regard for our democracy and humanitarian ideals, but now they are beginning to doubt America's power – and its altruism.

The reasons for Russia's reluctance to permit Allied correspondents and observers to move about freely in the Balkans is obvious to anyone who has been there. She wants no outside witnesses to her unfolding purges and pacifications.

In February 1945, according to a report of Radio Sofia, about 150,000 Bulgarians thronged the square facing the Palace of Justice in Sofia to hear the official promulgation of verdicts against a hundred persons condemned as "war criminals." Members of Premier Kimon Gheorghieff's Fatherland Front government addressed the crowd, denouncing the "criminal rulers of Bulgaria." Certainly some of those sentenced, like Prince Cyril, brother of the late King Boris III, were genuine war criminals. But just as certainly, others were not; their only crime was a defense of democratic hopes.

It has long been one of Moscow's favorite methods to create "amalgams" of *innocent* and *guilt* so as to make their executions or prison sentences palatable to pro-Soviet liberals. It was a method demonstrated in many a Moscow purge trial. Now it was applied to Bulgaria. Among those who received life sentences were the "war criminals" Nikola Mushanoff, Constantin Muravieff, and two other leaders of the Agrarian Party, Athanase Buroff and Dmitri Ghitcheff.

When these men were first placed on trial as "war criminals," I protested publicly in a letter to the *New York Times* (December 28, 1944) where I pointed out that since the Bulgarian armistice terms had been worked out by the European Advisory Committee, of which the United States was a member, and were also signed by a representative of the United States, it was our duty to speak out on behalf of men like Mushanoff who have been our friends and allies. Subsequently I was assured by officials in Washington that everything possible would be done to save these men. Perhaps it was our intervention that saved the lives of Mushanoff and his friends. All the same, the great old democrat may spend his declining years a prisoner of the country for whose liberty he sacrificed his life.

Even more tragic was the fate of G. M. Dimitroff, leader of the left-wing agrarian Stambolisky Party. On June 2, 1945 Undersecretary of State Joseph C. Grew confirmed a report that was first broadcast by Moscow that our representative in Bulgaria, Maynard B. Barnes, accorded sanctuary in the United States Embassy to Dimitroff because the latter believed "that his life was in immediate danger from irresponsible elements." Although not without its ironic side, the Bulgarian leader's plight was not unexpected.

A life-long democrat and anti-fascist, who because of his views was subjected to terrible tortures under the dictatorship of the late King Boris, Dimitroff was, however, a staunch supporter of Soviet Russia's policies in the Balkans and an advocate of close collaboration with the Communists. After the Russian Army entered Bulgaria he returned to Sofia from a long exile in western Europe and the Middle East where he had headed the *Free Bulgaria Committee*.

At first the Russians and the Bulgarian Communists "tolerated" Dimitroff and even exploited his prestige with the peasant masses in their attempt to discredit the more conservative leaders of the Agrarian and democratic parties. But pro-Russian though he was, Dimitroff was after all a democrat and not a Communist! Such men do not readily fit into the picture of the Soviet sphere of influence. Moreover, as the General Secretary of the radical Peasants Union – a traditionally Russophile, democratic, and pro-Allied group – he was known as the "doctor of the poor" throughout the country. Dimitroff was thus too dangerous an element to be tolerated in a totalitarian state. At the appropriate moment the Bulgarian Communists charged him with "collaboration with the Germans." They demanded that he be dismissed from his post as General Secretary of the Peasant Union – a demand which was subsequently carried out by force. The denouement occurred in June 1945 when he was compelled to seek refuge in the United States Embassy. Whatever political sins Dimitroff may have committed, particularly with respect to his older and more conservative colleagues of the Agrarian Party, the tribute paid him by Undersecretary Grew as "a political leader representing a large democratic element with a long and honorable record of loyalty to democratic principles and the Allied cause" was richly deserved.[35]

The entire tragedy of Bulgaria was summed up by a highly placed American with about thirty years of dose association with Balkan affairs when he said in Istanbul:

I consider most alarming the sentence passed by a so-called people's tribunal in Bulgaria condemning to imprisonment the three outstanding democratic leaders of that country. It is alarming because Messrs. Mushanoff, Buroff, and Ghitcheff have throughout their lives been stalwart fighters for the democratic liberty of Bulgaria. These three men are internationally known for their unswerving faith in the principles of democracy.

I shudder at the thought that such indefatigable fighters against fascism should be doomed, just at a time when democracy is to triumph, to spend a whole year behind prison bars, which term at their advanced age they may never survive. The whole world at large has been fooled by Bulgarian political adventurers who control both the radio and the press of the country when they unceasingly proclaim that "Bulgaria now marches hand in hand with great democracies." Does the imprisonment of democrats like Mushanoff, Buroff, Ghitcheff conform even with the elementary principles of democracy?

Doesn't it rather prove that this group of political adventurers who succeeded in seizing power are trying to eliminate the real proponents of democracy in Bulgaria? But what I find most painful, indeed tragic, is the fact that the great democracy of which I am a proud citizen has neither officially nor through the press or public organization nor through the avowed propounders of the democratic faith manifested the slightest sign of protest against file dictatorial imprisonment of three genuine Bulgarian democrats.

United States' silence on this matter is a severe blow to American prestige in the Balkans. It is not only from a standpoint of Bulgaria that the miscarriage of justice in the case of Mushanoff, Buroff, and Ghitcheff calls for a strong protest from the American Government and public, but from the standpoint of American honor. The Bulgarians, who always believed in the

35   New York Times, June 3, 1945.

consistency of America's manifestation and support of the democratic faith, are now bitterly disillusioned.[36]

For the United States, at a moment when three of the most loyal devotees of democracy in Bulgaria were languishing in prison, not to give a single sign of protest, our Balkan representative pointed out, was suicidal to our national prestige in the Balkans and even with the Allies. This initial neglect on our part is bound to increase the tragedy in the further settlement of post-war problems.

Bulgaria feels betrayed and abandoned by the Western democracies. And Bulgaria is typical in this respect of the Balkans as a whole.

36   Quoted by Joseph M. Levy in the New York Times, Feb. 9, 1945.

Yugoslavia

Stephen Bonsal; 1890:

Excerpts from *Heyday of a Vanished World*; New York: W.W. Norton & Co.; 1937.

14. SERBIAN TRAGEDY, MAGYAR DIVERTISSEMENT

It may be helpful to the reader for me to explain at this point in my narrative that my Serbian experiences ran concurrently with the Bulgarian episodes which I have already described. Within a month after my first arrival in Sofia, and after making my bow to Prime Minister Stambouloff in Sistova, I had steamed up the Danube through the Iron Gates of Orsova on an Austrian Lloyd vessel which carried excellent beer well-refrigerated, and landed in Belgrade, and this, with variations, was my procedure throughout the twenty exciting months that followed.

This river journey, although often repeated, never became monotonous. To get through the narrow Pass of Kasan we would often be compelled to transship to a smaller boat. The gorge through which we passed was immensely picturesque and only about a hundred and fifty yards broad, but the volume of water that rushed through it was nearly two hundred feet deep, and out of it rose a great rock (much feared of the pilots) around which swirls the famous whirlpool in which so many river craft have become involved with disastrous consequences. At Turnu Severin you could still see a few upstanding pillars of the great bridge the Roman Emperor built to carry on the war against the Dacians, and at Dulbova we walked along the road which Trajan built with the avowed purpose of carrying the blessing of civilization to the outside barbarians. Only a goat track here and there indicates where the great military road ran, over which the legions and the cohorts marched in their invincible strength, but you can still see and, in part at least, decipher the arrogant memorial to the Roman conqueror inscribed upon the granite wall of the great Pass. "Imperator Caesar! Trajanus Augustus Germanicus! Pontifex Maximus! Pater Patriae."[1] He made this highway for all time. It was the vital artery of the Empire upon which it was thought the sun would never set, but today the bridge and the highway of conquest have disappeared and the proud memorial is all but obliterated. On the deck of my steamer the conquerors of the day, the Bulgars, the Serbs, and the Macedonians, smiled with contempt at the ruins of the empire of yesterday and, talking boastfully of their rising kingdoms and principalities, ignored the handwriting on the wall of the Pass.

It may be recalled here that my only, but often repeated, instructions from the Commodore were, "Move about as you please, but I shall expect you to be on hand when and wherever Hell breaks loose." In these circumstances I could not remain long in one place. A report of the Volcanique, as we called it, would send me hurtling from Bulgaria into Macedonia, or from Thrace into Roumelia or Albania, and while my haphazard method of re-counting these experiences may not result in a clear picture, when in my notes I have followed the chronological sequence the result has seemed to me something very like "confusion worse confounded."

I hope to disarm my critics by frankly admitting that what I place before them is not history, but a staccato medley of news alarms and breathless ru-mor chases, and that there are gaps in my story. On the first day of my so-journ in the Serbian capital I heard the Finance Minister of the day present his annual budget to the deputies of the Skupshtina, or national assembly, in sonorous blank verse. May I add that when, during a lull in the debates of the Peace Conference in Paris, thirty years later, I sought to rescue this po-etical financier's name from oblivion by interrogating Prime Minister Pashitch, that venerable statesman shrugged his shoulders and said, "In those Arcadian days it was our custom to break out into verse on all occa-sions." And then with a gesture of contempt he added, "Today the budget is presented by accountants and, of course, no Serbian can follow the stupid rows of ciphers."

The misery and squalor that prevailed at this time in the Serbian capital, so closely associated in the minds of Westerlings, at least, with Prince Eu-

---

1   The inscription has recently been restored by the Serbian government, but the text is
     still a subject of hot discussion between learned Latinists and archeologists. S.B.

gene, the "noble knight," is indelibly impressed upon the tablets of my memory. While I was on quite intimate terms with all the members of the discordant royal family, I stopped at a tavern which was widely and most unfavorably known as the Inn of the Red Dog although I am not quite sure whether this was its official name or merely the sobriquet bestowed upon it by indignant guests.

At this time we had no permanent diplomatic representative in Serbia. There was, it is true, a peripatetic minister extraordinary from the United States accredited to Belgrade, Cettinje, and to Athens. The post was a party plum and the occupant, when not at home looking after his political "fences," wisely sojourned in Athens. The archives of the legation were in the keeping of an amusing Scot of the name of McClure. He also took his meals at the Red Dog Tavern and on more than one occasion he waxed indignant at my attitude toward the food that was served there. "With you it is only a matter of weeks or a couple of months," he explained, "but with me it looks like a life sentence." I asked for an explanation and it was promptly forthcoming. "No correspondent survives long in Belgrade. Sooner or later, and generally sooner, he is escorted across the river to Zemlin by the political police. There on Hungarian territory they live in a very comfortable hotel and their telegrams, as long as they are unfriendly to Serbia, are forwarded with the utmost dispatch. But they don't like it. They feel that they are lacking in prestige and then the news that dribbles across the river is fragmentary and unreliable. They find it difficult to interpret what is going on in a country from which they have been exiled."

When I asked if his place were not also subject to the dangers that beset all political positions in the foreign service of that day, he assured me it was not. "You see, I m a commercial vice-consul. I retain half the fees that are paid for invoices, but as there is no trade I never receive any. If I did " Here McClure lapsed into eloquent silence, but it was quite clear that the moment he had the funds he would leave Belgrade.

The only thing that remains of the Belgrade I came to know so well in these years is its picturesque situation on the banks of the Save with the broad but never blue Danube flowing on in the near distance. The details of the picture have changed completely. In the Great War the city was bombarded and reduced to smoking ruins. When I came there after the Armistice of 1918 I lost my way in the still smouldering debris. This panorama of desolation by which I was bewildered was the handiwork of the Austrian monitors that came down the river and fired the first big guns that heralded the holocaust of disaster.

While the Turkish garrison had been withdrawn in 1867, or twenty years before I came this way, they left behind them many traces of their prolonged and heavy-handed domination. The streets were narrow and crooked and dusty or muddy, according to the season. The royal descendants of the swineherd Obrenovich housed higgledy-piggledy in the ancient *konak*, the new palace not having risen above ground in all its incredible ugliness. The Terasia, then as now the main street, was a popular pig-wallow, but through quagmires and filth it led into the street of Prince Michael the Liberator. From here you could climb up to the medieval fort[2] that was for so long in the epic days the objective of Prince Eugene's artillery. From its dismantled battlements and crumbling walls there was unfolded a wonderful panorama which embraced a dozen battlefields where so often throughout the ages Christian and Moslem hosts had been locked in deadly struggle.

What the Turks had not been able to destroy on their enforced departure, though they tried to, was the deep cistern fed by springs within the walls of the fort which was, I dare say, its most valuable defensive arm during many a prolonged siege. You descended to it by four hundred steep stone steps worn away by the tread of the callous feet of many generations of thirsty, hard-pressed soldiery. Beyond the fort extended a rambling country road which later was given the name of Nathalie Boulevard in remembrance of the unhappy queen of my day. It led to Topchider or the vale of the Cannoneer. In its midst rose a simple country house where the boy king Alexander entertained his friends with sweets and delicious coffee luring the hot weather. This royal retreat was surrounded by a forest of magnificent trees

2   Originally a Hungarian border-fortress, called Nandorfehérvár, where, on July 20, 1456, John Hunyadi, "the Scourge of the Turks", with the aid of a crusader army led by John Capistrano (noted for the swallows) has broken the siege of a 150,000 strong Turkish army. This victory delayed the eventual fall of Hungary to the Turks by seventy years. By order of Pope Calixtus III, this event is commemorated by the daily toll of bells in Christian churches at noon. -Ed.

and an extensive deer park. Here after refreshments, in the cool of the evening, we often strolled about and frequently passed the spot where, as the memorial stone indicates, Prince Michael, the great-uncle of our host, was set upon murdered. We little thought then that assassination had not abandoned by the Serbs as a political weapon and that the little boy, who led us through the labyrinth of shrubbery, was destined, together with his wife, to die a violent death; or yet that the son of his successor, King Peter, another Alexander but of the Black George[3] line, should come to his death at the hands apparently of one of his own people, although on foreign soil.

King Milan was in Vienna upon my arrival in Belgrade, but Queen Nathalie was present and living in a small private house not far from the ancient *konak*. With her was a charming lady-in-waiting, a bright vivacious creature who unhappily some years later was displaced by Draga Mashin, who brought about the downfall of the Obrenovich dynasty. My first contacts with Serbian royalty were with and through them, but I can say that what developed into an intimacy was in a manner forced upon me.

The leading Regent at this time, and for the period of the boy king's minority, was Ristich, an ancient war horse of Serbian politics. Serving with him as co-Regents were two military men, Protich and Belomarcovich, who were known throughout the Balkans as the "tarnished generals." I believe this unsavory appellation was bestowed because of their failure to distinguish themselves at the battle between the Serbs and the Bulgarians at Slivnitza four years before. But as I do not know whether these charges were well-founded or false, I should say that I use the uncomplimentary adjective that was always hitched on to their names merely for the purpose of identification.

I was pleased and I must confess somewhat surprised when upon my first call Ristich greeted me warmly, almost with enthusiasm; indeed, when the bemedaled Belomarcovich was called into the conference, I was introduced to him as "a messenger from heaven." The explanation of this unusual welcome was not long delayed. It soon developed that two weeks

3   Karageorgevitch dynasty. -Ed.

before there had reached Belgrade an interview with Queen Nathalie written by a famous American newspaper correspondent who spent most of his time in London. In the course of the interview very unpleasant things were said about the Regents, and the situation in Serbia was depicted in most unflattering terms. Some of these strictures were said to be the very words of the Queen, others were admittedly the conclusions the writer reached after what, he claimed, was a careful survey of the Serbian situation. The Regents had ascertained that the writer in question had not been nearer to Belgrade than Munich, and I was informed that the Queen had never seen him and that she denounced the article as a fabrication. I had no particular interest in the matter; the correspondent, I knew, was a man of high standing, it seemed incredible that he should have perpetrated such a barefaced fake and, after all, it was water gone over the dam and did not concern me.

But, of course, it interested the Regents immensely and on the following day I was escorted to see the dark-eyed heroine of the interview whose status at the time was uncertain, for by all reports the church divorce that King Milan had secured from her through a corrupt bishop was wholly illegal. She was most gracious and we ate sweetmeats and drank tea for some time before I was able to fasten her attention on what was really the purpose of my visit and, indeed, its sole excuse.

"The Regents wish me to issue a denial of all this talk," she said, "and I can well understand their point of view." Here the dark-eyed woman laughed in a way that seemed to indicate that she had enjoyed the strictures on the great men of the moment hugely. "And they have proved through the investigations of our consular officers that this newspaper Monsieur never came to Serbia, and I have not been away for years. This was very unchivalrous of him but, on the other hand, this newspaper Monsieur has penetrated into the inmost recesses of my soul; he has laid bare my secret thoughts and put them into words as I have never dared to do.

What a wonderful man he is! What a menace to society! Are all American journalists as able as this?"

I answered that while opinion was divided on this point, in my judgment they generally required some assistance from the person involved in reading secret thoughts, whereupon the Queen blushed and the lady-in-waiting had what she called a fit of coughing and had to leave the room for several minutes.

"No, I m afraid to take any steps in this matter," said the Queen in conclusion. "Of course, as the Regents have proved, the interview never took place, but on the other hand here is a man who, while at a great distance, can read my thoughts. Why, he might, if I made him angry, fill another page of his paper with well, things that the Regents would like even less than what has already been published." I told the Queen that I thought she was wise and, in parting, she gave me a very friendly shake of the hand. I was led back to the Regents and they were disgusted with me when I told them that, while the interview evidently had not taken place, the Queen had decided not to dignify the article with a formal denial. The fact that I had refused to play their game rankled, and two years later, when my position in Belgrade was shaken by an incident I shall in due season relate, the displeasure of the Regents weighed heavily against me.

I was convinced that in some clandestine way the Queen had furnished the correspondent in question with the information which, with or without authority, he had put in the form of an interview, and the Regents, though they tried cajolery and even veiled menace, were never able to induce me to enter into the controversy which was distinctly not my affair. And the Queen was grateful, and also the bright, vivacious lady-in-waiting.

In a few days, however, Milan appeared once more on the scene and became, as was apparent, an unwelcome guest at the Palace; but, as the jovial ex-monarch asserted when I waited on him, as in duty bound, "No man can allow his father to lack for food and shelter, be he prince or commoner." And if the boulevard sheets were to be believed at this time, his Paris creditors were constantly harassing the ex-King. It is, perhaps, advisable at this point to describe, as briefly as possible, the circumstances under which only six months before King Milan had joined the circle of kings in exile who were sojourning in the gay city on the banks of the Seine.

In January 1889, Milan, after having ruled the country most capriciously for a number of years, suddenly promulgated a liberal constitution and three months later, to the amazement of all, abdicated in favor of his son and, although the boy was only twelve years of age, had him proclaimed King. A Regency of three was constituted to rule the country until the boy came of age. At this late day it would be difficult for me to describe correctly the political situation by which, at the time, the country and I, as a political observer, were confronted. The *Skupsktina*, or national assembly, had a majority of Radicals, the Ministry claimed to be Liberal, and the Regents, whatever else they may have been, were certainly conservative in politics. In these circumstances the ordinary processes of administration were impeded and, as the political anarchy continued and increased, four years later the mechanics of government broke down. At this juncture young Alexander acted energetically. He dismissed the Regents, proclaimed himself King, although he was only seventeen, and then invited his father to return from exile and advise him out of his knowledge of men and affairs how to steer the ship of state away from the lee shores of bankruptcy and anarchy toward which it was drifting rapidly. The return of Milan to Belgrade, at least, proved a mistake. He had been formally exiled by the Regents for good and sufficient reasons, but I must not anticipate. In 1889, when I saw him for the first time, he was the guest of the nation and he had returned to his native land simply to explain that the prestige of their country, dear to all Serbians, would suffer if he were compelled to make both ends meet on the meager allowance which had been assigned to him on his departure.

In this the first of many talks which I had with the ex-King he dwelt at about equal length upon his financial and his matrimonial misfortunes. He asserted money was no object to him. He would gladly live upon a crust if by so doing he could enhance the prestige of his beloved country. But, unfortunately, the contrary was the case. The more he economized the more his people lost standing.

If they could not keep one former king in dignified affluence no one would believe that the Serbs were the coming people in the Balkans. Did I not see that? Here I, wisely I think, dodged the expression of an opinion upon a subject on which I, as a transatlantic democrat, had but little information.

Then the King, who spoke French rather badly (at least at this time) but with an amazing fluency, took up the subject of his marriage which he asserted had wrecked his career. His union with Nathalie had been a love match and it had turned out badly. He admitted he had turned a deaf ear to the counsels of his advisers who pointed out how advantageous it would have been for the dynasty and for him to marry into one of the royal or even into one of the old ducal families who would have welcomed such an alliance. "That is what I should have done," protested the repentant Lothario on more than one occasion. "I should have made an alliance that would have insured me and my family support in either Russia or Austria. But I was ensnared by those flashing black eyes, those billowy masses of jet black hair, and I married the Roumanian gentlewoman, or so she seemed."

This romantic comedian made no secret of the fact that the marriage was a failure from the very beginning, or that after the birth of the unfortunate pledge of the union the tie that bound the pair became merely nominal. Milan complained to all and sundry, and even to me, a wanderer from a strange land, in a way that was unusual in those reticent days, of the frigidity of his wife with the burning black eyes. He insisted that this revelation should be published (I never complied with his request), because this unhappy condition was in his judgment ample excuse for the constant, or inconstant, philanderings which lured him so often, and with such unpleasant results, far from home and fireside, first in Belgrade and, later, in Paris and Vienna.

Much that Milan said was doubtless true, and it is equally certain that the first announcement of the King's marriage to Mlle. Kechko was a surprise and a rather unpleasant one to his people. Several Russian princesses had been thought of in connection with a suitable alliance that should not long be postponed, and indeed preliminary steps had already been taken, but Milan's mother, Princess Helene Obrenovich, had selected the bride, Nathalie Kechko. It was she who brought about their meeting in Vienna, which was represented as accidental, and, as he always admitted, the King at first was delighted with his mother's choice. The Queen must have been a very beautiful girl at this time when barely seventeen, and she was still a very handsome woman with wonderful eyes and charming features when I met her fifteen years later.

As to who the Kotchkos were many stories circulated. There was a story that Nathalie's mother was a princess from the Caucasus, and certainly the Queen looked like a Georgian. Only one thing is certain her father came from the lesser Moldavian nobility and had served for many years in the Russian army as Colonel of a crack cavalry regiment. The wedding day opened auspiciously and the people of Belgrade were charmed as they saw the happy young people driving to the cathedral where on a beautiful October morning the marriage was solemnized. By procuration the Great White

Tsar gave the bride away, and this added immensely to the éclat of the brilliant ceremony. Then suddenly the omens became adverse. The horses of the wedding equipage balked for minutes as they were driven away from the cathedral and a violent storm, at the same time, burst suddenly over the so recently sunlit city, and these things were regarded as of evil augury.

While all people are superstitious, none are more so than the Serbians, and it was soon recognized that the young royal couple had gotten off to a very bad start. The Serbians believe that a man's fate is decided at his birth and that there is no way of escaping an unfavorable destiny. The sequence of stark tragedy which followed, which I shall briefly relate, had been foreseen by the famous seer of the mountains, old Matche Krema, and his words of ill omen had gone through the kingdom and were on many lips. The unfortunate thing about them was that, in the past, his predictions had come true on many occasions. It was a pity that so bright a future should be darkened by the presage of disaster, but the swineherds could only be sorry and shrug their shoulders; in the future, as in the past, the powers of darkness would prevail. It was *kismet*.

As a matter of fact old Krema, the mountain bard, would have ranked high as a seer even among a more prosaic people. Years before the murder took place, he had foretold in moving verse the assassination of Prince Michael that occurred in 1868. Long before the nuptials were celebrated, he had revealed that the marriage of Milan and Nathalie would prove unhappy, that only one child would be born to them and that he would be always beset by misfortune. He had forecast that Milan would live much abroad and die in a foreign land; that his son would marry a woman of the people and that with him the dynasty would perish. Even farther into the future penetrated his farseeing eyes. "A son of Black George will ascend the throne, a foreign army will invade and devastate our country. There will be starvation and suffering and the dead will outnumber the living, but after the years of sorrow by the aid of the blessed Virgin and of St. Michael, and all the angels, a Champion of God's people will appear; our enemies will be destroyed, and once again peace and happiness will descend from heaven upon all the Serbian lands."

These words of ill omen were given wide credence in the kingdom long before my arrival in Belgrade on my first visit. I would not venture to say that they sealed the fate of the family, but undoubtedly they exerted considerable influence in shaping the disastrous course of events. As the many dangers threatening the Obrenovich line became more apparent, even their loyal adherents confessed that they were powerless to combat fate while, on the other hand, its enemies were doubly armed by these words. Certain it is that in these circumstances the Black George conspiracy was hatched and many of the conspirators afterwards admitted they would not have had the courage to carry out their murderous plans but for the belief they had that the powers of darkness were on their side.

In this connection the vivacious lady-in-waiting, who was in attendance on Queen Nathalie when I first waited on her, in later years told me of an incident which would indicate that superstitious fears were not confined to the humble homes of the peasants. "For years the Queen would laugh to scorn the words of the Mountain Seer until one day in Paris," said the little lady, "she visited Mlle. Thebes, who was well-known then as the favorite *clairvoyante* of all the royal houses of Europe. She went incognito and quite alone and what was said to her she never told me. But from that day she was a changed woman, a very sad one, and the prey of many fears. Whenever anyone in her presence spoke of prophecy or mentioned the future she would always cross herself in the Russian fashion and become very pensive."

Rambles in the royal park were pleasant diversions to our humdrum existence in the close and humid atmosphere of the city. The little King often guided our steps. I say "we" advisedly, because we were generally accompanied, not only by one or more of the King's tutors, but by Douglas Dawson, a captain in one of the English Guard regiments, who at the time was serving as military attaché to the British legations in the Balkan States. Dawson[4] was as handsome as one of Ouida's guardsmen and in addition he was endowed with brains and with charm; the little King at whose birth so many fairies had been absent simply adored him and loved to walk hand in hand with him.

4   Later Controller of the Household of King George the Fifth.

One day it chanced that we chatted about our swimming expeditions and our races in the great river below in which, among others, Pallavicini, who later during the Great War was saddled with the difficult role of Austro-Hungarian Ambassador to Turkey, took part. The little boy admitted that he had never been taught to swim and looked quite wistful when I told him that all boys in America had access to a swimming hole and that most of them could swim like fish. Dawson was indignant and announced that this flaw in his education should be remedied immediately. Under the shade of the great trees he found a dark forest pool, and while the tutor in attendance trembled nervously, we were soon stripped and Alexander was splashing about not a little nervous, too. The tutor bleated out that the Regents should be informed, that perhaps they would not approve of the venture, but Dawson insisted the boy must learn to swim before he mounted the throne and that even the Regents must know that a king who could not swim would be under a heavy handicap.

Stripped, Dawson was the perfect figure of an Olympian athlete and his magnificent physique emphasized the strange and far from comely figure which naked and shivering little Alexander cut before our eyes. His head was much too heavy and he was terribly knock-kneed. His shoulders and arms were those of a man trained to carry heavy burdens, while his hips were weak and his shanks spindling and, indeed, none of his limbs matched up. It would seem that he had heired the physical discord that prevailed between his mismated parents. But he had a fine spirit and a stout courage and in a couple of weeks he could paddle across the pool dog-fashion. Dawson would start him from one bank with a vigorous shove and I would advance to meet him from the other side and hold him up when he sank. When he had accomplished the crossing, a distance of about thirty feet, the little chap was the happiest boy in the Balkans. "Now you need not tell the Regents that I'm being given swimming lessons by these gentlemen, my friends. You can tell them that I know how to swim." And so it was revealed, as I had long suspected, that the harassed tutor had not dared to mention to the Regents that the secret lessons were in progress.

In later years Dawson and I often plumed ourselves upon this exploit, but now that the chapter of his life is closed it may appear that in teaching the little King how to breast the waves (a manner of speaking!) we did him a disservice. Some years later when Queen had definitely abandoned Belgrade and was living in Biarritz on the Gulf of Gascony, Alexander went to visit her as in duty bound, and here on the golden strand he loved to disport himself and face the surf as it dashed in upon the beach. In his water sports one of the ladies-in-waiting, according to court gossip, became interested and, finally, Alexander in his turn offered to teach her to swim. They became greatly attached to each other and despite the weighty reasons against the union, and apparently they were many and valid, Alexander married Draga Mashin.

No children were born to the union which was so unwise politically, as in other ways, and finally the enemies of the regime, and they had become quite numerous, as well as the adherents of the Black George family, started the rumor that recognizing that his wife would not or could not present the kingdom with an heir, the King was about to designate the younger brother of Draga as crown prince. There was probably no more in this story than in another also current at the time that in a very few days, when the Queen had gone to Franzensbad where she had been ordered to take the cure, the King proposed instituting divorce proceedings.

I was in Belgrade a few months after the tragic murder of this luckless pair, in which also so many of their adherents lost their lives, and while many tried to make me believe in the first story, including the principal regicide, Colonel Mashin, who strangely enough was the brother-in-law of Draga, I have always been convinced that it was a political fabrication of the adherents of Peter, the king to come. And it was successful, for with Alexander died the last legitimate scion of the Obrenovich family. And so ended the feud between the Montague and the Capulets of the Balkans.

As they at this time exercised great influence on Serbian policy and a little later destroyed the dynasty root and branch it is necessary here to make a brief excursion, as brief as possible, into the unpleasant realm of court scandals. And while I should add that the events I am about to chronicle occurred some months before my arrival in Belgrade, they are fully authenticated.

The most charming place in the environs of the Serbian capital, especially in summer, is the Topchider Park. But to this pleasure ground King Milan would never take his wife, explaining to her that it was a place of evil omen to his family and that he could not bear to see the spot where at least one of his predecessors had been so foully murdered. For a long time the Queen did not question the truthfulness of her husband's statements in this regard, but a year or so later, doubtless primed by information from other sources (the "affair" was an open secret to everyone in Belgrade), the Queen penetrated one afternoon into the vale of Topchider and there found the King walking arm in arm with Madame Christich, the daughter of a Levantine lumber merchant of Constantinople and the wife of a Serbian diplomat who was always somewhere else. Madame Christich was at least ten years older than her admirer and she was exceedingly ugly in a country where ugly women are rare. But with all these handicaps she exercised a wonderful and certainly a most baleful influence over the King. Hers was not an easy yoke either. And many who knew the King's dictatorial ways and his love of creature comforts often wondered at the absolute control which this exacting woman exerted over him. One of her favorite forms of amusement was to summon Milan from the palace and order him to bring her to her house with his own hand, say, a bouquet of five hundred flowers. The King would be followed by a mob of curious idlers and not seldom he would be dismissed at the door of Madame Christich by a lackey, while those who lingered would see the flowers thrown out the window a moment later or deposited in a receptacle for garbage.

However, the King and Queen kept upon some sort of terms in public, at least until the high mass was celebrated in the Belgrade Cathedral on Easter morning in 1888. The Cathedral was crowded by the Court and by all the notables of the country, and after the ceremony they one and all filed past the King and Queen seated on their raised dais. It had been the immemorial custom for the ladies and gentlemen of the Court to say, as they passed before their sovereigns, "Christ is risen," and with the reply, "Of a truth Christ is risen," the King and Queen would kiss the cheek of each and every one of them, repeating the ceremony down to the end of the line. On this occasion Madame Christich had the audacity to place herself in the line but the Queen pretended not to see her and made no reply to her statement as to the Resurrection. King Milan was beside himself with rage. It is said he drew his sword, brandished it above his wife's head and shouted: "I order you to kiss her." When the Queen remained obdurate he attempted to strangle her, but the Court officers intervened and the ceremony ended in indescribable confusion.

While the sympathies of all Belgrade were with the Queen, Madame Christich left the Cathedral leaning on the King's arm and he tried to carry the affair off with a high hand. On the following day he announced to his amazed ministers that he proposed divorcing the Queen, and indeed an attempt to do so was made. Madame Christich was exceedingly extravagant and so was the King. They were always in money difficulties and soon Milan lost what little popularity he had hitherto enjoyed. It is to these days that one of his most despicable exploits dates. In a tight place financially he acquainted the Tsar of Russia with his embarrassment by telegram and, asking for a loan, offered certain estates of his as security. The Tsar helped him out of the unpleasant situation and a mortgage on the estates was duly executed in the Russian legation. But a few weeks later the Russian Minister M. Hitrovo found that the estates were already mortgaged up to their full value!

At this time politics in Serbia were at the very lowest ebb. This was not entirely due to King Milan, but he was certainly the largest contributing factor to a most unhappy state of affairs. There was corruption in the Court and there was corruption in the government everywhere. It was about this time that a tourist visiting the Skupshtina, or national assembly, was amazed to find all its members sitting upon one side of the house.

"Is there no opposition here?" he inquired.

"Oh yes," was the reply. "There are some opposition members but they find it safer to sit in the midst of the Ministerialists."

But there were many who had little confidence in parliamentary immunity, and of these quite a number were eating the bitter bread of exile. Among these was my wise friend M. Pashitch, who in happier days returned to Belgrade to serve as Prime Minister and to represent the heroic people of Serbia at the Versailles Peace Conference in 1919.

I had first and last many amusing experiences with King Milan, one of which at least it may be of interest to recall. He was a gambler and a spendthrift, and his word carried but little weight, either at home or abroad, but he had a rare and dangerous gift of eloquence that often, as in the instance I shall relate, stood him in good stead. At this time he had not been formally exiled, but certainly his repeated absences from Serbia were encouraged by the Regents and by all others in authority. He had gone abroad on what the government thought was a liberal allowance, but evidently the King thought differently. His overdrafts came pouring into the treasury from al-most every reputable banker and also from every disreputable money-lender in western Europe, and at last they were formally dishonored by the government.

At this juncture Milan returned from Paris to lay his case before his friends and enemies alike, and I went to where a party convention was being held. One of the announced purposes of this meeting was to denounce Milan for his reprehensible conduct and to support the government in its determina-tion to dishonor the overdrafts. The convention was held in the garden of the one hotel of which this ancient city boasted, a hotel which for many rea-sons all travelers from the West who have entered its gates will long re-member. I attended the session in the afternoon and was assured that if Milan appeared at the banquet that was to follow he would have a most un-pleasant reception. It was even announced that plates would be thrown at the unwelcome guest, and that if he did not withdraw he would be forcibly removed.

Imagine my surprise, therefore, when as I watched the scene from my room window, I saw the King, quietly attired in civilian clothes, walk through the garden and take a vacant place at one of the tables for the humblest guests. Nobody threw a plate, nobody paid the least attention to the interloper, and the King sat pat and ate his swine flesh and drank his plum brandy in si-lence just like the other guests. But when the time for speech-making came he rose, and after overcoming some heckling he delivered an oration which demonstrated that, after all, speech is sometimes golden. He said that as for himself poverty had no horrors; he was willing to walk barefooted around the world and to wear threadbare clothes; but, he said, it was the nation and the prestige of his people which was lowered by such a situation. He then drew illustration after illustration of the plight to which he was reduced, how the other kings in exile looked down with contempt upon the head of the Obrenovich family; with the result that in about half an hour he had re-duced many of his simple sheepskin clad hearers to tears, and coaxed money out of their pockets. As he was escorted by a committee back to the hotel, he was assured that his drafts would be met and he was again hailed as "our stalwart alone-standing fighter, the conqueror of the Turks." Mi-lan's words, unlike his paper promises to pay, were worth their weight in gold.

Perhaps the most inexplicable trait of the ex-King was his belief that he was lucky in war and that had his people but followed his leadership the "Great Serbian Idea" would long since have been realized. "Had they but followed their king who was lucky in war, today my son's kingdom would have embraced not only Bosnia and Herzegovina and Montenegro but also northern Macedonia and the Turkish *sandjaks* where, as you know, our musical language is spoken," he frequently asserted.

When I became more familiar with the details of recent Balkan wars I saw that the King's belief that he was fortunate in war was not without foundation. While he had been invariably defeated he had always been saved from the disastrous consequences of his foolhardy leadership. When the uprising took place in Bosnia (1877) he had thrown his ill-armed little host upon the Turks and was only saved from destruction by the intervention of Russia. Again when he went off in 1885 and threw his untrained men against the splendid little Bulgarian army which the Russians had trained to a high degree of efficiency, he was disastrously defeated at Slivnitza, and as the Bulgarians crossed the frontier and nothing stood between them and the Serbian capital but disorganized fugitives, they were stopped and Milan was saved by the appearance of the Austrian Minister who announced that if the Bulgarians advanced another step they would be met by Austrian troops. Nevertheless (or perhaps on this account) Milan was always planning new wars and dreaming of new Balkan lands to conquer!

I would not relate even in an expurgated form the terrible fate that overtook my little friend of the Topchider swimming pool, were it not for the sequel that I think important and which I believe leaves it without a parallel in the long roll of Court murders. It also reveals, as nothing else could, the anarchic conditions prevailing at the time in Serbia. I was in western Europe when the tragedy took place and did not return to Belgrade until some months later (March 1904). Pashitch was in control although he chose not to become Prime Minister immediately. King Peter was installed in the Palace and the old Turkish *konak* was still reeking with blood and sinister crime.

The Serbian capital was at last awakening to the fact, the very disagreeable fact, that it had been placed under a rigid boycott by the civilized powers, a movement which, be it said to his credit, had been inaugurated by King Edward of England. As I recall, at the time, the diplomatic corps in Belgrade was reduced to the agent of King Nicholas of Montenegro, whose daughter had married Peter and so became the mother of King Alexander (later to be assassinated in France) and a strange enigmatic creature who claimed to represent Prince Dadian of Mingrelia, a constant aspirant for any old Balkan throne.

The National Assembly had by unanimous resolution thanked the regicides, although it is only fair to say that many of its members acted from fear and under duress rather than from conviction. But among the people a more creditable attitude was becoming apparent. They had at last been impressed by the almost unanimous decision of the civilized powers to sever diplomatic relations. They had begun to look askance at the regicides and their puppet the unfortunate Peter who now sat on the bloodstained throne. now in power, subject however to the dictates of the regicides, asked me to call upon Peter, but I declined and only listened, perfunctorily I fear, as he pictured the benefits that would accrue to the Serbian people as the first result of the new economic era that was about to dawn.

After months of terrified silence those who knew what had happened began to talk rather hysterically. They were generally of the opinion that while Peter had been conspiring all his life against the dynasty he had not advised the barbarous methods by which its overthrow, and indeed its extinction (for there were left no members of the family in the legitimate line), had been accomplished. In these circumstances it was doubtless wise to carry on as best one could with the Black Georges, and this with ability and persistence Pashitch set out to do.

Whenever I called, Pashitch rambled along for hours. To me, at least, it was not a surprise when fifteen years later in Paris he was unanimously recognized as easily the champion of all the long-winded ramblers who came to the Peace Conference. At times he placed responsibility for the tragedy that had in the eyes of the world disgraced his people, upon the Russians, and then only a few minutes later he would put the Austrians in the pillory. Of course, he absolved his party, composed of the Radical groups, of all guilt, and then again he begged me to call at the Palace and have a talk with "gentle" King Peter. This request I again declined, feeling that a correspondent, though he must be more catholic in his associations than most men, was entitled to draw the line somewhere.

Among the officers with whom I renewed acquaintance was one I would like to name were it not for the pledge of absolute secrecy which I gave at the time. In the Great War he died a gallant death, and if he was, as many thought, a leader of the regicides, at least in some measure his soul was purged of his guilt by a noble end. Of course, I should say that I had declined to meet any of the notorious regicides, the murderers of my poor little friend of the swimming pool, who were now in the saddle and riding King Peter with a cruel bit. But this man was different, and I came to spend many evenings with him. He admitted that he had gone to the Palace with the regicides, but he protested he went in the hope of restraining the band from carrying out what he suspected was their fiendish purpose.

"I was quite willing that they should force Alexander to give his kingly word of honor that he would not designate brother as his successor, and I must tell you that there were at least three or four other officers who went along with this purpose. But, maddened by drink and by the delay in finding the concealed pair, fearful of a rescuing party whose approach from the barracks was announced by the firing that had sprung up, the conspirators went ahead and in a general way you know what they did, and how we failed.

"But there are many mistakes in the accepted story. One is to the effect that the King was alive when thrown out of the Palace window, and that when he hung on tenaciously to the window sill, his fingers were chopped off by one of the brutes. This is absolutely untrue. He was quite dead, and as a matter of fact his body, and that of his wife, were thrown out of the window with a laudable purpose to save further bloodshed."

"But how can that be?" I gasped.

"You see, soldiers were coming from several quarters who were not in the conspiracy. They were partisans of the clan, or police, who only knew that a group of strange men had taken possession of the Palace, and by throwing out the bodies, that ended the fighting at the Palace, at least, because there was not left a single member of the family to fight for, no descendant of the great Milosh – except Milan's bastard son."

"It was also a measure for the preservation of the conspirators against counter-attack, as I see it."

"Perhaps, but it ended the greater bloodshed. But what I really wanted to tell you was this. Both the King and his Prime Minister died under a wholly mistaken impression."

"In other words, they died as most politicians live," I suggested. Paying no attention to this remark, the officer continued. "Only a few hours before the midnight murders the King and his Prime Minister, General Marcovich, had a long and unsatisfactory conference. Marcovich had been ruling the country at the King's command, but he had little popular support and but few adherents in the chamber and he, on this evening, asked to be relieved of his responsibilities. He admitted that his task was hopeless. This statement angered the King, but finally he asked Marcovich to remain on at least for a few days longer so that he might look the political field over for a suitable successor.

"Now the King, when he was shot down trying to shield the Queen, fell crying , Mito! (The given name of Marcovich was Demeter, and this the affectionate diminutive.) How could you do this thing to me? What of your oath of fidelity?'

"An hour later I went with a company of soldiers to the nearby house of the Prime Minister. Captain Radokovich was in command, and what his real instructions were from the ringleaders I had no idea. Ostensibly he was sent to bring General Marcovich to the Palace to turn over the seals of office. The General we found working in his study, though it now must have been after two o'clock in the morning. The Captain said very politely, as he confronted us, 'I am ordered to place you under arrest and to guard you in your own house – until further orders.'

"'I will endeavor to make your duty as pleasant as possible, said the General, who was apparently entirely ignorant of what had happened at the Palace. We sat and smoked for a time and then the General said, 'Let's have some coffee. He rose to give the order, and as he turned his back Captain drew his revolver and fired three times. He then turned upon me and said sternly, 'Of course, you understand these were my orders from the Regents who will rule until King Peter arrives.

"I lifted up the poor man's head. 'Sire, Sire, he exclaimed, 'I have been faithful, I have not deserved that this thing should be done to me. Then there came a choking sound, a rush of blood from his mouth, and the General moved no more. I closed his eyes and covered his body with a cloak."

Strange as it may seem, I found this description of what occurred on that dark night rather comforting. Men who escaped from the atmosphere of distrust and suspicion which reigned in the royal circle at this time could hardly be regarded as victims. They were lucky to get away from such a world by almost any exit. For me, for a season now, Belgrade was peopled by strange pitiful figures, some living and some dead, and I shuddered whenever I came upon poor little Sandra's swimming hole, nothing like as good a swimming hole as is the birthright of every American boy. I was happy, indeed, when a few days later orders came sending me to Constantinople to sojourn for a season among the "unspeakable Turks."

I would be remiss and indeed ungrateful if in this chronicle of my days in southeastern Europe I neglected to mention the many happy weeks I spent in Budapest as the guest of the chivalrous and horse-loving Magyars. While, of course, this magnificent city, so long held and always coveted by the Ottoman Turks, was well within my newsgathering "beat," it was a "quiet sector" and my repeated visits had the added charm that always goes with the enjoyment of forbidden fruit. While the Magyars had, and seemed to enjoy, many and distinct grievances as a result of the Ausgleich or Composition with Austria (in 1867), still the interest in these matters as far as America was concerned was slight, and I cannot recall that any of my dispatches from here reached the bulletin board in New York or were blazoned to the world by impressive headlines except when I described the passing of the great Andrássy[5] who, after having been outlawed and condemned to death in *contumaciam* because of his allegiance to Kossuth[6], became the most substantial pillar of the Dual Monarchy and was followed to his grave

5   Count Julius Andrássy Sr., after having been hanged in effigy by the Austrians following
     the 1848 Revolution, conducted the coronation of Francis Joseph as Hungary's prime
     minister on June 8, 1867. Later, in 1871, he became foreign minister of the Dual
     Monarchy. His son, Julius was the last foreign minister of Austria-Hungary.

6   Louis Kossuth was the leader of the Hungarian Revolution in 1848-49.

not only by the people he loved so well but by a score, at least, of Austrian archdukes.

Of course, my undoubted unpopularity in the official circles of Sofia and Stamboul was an excellent foil and did emphasize my appreciation of the hospitality of a warm-hearted people that was so generously extended here. The morning after my arrival on my first visit (in 1888) there came to me, carried by a gorgeously attired messenger, a note in the trembling hand of an evidently aged writer, which read, "For forty years, until I reached the age of seventy, I have always called immediately upon everyone who came to our city from dear America. Now I'm seventy-six and I hope you will call upon me, Ferencz Pulszky."

Pulszky! Pulszky! The name was familiar, but for the life of me I could not recall where or in what connection I had heard it. But I was not left long in my ignorance. From my hotel, throughout the city, the news traveled with the speed of a prairie fire that the young American had received a note from Pulszky, the glory of Hungary, past and present, the trusted companion of Kossuth and Deak, the historian of the Magyar Revolution, the custodian of the patriotic archives in the Royal Library!

Within the hour I was at his desk and confronted by a handsome man with a hawk-like face and a piercing eye, who talked about Webster and Clay as familiarly as we were accustomed to discuss Cleveland and Blaine. With great modesty he said that in the capacity of secretary he had accompanied Kossuth during his historic tour of America[7]. It is unfortunate that I can only recall in a general way his impressions of our country, but they were all appreciative. He said he well understood the reasons why in that far-off day we could only give our moral support to the Hungarian insurgents, but he was quite confident that the time was near when America would gladly accept its responsibilities and perform its duties as the great liberty-loving world power. I do recall, however, a family anecdote of my own which amused the old gentleman immensely and the substantial accuracy of

7   After Lafayette's historic visit, Kossuth was the first foreigner ever to address the Joint Session of Congress on January 7, 1852.

which he admitted. My father, at the time a young man, was a member of the very large reception committee in charge of arrangements during the visit of the Hungarian Revolutionist in Baltimore. There was much oratory and many ovations were showered upon him and lectures were given by the visitor. The ovations were participated in by thousands, but the lectures for which an admission charge was made were not so numerously attended. When the proceeds were turned over to him Kossuth accepted gratefully, but he was disappointed as to the amount and my father heard him say *sotto voce*, "Too much committee, too little money."

Pulszky laughed quietly and said this was not an isolated experience; then he added most charmingly, "But you were all so far away from the political conflagration in Europe! The Liberator thought, and I thought, it was wonderful how much you did in the circumstances. Others talked, but you sent a man of war to save us when the Turks were about to deliver us to the Austro-Russians. The Liberator always said, 'America is the hope of the world."

More, much more I fear than the diplomatic discussions with Count Albert [8], the Tiszas [9] and the other men of mark with whom I foregathered in the Hungarian capital, or even the long stories about the lost cause of Kossuth and the heroism of Klapka and Görgey (how like they were to the memories of Lee and Jackson which I listened to at my mother's knee!) I enjoyed the frequent excursions we made to the great stud farms and the race meetings which my horse-loving friends would there improvise.

I recall with particular pleasure a frolic at Totis [10], one of the Esterházy estates. We went down by train and were met at some way station by box wagons filled with straw and painted all the colors of the rainbow. In these

8   In 1913, he was the third foreigner in American history who was invited to address the U.S. Congress. Later he represented Hungary at the League of Nations.

9   Count Kálmán Tisza was a leading statesman. His son Istvan was prime minister of Hungary during WWI. Was murdered by vagrant soldiers in 1818.

10   Probably he meant the town of Tata -Ed.

we shook down and were driven along the heavy mud roads to the large but by no means imposing castle. It had been well described to me as a horseman's paradise. While our quarters lacked much that we were used to and considered indispensable, the stables left nothing to be desired.

On the following morning we entered the paddock where some twenty horses were on display, and each of us chose his mount for the coming contest. Despite the warning of his three white feet, I picked out a bay horse that seemed very fit and up and coming. Six other guests entered the race, as did two of the horse-herders who enjoyed fraternal relations with the territorial lords present that were altogether charming. It was agreed that we were to race twice around a one-mile track with about a dozen low bush hurdles, which any horse that knew his business could take in his stride. Several things which happened before we were started led me to think that while it was not arranged everybody wanted to see the stranger from America win the race.

After the first mile was completed I saw that my most dangerous opponent was a gray mare (most unusual color in Hungary) ridden by "Rudi" Kinsky, the famous gentleman jockey. I would not venture to say that Kinsky did anything so disgraceful as to pull the mare, to realize the hospitable plan, but before and since I have seen him ride in the Freudenau and at Baden and never have I seen him in the role of a passenger on his mount as he was this day. However, the gray mare was not as chivalrous as her rider and she won by a short but undeniable head.

And then occurred an incident that revealed that life even in Hungary was not all beer and skittles. In the evening we were at a country dance at a nearby *czarda*. During a lull in the dancing several stern-looking men approached and quickly roped a dancer, one of the herders who had ridden in the race. At first I thought it was a practical joke, but I soon learned that these were the men of the county draft and that when called the youngster had not presented himself for military duty.

But the interruption to the dance turned out more pleasantly than I had anticipated. The herder asserted that he had not the most remote wish to escape army duty but he did not want to be "unhorsed." Some of the other boys of the county had been drafted into infantry regiments and this was a humiliation that he could not face. His words were so sincere and his point of view so convincing to horse-lovers that even the agents of the draft were moved and they assured the boy he would go to the hussars. They then unbound the prisoner who became the hero of the evening. All the girls danced about him flapping their many-colored skirts and shouting "Hussar! Hussar!" and presenting goblets of the muddy red wine of the country. Then Kinsky assured him that he knew very intimately the Colonel of the Radetsky Hussars, the crack regiment of the Hungarian cavalry, and would see to it that he serve his time with these famous riders. This, or the muddy red wine, well named "bull's blood," was too much for the boy and an hour later we had to carry him into the inn and put him away in one of the strange and almost suffocating box beds of the country.

I fear that in those days we paid little attention to the submerged nationalities, later on to play such an important role in the history of the Balkan peninsula indeed of the world. I was, of course, pro-Christian, and when Tashin Pasha, the "burden bearer" of the Red Sultan, accused me of being a Gladstonian in my attitude toward Turkey, I could not deny it, but I do not think I differentiated between the Christian tribes, or was greatly concerned as to the outcome of the church rows or the language troubles. And doubtless this is why, when years later, in August 1918 to be exact, I was called upon to represent the United States in their congress to concert war measures, I presented myself at the Palais Bourbon, where the delegates of the Submerged Nationalities assembled, with an uncomfortable feeling. After all, I had had the opportunity nearly thirty years before to lay bare the wrongs of many of these unfortunate people and had failed to do so.

I confess that I do not remember having, at this time, even heard of the Slovaks, as a people quite distinct from the Hungarians, although I often went shooting in their districts north of Pressburg[11]. But I did try to break a lance for the downtrodden Croats even when I was completely under the charm of the horse-loving Magyars. I suggested that their treatment in Parliament did not square with my idea of what a fair deal should be. At this time it seems, as a compromise on the thorny language problem, the few, the very few, Croat delegates were allowed to open their remarks with a sentence in

---

11   Today Bratislava, capital of Slovakia.

the South-Slavic tongue, but then if they wanted to be listened to, or reported, they had to switch to Hungarian.

"But they are such insufferable swine," was the answer of an Erdödy or a Zichy to my mild reproof. "Now listen and you will understand the situation perfectly. Their Ban Jellachich[12] helped the Russians to trample under foot the glorious republic of Kossuth – that, of course, we can understand, politics being what they are. But that was only the beginning. Only when the unequal struggle was over and the Russians and their allies marched into our capital did we realize what Slav blood and Slav breeding is and can't help being. They tore down our flags which in war they had been unable to capture, and tried to steal the crown and the precious regalia of St. Stephen, but these, of course, we had hidden away. And then what do you think they did? You could not guess in a hundred years so I may as well tell you right away. Those Russian brutes dragged the Princess Batthyany from her palace out into the market-place and there spanked her publicly because, forsooth, her sons like all true Magyars had fought in Kossuth's army. You remember the little Prince, her youngest son who still races in England – ?"

"Well, but the Croats," I inquired, "where do they come in?"

"Ban Jellachich and his men stood guard while the spanking of a lady – all of whose forbears had sat at the table of Magnats – went on! Now I think you will agree with me, we treat the Croats too gently. They should be hung to trees with their own cravats![13] Fortunately, there are not so many of these vile people as there were. They are going to America in great numbers to work in the coal mines. Believe me, my dear friend, they are a bad lot. I advise you to keep them underground." That was the only lance I broke for the Croats in those days, and a feeble one it was. I am glad to say I have done better since.

---

12   In the 1848-49 Hungarian Revolution the hostilities when General Jellasich, heading an
      Imperial division, attacked Hungary. The attach was repulsed by another Imperial
      division commanded by General Moga. The only difference between these soldiers was
      that the former was sworn to young Francis Joseph, the other was sworn to the old
      Ferdinand, who was just deposed in a palace coup.

It had been decided by my generous friends that I should be given a dinner, or as they called it a banquet, of welcome during my last stay of any length in the Magyar capital. While the preparations were under way there came a telegram from the Argus-eyed Commodore in Paris telling me, as so often before, "Return to Macedonia – outlook stormy." It had the effect of hurrying up the dinner date and changing it to a ceremony of farewell rather than one of welcome; Jókai[14] threw himself into the affair with energy and zest. It was to be an important occasion and I must make a speech that would be equal to it. Fearing that my unaided efforts would result in a jumble of drab words he wrote out the peroration himself. He liked it and so did I. When shown to Vámbéry[15] he agreed that this speech would go far and be long remembered. There was still another surprise for me and for the guests at the banquet. My mentors decided that I was to recite at the conclusion of my remarks the first five lines and the last two of Petöfi's wonderful war song of the Magyars, the Talpra Magyar[16], the call to arms of 1848 which cost the inspired singer his life and gave him immortality.

I, of course, agreed. There was really nothing short of murder. I would not have done to spend the magic hours that now were mine in Jokai's little study where he could weave better stories than I could find though I ransacked the world in search of them.

13   When the Croatian Lancers came to Paris with the allied armies in 1815 they introduced
        to the Western world their choking neckwear, and it was in their honor baptized
        "cravat" by the haberdashers.

14   Maurus Jókai, one of the revolutionary youth in 1814, was the preeminent novelist of
        Hungary in the 19th century.

15   Armimius Vámbéry, (1832 - 1913) internationally known orientalist.

16   "Rise up Magyar, the country calls! - It's 'now or never' what fate befalls... - Shall we
        live as slaves or free men? - That's the question - choose your 'Amen"! - -God of
        Hungarians, we swear onto Thee - that slaves we shall no longer be!" is the first
        stanza. From Adam Makkai Ed.: In Quest of the Miracle Stag: the Poetry of Hungary,
        Univ. Of Ill. Press, 1996. -Ed.

Often in the midst of the sing-song lessons that followed Jokai would embrace me and assert, so boundless was his imagination, that my Magyar accent demonstrated clearly what he had often suspected, that the Americans were a Turanian people. And then the stay-at-home romancer would sigh, "How beautiful is your life! Here today and gone tomorrow – before stagnation follows. Always romance, always in action – while I sit here and dream of people and places I have never seen."

Vámbéry who often dropped in would join in the praise of my vagrant career and at times he would grow tearful as he realized what he had been and what he had become. With rapture he described the years he had spent as a beggar and a prayer-brother on the Central Asian plains with no thought of the morrow "when my only care was to secure my daily bread," he said. Then with sudden earnestness, "Young man, never settle down. That was the mistake of my life, but you see they tempted me so cunningly. Five hundred golden dollars a year they gave me, the beggar-man, to lay aside his pilgrim staff and become the professor of Oriental languages in the Royal University. I listened and succumbed. I shall regret it always. Always I would leave the bleak halls of learning and return to the living world."

In view of the very different feelings which my arrivals and my departures from some of the Balkan capitals, notably Sofia and Stamboul, had excited, the kindly sentiments expressed on this evening were most pleasant to hear. It was a gorgeous hour and I enjoyed every minute of it. The elder Pulszky, the companion of Kossuth, was ill and could not come but he sent his harming son with his regrets and a message so flattering that I dare not repeat it. Count Apponyi presided and the Erdödys, the Zichys, and the Bornemisszas were there in full force, all the rough riders of the Hungarian plain, and not a few who had the right to sit at the table of the Magnats and wear the leopard-skin dolman of the Royal bodyguard.

Jókai, of course, made an impassioned speech and so did Vámbéry, but the words of the great Orientalist ended in a warning, almost a menace. He evidently had a suspicion that would not be quieted, that in my heart there was a dream of a placid future and a farm, somewhere between the Susquehanna and the Potomac, in the land where I was at home, and so he shouted, "You must come to the Magyar land at least once a year and if you ever settle down, I, and all the evil *djinns*, will haunt your pillow."

The *Pesti Hirlap*, the old Kossuth organ, devoted much space to the occasion and dwelt upon the real feeling I displayed in reciting Petöfi's patriotic words. It was very pleasant and, of course, I had not the remotest idea that a few months later when the Pig War was on and the relations between Hungary and Serbia had become more than usually embittered, my recitation would be seized upon by my enemies, "the tarnished generals of Belgrade," as proof positive that I had departed from the neutral attitude which an American journalist should maintain in European affairs. Then as always, fortunately, the future was a closed book and I enjoyed a happy cloudless evening.

16. BELGRADE AND THE PIG WAR

The political situation in Serbia at this time (mid-summer 1890) is difficult to describe and perhaps it would be futile to attempt it. Political morals were at a low ebb and the future seemed to depend upon the antics of ex-King Milan, the prodigal parent with his unfortunate homing instinct, and the success or failure of the deep-laid schemes of Monsieur Hitrovo, the Machiavellian minister from Russia. There were active in the political arena all the parties that I have previously mentioned, and a brand-new one besides. Its members were called the Possibilists and their policy was to keep the Balkans boiling and to get just as many rubles as they could out of the Pan-Slavs of Moscow without interrupting for a moment the flow of forms that came to them from Vienna, from the men who believed in the vital urge that lay behind Austria's historic advance toward the East and, to be specific, toward Salonica and the Aegean.

Serbia was very hard-up and the army was being starved. Try as they would to balance the budget the accounts were always upset by the arrival of Milan's overdrafts from Paris and other uncontrolled expenditures. In a fit of righteous anger the radical assembly not only dishonored the last flock of drafts but cancelled the King's allowance altogether. They soon had much reason to regret this natural but ill-considered action. Within the week Milan stepped jauntily off the Orient Express, drove to the palace and told his son, the unfortunate Sandra, that he had come to take refuge with him against the disloyal strokes of a cruel world. A very few hours later, he

whispered to me that the boy king had called him home to take charge of
the army which needed "jacking up."

It was soon evident that the relations between father and son were greatly
strained. Milan, however, held his ground and maintained separate apart-
ments in the palace from which his son could not expel him, much as he
doubtless wanted to. Still the ship of state sailed on, although the waves of
discontent were rising to formidable heights, and what was a source of constant surprise to McClure, and of indignation to my exiled colleagues
across the river in Zemlin[17], despite cabals and backstairs gossip against me
I maintained my position as the only correspondent in the capital with un-
hindered access to the wires.

Perhaps my attitude, however successful, was not very creditable, but as an
extenuating circumstance may I stress the fact that there was being debated
in the political arena no great question upon which, as a Jeffersonian democrat, I should have taken an appropriate stand. It seemed to me, rightly or
wrongly, that I was not called upon here to suffer for a great political and
moral principle as I had in Sofia, and so it came about that, in an academic
way, at least, I conspired freely with all the conspirators (and heaven alone
knows how many there were!) with but little or no regard to creed or political complexion. I played *tarok* with the Radicals in the morning and
tric-trac with the Conservatives in the afternoon. I rambled through the forest and swam with little Sandra in the park of Topchider and ate the cloying
sweets which Milan had served in that part of the palace where he had established himself. And I will confess that even when he gossiped about his
expensive, and as some thought extravagant, *menus plaisirs* in Paris I did
not feel called upon to interject a word about economy or the sanctity of the
home.

Probably I was becoming Balkanized. This had happened to others before
me, but the explanation of my attitude which I prefer is that I was increasingly anxious to return home. There were people I wanted to see again of
whom I frequently thought during my lonely vigils. I had saved what

17   Hungarian bordertown.

seemed to me a great sum of money, particularly during the last two years in the Balkans where there was nothing, that money could buy, that I wanted. There it was stacking up mountain high in the *Herald* office in Paris by reason of my underdrafts for the salary account. It was not drawing interest, but it was growing rapidly because often I only drew half of my salary and never more than three-quarters of it.

It was a pleasure to dream of what I would do with all this money when my responsibilities for these turbulent regions ceased and my Balkan assignment was at an end. I would, of course, replenish my wardrobe in London. I would discard those ill-fitting Stamboul clothes which the Greek tailors on the Rue de Pera turned out for me, and then with my hard-won prize money I would buy a farm in Maryland, or at least I would make a partial down payment on it, which would be in accordance with the custom of our county. I would plant tobacco and start my Diamond Back terrapin breeding establishment. I would, equally of course, acquire two or three brood mares and some day at Pimlico I might see a colt carrying my colors pass the winning post in the four-mile heats. Mine would be real horses, not the racing machines for the short and silly dashes which, alas! were coming into fashion.

This was the state of affairs and my frame of mind toward the end of the fourth month of my longest sojourn in the Serbian capital. I had become there, or so it seemed to me, as stable as the town pump. All the plots of my former colleagues, living in exile across the river, had failed to shake my position. Now indeed they were cringing before me, and I? Well, I was letting bygones be bygones. Sometimes I even went to the extreme of generosity by furnishing them with the news I had cabled the day before! Some of the local papers spoke of my continued presence in Belgrade as one of the more encouraging signs of the times, and I was several times referred to in editorials as a sympathetic colleague.

But from the American viewpoint, and I always clung tenaciously to that, affairs in the Balkans were growing dull and, of course, we from across the Atlantic were only interested in Balkan fireworks. Every morning I expected to receive from the Commodore one of his long telegrams, or one of his short letters, telling me to move on to some more exciting front of world news, when suddenly out of a clear sky there thundered the bolt which in-

augurated the first skirmish of the Balkan Pig War which, as all economists
know, was the prelude to the great disaster of 1914-18.

How it happened was not clear then, and it is not much clearer now and
much less important. Perhaps, as rumored, the Austrian agents discovered
that M. Hitrovo, the Russian Minister, was smuggling into the country by
the way of Semendria hand grenades and bombs, indeed anything in the
way of a weapon in any way suitable to block the progress of Felix Austria
across Macedonia or Albania to the sea and so to strengthen the barricade
the PanSlavs sought to erect against the German *Drang nach Osten*. Austria sulked and Berlin growled, but better than that someone in Vienna or in
Budapest put on his thinking cap to good purpose. Who it was I have no
idea. The clever Andrássy, who would have been immediately suspected,
was dead, but whoever he may have been this great anonymous conceived a
plan of economic boycott which brought Serbia low in a few days and perhaps laid the fuse for the terrible conflagration in the years to come.

This fulmination took the commonplace form of a telegram from Vienna to
the effect that hog cholera having been discovered in many Serbian pig-
sties, no more Serbian pigs would be admitted into the Dual Monarchy.
People who now, as then, are ignorant of the intimate relation between a
prosperous budget and pigs in Serbia will hardly appreciate the force of this
stroke. "How is that?" they inquired, "with all the pigs penned up at home,
food, or at least pork, must have been plentiful and cheap and certainly no
fear of starvation."

But the people who indulge in such remarks merely show their ignorance
of the idiosyncrasies of the Serbian pig. The pig in Serbia is not eatable.
Upon his native heath he is wonderfully prolific, but still only skin and
bone and bristles. The pigs are driven up to Belgrade from their inland
swamps, lean as greyhounds and hungry as wolves. But once across the
river in the green pastures of Hungary[18] they fatten rapidly and are highly
prized in the European markets. With Hungary closed, its lush fields em-
bargoed, a tantalizing dream and yet one you could plainly see across the
river with an ordinary field glass, there was nothing for the Serbian pigs and
the Serbian swineherds to do but starve.

Perhaps I was incautious at this juncture. Frankly, as I have admitted, I was
taken by surprise, and perhaps I did not appreciate the far-reaching conse-

quences to myself as well as to Serbia of this new economic policy. But a man, certainly not a newspaper correspondent, cannot hold his tongue forever, and besides I recognized that the popularity in which I basked at the moment was not a permanent asset. I felt I must keep bidding for it and consolidating it all the time. So I bid. "That is not diplomacy," I said for publication. " 'Tis a disloyal stroke – a blow beneath the belt." And the next morning the *Male Novine*, the greatest of the Belgrade papers, hailed me as an outstanding friend of Serbia and a protector of the pigs.

Three days passed and the press of pigs in the Belgrade streets was so great that one found a place to put one's feet with difficulty. On the evening of the fourth day a famished drove broke into the restaurant of the Red Dog Tavern and ravenously devoured the crumbs that had fallen from our round table. Raskelvich, the Chief of Police, did what he could to protect me, as often before. But prestige, or even a Browning, are not effective weapons against famishing pigs. Raskelvich was a good friend of mine who had worked in an American packing establishment where he had acquired a taste for our dime novels. This taste of his I pandered to by securing for him copies of the *White Savage*, the *Wild Man of the West*, and above all, *Jack Harkaway in Search of a Mountain of Gold*. So that night Raskelvich sat late with me over his plum brandy, reflecting on and discussing the parlous state of the kingdom and *how the white-coated, white-livered Austrians could be bested.*

Suddenly an inspiration came to him. "You can do all kinds of things with pigs in America. In Chicago, I know, they put a pig in one end of a pipe and presto! he comes out at the other divided into a dozen neatly wrapped parcels. You lose nothing but the squeal."

18   Bonsal refers to the former Hungarian province now called Voivodina. In 1390, after a failed attempt by the Habsburg Monarchy to push the Turks out of Serbia, and after a suppressed Serb revolt, the Serbian Orthodox Patriarch of Ipek, Arsen Chernovich requested permission from Austrian Emperor Leopold to bring 200,000 of his people to this area as refugees. He was granted admission on a temporary basis, along with partial autonomy, in return of serving as a military district guarding the border.

Here I had my first inkling of what was coming a presentiment of how near I who had so long escaped the shoals and the whirlpools of Belgrade waters was to shipwreck. Yet could I, merely to safeguard my personal position, forswear one of the most envied garlands in our commercial crown?

"Yes they can do a lot with a pig in Chicago," I admitted. I was about to add and self-preservation being the second if not the first law of nature it seemed only fair that I should that we could, because of the tariff, only work these wonders with native-born pigs; but Raskelvich was gone with a ray of intelligence in his eyes which I could not ascribe wholly to the plum brandy.

The next morning, as I had anticipated, I was summoned to the Presidency. There sat Belomarcovich and the man who had taken the place of the late Protich. This substitute looked upon me with evident ill-will. When the vacancy occurred, the surviving Regents, who were very friendly and even deferential to me at this time, asked my opinion how to fill it and I had suggested Pashitch. They thought the man who had often eaten the bread of exile with me in Philippopolis and in Tsaribrod a bit too radical, and the clever fellow who in later years became the perennial Prime Minister was turned down. All I had really said was that often the wisest way to handle a radical was to draft him into a conservative administration and then he would probably hold his tongue; but these wise words had been distorted and the man who got the place, as I have said, on this notable occasion regarded me with ill-concealed dislike. However, Belomarcovich was, as usual, charming, and he "after compliments" got down to business even before I had eaten the customary sweet.

"You cannot ignore," he began, "the deplorable condition of the pig market, the principal product of our country, and our money crop?" I admitted that I was well aware that the pig market was – ahem – a little congested and then, foolishly enough, went on to say that with the greatest difficulty we had succeeded in keeping several droves of them out of the Red Dog Tavern on the previous evening. The man who had taken the place of Protich frowned at this and I was, or at least should have been, warned of his hostility. But, smiling amiably, Belomarcovich continued.

"You, Sir, as we all know, are an important man in your happy country. There are thousands there who hang upon your words."

Of course, I made a deprecating gesture such as modesty demanded, but the ranking Regent went on with a eulogy which, dared I recall it, would excite ribald laughter among even my friends and how my enemies would enjoy it.

"As such, and in appreciation of your position, you have been received and honored by all those who move in court circles and also by the lowly. And therefore we frankly put our problem up to you, for you, and perhaps you alone, can save Serbia from bankruptcy, her people from starvation and Europe from the outbreak of war." Then he snatched up pen and paper and began to figure out the situation. The result he achieved was then communicated to me in fact, to all of us, and I should add that at this time Raskelvich joined the group with an enigmatic smile upon his face. Well, the conclusion of the figuring was about this: With pigs selling in Belgrade or as perhaps I should put it with pigs to be bought in Belgrade, for six cents apiece, there would be a handsome profit in importing them and distributing the bacon on the American market.

"Indeed," interrupted the new and junior Regent who so evidently did not like me, "you could send them first-class by the Cunard steamers from Trieste or Fiume and yet so dear is swine flesh in your country there would still be a handsome profit for the importers."

"True," I assented, "but there are difficulties. How could we get the pigs to the port of shipment? There stands the Dual Monarchy like a stone wall. They might not even let the pigs pass in bond and, of course, they would refuse to admit to bondage pigs of which it has been said, most falsely, I know, that they are tainted with hog cholera. Mine is a commercial not a warlike people. We don't want any trouble with the Austrians, and this is particularly true of our pork-packers because the Austrians are among their best customers."

"Fortunately, we can and shall avoid all those complications," asserted , "although, I must say, in my judgment you magnify them somewhat. We ll raft the pigs down the Danube to the Black Sea. Thank God and Prince Michael, the Danube is an international river. Once on the Black Sea you can pick up the pigs with your cattle boats and shoot them to Chicago. It's easy." "It's easy," chimed in that devil Raskelvich with a wicked smile.

Strange as it may seem, at this time I did not know a single pork-packer in Chicago, or anywhere else for that matter, even by name, but I did know a Chicago grainman, the Caius Metellus of our day, the same who by his partisan contribution had made of me such a favorite in the Boulanger camp two years before. Surely he would have close relations with the pork-packers so I cabled him a statement of the situation in which I had become involved, and as I prepaid the answer I expected an early reply, but the eighth, ninth, and then even the tenth day of the Pig War came and went and still no answer. The explanation I made to Raskelvich, as sulky and alone, he sipped his plum brandy in a corner of the tavern, that perhaps the wires were down, was received in unbelieving silence.[19]

And then the unfriendly campaign in the press began. It opened with a squib in the *Male Novine* which read, "There was a man named Bonsaloff with the Bulgarian army at Slivnitza and Pirot. He glorified our enemies – was violently anti-Serbian. He claimed to be an American, but he came from the Ukraine."

"They are going to put you on the skids," commented the wise McClure. "You had better reserve a room in Zemlin. It's rather crowded, you know, with your colleagues."

On the following day, the disreputable but influential organ opened with heavy artillery. This announcement read, "Last year in Budapest at a Pan-Turanian banquet, to the delight of the Magyars, a certain alleged American, well-known here, truckled to our hereditary enemies by reciting Petöfi's infamous ballad calling upon the Huns to throw themselves upon the Slav world."

There was in this statement that mixture of truth and fiction which is so dangerous and often indeed convincing. There seemed nothing left for me to do but to pack up. Of course I had wanted to leave Belgrade, but certainly not in this way.

19   Later it developed that my good friend was in China.

And then, almost miraculously, the atmosphere cleared, and I was in a position to snap my fingers at the Regents and my other false friends. Silvano, an Italian porter on the Orient Express with whom I had long enjoyed confidential relations, slipped into the tavern and presented me with a magazine which he assured me I would find interesting reading. And indeed I did. Tucked away between the covers was a telegram from the Commodore ordering me to Vienna as fast as I could get there. I was half-packed already, but now in a triumphant mood I continued the operation. It was clear I could get away next day on the noon train...

I can hardly blame my colleagues in exile at Zemlin for their misunderstanding of the situation that had so suddenly developed. Of course, in sending the news to western Europe that at last I had been toppled from the pinnacle of favor I had so long enjoyed, and other misinformation, they were simply running, and wiring, true to form. Indeed, even in Belgrade in high circles these absurd rumors were credited. While I was still packing my bags the adjutant of the King (that is of the ex-King Milan), sneaked into the Red Dog Tavern by the back door and I must add the cowardly fellow was in uncompromising mufti. "His Majesty charges me to say that his affectionate good wishes go with you. He knows you will understand that it was only because of those overdrafts he could not interfere." I was in a hurry so I simply thanked the adjutant and then added somewhat cynically, "Of course, I understand. Sooner or later overdrafts have to be met."

The incognito which marked the visit of the King's messenger was successful and so this timid gesture of friendship escaped the attention of my long-envious but now jubilant colleagues in Zemlin, but I must admit there were other circumstances attending my departure which lent a certain color of plausibility to their version of the event to which they gave the widest publicity in western Europe. At the station did appear both Raskelvich, the Police Chief, though in fatigue dress, and McClure, the Scot, who was substituting at our fee consulate where to his sorrow no fees came in. McClure presented himself in rather formal attire.

Naturally enough these, as always, ill-informed correspondents, felt justified, with these facts to go on, to announce that Raskelvich was there to see that I should not evade the expulsion order of the Regents, and they had the audacity to add "as I had so often before." The presence of McClure they chose to interpret in an equally unfriendly way. They asserted that while, of course, the Consul was convinced of the justice of the edict that sent me into exile, still he came to defend me against the indignation of the populace, righteous as this was, as the Consul well knew, in view of the articles that I had written so misleading as to the actual situation in the kingdom. Reluctant as the Consul was to become mixed up in the matter, and while he made no secret of where his sympathies lay, still his sense of duty had brought him to the station to see that such rights and privileges as an American citizen I had not forfeited, were safeguarded by his presence.

Of course I did not condescend to answer the ravings of these fellows. It would have been but a waste of my valuable time, and indeed I regarded the abuse they heaped upon my head as the inevitable reward of anyone who pursued higher politics in the Balkans in the conscientious way that had always characterized my activities. But today I see no reason why I should not reveal the real purpose of these gentlemen as they came to salute me at the moment when I hoped that I was saying goodbye to Belgrade forever. Raskelvich came to beg, indeed to beseech me not to allow anything to interfere in the future with the flow of dime novels with which for so long I had been furnishing him. He admitted this had become his necessary mental pabulum. I gave him my solemn promise to continue these favors and I kept it, too, as far as my vagrant career permitted. I could not have done this, of course, had Raskelvich been a party to my mythical expulsion. As a matter of fact, I harbored no ill-feeling against him and should not have done so even had the blessed letter of release from Mr. Bennett not come and things gone on to what seemed, only twenty-four hours before, to be the logical conclusion. In this case I was enough of a philosopher to recognize that we would both have been the helpless victims of an economic revolution. I personally have been inclined to think, when similar disaster has overtaken me in other parts of the world, that it was the appearance of spots in the glorious orb that should give light to all, but doesn't, that was responsible, and not the machinations of mere men.

And McClure? Well, he was there because he was my faithful friend and then he was completely possessed by a financial project which he wished to lay before me. He was confident that if I could only get the right people interested it would make me immensely rich and also furnish him with the funds necessary to effect his escape from Serbia which was his ardent wish.

"The fact that pigs are a drug on the market today in Belgrade," he explained, "should not blind us to the fact that the market furnishes other short-cuts to fortune. For instance, look at kids. They practically have no value at all. Have you not heard them bleating in shame and despair over by Bulova and Krushevatz the live-long day?" Indeed I had noticed their complaints though the kids were not so intrusive as the pigs. And so I listened patiently to McClure's get-rich-quick scheme as I have to many another, to the plan for a salmon cannery on the banks of the Amoor, so dear to the hearts of the Cossacks in that lonely stanitza, to the opportunity which the Paraguayans on the banks of the Parana gave me to become the maté millionaire. But I did not have the Midas touch, and fortunately knew it.

"Just as soon as you reach civilization," was McClure's plan, "get in touch with a glover. I mean, of course, a large-scale manufacturer of gloves. With a thousand dollars in hand I can control the kid market here which is capable of expansion – if necessary. I will draw up iron-clad contracts and not a single kid shall escape us. All the goats, billies as well as nannies, will be working for us and our fortune will be assured, and further, and this is most desirable, kid gloves will be within the reach of the underprivileged – which is not the case today."

I thanked McClure for letting me in on this Pactolian project and promised to lay the matter before the next glover I came across. I mean, of course, a glove man on a large scale, but as such a one never presented himself I never did. So far as I know the field is still open to pioneers who may wish to try their luck in foreign fields. As for myself, I can only list it as another one of the golden opportunities which came my way and which I missed because well, because I was predestined to the pursuit of higher politics for all time, from its enticing beginning to the ragged out-at-the-elbow end.

Other and not a few less compromising friends were on hand at this trying moment and we had a stirrup cup, in fact several of them, in the dining car as the train was shunted about and the wheels well greased before it began the run in the blessed westerly direction.

"*Shogum! Shogum*! Go with God and may He accompany you," was the heartfelt prayer of this faithful group. Of all save Pope Gregori, the sophisticated chaplain of Milan, who had accompanied the ex-King on many European tours and seen things. Hearing these pious wishes he raised his arms in holy horror and shouted in his great bass voice, "No! A thousand times no! Wishing our friend Stefan Stefanovich a pleasant journey is one thing, but calling upon God to accompany him is quite another. Dullards and swineherds; have you forgotten that Stefan Stefanovich is going to Paris?" And in a moment I was gone – but as a matter of fact I did not know where I was going I only knew that definite instructions were awaiting me in Vienna at the Imperial Hotel.

As is often the case when you return to a place of happy memories, the few days I now spent in Vienna were disappointing. I was hungry for human conversation; I wanted to hear words that had no bearing whatsoever upon South-Slav problems. But it was Sunday when I arrived and most of my friends had gone up to the Semmering or were sojourning at Baden or somewhere under the trees of the Wiener-wald. In our corner of the Imperial Café I came upon Theodore Herzl and he was friendly and charming as always. But he was very busy; with muddy ink and sputtering pen, all that the cafe afforded, he was driving along upon his weekly feuilleton for the *Neue Freie Presse*. Perhaps he was working on that epoch-making and possibly war-breeding article in which for the first time he outlined his dream of the Zionist State, a national home for the Jews in Palestine.

I have another memory of those days in Vienna which, though it seemed trivial at the time, has grown in importance with the passing of the years. It comes back to me very clearly whenever I have heard the cannon roar and failed to locate the responsible battery and heaven only knows how often that has happened. It is my recollection of a Legation dinner that was not boring and where the conversation was not banal. That would mark it as epoch-making in diplomatic circles, but it was even more remarkable than that. Our Minister at the time was Colonel Fred Grant, a son of the Great Commander whom I was to know better years later in the Philippines where he commanded a division. Here in Vienna he had nothing to do and did it very well, and he was ably supported by his gracious lady who had both tact and brains. The dinner was a small affair, half a dozen members of the corps and a Prince Schwarzenberg, the descendant of the sluggish Austrian General whose tactics Bonaparte found so amusing in the Napoleonic Wars. Another guest, obviously a misfit, although he did not seem to know it, was introduced as Mr. Hiram Maxim from Maine. "A remarkable inventor," whispered Mrs. Grant to me.

I came to the conclusion that Maxim must be the inventor of the machine gun in which so much interest and so much ignorance was being displayed in the military journals. He was a tall, powerfully built man with a ruddy complexion and a great upstanding shock of iron-gray hair. His expression was kindly, his eyes friendly almost meek. It was hard to believe that such a benevolent figure had produced the new and terrible instrument of warfare. He was silent for a long time, but when he began to talk he monopolized the attention of all.

"I was a barefoot boy in Maine," he said, "and I hoped to become a tinker. That is, I was always tinkering with pots and pans and thought that some day I could make a living by mending them for the housewives of our village. Then suddenly an idea came to me. I saw I had hit upon something that seemed important, at least to me. It was a mechanical device which once attached to the sewing machine would save the seamstress all her tiresome treadling. But it didn't go at all. No one seemed to want to relieve the sewing mothers from their treadmill, and so I adjusted my device to a gun and people began to take notice. With this device attached to his rifle a soldier can continue firing incessantly. He will not have to lift a finger. He will only have to keep his finger on the trigger and his fusillade will continue indefinitely or as long as his ammunition lasts."

We all expressed interest in this new and terrible weapon – all except the Schwarzenberg Prince. He registered dissent by saying that nothing mechanical would displace the regularity and the reliability of the trained soldier, at least not if he had been trained in the school of the late Archduke Charles. The inventor smiled courteously. "Perhaps you are right – only time will tell." And then, after a pause, "But I have in my pocket something that will change the whole aspect of warfare, indeed revolutionize it." We sat up at this – even the Schwarzenberg Prince opened wide his sleepy eyes. And as he began to talk Maxim turned deferentially to the grandson of the man who was great, at least in the number of troops he trained in the wrong way.

"Do you officers of the army not say 'A battery discovered is a battery destroyed?' The Prince nodded assent and the inventor went on, "Well, with my new powder, *maximite* I call it, it will be almost impossible to locate a battery. It is smokeless. Battalions will be mowed down and black powder guns in battery will be dismounted and no one will be able to say from whence the destructive fire comes." All expressed interest and while he tried to conceal it even the Prince betrayed a certain amount of curiosity, so Maxim bowing to our hostess said, "If you will let me have a deep plate – but not a valuable one – I will show you how it works."

The deep plate was forthcoming and Maxim produced an envelope from which he poured a gray powder. He lit it with a match and it burnt for several minutes with a clear bright flame until the powder was consumed without even a wisp of smoke arising from the fire.

It developed in the following days that the inventor was in Austria to push his new-style munitions which he had just patented, but he was getting nowhere. The vested interests in black powder were up in arms and then his Old Testament name of Hiram was a heavy handicap to a fair consideration of his remarkable discovery. At the War Office Hiram Maxim was ticketed as a Jew and that was that. On the following day, at the suggestion of Colonel Grant, I called at the Ministry and told my friends there that far from being Semitic, Hiram Maxim was of straight Aryan descent, although I did not then misuse that term as we do so frequently today.

Nevertheless the school of Schwarzenberg and the ideas of the late Archduke Charles prevailed, and in Vienna the American inventor was rebuffed. He soon went to England and there *maximite* was quickly appreciated. The inventions of the kindly old man from Maine, and those that have followed upon them, ushered in a new era of carnage in comparison with which the wars of the Middle Ages were milk and water affairs. The smokeless powder and the concealed batteries helped to extend the rule of Britain in many lands and over many savage peoples who were brought to heel. And in the end the tinker from Maine grew immensely wealthy and King Edward raised him to knighthood!

.....

In due season the expected instructions came and once again I hastened across the wildest sections of the Balkan countries, at times on horseback and then again in the springless carriage called a *paitan*, but I was fortunate and made good time which permitted me two days of rest in Cettinje, the eagle nest of the Montenegrins. On the morning of the second day Prince Nikita, that charming old buccaneer of the Black Mountain country, waited upon me, supported by his stalwart henchmen, and asked me to sit with him upon his "bed of Justice" outside his lilliputian palace and watch him as like Ulysses of old he dealt "unequal laws unto a savage race." And he did it very fairly, it seemed to me, and certainly in the patriarchal manner. I little thought then I should, twenty-nine years later, see the handsome old man as a suppliant in Paris before the world "bed of Justice" and hear his sentence of deposition, a very unfair one I have always thought. That afternoon I coasted down the steep descent to the Bocche di Cattaro[20] and an hour later the *Namouna* steamed into the picturesque port.

Stephen Bonsal; 1920:

Excerpts from *Suitors and Suppliants – the Little Nations at Versailles*, 1946. Reissued by Kennikat Press, Port Washington, NY, 1969.

CHAPTER V

King Nicholas of Montenegro and Essad Pasha of Albania: The Black Mountain Folk vs. the Sons of the Eagle

December 4, 1918

Of the many suitors and suppliants who, awaiting their critical hour at the bar of the Great Assizes [Bonsal refers to the Paris Peace Conference where he was a Balkan expert attached to the American Delegation], are gathered here, King Nicholas of Montenegro and Essad Pasha, who represents many of the Albanian tribes and perhaps all who are Moslems, while not the most important, are certainly the most picturesque. I visited both their mountain fastnesses years ago, and today I find them sympathetic and extremely interesting. They are both men of magnificent thews and sinews,

20   Today Kotor.

and of the visiting monarchs of the West, only the gallant King Albert of Belgium need not fear physical confrontation with their stately figures.

They come as suppliants, it is true, but not on bended knee. In fact they are quite stiff-kneed, and perhaps that is why I like them so much. (Here are so many who crawl and creep around, falling on all fours whenever obsequiousness would seem to further their plans.) I do not play favorites as between these stalwart champions, but I must admit that my Colonel[21] has frequently chided me for the strong preference I show for their company a preference I have never sought to conceal because I know by unfailing signs that my chief shares my sentiments and would like to see more of them.

Nicholas has maintained his sovereignty over the Black Mountain country and fought for the Cross in the benighted Balkans for six decades, although from his fresh appearance and upstanding figure you would never suspect that he had passed the half-century mark. He is well aware that he is in danger of being deposed by enemies assembled here more versed in intrigue than in open battle in which they were always worsted. too, under the Crescent, has taken a leading part in many of the long and pitiless campaigns that have been waged by the discordant races and the militant churches of the dark peninsula. He now aspires to lord it legally, quite legally he insists – that is according to the Law of the Mountains – over that gaunt pile of rocks that juts out from the east coast of the Adriatic, the aerie nest of the sturdy Albanians who have defended it against all invaders and would-be conquerors back to the days of the Greeks and the Romans.

Unfortunately today the Neo-Roman Imperialists regard this rock-bound coast as necessary to the security of their homeland and their budding empire. In any event they claim it as at least a token reward for their services to the Allies (services not held in high esteem here) during the World War.

More recently these champions of ancient feuds faced each other in mortal combat under the battlements of Scutari. Nicholas conquered and Essad ca-

---

21   Colonel House, Bonsal's boss in the American Armistice Delegation in 1919.

pitulated, but not to the Black Mountain men, at least that is his claim. "I surrendered," says Essad, "to the great ships of the comity of nations that most unjustly were allied against me, and they were more numerous than the gulls of the Adriatic. To them and to them only I surrendered, so that I might live to fight another day. And that will be a dark day for Nicholas."

Almost suffocated by the miasmas of intrigue that flourish so rankly in Paris, and confronted by the false faces that are seen here in every quarter, I find it refreshing and most cleansing to note the fierce hatred which blazes in the eyes of these champions whenever the name of the other is mentioned. This is real primeval stuff! These men fight and hate each other in the old style, much as did the Homeric heroes on the "ringing plains of windy Troy."

All those in attendance at the conference, whether delegates or observers, who are totally ignorant of Balkan conditions (and their name is legion), are talking continually of a confederation as the unfailing panacea for the situation in the Balkan Peninsula which has provoked so many wars and promises more in the immediate future. The economic advantages of a confederation and a customs union are obvious to everybody except the people immediately concerned, who seem to delight in little wars that have the unfortunate habit of spreading to other regions and setting Europe in flame. If argument on the subject could be maintained, the economist would only have to say the word Sarajevo.

Of course, there are many circumstances and cogent reasons which explain the warlike proclivities of these unfortunate people, some of which unwisely I voiced not knowing what they would lead to. I explained didactically, as one will who has spent some years in the disturbed and disturbing regions, that Balkan is an old Turkish word which means mountains or very high land. Then getting into my stride I explained that a great geographer of the Gotha School had asserted that the turbulence of peoples corresponds to, and is in proportion to, what he termed the "rugosity" of the lands in which they dwelt. The people in flat lands are peaceful by nature, while those who dwell in regions that are "wrinkled or corrugated" are inclined to fight at the drop of a hat. I described at some length the failures of many movements for confederation and a better understanding among the people of Southeastern Europe, some of which I had witnessed. These admirable plans had always failed, although they had been eloquently and very ably advocated by men who should have been accepted as leaders.

"In the war-racked peninsula," I continued, "we are confronted with racial and cultural differences and above all by religious animosities and rivalries, and as Bacon said long ago in his book on the vicissitudes that afflict humanity: 'The greatest of these is the vicissitude of sects. The Bulgars still dream of the day of the great Czar Simeon, the Serbs hark back to the spacious empire of Stephen Dushan, and the Albanians are quite confident that the blueprints of Scanderbeg are not outmoded. Unfortunately also the churches are not very helpful to the peace-talker, although, of course, their intentions are of the best. The members of the Greek Church look to the Patriarch in Stamboul, the Bulgars are beholden to their Exarch, while the Croats and the Slovenes look to Rome for spiritual guidance; and this, as it filters through to the mountain folk, is not always of a conciliatory character."

Unfortunately for me, my expert knowledge proved impressive, and well before I knew it I was given the unwelcome task of bringing some of the fiery chieftains together and of talking to them convincingly. Reluctantly I began with the chieftains of the two smallest warlike tribes: King Nicholas of the Black Mountain folk and Pasha, representing a number of the eagle clans who have been squabbling for years over the possession of a few barren foothills that lie between their respective territories.

As I had visited both these Balkan chiefs on their native crags, I was urged to bring them as near as possible to the spirit of conciliation which it was thought should prevail at the Conference. I lunched them and I dined them – separately. My dream was, of course, to bring them together, to have them break bread at my table, drink plum brandy, and smoke the pipe of peace. My talking point was the frequent reunions in our happy land of the gallant men who wore the blue and the gray, who had fought each other for four long years and yet were now meeting so frequently on the very fields where the bloody battles had been lost and won. "After four years of fratricidal war, today they meet as brothers should. Why not you?"

"But we have been fighting those godless Albanians for four hundred years," demurred Nicholas. "That makes a difference." Indeed it does.

Then I tackled Essad. "Break bread with Nicholas? or any of the Black Mountain folk? Impossible that would be against the law of the mountains which we are all pledged to respect."

Essad had the dangerous gift of picturesque language and not seldom he gave it loose rein. Lie had served as minister of war to the Prince of Wied during the short and hectic sojourn of that German princeling in Albania.

[Prince William of Wied, cousin of the German Kaiser, was offered the crown of the newly autonomous Albania by the Western Powers after the First Balkan War and the crisis of 1913. Internal unrest and the outbreak of the World War forced him from his throne a year later. At this time (1918) Albania was occupied mainly by the Italians, but also by the French and the Yugoslavs. Its capital, Scutari, was under an interallied administration.]

"At the London Conference" [1913], Essad related, "the machinery of the new state was well set up, but the choice of the resident engineer was unfortunate. It soon became evident that the real purpose of the Prince was to weaken our people so that we might, without further resistance, drop into the lap of Austria and so cease blocking the march of the Germans to the sea. Soon we drifted apart, our relations became much less cordial, and I, though his minister of war, had to summon guards to protect my life against the machinations of my sovereign."

"The Prince surrounded himself with Austrian engineers who had come ostensibly to modernize the old palace on the coast where we, the members of the government, were living. But they really came to remove Essad Pasha from the scene; of course, in such a way that murder would not be suspected. This the Prince thought would be more easily accomplished down on the coast far from the atmosphere of freedom on the hills which is the birthright of my people. All day these alien intruders would be busy with their ostensible occupation, but at night they would prowl about the palace, and I soon saw that their sinister purpose was to learn where I and my wife were accustomed to sleep. When the veil of friendship was cast aside and the Austrian fleet bombarded the palace, a shell, which fortunately did not explode, landed in my official bedroom where, however, I was most careful never to sleep."

Essad if possible was still more critical of the behavior of the Italians in the last days of their first sojourn on the Albanian shore. [The Italians, *et al.*, fled before the Austro-Bulgarian seizure in 1916.] "I was out on the hills," he related, "ostensibly shooting woodcock, but really I was getting in touch with my mountain folk and seeking a plan by which we might escape the foul plottings of our enemies. At home and abroad I told them: 'We Albanians number five million, all with national consciousness, all hoping to retain our independence, yet we are given to tribal warfare and family vendettas, and it would be wise to ask for a dual protectorate, say of America and of England, until we have learned the difficult art of self-government and also have acquired a taste for peace'.

"This was my hope when suddenly the bombardment began and the Italian garrison in dropped their rifles and fell on their knees. 'Santa Madonna! Santa Madonna! they implored, but as no help came from Heaven or elsewhere they ran away like hares, only faster."

"There was a French colonel there heading the French Mission (Colardet), and I said to him, 'Let me defend the bridge with my men and I can assure you the Austrians will never get across!" But he said, 'No, I can better trust these battalions of rabbits than your band of wolves.'

"You see, those Europeans were very unfriendly to one another, but most of all they feared my gallant tribesmen. Then the cowardly Italians sneaked down to the port and made for the boats; but before they went they had thought of their bellies and they cut the throats of my two magnificent chargers which I had bought in England at a cost of half-a-million francs. They were magnificent animals, completely war broken; and those miserable rabbits took their noble carcasses along with them to serve as meat rations on their ignominious flight."

December 5, 1918

At a lunch with him last week, to which he invited me in a formal manner, honored me with a commission that showed that he was broader-minded in religious matters than many, including myself, had supposed. It was a strange repast. We were quite alone, because, as he said, he had an important communication to make, one which if it prospered would exert a benign influence upon the turbulent conditions that prevail in the Balkans.

Behind his chair and also behind mine stood heavily armed servingmen, their blue tunics bulging out with pistols and their gorgeous belts bristling with yataghans. They stood to guard us only, and the food was served by the Parisian waiters of the tourist hotel who tried, not quite successfully, to ignore the strangeness of the scene in which they were involved.

Now and again, vexed by a tough morsel on his plate, Essad would drop his ineffective fork and, picking up the hunk with his fingers, would throw it disdainfully over his shoulder. The servingman never failed to catch it in his mouth and seemed to enjoy his share of the feast. The spectacle carried me back to experiences in Prisrend and Prishtina and even in more civilized Usküb on the Vardar years ago.[22] Then I too had in this manner thrown tidbits to my servingman; but today I was out of practice, so when the repast was over I simply slipped a twenty-franc note to the guardian behind my chair and he seemed to be perfectly satisfied. Evidently Paris had corrupted him as it has so many others.

Over the coffee, which was brewed in the slow, deliberate Macedonian way, Essad broached the subject that had evidently been on his mind for some time.

"An Albanian friend who has lived long in Boston brought me last week an item of disquieting news," he began. "He says your honored President is an Elder of a church which some consider, doubtless unfairly, as narrowly sectarian. Whether this be true or false, this rumor has decided me to reveal what may be regarded as my religious outlook. While my people are divided as to churches a division which the Tsar[23] in Stamboul, until I helped to dethrone him, and the Emperor in Vienna always fostered you must have seen how very liberal and catholic my people are when left to their own devices. You surely have noticed during your visits to Albania that when our peasants prepare to sow their crops they not only ask the Moslem mullah to

22   See Albanian chapter in the author's Heyday in a Vanished World (W. W. Norton, New York and London, 1937)

23   The Albanians and many of the Balkan peoples often, to the confusion of the Westerling, referred to the Sultan as Tsar.

bless their fields and their labors, but also the good will of the Christian priest was asked and paid for by them if they could afford it. I think your President should be advised of the situation in my land and of my personal attitude which, you can assure him, I would never allow to become a barrier to the happiness of my people.

"To begin with, I want you to explain what happened in our country after Kossovo [1349] and the tragic battle that was fought there. The Turks with their green banners and their horsetail standards overran our lands killing all who would not praise the one God and his prophet Mahomet. We had always been Christians; in my family many had suffered martyrdom, and my forbears would gladly have accepted the fate which the fortune of war imposed if only their lives and their property had been at stake. But this was not the case. The lives and the property of the Albanian people were in the balance, and my ancestors did what I have always considered was the proper thing for them to do. They bowed down before the green banners. They admitted the truth of the proverb, Where the sword is there also is the Faith, and by so doing they saved their people and their land from utter destruction."

In an aside Essad now drew a parallel which he thought was devastating to the forebears of the hated Nicholas. "How stupid those Montenegrin bishops were," he commented. "Instead of admitting that there are many roads to Heaven and that no church has the exclusive control of the entrance gate, they fled to the mountains and took refuge in the caves. They saved their faith, it is true, but they lost their civilization. They sank to the lowest level of the human race. Even your Nicholas, who has been presented at many courts, is under his gorgeous trappings but a boor."

And now came the definite proposition. "My fathers saved our people and we served the Ottoman Turks faithfully until the moment came to overthrow their sultan, which we gladly seized. Today if my religion, which was imposed or at least accepted only under duress and to save our people, is an obstacle to our return to the Christian fold, I – we – would all recant as did our forebears, and to save our people accept once again the creed of long ago."

I told I would not fail to advise Colonel House and other delegates of his patriotic reasonableness, and I did so. But, doubtless wisely, our commission refused to have anything to do with the Albanian settlement. Like so many other problems it is allowed to drift along, and a deluge of blood will be the result.

[At this time, doubtless under instructions from Rome, Signor Nobile Chiesa, aviation expert of the Italian delegation, made a terrific attack in the French and Italian papers upon the stalwart Essad. He said that, while Essad was quite ignorant of any civilized language, he was very familiar with all European currencies and would accept bribes in any one of them. In the matter of language, at least, Chiesa is quite mistaken. Essad spoke a baffling French although apparently he wrote it with distinction, but he had a good knowledge of Italian, with which we eked out our conversation. Certainly it was not the *lingua Toscana*, but his meaning was always unmistakable. How he hated the Italians and how he loved to vilify them in their own language!

In his mountain tongue, though, Essad sums up with a song his feelings on this subject: "What is it that sports feathers but is not a bird? That carries a rifle but is not a soldier? That wears trousers but is not a man the Italian Bersagliere!"]

December 6, 1918

One of the dreams I cherished in the first hopeful days of the Conference (as mentioned in a previous entry) was to bring Nicholas, the undoubted champion of Balkan Christendom, and Essad, the Saladin of these modern crusades, together at my table; not, of course, at the Crillon where we would be exposed to the Argus-eyed gaze of the press, but in some remote restaurant, well out of the path of the conferees. The denouement of the plot was to tip my Colonel off and have him drop in casually at the place of meeting in his rôle of apostle of peace, and have him once again pronounce his familiar lines, so often effective: "All men are brothers. There are but few points of friction between us, and with but a little patience and good will, these can be ironed out."

However, the Colonel soon ruled out as unthinkable all thought of a formal meeting with these champions of the Balkans. He said it was not permissible under the Protocol, but I could see that he toyed with the idea of a chance or clandestine meeting.

Once he admitted: "I always get along best with mountain men. We seem to understand each other right away. My anteroom is crowded with lowlanders talking about dollars and cents, debts and trade privileges, and I confess they bore me. I envy you your contacts with the highlanders. How I would enjoy sharing them with you! But of course it is impossible. And you must not tempt me. From what you tell me I picture the hard-bitten Nicholas as a John Sevier, – who with 'over-the-mountain men'– walloped the Red Coats in the Carolinas; and Essad I picture as a ringer for Big Foot Wallace of the Pecos country, who would ride for a week in the tropical sun if only at the end of the journey there was a chance of a gun battle. I should like to meet them, but, of course, it is impossible for the present."

Clearly my Colonel was weakening.

Another reason why I was never able to pull off what might well have been a confrontation of incalculable consequences to the Balkan situation was the increasing reluctance of to leave his comfortable quarters in a Champs Elysées tourist hotel generally patronized by cosmopolitans. Adored and even idolized as he was by at least half the Albanian tribesmen, the Pasha was cordially hated by many others. He went out as little as possible, and when he did he was surrounded by heavily armed followers and he himself carried with him quite a battery of Brownings.

[Despite these precautions, within a few months Essad Pasha was dead. In June, 1920, the National Assembly, in which most of the Albanian clans were represented, recognized the position of their delegate to the Conference in Paris and proclaimed him king. On the thirteenth of that same month, as he was about to leave to be crowned in Tirana, he was assassinated in front of the Hotel Continental in Paris by a certain Averni Rustam, a fellow countryman whose clan had waged a blood feud with Essad's tribe for decades and who could not tolerate Essad as his monarch.

In the person of his favorite nephew, Zog, however, Essad reached the uneasy throne of the Albanian Eagles. In 1924 Zog became president of Albania and four years later, with a Napoleonic gesture, crowned himself king in Tirana, the forty-fourth successor to Scanderbeg, the legendary ruler of the Eagles.]

December 18, 1918

Today I feel that in all fairness I must put on record a more detailed account of my relations with Nicholas, his Royal Highness, King of Montenegro, which has been long withheld even from these confidential files. I must admit that these relations have not escaped misrepresentation in some quarters. They go back twenty-five years, and perhaps a few more, and I have for him such a deep admiration that when the problem which his future presented to the Supreme War Council came up, I felt it was only right that I should reveal to the Colonel, my chief, the ties of ancient friendship that bound us; and also to confess that on this subject my judgment might be colored by the admiration I had long felt for the "alone-standing, stalwart fighter" of the Balkans. This frank confession earned me a compliment that I cherish. "That is just like you," said the Colonel. "You have put your cards on the table. I shall of course be glad to discuss with you the Montenegrin problem, but when it comes to a decision I shall have to go it alone." And then the Colonel made the only ill-natured remark that I ever heard fall from his lips. "You are different from X; whenever he tips away to lunch at the Hotel Eduard VII where, as is well known, the Italians set a magnificent table, I feel in my heart that the Yugoslavs will lose another island."

"I never broke bread with King Nicholas," I protested; but weakening under the Colonel's scrutiny I confessed, "I had a few slivoviches with him, and once or twice, after the heat of the day was over, we pledged our respective countries in raki."

"That rules you out," decided the Colonel; "you must see that you cannot sit as a member of the jury before which the King comes as a suppliant." As I was excluded from the jury, I felt that I could go the limit as an advocate. "As a passing stranger, I sat with the King as an assessor or coadjutor on his bed of justice in years ago, and what I saw justified me in maintaining that Nicholas is a great and good man as well as a stalwart fighter. Yes, I sat with him and saw him, as did Ulysses of old, 'deal unequal laws unto a savage race.' While it was certainly rough and ready justice, strictly according to the Law of the Mountain, in only one instance can I recall a verdict perhaps not in strict accordance with the evidence. The King did close an eye to help an old soldier who had stood by his side in one of the many battles for the coveted port of Scutari. A magnificent-looking fellow he was, who fed his flocks on the mountaintops in summer, in the valleys in winter, and who was ready to fight the Turks, or anyone else, whenever the signal fires on Lovcen blazed."

"In that I see no basis for your exclusion," said the Colonel. "We all love the soldier, but I fear you are holding back the gravamen of the charge."

"Give me time," I stuttered. "It was this way. A lowlander, a villager, a measly looking fellow who sat quite still in the days when brave men were arming, now declared that this mountaineer soldier had herded into his flocks sheep and goats that did not belong to him.

'Tis a lie an atrocious lie!' answered the mountain man. 'Had I been in want of sheep or even goats, I had only to tell my Gospodar, my King, and he would have helped his soldier in need.'

" 'True, true,' said the King, 'that is the course I would have pursued.'"

"Then the King argued with the accusing villager. 'May you not be mistaken?' he suggested. 'Wise indeed is the shepherd who knows his own sheep. And then, of course, if they are there, your sheep may have forced their way into Perko's flock without the least inducement from him'."

"The King now lit a fat cigarette and with a dark look at the villager announced, amid applause from the many who had gathered under the great tree where the bed of justice was held: 'The case is dismissed. I cannot convict an old soldier on evidence as flimsy as this'."

'But my sheep! my goats!' screamed the villager. 'My brand marks on them are perfectly plain.'

" 'Well! well! said the King, 'it may be so. Yet perhaps your goats forced their way into Perko's flocks of their own volition. Bring me the evidence on this point set out in writing by the Elders of the village this day fortnight when, God willing, I shall once again dispense justice.'"

The Colonel grew thoughtful. He was evidently interested now in the monarch of the Black Mountain. "I must meet King Nicholas. Clearly that is my duty," he mused.

December 28, 1918

It had been a long week of economic discussions and plans for reparations and plump indemnities that were no more substantial than fairy tales, as the Colonel sorrowfully admitted. I had plagued him so constantly that at last he consented to visit the King of Montenegro, who had now moved into town from his suburban residence and was residing so conveniently down the *rue de* at the Meurice.

"Let's take a car," the Colonel suddenly agreed. "I am bursting with impatience." Then a shadow of care swept over his face which, in anticipation of the long-desired but often postponed meeting, had been so sunny. "But you don t think he will ask for a loan?"

"Not a chance," I reply gaily. "All he asks for is a passport to return to Lovcen – for the rest he will manage himself."

I must say that on this occasion, so important from every point of view, the King did not demonstrate the subtle qualities for which he has been long famous throughout the Near East. The moment after bidding us welcome and ordering Danilo, his heir (with a sturdy frame but a decidedly weak face), to go for coffee and sweets, he danced over to a lacquer cabinet and produced a number of ribbons and rosettes and crosses with yellow metal attachments that glittered and may have been gold.

"You are my true friends, or you would not be visiting a dethroned king. I beg of you to honor me and our friendship by wearing these tokens of my high esteem and my admiration." With that he tried to attach what was, I believe, the highest class of the Order of Danilo the Great upon the Colonel's coat, and upon me he thrust an order almost as high. The Colonel drew back and we both, gracefully I trust, waved away the temptation. We had by this time a regular form refusal for compromising gifts or decorations of any kind.

"We cannot accept," said the Colonel, with a pained expression on his face which did honor to his Thespian ability, "because our government is not in a position to reciprocate with a corresponding honor." And then the Colonel went on: "But for this barrier, the temptation to accept these signal honors from your Majesty's hand would be irresistible, but even so, would it be wise? Would not our desire to serve you be handicapped? Would it not be said that, after having been showered with the highest honors, is it possible for these American gentlemen to maintain the judicial attitude they should when Balkan questions come before the Conference?"

King Nicholas was not slow to see the force of this remark, and soon the decorations were safely housed again in the lacquer cabinet. After a few sips of most excellent coffee, the real business of the meeting got under way.

"My Colonel," began the King, "it distresses me that the fate of my land and that of my line is causing you anxiety. Permit me to say it should not. Lend me but for a few weeks your commandant here as a symbol of American sympathy; secure for me the passports so long denied which will permit me to reach the frontier of my native land, which your commandant knows and also loves, and the problem will vanish as does the snow on Lovcen when the sirocco blows. I am an exile and a man under an unholy ban, but once I cross the border the soldiers of my son-in-law and of my grandson would flee and I would not deign to pursue them."

Having settled in this summary manner the diplomatic and military features of the problem, the King now took a lighter and a more personal view of the situation.

"Let your commandant go with me as your plenipotentiary and as the representative of liberty-loving America. What a time we shall have," and the King in anticipation roared with laughter. "We shall go shooting in the mountains, in my beloved mountains; we will bring down chamois and mountain goats and bear and wolves, particularly the wolves which have become a pest to our peasants because the Swabs[24] who have overrun the low land are afraid to follow them to their lairs as we do." Then turning to me and rather leaving the Colonel out of the shooting symposium, the King went on: "I promise you a great big bag of *jarebica*, the most beautiful bird that flies. It is larger than the partridge, has red legs and a red bill, and I can tell you we shall have to climb the highest peaks to get a crack at him."

24   A term the Montenegrins and other South Slavs use when they wish to speak
      disrespectfully of the Germans – and that is generally their wish.

"But what about your mission of pacification?" this from the Colonel, who, it seemed to me, was not a little nettled at being left out of the shooting party.

"That will be accomplished in a moment," said Nicholas. "When my people hear the crack of our rifles on the mountain peaks they will rejoice, and down in the valleys there will be peace and joydancing..."

A few minutes later a change came over the spirit of our host; the sturdy old king who had survived sixty years of constant warfare fell into a reminiscent and indeed a somewhat bitter mood.

"Our national life which we preserved from our enemies is now threatened by our friends. All the battles we fought are forgotten. It is little remembered that we served as the bulwark of Christendom against the infidel Horde for centuries, and little help came to us from the people we shielded; only Russia helped us, and she, being far away, could help but little. By persistent fighting we recovered the lands that belonged to us and we liberated our Serb brothers of the plains who had been overrun and submerged. We did not rest until we secured our seaboard towns our windows on the world of the West, where men were happier because we had protected them and we raised the cross once again over Antovari and Dulcigno. The world then hailed us publicly as gallant fighters for the true Faith, but they whispered that we were savages and that indeed few of us could read or write.

"And in a narrow sense that was true; I admit it. The school of the Montenegrin boy, and girl too, had been from the day the Horde arrived in Europe unrelenting mountain warfare. We had no need to write down the story of our race that our boys and girls imbibed with their mother's milk, and they sang it as they defended the mountain crags that were at once our home and our refuge. Yes, we did become illiterate because we had to fight day and night for our creed, our independence, our faith, our man – and our womanhood. But before the Horde came, mine had been an enlightened people loving the ways of peace. In those days Obod, today a battle-scarred village, was the Athens of Southeastern Europe and from there the records of our faith and our civilization were communicated m our tongue to the outside world still in darkness." [25]

Suddenly the old King sobbed aloud. "It is forgotten now," he said, "even by our own people, but it is God's truth that those leaden types of Obod were melted down to make bullets with which we stopped the enemies of our creed, and the precious manuscripts which revealed the glories of our race were used as wadding for the guns that saved Christendom. Had we not made those sacrifices, there might well have been no printing in Western Europe today. It might have become there a lost art, as it has with us; and the spoken language in the West might well have become Turkish. History reveals that some nations have short memories, but today in our hour of need it seems incredible that these services should be completely forgotten."

"That shall never be," said the Colonel, who was deeply moved. "In some way which we do not see plainly at present Montenegro will be restored to her ancient glory."

....

Back at the Crillon I slipped to the Colonel Tennyson's great sonnet and he read it and read it again.

O! smallest among people, rough rock throne
Of Freedom, warriors beating back the swarm
Of Turkish Islam for five hundred years,
Great Tzernagora, never since thine own
Black ridges drew the clouds and broke the storm
Has breathed a mightier race of mountaineers.

25   The British Museum possessed, before the Blitz at least, a book from the Obod Press printed in 1495 – the year after the discovery of America! And there are said to be many other books bearing this imprint in the monasteries of Ryllo, but I have never seen them.

"We must leave nothing undone to help these gallant people and their noble king. If the Powers fail us, I shall ask Texas to take Montenegro under her wing," concluded the Colonel.

December 21, 1918

Today Andrew Radovich, the former prime minister of Montenegro and at present the bitter enemy of King Nicholas, tracked me down to a restaurant in the Passage des Princes where I often take refuge from my ethnic factors. He brought with him a young fellow countryman just liberated from an internment camp through the intercession of King Alfonso of Spain. This hard-bitten youngster is a nephew of King Nicholas' queen and so by marriage is related to the House of Savoy. The royalties are evidently standing by each other, and unless I misread the signs of the times it is none too soon for them to be doing so.

Radovich had often delighted me with his stories of the Black Mountain boys who had taken to the high hills and harassed the Austrians, but his obvious purpose today was to convince me that King Nicholas had during the World War abandoned organized resistance much too soon and that for all his stalwart appearance he is really a tricky fellow who would bear watching. In the course of one of their disagreements, the King, according to Radovich, had yanked him from the premiership and with shackles on his limbs had thrown him into prison.

"The shameless fellow then visited me and with no idle purpose," said Radovich dramatically. "He had tears in his eyes, and he added he would not be happy as long as I was in chains and I well, I told him: 'Bishop-King, my arms and legs are in chains but my soul goes free, as it never did in the days when I served you and tried to follow your serpentine path."

Apparently the Serbians when they rushed into the Black Mountain country liberated the former premier and, as some maintain, sent him to Paris to make all the trouble he could for King Nicholas. One of his talking points is to the effect that Montenegro could have held back the Austro-German armies for years, as they had held back the Turkish horde for centuries, but for the perfidy of the King.

"If we had only fought shoulder to shoulder with the Serbians, the Germans would never have been able to pollute our soil or devastate our fields and villages. For fifty years he kept the Serbs and our Black Mountain folk apart, and now you see the result: no railroads, no communications, no modern weapons; only our stout hearts against modern artillery, and, inevitably, the result was defeat." So runs the story of Radovich.

I turned from politics and listened to young Djourovitch, who had an interesting tale to tell. He was a law student, and when the Austrian invasion came he went to the hills where he was soon joined by many other fearless spirits. At least half of them, he said, were Montenegrins from America who had worked in the mines and the lumber camps of our Northwest until the tocsin sounded that brought them home.

"We were splendidly equipped," he maintained, "in very short order. We drew our rations and our guns from the Austrian transport trains. Soon wandering Polaks and Czechs joined us and we led a merry life. Often in Austrian uniforms we would descend into the garrisoned villages and, with false information, send the invaders into the mountains on wild-goose chases. Then we would kill the officers and men who remained behind and we would also kill the very few of our countrymen who were so traitorous as to do business with the invaders and make profits out of our misfortunes. Not many, but some of the women had been so shameless as to consort with the Austrians; in one village we found nine of these. These we marked for life, that is, we cut off their noses."

The young bloodhound was particularly bitter against Serbs; indeed, he thought well of the Albanians who had harassed the retreat of the shattered Serbian forces on their march to the sea. "The worst of it is," he continued, "the fact that many of them [Serbs] are our blood brothers. Take the Mirdites, for instance, that infamous Albanian clan; they are really Serbs or Bosniaks who flinched and fled to the highlands while we held our ground against the Turks.

"When I return home I shall devote my life to exterminating these robbers and murderers who disgrace the Serb blood that flows in their veins. They are men who will kill their blood brothers for a pair of shoes."

I left the young barbarian with gloomy forebodings as to the nature of the peace we are bringing to the Balkans. There the melting pot will boil over with gore before the hostile tribesmen settle down again to the workaday world that awaits them if any of them survive.

January 6, 1919

King Nicholas has filed with the Secretary General of the Conference his protest against the situation in Montenegro for which he holds, with some justification, the Allied Powers responsible. It is but little toned down from the advance copy he gave me some days ago. It is a sweeping indictment of the Serbian authorities and their armies that surged into the Black Mountain country to replace the occupying Austrians during the last days of October, 1918. He says that at least four thousand of his men and several hundred women are now in prison and have been or are shortly to be brought before military courts, "because they oppose the annexation of their country to Serbia." [King Nicholas himself had bitterly opposed annexation with Serbia (his son-in-law, Peter, was King of Serbia) during most of his reign (1860 - 1918).]

"All of these men are patriots," the King insists, "and at least eight of them were ministers in my government when, without a moment's delay and without asking for guarantees of any kind, we threw down the gage of battle to the Central Empires, although we well knew that owing to our geographical position immediate help from the Western Allies was impossible.

"Furthermore, among these men arbitrarily held under most uncivilized and unsanitary conditions there are many priests and civilians who at great risk to their lives and property opposed and greatly harassed the Austrian invaders. As a matter of fact, to these gallant men and women the Serbian army of today owes its very existence. These are the people who in 1915 saved the Serbian forces from annihilation or ignominious captivity when, driven from their own territory by overpowering numbers, they undertook the march over the mountains to the sea.

"The only charge that can be brought against these patriotic people is that they have protested against the annexation of their homeland, secretly ordered by the Belgrade government, and that they have opposed, sometimes with arms, the way in which the invaders who claim to be 'blood brothers take possession of their villages, devastate their fields, and steal their flocks. It is said that some of these bandits have been murdered. This charge is true; my people admit it; but such acts are not reprehensible. This is the attitude my gallant people have always maintained against those who sought to despoil our country. Not a few of my people, with the recklessness characteristic of men who have always been free and are determined to remain so, have refused to submit to this treatment and many, very many have been shot down lightheartedly as though they were rabbits when they attempted to escape from the wired concentration camps.

"Last month when the French government, speaking for the Allies and the Supreme War Council, requested me not to return to my beloved country until conditions were more stable, I acceded to this most unwelcome delay because the government of the republic gave to me and to my people the most solemn assurance that the 'Allied troops would respect the sovereignty of our state and the liberties of my children. 'Allied troops, as it developed later, were only Serbian bandits and marauders. While at first these assurances were only given verbally (to save time, I was told) they were formally confirmed by M. Pichon, the French Minister of Foreign Affairs, in a letter dated November 4, and later, if possible even more authoritatively, in a letter from His Excellency, M. Poincaré, the President of the French Republic." The King then showed me both the letters, and they are textually exactly as he has represented them to be.

"Despite these solemn promises," continued the King, "the Serbs, in the name of and apparently with the authority of the Allies, continued to dragoon my people and enforce their authority by what is called by some observers an Asiatic terror, although we are bound to admit that the outrages of the Turks in the old days were milk-and-water affairs in comparison to what we are now undergoing at the hands of our 'blood brothers."

January 22, 1919

My repeated arguments to the effect that the Serb, Pasitch,[26] and the Belgrade government are ignoring Point II of the famous Fourteen [freedom of the seas], and that the present actual invasion of the Black Mountain country by the Serbians is even less defensible than the former onslaught of the Austro-German forces, at last carried conviction, and when the matter was brought before him President Wilson took his first affirmative action since his arrival in France. He approved of the memorandum which I had drawn up, and what was more, he secured for it the approval of all the great men assembled in the second session of the World Assizes. It declared that all the Serbian troops, irregulars as well as regulars, who were overrunning Montenegro and dragooning its people must be immediately withdrawn. If an army of occupation proved necessary to maintain law and order and to prepare the country for the American panacea of a "free and fair election," the troops of a neutral power should be substituted for the Serbian forces.

To accompany this decision, I had drawn up for King Nicholas to sign an appeal to his people which I was quite hopeful would aid in the pacification of the disturbed districts. In it, the King called upon all loyal to refrain from hostilities and return to their homes to avoid armed conflicts whatever the provocation; and it concluded with his hope expressed in these words: "I am confident that in accordance with President Wilson's noble program, now ratified by all the powers, the people of Montenegro will be given a full and early opportunity to decide upon the form of government they may desire."

I had great difficulty in inducing the King to sign this appeal, but as this was a part and a most important part of the bargain, I had to insist upon it.

It is difficult to say exactly what happened to this manifesto of the Powers and the appeal of the King that went with it. Both were radioed from the American, the British, and other naval vessels that were patrolling the Adriatic, but the French and the Italian ships, which were far more numerous in these waters than ours, showed little zeal in bringing the news of the peace policy to the distracted country. Even the English, apparently out of homage to Belgrade, showed little energy in passing on the good news. At least this was the information that reached us through American naval channels. However, some steps toward pacification were taken. Several brigades of Serbian troops were withdrawn and the assembly at Podgoritza which had been upheld by Serbian bayonets and which had declared the de-

26   Nikola Pasitch, called "the Old Fox of the Balkans," was a wily, violent, ex-radical who, after a youth spent in being condemned to death and banished for his anti-royalist plots, served as premier of Serbia and its successor state, Yugoslavia, 1906 -1926.

position of King Nicholas collapsed. The call of the King addressed to his people to return to their homes and refrain from active hostilities secured in some mysterious way a much wider circulation than did the assurance of the Powers that the harassed mountaineers would be given an early opportunity to decide for themselves what form of government they preferred and that was most unfortunate.

I am compelled to admit that my plan was not a great success and that, while crediting me with the best possible motives, the King regretted he had followed my advice. A few days later he told me (he was in "grape-vine" communication with his partisans at home throughout the Conference) that many misleading versions of his appeal had been placed in circulation and that by not a few it was considered a complete surrender and even a suggestion that the people should make the best possible terms with Belgrade.

"And of course that was the very last thing I wanted them to do," protested the King. "The very last thing I wanted them to do was to lay down their arms. I am a fighter, they are fighters. I wanted them to fight for the freedom of the Black Mountain to the last man."

March 12, 1919

Today I must note in my locked diary one of the most "hush-hush" of the many graveyard secrets, to use the Colonel's expression, that it contains. Ten days ago King Nicholas showed me the original of a cable which he received from President Wilson in the summer of 1918. It appears that his agent in Washington at this time had approached the White House with the request that recognition and encouragement be afforded the struggling Black Mountain folk who, by their guerilla tactics, were harassing the Austrian forces of occupation quite as effectively as have the Poles and the Czechs indeed all the oppressed and overrun peoples in their respective territories. The cable apparently resulting from this *démarche* is dated July 12, 1918, and on the face of it certainly confirms the position which the President took in enunciating the eleventh of the Fourteen Points [guaranteeing Balkan states free access to the sea], the world-wide Magna Charta of all the at-present submerged peoples. The cable reads:

"I am confident that neither you nor the noble people of Montenegro will allow yourselves to be cast down by the present untoward situation but that on the contrary you will have implicit confidence in the firm determination of the United States government and people that in the final, certain and assured victory, the integrity and the rights of Montenegro will be recognized and safeguarded."

Woodrow Wilson

Of course the cable may be a forgery; if it is, I am confident that the King is its victim and not the perpetrator of it. My Colonel has of course tried to elucidate the matter, but down to the present without success. In the files that the President brought with him from Washington there is no copy of the cable, much less the original record, and the King frankly admits that a confirmation of the cable by mail, as would have been the usual practice, never reached him. President Wilson recalls an interview with the Montenegrin envoy at about this time and also that he spoke encouraging words to him; but he has no recollection of having sent the cable, although he is not willing to deny that he sent it. This may be another instance of a typewriter near at hand and a dislike of secretarial assistance having resulted in embarrassment for our chief magistrate. The failure of a mail copy to authenticate the cable is not remarkable. At this time King Nicholas had taken refuge in Italy, and mail to the Allies, owing to the activities of the U-boats, was most uncertain and precarious.

The King is determined to show the cable to President Wilson and is insistently demanding an opportunity to do so. And nothing could be more understandable. The Italians are withdrawing the slender support they at first gave to the father of their Queen, and unless help, indeed real assistance, comes from Wilson, the King's chance of returning to his battle-scarred kingdom is slight indeed.

This change of policy in Rome is not an enigma to those who believe that the teachings of Machiavelli are still honored and practiced at the Consulta. To them it is clear that Italy wishes to further weaken the by-no-means harmonious confederation of the Serbs, Croats, and Slovenes by the addition of the Montenegrins who, they are confident, will soon be in chronic insurrection and so, indirectly at least, will aid Rome to control the Adriatic sphere. This I believe is a correct assumption. I am confident that a great majority of the Black Mountain people want to maintain their political independence of Belgrade whatever the economic disadvantages may be, and that they are willing and eager to fight for it.

March 24, 1919

My admiration for King Nicholas (which some denounce as blind partiality) has caused many of the Serbs to make statements which in my judgment do not tally with the facts; some indeed are laughable. This morning de Giulli and two of the other Belgrade propagandists came into my room and announced that in examining the Holy Scriptures of St. Cyril and St. Methodius they find that the deposition of Nicholas was therein decreed and sanctioned by these good men centuries ago. Their attitude induces me to think that the world is going mad and perhaps that I am getting "nutty" myself. They brought with them a Bible in Old Slavonic and began to read from it.

"In these holy writings," they insisted, "we find authority and justification for the course we are determined to pursue. Here is a sign and a portent which must be heeded if our people are to be saved. The Armistice came into effect at the eleventh hour of the eleventh day of the eleventh month. Clearly that is not an accident; it is an indication for our guidance, and following it what do we find? Listen, in the eleventh verse of the eleventh chapter of the eleventh book of the Old Testament we find these words: *And because he was a bad king his kingdom shall be taken away from him and he shall be despoiled.*

For a moment I was tongue-tied, but soon I rallied. "You quote from a schismatic bible," I answered, "and from a text which I cannot accept. If the Conference is to be guided by the Scriptures, and as yet there is no agreement on that point, we shall insist on the King James version." They left me very much disgruntled but announced the coming visit of Ante Trumbitch, their leading delegate, with data greatly to the disadvantage of King Nicholas – and much more up to date.

There are, of course, many stories in circulation very unfavorable to the course the Black Mountain monarch has pursued in the years of confusion and tumult. They carry weight with those who unlike myself have not been immersed in Balkan miasmas for years and are, as I am, consequently inclined to disbelieve any story that comes from that quarter, especially if it is plausible. Many of the lesser Belgrade people assert that Nicholas, so far from having been, as I and many others claim he was, "an alone-standing, stalwart fighter for freedom," from the very beginning of the World War was at pains to be on friendly, indeed intriguing, terms with both camps. "And then he was always a subsidized mercenary of the Tsar," they assert.

I confess this last blow below the belt robbed me of my diplomatic composure and I answered it in a wholly unseemly manner. "Just as you are, no more and no less, the mercenaries of Uncle Sam. He provides the money, the food, and the ammunition. And you? You provide the secret treaties which make the world unsafe for democracy!"

After explosions such as this, we disarm and shake hands and try to talk sensibly. I must say, however, that old Pasitch, knowing as he does better than anyone else how vulnerable is his own record, lends little or no official countenance to these scandalous stories. He bases his demand for the deposition of the King and the union of the two Serb states upon higher ground. "Montenegro is too small and too poor to survive in this troubled world. For the last three decades she only made both ends meet by the subsidies which came from Russia." He then added: "I do not suggest there was anything dishonoring in the acceptance of this assistance. Far from it. That money was earned by the brave Black Mountain boys on many a bloody battlefield with the Turks. But today Russia has vanished from the scene and the great White Tsar is no more. We must welcome back into the Serbian fold our brave brothers of the Black Mountain"; so says Pasitch.

But to avoid the charge of partisanship, if that is possible, I must not entirely ignore the other accusations against the King that are in circulation here, even if that circulation is due, as it is almost entirely, to high-powered propaganda. You hear in many quarters that the King quit fighting too soon and that before he sought refuge in Italy under the wing of his daughter, the Queen, he was not as helpful as he might have been to the Serbians, greatly harassed as they were by Albanian bandits on their desperate retreat to the sea. Judgment on these and kindred matters, to be worthy of consideration, requires intimate knowledge of conditions in this sector of the Balkans at this time, which few of the King's critics possess.

It should be recalled that for years a party had existed in Old Serbia, a by-no-means insignificant party, strongly in favor of the annexation of the Black Mountain principality to the kingdom. While the plan was often sugar-coated under the slogan of "union of all the Serbs," it always aimed at the deposition of the hard-fighting Nicholas. The result of this agitation was unfortunate. The brotherly feeling that should have existed between the two branches of the Serb family was seriously impaired. When Belgrade was bombarded by the Austrians, and the politicians who had for years plotted his downfall were in flight, I rather think that Nicholas accepted this with Christian resignation. But it is quite certain that he never joined with the hired bands of the Central Empire and the local Albanian bandits in harassing the heroic retreat of the Serbs across the snow mountains to the sea. Indeed, he helped them all he could.

Those who are determined to place the more unfavorable construction upon the King's activities throughout the war, and particularly during the darkest moments of it, exhibit what purports to be a letter from the King to the Emperor Francis Joseph offering peace and the assistance that Montenegro could still furnish, if he were assured the possession of whatever Serbian lands might remain after Austria had appropriated what she might consider necessary to safeguard her road to the Aegean. I never saw the original of this letter (although I asked for it, it was never forthcoming), but how any Serbians, after their quite recent experience with the Viennese forgery factory, as disclosed in the Friedjung treason trial,[27] could credit its authenticity for a moment passes my comprehension. And of course they did not; it was merely another bit of mud with which they hoped to plaster the heroic figure of the man who stood and still stands in the way of their selfish plans. Perhaps the letter should only be taken into consideration as indicating the low level to which the war psychosis had reduced some members of the Belgrade gang of character assassins.

27   Dr. Heinrich Friedjung was a historian of some standing in Austria who in the Viennese press published a series of articles charging a number of Serbo-Croat politicians with treasonable practices. He was sued for libel by fifty-two of these aggrieved statesmen. In the course of the trial it was proved that the unfortunate historian had received most of the documents upon which the charges were based from the Austrian Foreign Office and also that two thirds of them were bare-faced forgeries.

It is, however, an awkward fact that throughout the war and down to his death in October, 1918, Prince Mirko, the second son of the King, was in Vienna. Upon this fact the accusation that King Nicholas maintained a footing in both camps is based. It is further alleged that Mirko was authorized by his father to make proposals to the Central Powers whenever a favorable moment presented, and that these proposals were far from being in accord with the public pledges of the Montenegrin government. I took this charge up with the King and, far from being offended at my frankness, he seemed to welcome the opportunity to deny the accusation.

"My boy, Mirko," he said, "on the urgent advice of his doctor, took his wife to Vienna for treatment in June, 1914, and unfortunately was there when war came. The Austrians immediately placed them under guard, but I must say that at first and for many months they were both treated with some consideration, and that fact is the foundation for the story that they were on friendly terms with the enemies of our country and of the Entente Powers. Of course the Austrians later, under threat of placing the unfortunate young couple in a concentration camp, did try to make Mirko pronounce in favor of the Austrian Balkan policy, but he remained steadfast. Toward the end of the war the attitude of the authorities was much less considerate, and this circumstance, and the anxiety which he suffered because of the health of his wife and the uncertain future of our country, brought about his untimely end.

"But if my boy made any mistakes it was because he heeded my advice. I soon established a secret channel of communication with him and I made it quite plain that his duty now was above all else to survive. I urged him to listen to whatever propositions the Ball-Platz[28] would care to make to him, and this he did. In this way very valuable information reached me, and through the Rome foreign office I passed it on to the Allies who found it useful. I even told Mirko, and I am not ashamed of it, in the last analysis to consent to any steps, to any change of attitude the Austrians might insist upon. 'Once again in freedom you cannot be held to engagements you were forced to make while in captivity but I am bound to say it never came to

28   Foreign ministry of the Dual Monarchy.

that, and it may be said that on the whole my children were treated fairly well by the Austrians. Through Mirko they thought to exert considerable influence upon me. But the death of my boy thwarted whatever hopes they had in this direction."

[Full corroboration of this sad story came to me in 1935 in a surprising way. Under the guidance of "Steve" Stevovich, a Montenegrin guide with headquarters in Ragusa, I had the good fortune to make a number of motor-car excursions into the Balkan countries with which I had been familiar in the slow-moving horseback and Paietan riding days. "Steve" had not the most remote idea of my interest in King Nicholas, and I only advised him of my friendship after he had told me the following story.

"I was and had been for four years, ever since my return from America," he related, "the personal chauffeur of the King. In June, 1914, he summoned me and told me that the wife of Prince Mirko was very ill and that I was to take them to Vienna. In view of the condition of the roads in those days, I thought he wished me to drive them to railhead, to Skopje, or to Nisch at farthest. But no, he meant exactly what he said, and when we got under way I saw the reason of his injunction. After suffering from a nervous breakdown, Princess Mirko was out of her mind more than half the time, and travel on the railway would have attracted public attention to her unhappy condition. More than once we had to place the unfortunate lady in a strait jacket with which the doctor had provided us before we left Cetinje. After five anxious days I delivered the unfortunate couple at the sanitarium in the city that poor Mirko was not to leave alive, and I only got back into Serbia the day war was declared." So the old King told the plain unvarnished truth although with natural delicacy he held back some of the more distressing details of the unfortunate incident.]

April 26, 1919

Slowly but irrevocably, I fear, the Montenegro problem has faded from the picture. Sympathy for King Nicholas is frequently expressed, and in some quarters it is sincere; but the consensus is that nothing can be done about it or for the sturdy King, out of tune with the times.

After Wilson's illness early in April[29] – and how serious it was we are only beginning to appreciate – the President naturally, indeed inevitably, concentrated his energies upon main objectives: the Peace Treaty with Germany; the acceptance of the League and the Covenant by all nations. Strangely enough the active, the very active influence exerted against the little principality came from the officials of the foreign office of the land whose Queen [Elena of Italy] is the daughter of the king they seek to depose.

April 28, 1920

Through other channels, when Queen Elena became passive, King Nicholas, her father, continued his efforts to obtain authorization to return to the Black Mountain country. His requests were never definitely refused; he was always put off with the plea that he must wait still a little while, until the situation had "cleared up." Months later and still in exile, the sturdy Nicholas died, and although it was one of the Fourteen Points nearest to President Wilson's heart, the restoration of Montenegro to its former independent status was never achieved.

But it can be said, nevertheless, that the fate of the Petrovich family was more fortunate than that of the Romanoffs, their constant allies and unfailing protectors. Alexander, the grandson of King Nicholas, ascended the throne of what was planned to be the federated monarchy of the Serbs, the Croats, and the Slovenes [Yugoslavia], while Nicholas the Second, the son of the great White Tsar who had proclaimed the lord of the Black Mountain as "his only loyal friend," was butchered in the dark Ekaterinburg cellar to make a Communist holiday. And with him died the little Tsarevitch I had first seen on that memorable day in Tsarskoe Selo (1907) when, with pomp and circumstance and much barbaric splendor, he was proclaimed Grand Hetman of all the Cossacks and heir to the empire extending from the Baltic to the Pacific. And with him perished his sisters, the charming grand duchesses I had so admired as I saw them tenderly nursing the wounded soldiers in the overflowing hospitals of St. Petersburg in that war winter of 1916 when the dark shadows began to lengthen over what was then still called Holy Russia.

29   See Chapter XVII, "The Conference Runs into Heavy Weather."

175

And this is by no means a complete list of the misfortunes that have over-taken the "anointed" of the Lord, who until quite recently by some were considered immune from the changes and chances of fortune that beset lesser folk. Kaiser "Bill" is an unwelcome refugee in misty Holland, and Emperor Karl vegetates in Lausanne. The Sultan of Turkey, whatever his name may be (no one bothers to recall it today), is a lonely sojourner on an Aegean island. And Ferdinand "the felon," as he is rightly called, who, by cunning and duplicity, from an intruder in Roumelia worked his way up to become the Tsar of all the Bulgars, haunts the antique shops of Weimar and Coburg bent on completing his collection of ancient Greek coins. And speaking of coin, yesterday a Hungarian magnate, whom I knew in happier days, came in and touched me for five dollars. "What a world it is," he solil-oquized; "Until 1868 we, the E's, *frappéd* our own money."

When you call the roll of those who in the last few months have suffered the "slings and arrows of outrageous fortune," the lot of Nicholas Petrovich is not a particularly unhappy one; but this, I am compelled to admit, he would never concede. When on my last visit, I talked to the King in this strain, he nodded his great lion-like head, but his words showed that he did not acqui-esce in my philosophy.

"I shall write no more notes of remonstrance to the powers who are unwor-thy to receive them," he said, "but I will write and rewrite the songs of my people, and these songs will hearten and sustain them until once again the light of freedom and of liberty shines down upon them from the summit of Lovcen."

January 3, 1924

King Nicholas, still in exile, died on March 1, 1921. Even at the last, when life was ebbing, he refused to abdicate in favor of his grandson, Alexander, and it was because of this that he was not allowed to return to his beloved . I understand, however, that his ashes have now been interred in the soil which he loved and so gallantly defended.

John Flournoy Montgomery; 1947:

Excerpt from *HUNGARY – the Unwilling Satellite*; New York: Devin-Adair Co., 1947.

Appendix IV – Secret Contacts between King Alexander of Yugoslavia and Mussolini

Preceding Hitler's advent to power several attempts were made to bring about better understanding between neighboring nations which within a few years were to become victims of Nazi aggression. Italian-Yugoslav animosity was an inheritance of the Paris peace conference. It had led to serious incidents between Italy and Yugoslavia even before the advent of Mussolini to power.

The Corfu incident almost destroyed Mussolini's dictatorship in 1924 and from that time on he proceeded more carefully with his schemes concerning imperialistic expansion in the Balkans. Nevertheless, he distinctly favored disruptive tendencies aimed at the splitting up of Yugoslavia into separate national units, especially at the separation of the Croats from the Serbs. The resulting tension extending over all of the Adriatic coastline interfered with the general stability in southeastern Europe and affected the situation both in Vienna and in Budapest.

King Alexander reacted very firmly against Croat separatism. He even went much too far by establishing his personal dictatorship in Yugoslavia (1930) but credit must be given him for his tenacious attempts at coming to a better understanding with Mussolini.

The following excerpts from the file of my Italian friend, whose name I prefer not to divulge, are evidence of Alexander's good faith and of Mussolini's shady intentions. To my mind, this document is of interest as a behind-the-scenes example of the play of forces which swayed events in central Europe.

The conversations began late in 1930 when King Alexander discovered that my friend had direct access to Mussolini. On many occasions the king did not ask him to convey direct messages to Mussolini but merely expressed his opinions vehemently, confident that my friend would repeat them to the Duce. Much of the record is repetitious; much of it expresses Alexander's indignation against the Italian press, as on January 1, 1931:

"The papers continue with their attacks and when they have nothing to say, they invent. Recently they published the statement that there had been discovered here a conspiracy of generals, and that I don't know how many had been shot and hanged. There was not a word of truth in it, for at all events with our army, which is well disciplined, we are absolutely safe. I cannot understand why Italy acts this way to create difficulties for us when both our countries could obtain great advantages from a good friendship, since we are an agricultural and Italy an industrial country."

"We are accused of desiring war! Thanks! That would indeed be the last straw for the whole world. We have just come out of a war, and we know what it means. And what good would it do? What would we get? I assure you that I can think of no conceivable reason for desiring a war, for even if I had a ninety percent chance of winning it, I would not risk the ruin of my country."

"In 1921 our relations with Italy were most cordial and we were entirely willing that Italy should be free to do what she pleased anywhere except in the Balkans, where any question could have been settled after a reciprocal agreement. And then Italy goes and signs a treaty at Tirana without giving us the slightest warning. From 1920-21 on, France was determined to persuade me to sign a treaty of alliance and she was pressing me as hard as she could. I had steadily refused to sign, out of regard for Italy with whom I desired good relations, but as soon as I learned of the Treaty of Tirana I instructed my minister at Paris to sign. Subsequently, Italy signed a second treaty at Tirana, and after that we strengthened our ties with France; now we are committed to following the French line."

"People are astonished that we are arming when the threat of treaty revision is always present. Does anyone believe that I would submit to treaty revision being discussed at a table? My entire country would turn on me in a fury! Those who wish revision must fight for it. It is just as though someone came to take away belongings from your own home. It is because of this continual threat that we are compelled to arm. Do you suppose that I am pleased at having to spend billions to buy cannon, and aeroplanes and weapons in Czechoslovakia and France when all this money might remain in my own country which needs so many things? This year alone I have bought nine hundred cannon and it has cost me an incredible sum of money."

"Before the annexation of Fiume, I received a message that Mr. Mussolini desired to come to an agreement with me on the basis of a policy of sincere and frank friendship, providing I would not raise difficulties in this question of Fiume. I was delighted to seize this opportunity, and I replied that if the friendship of Italy and particularly of Mr. Mussolini were involved, I would yield in the matter and undertake to raise no difficulties – I myself accepted the entire responsibility and likewise I courted the displeasure of my entire country... I expected that the press would cease its attacks in order to prepare the ground and public opinion; but the press has not stopped its attacks, nor has anyone to date said another word about discussions or agreements. You know I believe that Italy is now no longer free: she must have commitments, of which I am not aware, with other powers binding her so that she can no longer come to an agreement with us."

Had the spirit of King Alexander been able to appear at the League of Nations trial concerning his assassination, there can be little doubt as to whom he would have accused. On February 12, 1931, lamenting the recent bomb incident at Zagreb, he said: "... – the bomb attempt was hatched and paid for by Italy."

To my friend's protest that he must be mistaken, he replied: "But my dear fellow, we now have the whole organization in our hands and we are well aware through our excellent police that *lire* were received in payment for the business."

My friend protested that if Italy had actually been behind the matter she would probably have paid in dollars. But the king was insistent:

... "On Italy's side it is really a policy of obstinacy; Italy is determined to create obstacles for us, but they will have no success... If I, as a soldier, wished to capture a position, I would, of course, do everything possible to that end; but once persuaded that I could not capture it and that I would merely lose my men and ammunition, I would withdraw... Italy should now realize that she cannot bring catastrophes upon us and that her policy of obstinacy is costing her a great deal of money without any results."

"It would be much better to decide on a good policy of frank and loyal friendship from which we would draw great reciprocal advantages... leaving aside sentiment, one could, from a purely selfish point of view, come to a commercial agreement; ... why should we not make an experiment of this kind, let us say for three years, and try to obtain the greatest possible advantages from such a commercial arrangement, at the same time practicing a frank and loyal policy? The policy of hostility can always be resumed if it is found to be more advantageous and if the commercial arrangement does not work... I particularly believe that this hostility is created entirely artificially, for neither among our people nor among yours is it a part of popular sentiment."

Late in February, when my friend asked the king whether he would be interested in meeting with Mr. Mussolini, his reply was emphatic:

"You may well imagine that I would be delighted, for you must remember that I have always spoken to you of Mr. Mussolini with admiration, understanding, and I would even say enthusiasm, and I would like to speak to him calmly and frankly; but I would wish to be sure that on his side he had a firm intention and disposition to find a way of agreement, and – when found – the desire to follow it."

"I would not wish our conversation to share the fate of all the other conversations between our respective ministers, which after having given us hope never led to anything. I am convinced that Mr. Mussolini is, generally speaking, not well informed. I do not say that Mr. Galli (the previous Italian minister to Belgrade) does not keep him properly informed, for Mr. Galli is a man of the best type – a real 'gentleman'– whom I hold in the greatest esteem; but he likewise is in a difficult position here, since he must carry a very heavy load left by his predecessor. Informers often make reports and shape them according to what they think will please the persons who receive them, thus hoping to do well for themselves; or else they exaggerate to create the belief that they are extremely well informed even about the most confidential matters."

"I saw Mr. Galli after the marriage of the Prince of Piedmont and he told me that he had spoken with Mr. Mussolini and Mr. Grandi at Rome and that he was under the impression that Rome was extremely well disposed toward us – but nothing more ever came of it. Later Mr. Grandi met Mr. Marinkovic in Switzerland, but after four hours of conversation the same negative results followed."

"If I could speak with Mr. Mussolini I wish we could push forward without being discouraged at the first difficulties, for I can well understand that after all the fuel which has been thrown on the fire by the filthy press, any suggestion of agreement would at first be most unpopular in both countries. Soon, however, the material and moral usefulness of an agreement would be realized and satisfaction would follow. As for myself, I know definitely that I could obtain its willing acceptance, for, in my own country I am esteemed and well-liked and above all they know very well that I have no other thought nor aim than the welfare of the nation."

"In Italy they believe absolutely that our country is under the domination of Zifkovich – another matter wherein they are badly informed, since I have everything in my hands, and I myself brought in Zifkovic as prime minister for the simple reason that I wished a man in that position who had nothing to do with politics. General Zifkovic has no political ambitions and he serves his king as a faithful servant with intelligence and devotion; but he is ready to leave his place and go back to his regiment whenever I wish."

As far as General Zifkovic' political ambitions were concerned, the king was certainly mistaken. General Zifkovic tried to seize power in Yugoslavia immediately following the death of King Alexander. He was prepared to go so far as to provoke a war against Hungary to serve his political ambitions. He was prevented from doing so by the foresighted action of Mr. Jeftic – who had succeeded him as prime minister before Alexander's death – in settling the Marseilles affair through the instrumentality of the League of Nations.

Alexander went on:

"Mr. Mussolini has often declared in favor of treaty revision without particularly stressing that such revision must necessarily be directed against Yugoslavia. If we could converse, we could most probably reach an agreement on this delicate and important question – perhaps the most delicate and the most important of all – but naturally until that time I am on the side of those who are against revision. It is said that because of this we are the vassals of France. We are nobody's vassals, but we have with France treaties which bind us reciprocally, and it is scarcely surprising that we are and continue in agreement with those who, like ourselves, are interested in preventing treaty revision."

Late in March 1931, the king spoke of France again:

"As I told you, I have a treaty with France and we are reciprocally bound. If sometimes France uses a somewhat high handed tone to Italy, she does so because she believes you isolated and because she knows that she is supported by us and – of course – by the entire Little Entente. She would no longer do it if Italy had with us – and naturally with the Little Entente – a frank and loyal agreement. Isolation is to be avoided; what does Italy think she will get out of alliances with Hungary, Albania, Bulgaria, etc? All these people tie on to Italy in the hope of getting her to pull the chestnuts out of the fire; but these alliances will cost Italy appalling amounts, and in her day of need she will get nothing from them: believe me, it is a bad investment."

An interesting sidelight on Hungary's ceaseless attempts to break up the Little Entente is a note which appears in my friend's file concerning a conversation he had in Budapest on his way back to Italy at this time. The Italian minister to Hungary, Mr. Arlotta, told him that "Count Bethlen and also the Hungarian minister of war, Mr. Gömbös, would be far from displeased with an agreement with Yugoslavia and Rumania isolating Czechoslovakia" and authorized him to tell that to Mr. Mussolini.

In May definite plans were made for the king to meet Mussolini in Italy that summer. The king was impatient for the meeting to take place. At this time the Yugoslav minister was meeting in Geneva with Mr. Grandi, and Alexander had high hopes that the meeting would bring about constructive results which could be the subject of discussion with Mussolini.

But Marinkovic sent a discouraging report of the meeting and the king was much grieved.

Returning to the discussion of the necessity for an agreement between Italy and Yugoslavia Alexander said:

"You see, an agreement with Italy means changing my whole policy and turning it completely up-side-down. My present policy is based on the possibility of a war: it is the policy of treaties of alliance securing defense in case of attack, the policy of armament. Doubtless it is a good policy and, in view of present circumstances, we are compelled to follow it – but there is a far better one. The present-day policy is a negative and ruinous one; a policy which destroys the riches of our countries, which compels us to spend billions, mostly abroad, for armaments. On the other hand, the policy which we could pursue if we had an agreement with Italy would be a positive one, a policy creating riches in the line of commerce and industrial development. We could reduce our expenses for armaments, without counting the enormous benefits which we would reap through tranquility and confidence once the danger of war in Europe had been averted: for, after all, we have no other enemies to fear except Italy, and Italy has none except ourselves. If we continue – and let us call a spade a spade – as enemies, the day will come when war will be inevitable, even with the best will to avoid it; for we will be in such a state of excitement as to be at the mercy of some mad Dalmatian or Croat, who, without being able to avoid it, will fire the powder magazine on account of a mere nothing. The war would inevitably be a world war – or at least a European war – and this would be the last straw for Europe: what a result! Heaven preserve us!"

"Let us suppose that Italy makes war and wins it: what would she get from it? At most she would be able to take from us Dalmatia. If we suppose a victory for Yugoslavia, we might get Albania, Istria, and Trieste; but, as I have already told you, I would not take Albania as a gift; Istria isn't worth much, and Trieste we could not hold because of German pressure, since the Germans wish to get it so as to have their own port on the Mediterranean. Even if we could hold it, it would only yield expense and worries for us, since we already have our hands full with Susak and Split, and Trieste would be for us a port with a passive balance – just as it now is for Italy."

"One of the capital questions is the question of Albania. Italy concluded the Treaty of Tirana to protect and defend the independence and integrity of Albania; but on this point I am in complete agreement and I have also expressly declared in public that I myself am likewise ready to guarantee the integrity and independence of Albania...."

In June, discussing the proposed meeting still further – for despite his discouragement over report he still wished to meet with Mussolini – Alexander again brought up the subject of Albania as the most important one between himself and Mussolini. He remarked that "Italy constitutes a real military base against us in Albania which is like an arrow in our body." Stating that one "could not find a better time for reaching an agreement than the present when there are no parliaments to begin an endless fire of interpellations," he went on: "At present the matter only depends on the two of us. . . . Once an agreement has been reached it doesn't matter who comes into power; unless they are completely mad they cannot but approve my action and maintain the agreement."

In July, on my friend's return from Italy where he had conveyed the king's earnest desire for a meeting, Alexander wanted to know what had been said about the Albanian question. When my friend replied that Mr. Grandi had said Italy would not renounce the mandate which had been given her and which had been affirmed both by the League of Nations and by the Conference of Ambassadors, Alexander exclaimed: "But don't you see that this is a mistake! It is not a question of a *mandate*: Italy was given the mission of protecting Albania *in case of attack by third parties*, but if Albania is not attacked... and besides, by whom should she be attacked if not by us?"

Mr. Mussolini had sent word to the king at this time that the proposed meeting would not be convenient to him until September 1931. To this delay Alexander readily agreed.

On the following day the king explained his political point of view concerning the situation in Europe and all over the world:

"As regards our neighbors, the Hungarians, the Rumanians, the Bulgarians, etc., it is believed in Italy – on the basis of I do not know what kind of reports – that we have aggressive and invading tendencies... I can assure you that this is absolutely false because, since we have already obtained by the treaties all that we could desire, we ask nothing better of our neighbors than to live in peace with them and to develop as far as possible our good rela-

184

tions of vicinage, commerce and peace; we do not covet their territory, nor do we desire to mix in their affairs."

"As regards the international political field, we have no expansionist ambitions as we do not desire either colonies or mandates. Our policy is a local policy since we have many provinces which, like Montenegro and others, are large and incredibly poor. Nothing grows in them and we must provide for them and send them wheat, corn and everything else... We are only interested in central European questions which may have a reflex action on us. Italy, being a great power, must pursue a world policy; she must be interested in Asiatic and African questions, etc. – all matters concerning which we will never have anything to say and regarding which there will consequently never be any conflict between us. As regards European and particularly central European questions, we will have the same interests to maintain once we have reached an agreement."

"Mr. Grandi once said that he wanted to make Albania another Belgium; a neutral state guaranteed by treaties. I would accept this idea willingly and I am ready to give to this end any guarantees which might be desired. Is this still the intention of Italy? I wish to be informed exactly of the political point of view of Italy on this question of Albania, as it is the only one which is of capital importance between us."

"As this is a complex question I would suggest to Mr. Mussolini either to send me here with you a person thoroughly and technically conversant with the matter, or to allow me to send to Rome with you the person whom I consider best adapted to this purpose and who, having been with me a number of years, knows my ideas on this subject. I am speaking of Mr. Jeftic, the minister of the Royal House, who officially has nothing to do with politics and who is a most discreet and loyal person."

"Nobody in my entourage is aware of our discussions, for even Mr. Marinkovic is ignorant of them. Once the meeting has taken place and the agreement has been reached, I will say to Mr. Marinkovic: 'This is the policy to be pursued' – and he will pursue it."

Mr. Jeftic's subsequent visit to Rome proved to be completely futile, as he was not even received by Mr. Mussolini. King Alexander was incensed. "Our propositions," he complained, "are neither intangible nor unchangeable; why then are we met with this attitude of unwillingness to discuss them? We drew up our ideas in writing: why did Italy not do likewise?"

The September meeting did not take place. But early in 1932, the king had a visit from Mr. Galli, Italian minister to Yugoslavia, who was just back from Rome and came as the bearer of an agreement "complete in every detail."

The king described the interview to my friend upon his arrival in Belgrade on February 21, 1932. When Alexander had asked Galli whether he had spoken with Mussolini regarding the Albanian question, the latter had replied: "Naturally, Your Majesty, but on this point Italy cannot renounce its rights...

"At this point I really lost patience," the king told my friend. "This was really making fun of me, as it was the only matter on which I had asked Italy to yield. In all other matters I am ready to accept the Italian point of view completely." King Alexander discussed the problem further on the following day:

"If Albania is a free and independent country such as, for instance, Greece or Hungary, then there is no reason why Italy should mix in its internal affairs, just as Italy would not think of sending troops if tomorrow the Greeks and the Hungarians were to quarrel among themselves."

"If Albania is an Italian colony, then I am faced with another Italian front in Albania. If we are enemies I can look at it in that way, but if we are good allies I cannot admit that Italy should keep the right to send troops on that part of the frontier whenever she pleases and on some pretext which can always be found."

"If Italy refuses to consider this point of view, she must inevitably be concealing ulterior motives hostile to us, either to leave herself an opening to pounce on us or to take Albania definitely for herself. In such case it would be useless to talk of a loyal agreement."

"The agreement between us must be either absolute and complete or cannot exist at all. We are too close to each other, and our interests have too much in common; we must either be very good friends or enemies: there is no middle course."

"In Italy they say: 'The Adriatic must be ours.' Is it not yours? Can we with our four ships compete with Italy? 'Italy must have the key of the Adriatic,' but has she not already got it with the islands? And once we are united by a good friendship, will we not have the same interest to guard together the key of the Adriatic? In that case I would be willing to give you the Bocche di Cattaro, to defend together our common interests in the Adriatic against third parties."

Finally, on being reassured that Mussolini had expressed definitely a wish to go on with the meeting while my friend was last in Italy, Alexander said: "Go and see Mr. Mussolini and tell him my general ideas," and he proceeded to outline them as follows:

"*Foreign Policy:* Peace and cordial agreements with our neighbors and with distant countries. Full liberty for Italian expansion. Italy naturally needs to expand, because of the too great density of its population, either in Africa or in Asia. If other great powers wish to block these aspirations of Italy, we will always be ready to support her. We have no colonial aims, as we have sufficient to occupy us at home."

"*League of Nations*: We undertake to support the Italian policy and to 'pull together' in all questions. The agreement would bring disarmament as its immediate and automatic effect, for we are arming exclusively against yourselves. We could, therefore, support at Geneva Mr. Mussolini's ideas on disarmament."

"*France*: We have nothing against France, and I will not do anything against her because I am under too many obligations toward her; but I will merely say to her frankly and freely: 'We are very good friends, but I have also other good friends, our neighbors the Italians'– and that is all. France will have nothing to say."

"*Internal Policy:* We have nothing to change, nor any pretensions to territorial enlargement. War to the death against any possible Bolshevik infiltrations into the country. No tolerance nor indulgence nor asylum for any Italian anti-fascist emigres. Encouragement of cultural and commercial development, etc., reduction of armaments to the strictly necessary amount, and employment of our enormous military investments for the benefit of peace industries."

"*Commercial and Financial Policy*: We are ready to undertake to buy all Italian products, excluding by customs tariff the products of other countries. We are disposed even to go as far as a kind of customs union and abolish frontiers, even bringing Hungary into the combination, since we have no special or serious reasons for conflict with her. Encouragement and protection for the organization of Italian banks in the country; preference for Italian capital. If the agreement becomes a fact, it will be as though a partition-dam were opened in a water reservoir: the waters will mix naturally and inevitably and will require no one to make them do so. Manufactured products, money, everything will go from one country to the other according to needs and natural interests – and this will be a real and sensible and thorough agreement. After all, individual interests make up the general interest of a people and the bonds of interest are the most natural and the most durable."

"*Albania*: On this subject I have already spoken to you sufficiently, but I repeat and I declare that I have no pretensions and no concealed ulterior aims regarding Albania; I repeat that I will have none of Albania nor of the Albanians. I am ready to guarantee with Italy the integrity, the liberty and independence of Albania in the most thorough fashion which Italy could ask, – even by bringing in a third great power (England) as a party to the contract. The formula adopted with and for Belgium should be ideal for Albania."

"Generally speaking, I think that we are in agreement with Italy. I might add that England has informed me through her minister that she would see with satisfaction an agreement with Italy and a drawing-away from France; that the most influential persons in Yugoslavia are all favorable to such an agreement."

"It seems to me that I have said everything. Go and see Mr. Mussolini and give him my assurances of good will and confidence in him; but I would ask you to tell him from me that I entreat him to take the matter into his own hands: we have had enough of 'spokesmen'."

In reply to these statements my friend was given the following message by Mr. Mussolini in an interview on March 1, 1932:

"Tell His Majesty that I first listened to and subsequently carefully read the very interesting statements which he has transmitted to me and ask him now to leave me the time to formulate an agreement which shall be for our common interest and gratification."

"As a preamble to this agreement we must first say that it is derived from the desire for peace not only between our two peoples, but for the peace of *Europe*.

To this end:

1) Italy and Yugoslavia declare that for the purposes of this peace, they have the same common interest in the integrity and independence of Albania.

2) Yugoslavia, however, declares that Italian interests prevail in Albania, as has, moreover, been acknowledged by the treaties and by the Conference of Ambassadors.

3) Italy undertakes not to avail herself of the rights granted her by the treaties in any way which might be harmful to the interests of Yugoslavia or might weaken the pact of friendship."

In regard to having a third power guarantee the agreements, Mussolini said: "There are only two of us in the Adriatic and it is best to avoid any pretext which might allow a third great power to stick its nose in there."

In regard to the treaties of commerce, which would be drawn up by technical experts and which might even go so far as the possibility of a customs union, Mussolini expressed the opinion that there should also be constituted a *single* Italo-Yugoslav port authority for Fiume and Port Baross. "As it is now," he explained, "Fiume cannot live because it has no 'hinterland', and Port Baross cannot live because its 'hinterland' is not sufficient."

Mussolini went on:

"This draft of a treaty will be drawn up within a month and will afterwards be submitted to His Majesty for approval; then our meeting can immediately be arranged.

Tell His Majesty the King that he will find me in the best possible good will, as this agreement must be complete, loyal and productive of results if it is to be a lasting one.

Toward the end of the month you will come to me to get the drafts; but let me know immediately the opinion of His Majesty on these general matters."

On March 15, King Alexander dictated a reply to Mussolini's statement, which my friend had presented to him ten days before:

"We acknowledge with pleasure the clearness of thought and the loyalty with which Mr. Mussolini has treated the essential elements of a lasting agreement between our two countries. As it seems that we are in agreement on the general lines, it only remains for us to reach a definite agreement by drawing up a clear and precise draft.

To our regret, however, point No.2 of the preamble proposed by Mr. Mussolini, namely, – 'that Yugoslavia, however, declares that Italian interests prevail in Albania, as has, moreover, been acknowledged by the treaties and by the Conference of Ambassadors,' does not seem to us in conformity with the principles of the independence of Albania, recognized by the two guarantor countries. We could not in principle recognize such a prevalence of Italian interests in Albania. We see therein a constant danger to our agreement. This 'prevalence' is vague and ambiguous: it will lead to distrust. Undoubtedly, the economic and financial interests of Italy in Albania are greater than those of Yugoslavia, and in the future will be even more so; we do not deny this *de facto* situation and *we can undertake to do nothing to interfere with* (or, perhaps, 'endanger') *Italian interests in Albania.*"

"Since our agreement must be perfect, loyal and deeply sincere, the Albanian question automatically disappears; hence we see no reason for any special acknowledgment of the *prevalence* of Italian interests in Albania. As regards the remaining questions we are in agreement and we share Mr. Mussolini's point of view. We are awaiting with great hopes and will receive with the best good will the treaty draft which Mr. Mussolini expects to send us."

The King discussed the question of Italy's wisdom in leaving armaments in the hands of a childish people like the Albanians, and went on:

"We will do something great. Even France, once she knows that we are entirely reconciled with Italy in a lasting and loyal way, will feel the need likewise to draw nearer to Italy. Ours will be the first really serious and positive step which will set the good example; one must not mark time too long on a given spot, and if we decide, the others must inevitably follow us. Although the questions which divide Italy and France are much more serious – for they comprise colonial questions, the question of Tunisia, the question of naval parity, etc. – I do not doubt that after our agreement France will be much less exacting."

"When I was in Paris I spoke to Mr. Laval, who told me that he intended to get on better terms with Italy and asked me – as did Mr. Tardieu – if I objected or at any rate would be displeased. Naturally I answered that I had nothing against it and that it would give me great pleasure. The French minister at Belgrade asked me the same thing the other evening, and I gave him the same answer."

When asked what he thought of the proposal for a Danubian agreement, Alexander replied:

"I am very skeptical and I do not think that anything will come of it. I think, however, that as the world does not know that we have been preparing our agreement for a long time, it might be believed in France that we had hastily thrown it together to torpedo Mr. Tardieu's plan for a Danubian understanding. As for myself I am not in the least disturbed about what may be said or thought: I am entirely indifferent and I hope that Mr. Mussolini will think as I do."

"Besides, as I said before, I am sceptical. We are too much accustomed to hearing every minute of new proposals which are given out without any solid preparation – and then there follows conference after conference always with the same result: disillusion. I think one should do the opposite, as we have done: prepare beforehand, study the details and interests involved, discuss them, and when everything is prepared, present a positive, concrete, vital and definite achievement. This is the great difference."

"Ask Mr. Mussolini to give you the draft which I await with hope, confidence, and good will – just as I await with impatience the setting of a date for our meeting. Go, then, and may God be with you."

However, the draft did not arrive, nor was a meeting arranged.

In October 1932, when my friend saw the king the day after he had received from his ministry of the interior reports on the recent riots at Lika, he found him very much aroused because the report was drafted in such a way as to indicate clearly that the propaganda, the weapons and the bombs had come from Italy. Alexander firmly believed this and his remarks at this time were prophetic:

..."I am disgusted; this is what the Italians are constantly doing to us; they try to stab us in the back and they hope to obtain success with these disloyal attacks. Is it possible for a country like Italy to use such means in trying to increase the troubles in our country and provoke us! Do they believe in Italy they will get anywhere with such pitiful methods unworthy of a great and self-respecting people? They will not obtain any radical political success by stirring up some poor ignorant peasants and killing some farmer who asks nothing better than to live! Tell them that in Italy, and say to Mr. Mussolini from me that to stir up serious disorders in Yugoslavia or to obtain a change of regime they will have to shoot at me and be very sure to kill me, for only in that case will there be any changes here; I repeat that you will have to kill me and kill me thoroughly! You may say also that if it were necessary for the good of the country to shed rivers of blood I would be ready to do so, for I am conscious above all of my duty and of the responsibility of my position. I desire the welfare of my country."

Henry Pozzi; 1935:

Excerpts from *Black Hand over Europe* [Original French title:"La Guerre Revient]; Paris, 1935.

Author's Preface to the English Edition

I wrote the following chapters fifteen months ago, on my return from a long trip I had just made in the Balkans and in Central Europe, where I had been so often since the War to study the state of things created by the peace – by the false peace.

Since 1912 I have taken part there in all the events of the day; I have known intimately all the statesmen, I have had an entree everywhere, and I have received the confidences of ministers and revolutionaries. All doors have been open to me, and all means of information, official and private, have been at my disposal.

I knew about the preparation of the Sarajevo attack three months before the assassination of the Archduke.

I knew all about Serbian guilt in the preparation for the War (in league with Russia) for I held the proofs in my hand that Serbian officials themselves had given me.

I knew all about the Bulgarian intervention against the Allies in 1915; I knew how it could have been avoided, and I know the men who were criminally responsible for it. I know all about the machinations, the dishonesties, the maneuvers and the traffic of consciences which took place during the peace negotiations.

It is because the guilty ones knew I held all these secrets and was determined to reveal them that the publication of my book produced in France the effect of a bombshell. It was not possible to prohibit its sale for, – thank God! – France is still a free country; but, at the request of the Legations of the Little Entente, all the great French newspapers were silent about it and even refused to accept the notices offered to them by my publisher. Only a few independent journals, mostly provincial papers, spoke of *"La Guerre Revient"*, as my book was called in France.

But nothing could stop the diffusion of the truth. In a few months more than 30,000 copies have been sold in French-speaking countries, and about 10,000 copies have gone abroad.

I have received hundreds of letters of congratulation. Two were signed by former French Ministers of Foreign Affairs. I have been asked to give more than fifty lectures in France and Belgium. Only a month ago I spoke at Louvain, the martyred city, before the students of the great Catholic university there.

All the great newspapers of Belgium, Germany, Italy and Austria have devoted long articles to my book, and in England *"The Contemporary Review"* has given it prominence.

The assassination of King Alexander at Marseilles (which I had predicted) gave a new force to my words.

In the issue of *"L Oeuvre"* dated 12th October, 1934, Senator Henri de Jouvenel, former French Ambassador in Rome, called me "a prophet". It is not very difficult to be a prophet if all one has to do is to tell an obvious truth!

Two months after the publication of my book the Supreme Court of Belgrade sentenced me by default to twenty years of hard labour and the White Hand (the Pan-Serb terrorist and military organization) sentenced me to death. I have been warned that if I attempt to give evidence at the Marseilles Trial I shall be assassinated.

But this is just one more reason why I should go! One of the things I am the proudest of is to have in my veins, by my English mother, the blood of the great Hampden, who held his own alone against the tyranny of the Stuarts; and, through my French ancestors, the blood of the Huguenot refugees, who preferred exile and the galleys to the denial of their faith. Do what they will, I shall go to the trial and place my book upon the stand as evidence of the tyranny of the regime which the murdered king represented.

Since I wrote my book fifteen months ago events have taken place rapidly in Central and Eastern Europe.

There have been in quick succession, the Balkan Pact, the dissolution of the in Bulgaria, the Serbo-Bulgarian rapprochement, the assassination of Chancellor Dolfuss at Vienna, that of King Alexander at Marseilles, the Hungaro-Yugoslav conflict, the German re-armament, and finally, a few days ago, the Italo-Yugoslav rapprochement.

I owe a few explanations of these more recent events to my English readers who are as interested as my French compatriots to learn the truth.

We must not let ourselves be hypnotised by the German question. The German danger which people pretend to have discovered during the past few weeks was not born overnight; it has existed for months, and all the governments in Europe knew of it.

This danger may eclipse, but it does not lessen, the gravity of the Balkan problems; problems born of the fraudulent and violent peace of Trianon. On the contrary, it aggravates them, because now the people who have been the victims of the false treaties, and to whom justice has been refused for sixteen years, know where to go to obtain justice and they are going there!

Let us take the above mentioned events one by one.

The people of France and England have not understood the significance of the coup d'état in Sofia in the May of 1934. A very clever Serbian propaganda has distorted the truth. The truth is that when the Bulgarians learned, through their knowledge of the Secret Protocols of the Balkan Pact (the text of which the reader will find farther on), that the Pan-Serbs were determined to take as a pretext the first incursion of ORIM *comitadjis* into Macedonia in order to destroy once and for all the organizations defending the cause of their martyred brothers, they sought for a means to avoid the catastrophe menacing them.

As Bulgaria has no army, the only way was to bow before Belgrade. Bulgaria preferred humiliation to annihilation. The Bulgarians in the pay of Belgrade took advantage of this situation to make the coup d'état. Understanding that this was the only way to save the independence of his country, and his own life, King Boris ceded. The present Bulgarian government is an anti-national government, detested by the great majority of the country. It maintains itself in power only by the support of Serbia, who threatens to intervene if it is overthrown. The ORIM has not been destroyed; it is stronger than ever. A month ago in Paris I talked for an hour with one of its new chiefs. As for King Boris, he is only waiting for the right moment to rid himself of the ministers whom Serbia has imposed on him. Taking advantage of the difficulties which Belgrade was undergoing as a result of the death of King Alexander, he has already shaken off the more compromised of them.

In spite of appearances (and I insist on this point) the Bulgarian national sentiment has not changed, any more than the Pan-Serbian hostility towards Bulgaria.

The mad dreams of the Belgrade imperialists have not changed either. No one in French official circles is ignorant of the fact that definite pacts were signed in Belgrade last June (1934) between Nazi delegates and the government of King Alexander. It was agreed that in exchange for her neutrality, should Germany try to enforce the Anschluss, Belgrade was to annex Austrian Carinthia. If Italy came to the aid of Austria, Belgrade would intervene against Italy. You will observe that Belgrade would not intervene as a friend of Germany but only as an enemy of Italy. The Pan-Serbian policy is made up of this sort of hypocrisy.

After the assassination of Chancellor Dolfuss, when Italy mobilised 50,000 men in the Brenner pass, the Serbs mobilised 100,000 men near Maribor, at the Carinthian frontier. The Serbs were in with the Austrian Nazis to such an extent that the latter crossed the frontier freely with their arms and trained themselves for two months in the region of Maribor; and after the failure of the putsch on July 25th the defeated Nazis were able to find a refuge in Yugoslavia, where the police did not go beyond disarming them. And they still move there freely to-day.

The Pan-Serbs of Belgrade were the direct accomplices of the assassins of Alexander; just as they had been the accomplices of the assassins of the Archduke in 1914, and for the same reasons. They hoped to profit by the disorders, and even by the war that might be provoked by the death of the Austrian statesman. They accused the Hungarians of having aided the assassins of King Alexander. They knew very well that this was not true, for they know better than anyone why and by whom the king was killed. But they saw in it a convenient pretext to destroy Hungary because she obstructs the Pan-Serb imperialism.

The English people do not know, any more than do the French people, that last December the Little Entente had everything prepared for a general attack against Hungary. They counted on France to paralyse Italy. They were some tragic scenes at Geneva between M. Laval and the Czech and Serb delegates. War was near then. The attitude of Mr. Anthony Eden, the Italian delegate, Baron Aloysi, and of M. Laval (who frankly declared to Yevtitch and Titulesco that the French public opinion would refuse to make war under these conditions) would not have prevented the catastrophe if an unexpected intervention had not taken place. This came from Poland, who informed M. Laval that if the Serbs and Czechs attacked Hungary the Polish army would attack Czechoslovakia.

This alone, last December, saved peace.

As to the murder of King Alexander, it was prepared by Croat patriots. The King had already missed being the victim often attacks launched against him. The Croats hold him responsible for the regime of terror which they suffer and which is inconceivable to a justice-loving Englishman, as he will see as he reads these pages. All Croatia, all Slovenia, are determined to free themselves from the atrocious tyranny weighing on them. They are determined to cut loose from the Pan-Serb exploitation of which they are innocent victims. At the time of the funeral of King Alexander the French newspapers told how the entire population pressed crying and sobbing along the railroads (I have seen tears in the eyes of Frenchmen reading these accounts) to salute the body of their "beloved sovereign". They published photographs. The stories were deceitful and also the photographs.

In reality, the police and the Pan-Serb organisations had mobilised the populations in their villages and had conducted them by force to the stations and into the cities, and had ordered them to cry, to sob, and to throw flowers.

The Croats and Slovenes, however, displayed their real sentiments on this occasion. At Zagreb, while the crowd filed (by order) before the royal coffin, and covered it (by order) with flowers, the widow of the great patriot, Stefan Raditch, publicly spat on the coffin. The Serbian censorship over-looked a photograph, which appeared in *"L'Illustration"*, and which shows Slovenes standing behind the police and laughing and nudging each other as the coffin was lowered.

Continual riots, which amounted to revolutionary attempts, have taken place in the last five months from one end to the other of Croatia and Slovenia. Those at Zagreb, Bled and Ljubljana have been terribly bloody. At Bled, more then 25,000 peasants attacked the Serbian troops, who fired on them with machine-guns.

The assassins of the King are considered by the five million Croats and as heroes. The Pan-Serbs have asked the French government to "arrange" the trial of these men and to guarantee their death in advance. Their requests have been granted, and all the documents essential to their defence, all the documents revealing the bloody and corrupt regime that the King had authorised and favoured in Croatia and Slovenia, have been removed from the brief. At Marseilles, the Serb Secret Police, composed of veritable ex-convicts, menace the witnesses, and closely follow the examination in which delegates and the police of the Serbian White Hand participate in the most scandalous and illegal fashion. It can be said in advance, and I say it with a heavy heart, that the trial will be a parody of justice, and that every-thing will be done to silence the voices of those free men who will try to tell the jury the truth about the cause of the murder of Alexander Kara-georgevitch.

I can affirm, and I have this information from an absolutely responsible French source, that the French government has promised Belgrade that the accused will be sentenced to death and executed as rapidly as possible thereafter. It would have been done already (for everything had been pre-pared to have the trial take place at the end of March) if the defence had not made an appeal before the Supreme Court against certain violations of the law by the examining magistrate.

I affirm, moreover, that the accused men (who were not at Marseilles on the 9th October) are held responsible, not only for the death of M. Barthou, but also for the deaths of two women killed near the royal car. Now, the film taken that day, which is not allowed to be shown in France, proves that neither M. Barthou nor the two women were shot by the assassin. This is why, without a doubt, they have refused to let the people of France see it and judge for themselves. As for me, I have been warned from an official source that if I persist in my desire to appear at the trial I shall be assassinated.

Certain people who believe all they read in the French Press will say that Belgrade and Rome are about to become reconciled. Before the German menace Serbs and Italians forget their old hatreds and listen wisely to the French counsel of reconciliation. Significant conversations were exchanged at Belgrade three weeks ago between the special Italian ambassador and the Prince-Regent Paul.

Conversations, and especially diplomatic conversations, are only idle talk. The only things that count in the lives of individuals as in the life of peoples, are facts.

Now, the facts that had caused the hostility between Italy and Yugoslavia still exist. They are the Italian claims upon the Balkan regions along the Adriatic which are inhabited by Italians, but which have been given to Belgrade (in violation of the Treaty of London, April 26th, 1915), and the Pan-Serb aims on Venetia, Istria and Fiume (Rijeka).

Belgrade knows that Italy will never let the Serbs annex Bulgaria, Albania and the Austrian province of Carinthia, and Belgrade is determined to have them.

Rome is sincere, Belgrade is not. Rome subordinates everything to the desire to obviate the German peril; Belgrade (which is pro-German, for she counts on Germany to help her destroy Italy) conceals her German sympathies in order to rest on good terms with France who, for once, is in accord with Italy. It is important that the reader should follow the coming events with the closest attention.

That Germany is a menace to-day there can be no doubt! But it is our fault – the fault of those who did not hesitate in 1919 to make the peace one of "nonsense, violence and hypocrisy". Germany's claims for equality of rights are just, exactly as are those of the other vanquished nations – Hungary, Austria and Bulgaria.

But in order to avoid this danger, England, France and Italy should not rush to that other extreme which is leading us directly to war: under the inspiration of Benes, and the French politicians who share his ideas, they are recommencing the encircling of Germany – this encircling which led us to war in 1914.

There is where the mortal peril lies.

I fear that Great Britain's foreign policy, which would attempt to save peace by pacts and by the recognition of the rights of the conquered nations, will materialise too late. If she continues her hesitations, unable to choose between a France who cries PEACE but harbours war-makers, sadists and oppressors among her followers, and a Germany who has risen strong and defiant from the tomb of Versailles (and ready to offer a helping hand to those lesser nations who are bound in the chains of Trianon, Neuilly and Saint-Germain) then war will come. If she allies herself with Russia, France and the Little Entente before these reparations have been made, in an effort to preserve a peace of injustice that is fast tottering and crumbling, war will come. If she allies herself with the Machiavellian Benes and the Pan-Serb war-makers and oppressors, then also war will come.

We few who understand, in this Europe so sorely tried by the ravages of war and the horrors of an unjust peace, we turn to England asking: "Has the time come for you to declare yourself?"

Only England can answer.

Paris; April 5th, 1935
Henry Pozzi

II. The Serbian Scene: The Dilemma

A rat caught in a trap turns vicious not because it is full of power or of hate, but because it is full of fear. So to-day in Belgrade, the Big Men of the dictatorship, along with their minions, the petty officials and the police, are like rats in a trap, fighting against the power which their own ignorance and cupidity, handed down to them by the shades of Pasich and Company, has bound upon them. There is an old saying in China that he who rides upon a tiger dare not dismount, and that is true in Belgrade today. The men behind the dictatorship are riding upon their tiger because they can do nothing else. If the oppressed states of Yugoslavia have their dilemma of suffering, then also the oppressors certainly have their share of the dilemma, for the forces of nature almost are running against them – certainly the forces of human nature.

History is repeating itself in Yugoslavia. The lesson is not yet learned which Englishmen learned when they tried to coerce their brothers in North America. Co-operation is the secret of all national growth involving the absorption of unlike nations into a homogeneous whole. Co-operation begets co-operation as sunshine promotes growth, but coercion stiffens the muscles of the coerced and turns reasonable men into pig-headed obstructionists. Serbia, through the blind, greedy ignorance of its and their type, has set forces in operation which must destroy Yugoslavia either through war or through revolution. Meanwhile, the tyranny grows by what it feeds upon.

Once treason to the state becomes looked upon as a virtue (as treason to the Yugoslavian state is looked upon today by the oppressed minorities who regard it as nothing more than a vehicle of Serbian domination) then those who wish to maintain the status quo must either act or else stand humbly aside and watch the nation go to pieces. What is the natural human action in such cases? Is it not to fight blindly for the preservation of the established order? Is the crime of the Serbians any greater than that? No! The real crime lies upon the shoulders of those who conceived Yugoslavia as a cloak for Serbian greed and not as a free association of diverse peoples. Let us recognize the dilemma of the Serbian people and admit that the error lies not so much in the hearts of the people as in the fight against human nature to which they have been committed.

This fact does not unfortunately solve the problem. We may understand the dilemma, but we shall not disperse the gathering hatreds and the inevitable disaster by our knowledge.

Savoir tout, c'est pardonner tout, may be all very well as a philosophic statement, but it is of little use to men who feel themselves robbed of their inheritance to feed the vanity of a crowd of megalomaniacs who have no humanity and no respect for anything but their own desires.

And the great pity is that there are some things that cannot be undone except by explosion. You may easily pack a tree-trunk with dynamite and set the fuse ready for firing, but you will not find it so easy to withdraw the charge again. All you can do is to get as far away as you can form the scene and let the explosion spend itself in the air. So it is with Yugoslavia. The dynamite of human passion and thwarted desire is laid, the fuse is lit and the train is running to its inevitable end. The explosion must ensue. Away, then, France! Away, England! Cut the ties that bind you to the doomed tree, and retire to safety, lest the inevitable explosion find you in the path of its progress and sweep you, and with you Europe, into the dust of the Past.

The catastrophe, as in 1914, will come from some minor incident. As a high Serb official put it to me, "A single police operation in Bulgaria (and it just missed taking place six months ago) will lead to the intervention of Italy, and a French counter-intervention. In a few days the conflagration will cover all Europe – a second 1914."

The Pan-Serb part, which stands behind the government and directs the king, is inclined to play this card as soon as possible, as it is persuaded that a war against Italy would instantly re-establish the unity between the Serbs and Croats, the latter having an ancestral hatred for the Italians. In addition to this, the high Yugoslav officials are convinced that their country would come out of the conflict clothed with military glory and more than doubled in extent and power. In their eyes this is a sufficient reason for setting Europe on fire again, and it is possible that their calculations are right, though it is much more probable that they are false.

"I am telling you nothing," said my official friend, "if I tell you that Yugoslavia has offended all her neighbors since she has been directed by the Pan-Serbs, and this applies even to her allies. Under the double inspiration of Mustapha-Kemal and Venizelos (who know only too well that a new Serb victory, either over the Bulgars or the Italians would mean the loss of Constantinople by the Turks, and of Salonica and her Aegean shores by the Greeks) astonishing ententes have been effected against Yugoslavia. The people here in Belgrade are right when they complain that they are encircled by enemies. They are, and by their own fault! Only the Czechs support

202

them, but the Czechs have never been worth much as soldiers! On the day of danger, the Serb dictators can count on no one outside France. It is true that the weight that France would throw in the balance would be worth all the others put together, and it is because the present directors of Yugoslavia know it, because they have calculated that with France's aid they will be assured of the victory, that they will not hesitate when they believe the moment comes, to risk a war in order to avoid a revolution. This, at least, is my opinion."

It was not until King Alexander of Serbia made his visit to Paris in 1931 that he was able to realize to what extent French political circles were alarmed by the aggressiveness displayed by Belgrade towards Sofia and unanimously disapproved of it.

There were reasons to believe that the peril was averted, at least momentarily. But if war is averted, there is still revolution to fear. An old friend, a Francophile, and an advisor of Yugoslavia, said to me: "The second eventuality from which Yugoslavia will not escape is the revolution, even if its governors refuse to shoulder the responsibility of a new European conflict. Revolution is not, in my opinion, likely as yet. It presupposes an accord between powerful military chiefs and groups of the socialist and democrat opposition. If it takes place, it would involve a repetition of the drama that cost the lives of Queen Draga and King Alexander. It would sweep the good away with the bad. All those who in any way served the dictators would be its victims. Politically, by the general dislocation that it would lead to, this would be the end of Yugoslavia.

"Such is the dilemma: revolution or war. There is no escape. No one in France seems aware of what the situation really is here. In France they nurse the illusion of a powerful Yugoslavia and one, in case of war, capable of giving real support to her allies. No one knows anything of the Croat question, of the Macedonian question, of the furious opposition of former parties, of the progress of revolutionary ideas: of all causes which conduce to that state of things which in the event of war would abandon and betray the army from behind. France's blindness and ignorance in face of all this is almost touching because of its enormity.

"The worst, perhaps, is that the dictators have discovered the personality of the King. Before that, he was the refuge of parties; respected, if not loved, by all. He benefitted from the prestige which his father had enjoyed, and from the legend, cleverly established, that he served personally on the Macedonian front during the War. Today, the dictatorship has made a party chief of him. And what a party! It is called the Narodna Odbrana[30], in which is consecrated all the violence, all the blindness, all the appetites of Pan-Serbism: so from now on the Croats, Macedonians, and all the Serb opposition hold the King responsible for all the faults and abuses of his ministers, because they are convinced that they do nothing without having taken orders from him. And, unfortunately, it is true. They don't dare attack him openly because no one fancies hard labor, but most abominable rumors circulate about him. He has become the most unpopular man in Yugoslavia, after General Givkovitch and Jika Lazitch. Last April, thousands of students gathered before the royal palace. The furious charges of the gendarmes did not succeed in dispersing them, and there they stood hurling insults at the King, and accusing him of having enormous sums in the banks of Budapest and Basle, thanks to commissions he had received from foreign corporations and enterprises. I saw it with my own eyes, I can tell you the bones of old Pasitch would have turned a hand-spring in his coffin..."

"The revolution is rising, and hence war is coming."

Events must have marched terribly fast in Yugoslavia during the last few months, for no official would have said to me a year ago what so many among them have since done."

The dilemma in Yugoslavia is growing so intense that the floods of dissolution wash at very walls of the inner fortress of Pan-Serbism.

IV. Pan-Serbism

Those who did not know Serbia before the War, nor even just after the War, can have no idea of the transformation that has taken place within her borders.

---

30   This is not a new revelation. It has been clearly stated in the Austro- Hungarian
      Ultimatum (June 28, 1914) appended to this chapter.

Imagine a poor man, whose ancestors have lived for centuries in hovels, suddenly set free from his poverty by the wave of a magic wand. Imagine him, after generations of bowing to the lord of the manor, suddenly transported into the home of that lord.

If you can imagine that you will understand what has happened to Serbia and you will understand a lot of the feverish activity which is so foreign to the minds of countries whose history has been so dramatically changed by the War.

You will notice that I speak of Serbia and not of Yugoslavia. I do it deliberately because the latter is a mere hybrid that exists for Serbia. All that is called Yugoslavia is in reality only Serbia, for all who act, all who command, all who count in any way at all in the affairs of the nation are Serbian. The others have no influence at all upon the shaping of the national life. Considering also that the great mass of the Serbian people are illiterate, possessing the mentality of two centuries gone, it would be fair to say that Yugoslavia is not even Serbia – it is Belgrade.

In this Yugoslavia, with a territory about as large as that of Great Britain, lives a blind powerless amorphous mass of about fifteen million people which is animated, exploited and governed by a few thousands of Serbian officers, officials and business men installed in the Serb capital.

Yet nobody "in the swim" seems conscious of the enormity of the situation. Nobody seems to have analyzed the state of mind induced by the events. The more I hear, the more I am led to realize that an irresistible current is sweeping things and people in Yugoslavia towards no one knows what disastrous events. There is no guiding principle other than the fevered desire for more of everything. The hypertrophic development of Belgrade; the unbelievable revolution in morals and ideas which has taken place within the governing classes; the arrogance; the need to dominate and parade; the contempt for all that is beneath them; the hatred for all that is higher and stronger; the violent ambitions; and the aggressive imperialism, are all born of a too-sudden rise from obscurity to power.

The people of Belgrade who count by virtue of their official positions, their social importance, their fortune and their country in the eyes of the world, and who govern the rest of a nation as they choose, all live in a waking dream, a sort of collective hypnosis. To them prosperity is assured, and Belgrade, the metropolis of an all-powerful Yugoslavia, will tomorrow be one of the poles of Europe.

All the Serbs who today command Yugoslavia (and even those who combat the present masters and will replace them if the present regime is swept away by the excess of its abuses) have a common dogma, a similar faith in the unlimited future which awaits their race, and the irresistible and predestined force of expansion of Serbism.

All are Pan-Serbs.

In its origins and its manifestations, in the immense peril that it carries in itself, Pan-Serbism is an exact replica of Pan-Germanism and Pan-Slavism which have already cost the world a dreadful price.

Born of the dreams of a handful of doctrinaires; exalted by chauvinistic officers, by professors of a hasty and confused science, and by students enlightened by refugees encountered in foreign universities, Pan-Serbism is an affirmation of the Serbian pre-eminence over all Slav nationalities of the Balkan peninsula, and of its right of conquest over all the Slav lands south of the Danube. Its progress since it first appeared in the second half of the nineteenth century has been rapid, and its influence became immediately very great in all the elements of Serb society – excepting the poor and humble class.

The Pan-Serbs are responsible for the territorial ambitions of Belgrade towards the Adriatic regions on one part, and towards Bulgarian Macedonia on the other, which began to be manifested after the Peace of Berlin.

Repulsed by Austria, who hoped to drive them away from Bosnia and Herzegovina, the Serbs commenced by directing their efforts towards the south, on the Bulgarian border. Crushed by the Bulgars in 1885, they took their revenge in 1913. In the meantime, Serb professors and diplomats were affirming the integral Serbism of Bulgarian Macedonia, and thus peacefully paving the way for war.

Belgrade never lost sight of the Adriatic, but Austria-Hungary, for a long time, was too strong for her. The Serbs did not decide upon the move against Vienna until they were sure of Russian support. The day that it became a reality, Pan-Serbism, intoxicated as it was by the victories over the Turks and Bulgars, did not hesitate a second.

Ten million men paid for it with their lives; and the thousands of war memorials in the villages of France, England, Germany and Russia are matched by the statue of Princip, the assassin, which the Serbs raised at Sarajevo by national subscription.

In October 1908 during an assembly of all the military and civil notabilities of Belgrade held at the City Hall under the presidency of General Jankovitch, a Pan-Serb organization of propaganda and of combat was created. Henceforth Pan-Serb imperialism had a focus, a constitution and a name, and it was called the Narodna Odbrana.

Expression of all the aspirations, of all the hatreds, of all the great national expectations, the Narodna Odbrana did not tarry long in acquiring a formidable influence in Serbia: eighteen months after its creation it counted 223 local committees, it contained all the personalities of the kingdom, and its ramifications extended into Bosnia, into Herzegovina, into Slovenia, and even into Istria.

It was the Narodna Odbrana which condemned to death and executed King Alexander Obrenovitch and Queen Draga. It was the Narodna Odbrana which made a king of the refugee Peter Karageorgevitch, the father of Alexander since murdered at Marseilles.

The avowed official aim of the organization created by General Jankovitch was the development of a patriotic spirit and a national solidarity between all the Slavs of the Balkans under the direction of the Serbian race. Its real aim was the preparation for a victorious war against Austria which would permit the Serbs to realize their designs on Bosnia-Herzegovina and Croatia.

In May 1911, a second secret Pan-Serb society, Unification or Death, better known as the Black Hand, was constituted under the direction of Colonel Dragoutine Dimitrievitch-Apis, chief of the Intelligence Service of the Serb general staff. Its task was to "work for the liberation of Serbs living under foreign oppression." It was not long before it had absorbed the most active elements of the Narodna Odbrana, and had imposed upon them one of its chiefs, Milan Vasitch.

The Black Hand immediately entered into conflict with the President of the Council, whom they accused of cowardice and obstruction to the Pan-Serb idea. It was eventually outlawed in June 1917. Its chiefs were accused of revolutionary intent and were shot at Salonica as the result of a trial by the judges of the War Council, whose "decision" was really a written order of the Prince-Regent, Alexander.

But the Pan-Serb idea which these dead men had personified has survived them.

The imperialistic program of the Black Hand has been resumed, completed, carried to its height since 1917 by the White Hand, an official organization created on the model of the Black Hand by trustworthy men of the Narodna Odbrana, who were at the same time henchmen of King Alexander.

By the army, which is entirely its puppet, and by the administration in which it holds all the control levers so that none can hope to enter who are not its members, the White Hand is today absolutely and exclusively master of all the interior and exterior policies of Yugoslavia.

It has become the essential machinery of the State. It decided, and its members executed, the coup d'etat of the 6th January, 1929. The first dictator, General Givkovitch, is representative type of the Pan-Serb White Hand.

It was by the members of the White Hand, acting under the instructions of Belgrade, that the Venetian monuments of Dalmatia, in Croatia, were mutilated in December and January 1931; and so many others during the last ten years have been destroyed in Istria.

The destruction of the lions in Trojit was an act of defiance flung by the White Hand into the mouth of Italy. It was their way of demonstrating to the Italian populations in Dalmatia, and to Italy herself, that Yugoslavia intended to do just as she pleased on her own territory.

Pan-Serbism has not, unfortunately, restricted itself to destroying Latin and Bulgarian inscriptions and stone lions found on conquered territories.

It is today admitted without question that the double assassination at Sarajevo was its work. The material proof has been given, not only by the publication in 1930 of official stenographic notes and the debates *in extenso* of the trial of the assassins, but by documents revealed since the War by Messrs. Sidney Fay and Bogicevitch, which show that Colonel Dimitrievitch-Apis, chief of the Intelligence Service of the great general staff of Belgrade and grand master of the Black Hand, was the instigator of the 28th June, 1914.

Colonel Dimitrievitch, moreover, admitted in his written confession a few hours before he faced the firing squad, that he had placed at the disposition of the assassins of the Archduke all the service of the Serbian military espionage even down to the bombs and revolvers which came from the arsenal of Kragoujevatz.

The directors of Pan-Serbism were naively persuaded that the worst that could result from the attack would be a localized conflict in which Austria and Russia only would come in conflict, the rest of Europe remaining spectators of the conflict in which Slavism, they thought, was assured to carry off a brilliant victory.

Dragomir Stefanovitch, who was for fifteen years one of my intimate friends, and who was Serbian charge d'affaires in Paris, told me these things years ago.

In the course of our conversations on the subject of the origin of the War, at Paris, where I saw him daily, and at Belgrade, where he had become one of the chiefs of the National Bank, Stefanovitch revealed to me what his functions had permitted him to learn of the great conflict.

He did not cease to condemn the Pan-Serbs of the Black Hand and their official accomplices for the way in which they precipitated the World War. His conscience cried out against the crime that they had committed with such *sang-froid* against the peace of the world.

"They were miserable wrenches!" he said. "But they were so powerful, they had succeeded so well in concealing their actions, and in placing accomplished facts before those who, like Pasich, condemned their revolutionary methods of direct action, or more or less feared the consequences, that it was impossible to stop them. Pasitch knew! We all knew! But nothing could be done. If Russia had not supported us, if we had to submit to the inquest which the Austrian ultimatum exacted in July 1914, we would have been caught with our hand in the sack. Well, well! We have won the match - but will we win the next one, for there is going to be a next one. Those people at Belgrade take themselves for geniuses, but really they are only asses who have been intoxicated by success. They are persuaded that victory is their natural right. They want to start trouble again, and when they do start it we shall not, perhaps, have either Russia or you to save us."

The double victory in the Balkan War had already intoxicated the men of the Black Hand, and the miraculous triumph of 1918, in which they forget they played a most insignificant part, has made their successors lose all prudence.

They are convinced that the force of Yugoslavia will increase limitlessly and that its exterior alliances shelter it from all surprises. Pan-Serbists, the absolute imbeciles without scruples who admit neither contradiction nor opposition.

All those whom it regards as obstacles to its policy of indefinite expansion of Pan-Serbism looks upon as enemies; and there lies the explanation of all that at first appears incomprehensible, absurd or odious in the attitude which has been adopted since the peace treaty by the government of Belgrade towards the non-Serb portions of their country.

Those who have witnessed the violence, the abuse, the cynical contempt with which the Serbs have treated the Croats and are astonished that the Serbs do not realize that in acting thus they are working against themselves, compromising their future and undoing with their own hands the edifice of Yugoslavia.

But those who think in this fashion reason as Frenchmen, as Englishmen, as Americans; they judge and decide with their occidental mentalities; they do not judge as Serbs. If they did they would understand immediately.

The crimes which their best friends reproach them for having committed in Croatia, in Macedonia, in Banat, and in the Adriatic provinces are considered by the Pan-Serbs as thoroughly justified and necessary. In their minds, the acts of which they are accused are not faults, but on the contrary are the affirmation of the justice of their political intuition. All the things that appear to foreign observers as aberrations of judgment, heavy with perilous consequences, the Pan-Serbs judge excellent, and declare them indispensable to the consolidation and to the existence of this Yugoslavia which, according to them, cannot live, cannot develop itself, and realize its integral destinies, unless it has one mind, one thought, one destiny – the mind, the thought and the destiny of Belgrade.

This is literally the principle invoked by King Alexander and his Pan-Serb advisors to explain and justify the coup d'etat of 6th January, 1929, in which one of the first acts was to suppress, under pretext of unification, the very traces of the former administrative parties. Here, too, is a point which Frenchmen (and Englishmen also) might do well to realize. Pan-Serb circles do not love France. They dissimulate, but they do not even admire us.

Let us not harbor any illusions. The official manifestations, the academic discourses, the telegrams celebrating the fraternity of arms and the celebrations of victory, all that means precisely nothing. They are obligatory gestures and vain words. In reality, their respect for France rests on advantages which accrue to the government of Yugoslavia. Their respect will last so long as these advantages continue. Not a day more, not an hour!

The clique which directs Yugoslavia would have cast France off long ago had they been able to get along without us.

With the people it is different. The anonymous and obscure masses of the workshop and the fields, (among whom the veterans of the Great War and the refugees of the retreat of 1915 have sown the legend of the invincible force, the immense resources, and the fraternal camaraderie of the "Franski") these are the ones who love us, admire us, and are grateful to us for what we did for Serbia during the War. Their sentiments towards us are about the same as those which they held for the Russians before Bolshevism.

The Pan-Serb circles do not love France. How could it be otherwise? Their atavisms, their education, their political ideals, their principles of government, their ambitions for the future, their intellectual and moral formation, all are entirely opposed to those of France.

When they permit themselves to speak freely, Pan-Serb ministers and high officials sneer contemptuously at the weakness of our statesmen, the peril of our democratic institutions, and the blindness of the concessions to which we have consented during the last ten years. "Ah! If we had your army and your billions," one of them said to me. "How we would make use of them!"

Yet it is by the grace of France that their country is still existing; it is to France that they are indebted for all they possess. France has been their inexhaustible banker for fourteen years. Twice since 1918 she has saved them from bankruptcy. French power still today is the shield behind which the dictatorship of Belgrade protects itself against the popular wrath.

But what France has done and is continuing to do for them is nothing in the minds of the Pan-Serbs compared with what France has not done. We may have fought because of them, we may have saved their armies in 1915, but even so they cannot forget that in 1918 we halted the Serb regiments who were disposed to pillage Sofia. We made it possible for them to gain Macedonia, certainly, but they prefer to remember that we obliged them to evacuate Bulgaria and that we did not support their claims upon Fiume. We have fallen out with Italy because of them, but they hold it against us that we have not ceased for ten years to put pressure upon the government of Belgrade in order to constrain them to maintain peace in the Balkans.

The Pan-Serbs have forgotten the services rendered, and they do not pardon us for the other things because of those services. Let us not be astonished. Ever since there have been politicians who envy the property of others, history has been the same. The Imperialism of weak people has always turned to bottomless egotism when they have become strong.

Of this kind is the imperialism of Belgrade, and I will insist once more on this point – I do not say "the imperialism of the Serb people," because the people themselves are simple, calm, reasonable and terribly tried by six years of war. They ask only for peace for themselves and for others. They have no part whatsoever in the responsibility of the criminal errors of the governors, nor for the inconceivable madness of their schemes for expansion.

Here is what the officers and non-commissioned officers make their men learn in all the garrisons of Yugoslavia. It is taken from the *Soldier's Manual*, edited by Colonel Kostich of the general staff, under the direction of the government of Belgrade. I cite it word for word:

"All our provinces are not yet reunited to our kingdom. The Italians still hold all of Istria with Goritza, Gradisca and Trieste as far as Isonzo; the city of Zara and its surrounding country, the islands of Cherso, Lussin, Lastua and Pelagosa, as well as the southern part of Slovenia. Austria still holds the northern part of Carinthia, Steiermark. The Hungarians still hold the northern part of Baranya and of Prekomurje. The Roumanians still hold the eastern part of Banat. The Bulgarians still occupy the regions of Vidina and of Sofia. The Albanians still hold Scutari and a part of northern Albania."

In all the elementary and secondary schools of Yugoslavia, the same instruction is given each day to a half-million children, compulsorily and officially. The same mission of liberation of "brothers still oppressed" is presented to them as the sacred duty which will be incumbent upon them when they become men. This hatred is buried systematically in the hearts of children and young men who learn each day by hundreds of thousands that there are lands so-called foreign that are in reality Yugoslav and must be torn from those who retain them. Tears, ruin and bloodshed will follow on this for all the people who dare to remain bound to the destiny of Yugoslavia. Psychology teaches us that there is nothing so potent as an idea sown into a young mind – beware, then, of these babies educated to war.

You will understand why so much suspicion, so much hostility, and so much hatred in Central Europe and the Balkans surrounds Yugoslavia. Those who do no know and who are astonished about it attribute it to the jealousy which the prosperity and the power of Belgrade inspires in its neighbors.

Those hostile neighbors, whose aggressive spirit Belgrade does not cease to denounce, are hostile because they know the secret intentions of the men who dominate Yugoslavia. No one shelters the least illusion as to what is being prepared. Born of war, aggrandized by war, Yugoslavia is led by the megalomania of its chiefs towards a future war. Victorious three times in succession, tripled in territory, more than doubled in population, increased tenfold in riches and possibilities, she is not yet satisfied.

The *Soldier's Manual* is terrifying because of what it reveals to us of the secret projects of Pan-Serbism, and of the fearful mentality of conquering nationalism that it is trying to inculcate into the young Yugoslav generations. Yet certain geographic maps, officially edited at Belgrade, are even more terrifying in their import.

The one I have before me while writing this, and which is by no means intended for exportation to France, represents a "Greater Serbia" encircling Trieste, Fiume, all of Istria; extending up into Carinthia and towards the Austrian Tyrol to Gratz; and descending to Scutari, Drama, Thasos, and into Bulgaria well past Sofia.

It is not less ambitious than the maps which Pan-Germanism prepared to show the proposed annexation of Belgium, Denmark, the East and North of France, Basle, Geneva and Lausanne.

Do not tell the Pan-Serbs that their dreams of hegemony will shatter on insurmountable obstacles, and that they are preparing their country for a supreme disaster, for they will not listen to you. Whatever service you have been able to render them in the past, whatever friendship you have borne their country, you will become forthwith suspect and an enemy. They will accept the advice of no one, or if they are obliged to appear to accept it, they will not follow it. They will admit no contradiction. They wish neither to understand nor to know. They intend to follow to the end the road which they have traced for themselves. They do not believe that it was only by a miraculous stroke of destiny that the miniature Balkan kingdom of 1914 has become the powerful European State today.

The hypnosis of Pan-Serbism dominates everything. In the army, the diplomatic corps, the government councils, the great administrators, the men of Narodna Odbrana are everywhere, and even though they appear to occupy but a spot of secondary importance, in reality it is they who command, because all the forces of the secret organizations are behind them.

And let no one believe that this is a new phenomenon, a result of the state of intellectual and moral disequilibrium produced by the dictatorship and which will disappear if the dictatorship caves in. It has been thus at Belgrade since the day that these Pan-Serb organizations – first Narodna Odbrana, and then the Black Hand and the White Hand made themselves masters of the State.

Who, for example, was this Colonel Dragoutine Dimitrievitch-Apis, whose action was decisive in starting the World War? He was, I repeat, simply the chief of the Intelligence Service of the great general staff, that is to say, a subordinate.But this did not prevent him from passing over the heads of his superiors, over the head of the Chief of the Government himself, and deciding, preparing and organizing in its most minute details the attack of Sarajevo. He chose the authors of the attack, he sent them revolvers and bombs taken from the State arsenals of Kragoujevatz, he had them escorted to the frontier of Bosnia by officers of the regular army, he had them guided and cared for in Austrian territory by agents of the Serbian espionage, and he had them conducted in some underhand fashion to the quay of Miljocka behind which they (Tchabrinivitch and Gavrilo Princip) lay in ambush to strike.

Pasich knew what was being prepared, but capable Prime Minister as he was, he could do nothing against it. The forces of Pan-Serbism were behind it. The all-powerful minister met in the shadows something more powerful than he.

V. Propaganda

"The more they play the idiot in that house, the greater the results!"

That is what an American newspaper man said to me last year about the Press Bureau of the Presidency of the Council at Belgrade. His jibe was justified. This Press Bureau thinks and speaks for Yugoslavia. Its Director, working under the head of the government, forms opinion in the country and sends out official statements to newspapers not only in Yugoslavia, but all over the world, in which everything is coloured from the Serb point of view, and nothing contrary to the views and desires of the Dictatorship is allowed to pass. It is an amazing organization. I know, for instance, that in the summer of 1932 the Press Bureau held the key to the secret code of five foreign Legations – Great Britain, France, Greece, Bulgaria and Romania.

The foreign correspondents in Belgrade are carefully documented and closely watched by the agents of the Bureau. Those whose independence is liable to be embarrassing to the Government are made as uncomfortable as possible. As a matter of fact, a correspondent of *The Times* who told the truth about the political and economic situation had his home invaded by the police one night, his papers scattered about and seized, and he was conducted to the Hungarian frontier.

The Press Bureau is backed with money. It has a reserve of several millions – doubled by secret funds from the Presidency. It knows how to use them. In its propaganda work it has the help of the Telegraph Agency whose role it is to send to Yugoslav journals the official version of everything. It inundates the foreign Press with Balkan information dictated by Belgrade. But the Press Bureau not only sends out news; it collects it – from carefully primed and highly-placed observers in every European capital except Rome. Even the Secret Service and the State police work with them.

The Pan-Serb diplomats and propagandists are strikingly similar to those of Germany in that they always act as if they were dealing with imbeciles or blind men. They play their game with the cards on the table. Thus by feigning ignorance on a question with which they are thoroughly acquainted, or by manifesting incredulous surprise before certain affirmations which are brought to their notice, with a little cleverness the Press Bureau is certain to arrive at quite astonishing results.

The two men who at present share the direction of this essential cog of Pan-Serb politics are Dr. Marianovitch and his associate, Dr. Radovanovitch. Neither of them can tolerate any scepticism or contradiction on the part of their foreign interlocutors. Each works according to his own nature, Dr. Marianovitch with more distinction and finesse; Dr. Radovanovitch with a cordial vulgarity and an inexhaustible fund of talk. But neither expects you to leave them until they have convinced you.

In the summer of 1932 Dr. Radovanitch directed the Press Bureau alone. He arrived at the important post which he occupies by the support of secret organizations. Absolutely devoid of education, but of a pleasant temperament, he possesses one of the most prodigious faculties of elocution that I have ever encountered. As he knows he talks well, he expects to talk all the time.

I am indebted to him for enlightenment on the subject of the fate of Dr. Trumbitch, Dr. Korochetz, and M. Baricevitch, one of the leaders of the Democrat-Peasant coalition.

"We will have their hides," said Dr. Radovanovitch with fury, "I d like to have them here in my hands and boot them to death."

Dr. Radovanovitch would have talked all night about the enemies of Yugo-slavia, about the necessity of "striking first in order not to be stabbed in the back," and about the necessity of making French opinion understand this.

I went to see him prior to my departure for Macedonia where I was going to see things for myself I visited his office a few hours before my departure for Skopje and Southern Serbia. I asked him about the Macedonian question. "The Macedonian question," he said, "there is no Macedonian question. There isn't one because there are no Macedonian people. The regions which the Turks called Macedonia are in reality purely Serb. Their inhabit-ants, with the exception of a few tens of thousands, are Serb – just as the populations of the provinces that you French and the English have thought fit to give to Greece in order to thank her, no doubt, for having shot your sailors at Zappeion!

"These populations, you will say to me, speak a different dialect derived from Bulgarian. But why not? For centuries our compatriots of Macedonia have had no other priests, no other teachers than the Bulgars , because the Turks tried to Bulgarise them. But today all the youth of Macedonia has again learned to speak the ancestral language. You will see with what en-thusiasm the little children in our primary schools of Southern Serbia say, "I am Serb! I am Serb!"

"I shall convince you, when I tell you that the populations which, according to our enemies at Sofia, we terrorise, violate and exterminate, have asked us for arms and ammunition in order that they might defend themselves in case of necessity against the incursions of organised bands of their pre-tended brothers of Bulgaria."

I said: "But the Macedonians in Bulgaria say that the immense majority of the inhabitants of Souther Serbia hate you so much that nearly a half-million among them have already expatriated themselves. In order to put an end to this emigration *en masse,* you were forced to close your frontier over hundreds of kilometers with a barrier of barbed wire."

My interruption displeased Dr. Radovanovitch. "I know the story," he said dryly. "It is the sort of thing that Sofia serves up to the fools who listen to her."

"You are trying to suggest that the inhabitants of South Serbia are the Bulgarian race? The reply to this absurdity has been given by our great historian, Tichomir Djordjevitch in his famous book, *Nascha Juzna Serbia* (Our Southern Serbia). In it he proves that there exists at present hardly six or seven hundred thousand Bulgars of pure blood in all the Balkan peninsula. They are the last descendants of a tribe of Mongols who came to Europe in the wake of Attila, and who remained between Iskar and the Black Sea, the Danube and the Balkan Chain. Four-fifths of the so-called Bulgars who people Bulgaria, that is to say nearly five million inhabitants out of six, are pure Serb."

"Agreed, Doctor," I said, "but what do you make of the conclusions of the Commission sent by the Russian Academy of Science in 1900 to visit Macedonia and fix the question of nationalities? That Commission reported as follows: 'In Macedonia there still lives the same people who in the ninth century were already called Bulgar."

He hesitated an instant.

"The Russian Commission," he said, "have admitted they were paid by King Ferdinand to say what they said. That settles that!"

"Let us come to this pretended emigration of the Macedonian population fleeing from our bad treatment. When we entered South Serbia in 1913 we found there thirty thousand Bulgars, descendants of families who had lived there under the Turkish domination. These Bulgars preferred to return to Bulgaria and we made haste to facilitate their departure, only too happy to be rid of them.

"This horrifying story of a Southern Serbia that we have imprisoned behind a wall of barbed wire has nine lives. I certainly hope that you will help us kill it, if you still have time when you are down there to go as far as the frontier. It is true that we have had to wire certain defiles and gorges which we have found particularly favourable to Bulgarian bandits. But this does not exactly constitute hundreds of kilometers of steel walls, or lines of forts, or an hermetically sealed frontier which have been used in the propaganda of the revolutionary committees of Sofia and their Italian and Hungarian allies!

"As for the 'atrocities', to use your expression, they do not concern us. We Serbs do not employ these methods. The Inquisition is not a Serb invention, it is Italian." "Spanish, Doctor," I corrected him gently. "Spanish." "Spanish, if you will," replied Dr "It makes little difference! Spain is worth no more than Italy! The atrocities denounced in the report of the Carnegie Commission, if they really happened, were the work of the bandits from Bulgaria, who come to pillage and assassinate, and these we have exterminated."

"Moreover, it will take you a very few hours to see what the attitude of our Southern population is. I have given orders that you may get a clear idea of it all. Wherever you wish to go our officials will conduct you. You may see the affection and the respect which the population lavish upon the dutiful men, who are our administrators.

"But do not confound the sentiments and the opinion of the Bulgar official circles with those of the popular mass whom they oppress. Don't let them make a fool of you!"

"King Boris, for example, surrounded by Germanophile officers, and ignorant and dishonest officials, is detested by his subjects. Recall all the attacks directed against his life in the last few years."

I risked another interruption:

"These Bulgars affirm, and their declarations have been confirmed by the diplomatic corps at Sofia, that the ambush on the route to Kustendil was the work of individuals in the pay of your legation in Bulgaria."

Dr. Radovanvitch literally bounded out of his chair.

"Those people are capable of the most vile infamies," he cried. "Only they forget to remember that they commit more political assassinations in a month that do all the rest of Europe in ten years. We are not in the habit in Yugoslavia of assassinating or having our adversaries assassinated. They will assassinate King Boris without us!"

"The day he embarrasses the ORIM or the Macedonian National Committee, his account is settled. His Italian marriage has succeeded not only in alienating him from the mass, who do not pardon him having married a Roman Catholic, but also from the true Bulgar patriots who understand that it is not Italy who can re-establish the prosperity of their country, but we only, their racial brothers!"

"But," I ventured, "King Alexander himself declared in 1930, if I am not mistaken, that the incorporation of Bulgaria into the Yugoslav community would be most undesirable."

"Yes, indeed," rejoined the Doctor. "His Majesty said that. But events have happened quickly since then in Bulgaria and elsewhere. His Majesty has since completely changed his opinion, as I can prove to you, because he himself told me."

"Doctor, take care!" I said. "We are going into the realm of dreams. I spoke with too many people last year in Bulgaria not to know the truth; I questioned too many Europeans; there are too many of my compatriots established in the country since the War, who are thoroughly acquainted with it."

"Not in the realm of dreams at all," replied the Doctor. "No, in the realm of realities of tomorrow!"

"A Balkan Federation, eh?" I asked. "A first step towards the United States of Europe so ardently desired by Aristide Briand?"

"No!" thundered Radovanovitch. "As General Givkovitch said to you here last year, the United States of Europe is the panacea of a quack doctor, the politics of a paralytic for weak nations. We are a strong people, led by men who do not waste words, and are not paralysed, I can tell you!"

"A Balkan Federation such as certain irresponsible foreign circles advocate, which would leave to each of its members its administrative autonomy, its own political regime and even its finances and its personal army, is impossible! Those Utopias which certain lawyers would institute would have no other aim than to lull our vigilance in order to rob us!"

"Our idea is a Federation grouping together all the peoples of the Slav race established between the Black Sea, the Aegean, the Adriatic, the Alps and the Danube. It will not comprise Greece, but the present Yugoslavia, Bulgaria, Albania and the Slav populations still under foreign domination. Such an ideal is not possible, it is not desirable and it will not be realised, if it does not come into being by the crystallisation of all these peoples around the central nucleus, Serbia."

"That is how it will happen, sir. And it will inevitably happen either in peace or in war."

War! I did not criticise the word. I have heard it so often last year, and again since my return here. Yesterday I heard it again from the lips of a peaceful professor at the University at whose side I dined at the French Legation and who said to me: "War is terrible, of course, but without it the entire social body dies. Peace is decadence!"

How like the German professors of 1914!

I said to Radovanovitch: "So Serbia is destined to play in the Balkan Peninsula the role which has been assumed by Prussia in Germany?"

"Exactly," the Doctor agreed. "All the Slavs of the South, under whatever may be the region they inhabit, whatever may be the State which they obey today, all have the same origin – Serb. The day is near when all will group about their common source, Serbia, for the integral realization of the destinies of a great people!"

Enthusiasm transfigured the face of Dr. Radovanovitch. He was "living" his dream.

"Sofia, Skopje, Bitolj or Ochride are all Serb," he went on. "Salonica has never been Greek; it has a Serb city peopled with Southern Serbs. Its affiliation to Greece has been its death sentence! It will not revive, it will not find again its lost prosperity, until it becomes again the great commercial port of the Balkans towards the Mediterranean and the Orient. And it cannot become this great port unless it returns to Yugoslavia, of which it is a natural and historical dependency. It is the same with Drama, Seres, Janina, Kastoria, which have been of no importance since they were delivered to the degenerate Greek nation."

"In the meantime, I tell you frankly, we have had enough of the collusion between the government of Sofia and associations of bandits installed in Bulgaria, where they conduct an abominable propaganda against us, and do not cease to organize attacks in Southern Serbia."

"Our general staff itself will proceed with the clean-up that Bulgaria refuses to make. We shall start by putting Sofia in her place for the last time. If nothing changes, we will appeal to the League of Nations, on giving it notice that we, since Sofia is powerless, are going to proceed ourselves to carry out the necessary police operation. Once this is done, the first attack committed on our territory, or against one of our subjects in Bulgaria will be the sign for our soldiers to occupy the departments of Sofia, Petrich and Kustendil."

"And after that?"

"What do you mean, after that? What do you expect would happen? We will exterminate a few dozen brigands, to the great satisfaction of the peaceful populations whom they terrorise; we will burn their haunts; King Boris and his clique will be eclipsed, and a few weeks later, in an unanimous spirit, the Bulgars, liberated by us, will proclaim their intention to unite with Yugoslavia."

"And I, my dear Doctor," I said, "am persuaded to the contrary. The entry of your troops into Bulgaria will rise against you the entire country. In all Bulgaria there will be but one desire. The closest national union will surround King Boris. It will be a war to death."

Dr. Radovanvitch made no sign.

"But," I went on, "in all that, what are you going to do about Italy? you
don't suppose that if you invade Bulgaria, and especially if you express the
intention of remaining there, that Italy will watch you without acting, do
you? Italy will never permit you to install yourself at Salonica; she will
never permit you to incorporate Bulgaria into Yugoslavia."

"Your march on Sofia will call Italy up against you."

A gleam passed in the depth of his grey eyes:

"Italy will attack us," he agreed. "We know it! But what about that! She
may have tanks, artillery, technical means that we do not have. She may
have twice as many troops as we have. But what of that? Sooner or later it
will be necessary for their men to encounter our own, man to man. Then we
shall see. The Austrians had four men to our one in the Great War, but each
time the Austrian troops hurled themselves against our own, they were
crushed, and each Austrian (they proved it at) is worth two Italians. All the
carnivals and the parades of fascism have not changed the heart of those
runaways of Caporetto. Let them come if it pleases them! We will teach
them to run again.

"And what about France. Are you not our allies? If Italy attacks us, you
will be obliged to aid us. Your interest is our interest, for Italy menaces you
far more than she menaces us. She wants Albania, she wants Trieste, Istria,
and all the Dalmatian coast, but she also wants Corsica, and Tunisia and Al-
geria from you. Italy is much more your enemy than Germany is, but she
can do nothing against you because of us, nothing against us because of
you."

.....

Dreams of madness! Certainly, but dreams which all those who are masters
in Yugoslavia pursue obstinately and untiringly. Just as Russia, for three
centuries, pursued the mad dream of Constantinople.

These mad dreams will cost Europe much blood, and first of all France, if
she does not shatter them while there is still time by warning the men of the
Pan-Serb dictatorship that though we are their allies for the maintenance of
peace, we will never be their allies in adventures of provocation and rapine

which will cost Europe more dead and more than the revolver shot of the
Pan-Serb Princip!

....

NOTE: The following is not a part of Pozzi's book. It has been
inserted by the Editor in order to substantiate Pozzi's statements
concerning Serbia's responsibility for World War I..

23 July, 1914: The Austro-Hungarian Ultimatum to Serbia

The Austro-Hungarian Minister for Foreign Affairs, Berchtold,

to the Minister at Belgrade, von Giesl:

Vienna, July 22, 1914

Your Excellency will present the following note to the Royal Government
on the afternoon of Thursday, July 23:

On the 31st of March, 1909, the Royal Serbian Minister at the Court of Vienna made, in the name of his Government, the following declaration to
the Imperial and Royal Government:

Serbia recognizes that her rights were not affected by the state of affairs
created in Bosnia, and states that she will accordingly accommodate herself to the decisions to be reached by the Powers in connection with Article
25 of the Treaty of Berlin. Serbia, in accepting the advice of the Great
Powers, binds herself to desist from the attitude of protest and opposition
which she has assumed with regard to the annexation since October last,
and she furthermore binds herself to alter the tendency of her present policy toward Austria-Hungary, and to live on the footing of friendly and
neighborly relations with the latter in the future.

Now the history of the past few years, and particularly the painful events of the 28th of June, have proved the existence of a subversive movement in Serbia, whose object it is to separate certain portions of its territory from the Austro-Hungarian Monarchy. This movement, which came into being under the very eyes of the Serbian Government, subsequently found expression outside of the territory of the Kingdom in acts of terrorism, in a number of attempts at assassination, and in murders.

Far from fulfilling the formal obligations contained in its declaration of the 31st of March, 1909, the Royal Serbian Government has done nothing to suppress this movement. It has tolerated the criminal activities of the various unions and associations directed against the Monarchy, the unchecked utterances of the press, the glorification of the authors of assassinations, the participation of officers and officials in subversive intrigues; it has tolerated an unhealthy propaganda in its public instruction; and it has tolerated, finally, every manifestation which could betray the people of Serbia into hatred of the Monarchy and contempt for its institutions.

This toleration of which the Royal Serbian Government was guilty, was still in evidence at that moment when the events of the twenty-eighth of June exhibited to the whole world the dreadful consequences of such tolerance.

It is clear from the statements and confessions of the criminal authors of the assassination of the twenty- eighth of June, that the murder at was conceived at Belgrade, that the murderers received the weapons and the bombs with which they were equipped from Serbian officers and officials who belonged to the Narodna Odbrana, and, finally, that the dispatch of the criminals and of their weapons to Bosnia was arranged and effected under the conduct of Serbian frontier authorities.

The results brought out by the inquiry no longer permit the Imperial and Royal Government to maintain the attitude of patient tolerance which it has observed for years toward those agitations which center at Belgrade and are spread thence into the territories of the Monarchy. Instead, these results impose upon the Imperial and Royal Government the obligation to put an end to those intrigues, which constitute a standing menace to the peace of the Monarchy.

In order to attain this end, the Imperial and Royal Government finds itself compelled to demand that the Serbian Government give official assurance that it will condemn the propaganda directed against Austria-Hungary, that is to say, the whole body of the efforts whose ultimate object it is to separate from the Monarchy territories that belong to it; and that it will obligate itself to suppress with all the means at its command this criminal and terroristic propaganda. In order to give these assurances a character of solemnity, the Royal Serbian Government will publish on the first page of its official organ of July 26/13, the following declaration:

"The Royal Serbian Government condemns the propaganda directed against Austria-Hungary, that is to say, the whole body of the efforts whose ultimate object it is to separate from the Austro-Hungarian Monarchy territories that belong to it, and it most sincerely regrets the dreadful consequences of these criminal transactions.

"The Royal Serbian Government regrets that Serbian officers and officials should have taken part in the above-mentioned propaganda and thus have endangered the friendly and neighborly relations, to the cultivation of which the Royal Government had most solemnly pledged itself by its declarations of March 31, 1909.

"The Royal Government, which disapproves and repels every idea and every attempt to interfere in the destinies of the population of whatever portion of Austria-Hungary, regards it as its duty most expressly to call attention of the officers, officials, and the whole population of the kingdom to the fact that for the future it will proceed with the utmost rigor against any persons who shall become guilty of any such activities, activities to prevent and to suppress which, the Government will bend every effort."

This declaration shall be brought to the attention of the Royal army simultaneously by an order of the day from His Majesty the King, and by publication in the official organ of the army.

The Royal Serbian Government will furthermore pledge itself:

1. to suppress every publication which shall incite to hatred and contempt of the Monarchy, and the general tendency of which shall be directed against the territorial integrity of the latter;

2. to proceed at once to the dissolution of the Narodna Odbrana to confiscate all of its means of propaganda, and in the same manner to proceed against the other unions and associations in Serbia which occupy themselves with propaganda against Austria-Hungary; the Royal Government will take such measures as are necessary to make sure that the dissolved associations may not continue their activities under other names or in other forms;

3. to eliminate without delay from public instruction in Serbia, everything, whether connected with the teaching corps or with the methods of teaching, that serves or may serve to nourish the propaganda against Austria-Hungary;

4. to remove from the military and administrative service in general all officers and officials who have been guilty of carrying on the propaganda against Austria-Hungary, whose names the Imperial and Royal Government reserves the right to make known to the Royal Government when communicating the material evidence now in its possession;

5. to agree to the cooperation in Serbia of the organs of the Imperial and Royal Government in the suppression of the subversive movement directed against the integrity of the Monarchy;

6. to institute a judicial inquiry against every participant in the conspiracy of the twenty-eighth of June who may be found in Serbian territory; the organs of the Imperial and Royal Government delegated for this purpose will take part in the proceedings held for this purpose;

7. to undertake with all haste the arrest of Major Voislav Tankosic and of one Milan Ciganovitch, a Serbian official, who have been compromised by the results of the inquiry;

8. by efficient measures to prevent the participation of Serbian authorities in the smuggling of weapons and explosives across the frontier; to dismiss from the service and to punish severely those members of the Frontier Service at Schabats and Losnitza who assisted the authors of the crime of Sarajevo to cross the frontier;

227

9. to make explanations to the Imperial and Royal Government concerning the unjustifiable utterances of high Serbian functionaries in Serbia and abroad, who, without regard for their official position, have not hesitated to express themselves in a manner hostile toward Austria-Hungary since the assassination of the twenty-eighth of June;

10. to inform the Imperial and Royal Government without delay of the execution of the measures comprised in the foregoing points.

The Imperial and Royal Government awaits the reply of the Royal Government by Saturday, the twenty-fifth instant, at 6 p.m., at the latest.

A reminder of the results of the investigation about Sarajevo, to the extent they relate to the functionaries named in points 7 and 8 [above], is appended to this note.

Appendix:

The crime investigation undertaken at court in against Gavrilo Princip and his comrades on account of the assassination committed on the 28th of June this year, along with the guilt of accomplices, has up until now led to the following conclusions:

1. The plan of murdering Archduke Franz Ferdinand during his stay in was concocted in Belgrade by Gavrilo Princip, Nedeljko Cabrinovic, a certain Milan Ciganovic, and Trifko Grabesch with the assistance of Major Voija Takosic.

2. The six bombs and four Browning pistols along with ammunition — used as tools by the criminals — were procured and given to Princip, Cabrinovic and Grabesch in Belgrade by a certain Milan Ciganovic and Major Voija Takosic.

3. The bombs are hand grenades originating from the weapons depot of the Serbian army in Kragujevatz.

4. To guarantee the success of the assassination, instructed Princip, Cabrinovic and Grabesch in the use of the grenades and gave lessons on

shooting Browning pistols to Princip and Grabesch in a forest next to the shooting range at Topschider.

5. To make possible Princip, Cabrinovic and Grabesch's passage across the Bosnia-Herzegovina border and the smuggling of their weapons, an entire secretive transportation system was organized by Ciganovic. The entry of the criminals and their weapons into Bosnia and Herzegovina was carried out by the main border officials of Shabatz (Rade Popovic) and Losnitza as well as by the customs agent Budivoj Grbic of Losnitza, with the complicity of several others.

On the occasion of handing over this note, would Your Excellency please also add orally that — in the event that no unconditionally positive answer of the Royal government might be received in the meantime — after the course of the 48-hour deadline referred to in this note, as measured from the day and hour of your announcing it, you are commissioned to leave the I. and R. Embassy of Belgrade together with your personnel.

Leon Dennen; 1945:

Excerpts from *TOUBLE ZONE - Brewing Point of World War III ?*; New York -Chicago: Ziff-Davis Publ. Co., 1945.

CHAPTER FOUR: THE MARTYRDOM OF YUGOSLAVIA

1.

Of all the Balkan leaders I met during my long journeys through the Trouble Zone I shall always remember Major Lukacevich, friend and adjutant of the Yugoslav leader, General Draja Mihailovich. Young, tall, a giant of a man, passionately patriotic, Voja seemed to me the incarnation of bravery and suffering of the Serbian people.

After several years of continuous guerrilla warfare against the Nazi invaders of his country, Major and my friend Major Borislav Todorovich – subsequently Assistant Military and Air Attaché to the Yugoslav Embassy in

Washington – came to Cairo in April 1944 to request British and American authorities for military aid in preparation for an offensive against the Germans. From the first day of their arrival they found that despite their readiness to fight the Germans, their mission, for purely political reasons, was a hopeless one. The British had not yet openly recognized General Mihailovich's Stalin-appointed rival, Tito, but this was after the Teheran Conference and they were committed to do so.

In Britain's desperate struggle for the preservation of the Empire, loyalty and friendship play small roles. Instead of receiving military aid to carry on the fight against the Nazis, both Major Lukacevich and Major Todorovich were thrown into jail, as a gesture of appeasement to our Russian ally. Only after both men went on a hunger strike and the entire incident threatened to become a major diplomatic scandal were they freed, without so much as a word of apology.

There was resignation rather than bitterness in Major Todorovich's voice as he talked to me of the desperate plight of the Yugoslavs and of the treatment accorded him by the British. For many months he had been fighting the Germans. In his mountain hideouts he knew little of the moves and counter-moves that were being played out on the diplomatic chessboards in London, Moscow, and Washington. The whole thing puzzled him.

"They say that Draja Mihailovich is a fascist and collaborator of the Germans," he said, suppressing his tears with difficulty. "They say that I am a fascist. Why? Why are they spreading those lies about us? For over three years General Mihailovich and I, and thousands of hungry, ragged, and barefooted Yugoslavs with us have been fighting against the Germans and Italians. Thousands of our people have died in this fight. I am the son of a peasant. My grandfather and great-grandfather were peasants. Like them I am ready to die for the right of our people to lead a free life. Since my boyhood I have been a follower of the great Yugoslav democrat, Zivko Topalovich. Now they say I m a fascist! Why?"

There was no answer to the question. Three leaders of great powers had met in Teheran and decided that his country, despite the wishes of its people and their sacrifices for freedom, should become a "sphere of influence" for one of those powers. They had, as part of a larger bargain, consigned Yugoslavia to the area of totalitarianism. Voja was only one of thousands of his countrymen politically stranded by the very democracies which had first inspired them to oppose the Nazi beast.

A few months later, in September 1944, Major Todorovich and another Yugoslav leader, Colonel Zivan Knezevich, were sent to Italy by the American military authorities. They were to be parachuted into territory controlled by Mihailovich. Colonel Knezevich had been Commander of the Royal Guard and the Belgrade Garrison which staged the coup d'état on March 27, 1941, repudiated the Axis Pact and with the Serbian people brought Yugoslavia on the side of the Allies.

Upon arrival in Bari, Italy, the two men were interned by the British at the request of Soviet and Tito representatives. The fact that their orders were signed by the United States Chief of Staff, General Marshall, did not save them. The British even planned to deliver them to Tito, which would have meant certain death. Only the intervention of our Ambassador, Alexander Kirk, headed off this act of treachery Knezevich and Todorovich were finally forced to return to America without accomplishing their mission.

The Serbian people assuredly will never forget such episodes, typical of the whole complex story of their nation's ordeal at the hands of the democracies. They will never forget, for instance, that in and other areas under Mihailovich's control American planes, upon the advice and direction of the British, bombed and harassed the anti-Nazi Chetnik forces.

Our fliers, it is true, were not aware that they were bombing Mihailovich. They were intentionally misdirected by Tito and his British advisors, Brigadier Fitzroy Hew Royle Maclean and the British Prime Minister's son, Major Randolph Churchill. This was the reward Mihailovich's Chetniks received for rescuing six hundred American fliers who had been forced down in Chetnik or near-by enemy-controlled territory. Our American boys whose lives the Chetniks saved know the meaning of Serbian friendship and hospitality.

"Those of us who know the real conditions in Serbia," wrote Lieutenant John E. Scroggs of Kansas City, one of the American fliers rescued by the Chetniks, to Constantin A. Fotitch, former Yugoslav Ambassador to the United States, on October 18, 1944, "are enraged at the unfair attacks upon the Chetniks and their leaders. If only someone could open the blind eyes of the spoiled American people a wonderful group of men and women would receive due recognition."

"Unfortunately those of us who lived with these people are few and far between, but believe me that we whom they brought back to life shall never forget how the men and women of Serbia unquestioningly risked their lives for us, fed us, clothed us, and gave us shelter when they themselves were ill-clad, cold, and hungry."

"What did they give us? Black bread and goat's milk. We slept on piles of straw with only a crude blanket for cover or in rooms with dirt floors. The average American would laugh and tell you that this was very little. True enough: any American would give a stranger a few cents' worth of bread and let him sleep in his garage. But do you suppose you could find one American in a million who would accept you into his household if you were a total stranger and give the best he had and almost *all* he had? Do you think he would leave his occupation and walk for days and days to make possible your escape from enemy-held territory?"

"No, I m afraid he wouldn't. As a matter of fact, I know damn well he wouldn't. But there was never a question among the Serbs: we were to be given the very best they had and almost all they had, if necessary. The first night I spent with the Chetniks I complained and felt sorry for myself because I was housed in a peasant's only room and on a dirt floor at that. But the next morning I saw the mother and child of the family huddled in the pig pen!"

"Later when we joined the majority of our crew of ten men we noticed that we were always first. Everything the peasants possessed was placed on the table for us. When we were through, they ate what we left! I vowed to myself that if I could ever repay those people for all they have done for me I shall be the happiest man in the world. Unfortunately, what little I might be able to do would not even pay the interest on my debt to the Serbian people. I suffer with them in their present plight caused by the injustice rendered them by the American press and the American and British Governments. I sincerely hope that the true situation in Yugoslavia may be revealed to the public in some manner and that their national situation may be remedied. Those of us who know them salute the Serbs!"

Fortunately Lieutenant Scroggs was not swayed by higher diplomacy and political considerations. With the generosity and sportsmanship typical of American youth he has shed some light on the truth about Mihailovich and his heroic Chetniks.

2.

What is the truth about the man not so long ago glorified in the American press and in Hollywood as a very symbol of resistance to the Nazi beast? Is he, as Moscow's and Tito's propagandists claim, merely a reactionary and even a fascist, or is he, as millions of Yugoslavs believe, one of those legendary Balkan hero-liberators?

And what is the truth about Tito, the former Croatian metal worker? That he is a leader of the Communist Party of Yugoslavia and former "student" of Moscow's West School where foreign Communist agents are trained for operations in the democratic countries, is not disputed least of all by Tito himself. But is he merely Stalin's Commissar to weld the Balkans into a Pan-Slav union under Moscow's aegis, or is he, as even some liberals assert, a symbol of new revolutionary forces released by the war and stirring everywhere?

These questions are easier asked than answered. Tito's cause has been promoted in Britain by Churchill as an expediency of Empire politics. In the United States he has been successfully sold to the American people by groups of well-placed Communists and by pro-Communist propagandists like Louis Adamic. Tito also had at his disposal during his struggle with the Chetnik leader the Free Yugoslav radio station located at Tiflis, Russia, and the whole Soviet propaganda machine throughout the world. All of this has given him an overwhelming publicity advantage over General Mihailovich.

Nevertheless, out of the maze of conflicting and often invented information, those intimately acquainted with the Balkan facts are able to arrive at a semblance of truth.

Yugoslavia, made up in the main of about 8,000,000 Serbs, 3,500,000 Croats, and 1,500,000 Slovenes, is one of those hasty creations hammered together by the Treaty of Versailles. Almost from the day of its birth there arose bitter enmity between the majority Serbs and the minority Croats.

The two peoples belong almost to different civilizations. The Serbs are of the Greek Orthodox faith; the Croats, like the Slovenes, are Roman Catholics. The Serbs are a typical Balkan people – dour, brave, uncompromising. Unlike the Croats and Slovenes, who had lived for many generations under Austro-Hungarian subjection, the Serbs had their spirit of independence and national unity hardened in long and bloody struggles against Turkish rule and in the two Balkan Wars.

During the first World War, of all the Balkan peoples, the Serbs alone fought to the end on the side of the Allies. For nearly two years little Serbia barred Germany's path to the Middle East, at a fearful price in suffering and casualties.

The Croats, as subjects of the Hapsburgs, took on some of the polish and urbanity of the Dual Empire and have always regarded themselves as more European than the Serbs. For more than two decades they justly fought against Serbization by the numerically superior Serbs. It was natural that the Croats in particular should resent the dictatorship of the late King Alexander, exercised from the Serbian capital of Belgrade and administered largely by Serbians, and to regard it as a Serb institution. Alexander was assassinated in Marseilles by agents of Ante Pavelich, leader of the Croatian pro-Nazi terrorist organization called *Ustashi*. Subsequently, by the grace of the Nazis, Pavelich became the head of an independent Croatian state which joined the Axis and declared war on the United States and Great Britain.

The supreme test for Yugoslavia came on March 25, 1941. On that day the pro-German government of Regent Prince Paul joined the Axis Three-Power Pact. The Serbian people were passionately opposed to this move. *Encouraged by Great Britain and the United States*, the Yugoslav Army under the Serbian General Simovich carried out a coup d'état on the morning of March 27. Prince Paul was deposed, the pro-German government overthrown, and King Peter, who was then seventeen years old, ascended the throne. The Yugoslav government in exile was thus born in an anti-Axis revolt with Anglo-American support and guarantees.

It is a historic fact that the Croats did not join in this national revolt. Even Louis Adamic, himself a Slovene and violently pro-Croat, admits that the collapse of Yugoslavia was probably "not a wholly unwelcome occurrence" to many of the Croats and Slovenes who are today leading Tito's Partisans.[31] It is no less a historic fact that Yugoslav Communists and those under their sway would not join the fight against Nazism would not aid what Communists everywhere then called an "imperialist war" – until Hitler invaded Russia.

It was among Communists, dissident Croat Ustashi groups, and guerrilla bands roaming the countryside that the Partisan movement was born after Stalin was forced into the war by the German invasion. Tito later assumed leadership of this movement upon direct orders from an All-Slav Committee organized in Moscow.[32] As Leigh White, American correspondent who spent the crucial months of 1941-42 in the Balkans, put it: "For my part, I find it difficult to forget that Croatian Communists. . . . refused to fight for their country until the Germans invaded Russia."[33]

As a summary of the fratricidal war now going on, it might be enough to say that General Mihailovich is a Serb and a democrat while Marshal Tito is a Croat and Communist. But the picture is far more complex. The Balkans, as I have already pointed out elsewhere, have always been and remain today, pawns in the hands of the Great Powers.

On March 27, 1941, millions of Serbians, defying the victorious Nazi war machine, and without the remotest hope of aid, declared war on Germany. Winston Churchill stated in the House of Commons at the time that "the Yugoslav nation has found its soul." Hitler took a terrible revenge. At dawn on April 6, 1941, he launched an attack that made shambles of Yugoslavia's cities, towns and valleys. His Hungarian[34], Italian, Bulgarian, and Croatian

31   Louis Adamic, My Native Land (New York: Harper & Bros., 1945).

32   See Slavianie, official organ of Moscow's "All-Slav" Committee, Aug., 1942.

33   Leigh White, The Long Balkan Night (New York: Charles Scribner's
       Sons, 1944), p. 462.

34   The night before the German attack, Hungarian Prime Minister Paul Teleki committed
       suicide. Hungary did occupy Voivodina – a part of Hungary until 1918 – a week
       later,when Yugoslavia after was dissolved and Croatia became an independent state.

satellites joined in an orgy of murder. After twenty-one days, the country lay inert, broken, apparently dead.

Then, unexpectedly and dramatically, the name of General Draja Mihailovich and the deeds of his Chetniks began to thrill the anti-Axis world. When Mihailovich, after the Nazi invasion, retired to the mountains of Montenegro to organize his guerrilla forces, he was only an obscure officer in the Yugoslav Army. The government-in-exile in London knew little about him. At first the whole idea of guerrilla resistance seemed fantastic. The Germans regarded it as irresponsible romanticism very Balkan, picturesque, but futile. But by June 1941 they changed their minds. Engagements involving thousands of men on each side took place between Axis troops and Chetniks.

"Whether Mihailovich or Axis commanders provoked the earliest encounters," writes Adamic, Tito's most vociferous spokesman in America, "is not clear... But, he adds, "My guess is that many of them just happened." He admits, however, that Mihailovich was "killing Nazis, Italian fascists, and quislings right along," and that Mihailovich's chief aim was to prepare Yugoslavia's population for the day when the Western anti-Axis powers, Britain and America, would finally be ready to invade Europe."[35]

Following the Roosevelt-Churchill-Stalin conference at Teheran, Foreign Secretary Anthony Eden committed Great Britain to all-out military support of the Partisans. It was a foregone conclusion that the United States, following the British lead and at the insistence of Russia, would subsequently recognize Tito's "government." This Roosevelt did at the Crimea Conference.

The official explanation offered for this repudiation of the erstwhile Allied hero Mihailovich and his glorified Chetniks is that the Partisans were engaging a large number of German divisions whereas the Chetniks remained apparently inactive. What makes the explanation exceedingly curious is that Mihailovich had been engaging the Germans only in minor skirmishes

35   Adamic, op. cit., p. 48.

and conserving his main forces *upon the counsel of British military advisers who joined him soon after he had organized his Chetniks.*

This was not an exceptional policy for Yugoslavia but part of the over-all Allied policy for the underground movements in Nazi-held Europe. The resistance movements in France, the Low Countries, Norway, Poland and everywhere else were repeatedly cautioned not to undertake futile and premature military action; to limit themselves to harassment of the enemy while waiting for explicit orders to strike with full force.

It was a policy openly and vigorously attacked by Russia which demanded immediate action regardless of cost. The Soviet attitude was part of Moscow's larger demand for a second front at a time when Anglo-American leaders considered invasion of Europe not only premature but a risk which might throw victory into Hitler's lap. General Mihailovich, taking his orders from the Yugoslav Government in London, which in turn was co-ordinating its action with those of Britain and the United States, sat tight. He would not allow himself to be forced by Communist pressure into a hopeless adventure against the wishes of the Allied High Command.

We must understand the original quarrel between the Chatniks and the Partisans in terms of this conflict around the second front. Then we begin to understand, also, that the Chetniks have been punished and outlawed precisely because of their loyalty to the common cause.

Tito emerged as leader of the "revolutionary" Partisans only after June 22, 1941; that is to say, after Hitler forced Russia out of neutrality by invading her soil. Immediately the Moscow emissary insisted upon all-out action against the Germans, without thought of cost, to relieve pressure on Russia. The Chetnik leaders decided to follow Allied policy and explicit British advice in conserving their main forces until the Allied invasion of the Balkans projected for the future would make them most useful.

It was, in fact, this refusal of General Mihailovich to open a second front in the Balkans that served as signal for the powerful Soviet propaganda machine throughout the world to commence its campaign against Mihailovich.

Cables from London, Cairo, and Berne, Switzerland, began to stream into the United States with the startling charges that Mihailovich was a fascist and a Nazi collaborator. The principal disseminators of this information were the communist New York *Daily Worker*, the Soviet-controlled Inter-Continent News Agency, and the Free Yugoslav radio station in Russia. At the same time pro-Tito propagandists in the United States became extremely active in spreading these rumors against Mihailovich and his Chetniks.

The extraordinary success of the campaign may be judged by the manner in which the former hero is now smeared as a matter of routine in newspapers here that have no means of knowing the facts but merely fall in unthinkingly with prevailing fashion. Military actions carried out by the Chetniks have been attributed via Russia to Tito's forces. Mihailovich's frantic cables to the United States urging corrections, literally scores of them, have been ignored. His angry denials of collaborating with the Nazis have somehow failed to reach the press. Here, for instance, is one cable, dated October 6, 1943, from Mihailovich which never reached the American people though it was made available to the press here by Yugoslav representatives:

Woods and Mountains of Yugoslavia – The Communist radio station Free Yugoslavia informed the world, and this information was reproduced by the London radio, that the Partisan formations destroyed the bridges on the railway Uzice-Visegrad- Sarajevo, frustrating thus for a long time the use of this important railroad linking Serbia with Bosnia and the Adriatic Sea. A representative of the Democratic Yugoslav News Agency saw General Miroslav Trifunovich, Commander of Serbia in the Yugoslav Army commanded by General Mihailovich, from whom he received the following statement concerning the above Communist propaganda:

"I can tell you only this the four bridges of the railroad Uzice – Visegrad were destroyed by our units under my own command and in the presence of Brigadier Armstrong, Chief of the British Military Mission. . . . This happened at the beginning of October 1943. On the seventh of the same month, we took a 150 meter long railway bridge over the Drina River after thirteen hours of hard fighting because the bridge was guarded by one German and two Croatian quisling companies, protected by twenty-five block houses on both sides of the river. The bridge was taken by assault and using only hand grenades. We lost twenty-one dead and thirty wounded. This operation and the complete destruction of the bridge was executed in the presence of Brigadier Armstrong and Lieutenant Colonel Siez, Chief of the American Military Mission."

Like a hundred other messages from headquarters, this information was brushed aside by the American press. The credit for that Chetnik victory remained Tito's, and became one more tool used to undermine Mihailovich.

On October 22, 1943 that is to say, before the Teheran Conference Churchill's Ambassador to Yugoslavia, Mr. Ralph Stevenson, held a conference in Cairo with war correspondents accredited with the Allied High Command during which he discussed the internal situation in Yugoslavia.

"All the accusations of the Partisans that is a fascist, collaborating with the occupation forces," he said, "are completely unfounded and spring entirely from the efforts of the Partisans to blacken Mihailovich among the Serbian population and frustrate him when the moment comes to seize power in the country. General Mihailovich from the beginning of the struggle has loyally collaborated with the Allies, and no one can doubt his loyalty as "an ally or as the representative in the country of the Yugoslav Government."

But a year later, in October 1944, Winston Churchill had to make another of his pilgrimages to Moscow after a preliminary conference with Roosevelt in September. Things were not going too well with the British Empire, and once again Stalin made the great Prime Minister eat humble pie. Upon his return to London, Churchill made a public declaration that at his conference at the Kremlin he and Stalin had considered Black Sea as well as Mediterranean interests and that it all ended in "agreement."

Bulgaria and Rumania, being on the Black Sea, were recognized as part of the Soviet "sphere of influence." In this, to be sure, Churchill was merely reaffirming the decisions reached at the Teheran Conference (and to all intents and purposes reaffirmed by Roosevelt and the Prime Minister at Yalta). But Greece, as a Mediterranean nation, was included in the British orbit. Churchill would have liked a compromise on Yugoslavia and the Adriatic but apparently Stalin did not agree.

Thus in order to salvage Greece for the Empire's life line the Prime Minister had to sacrifice the rest of the Balkans. The prospect of Russia's becoming a Mediterranean power is so terrifying to Churchill that he was prepared to make important sacrifices. The irony of it, however, is that his sacrifices were self-defeating. In turning the Balkans over to Stalin, he gave Russia a preponderant position even in the Mediterranean.

The aged Prime Minister, who will undoubtedly go down in history as one of the greatest war leaders of modern times, must have swallowed hard when he was forced to stand up before the House of Commons on January 18, 1945 and announce:

"We have no special interest in the political regime which prevails in Yugoslavia. Few people in Britain, I imagine, are going to be more cheerful or downcast because of the future constitution of Yugoslavia. However, because the King and the Royal Yugoslavian Government took refuge with us at the time of the German invasion, we have acquired a certain duty toward the Government and people on the other side of the Adriatic which can only be discharged in a correct and formal manner, such as, for instance, would be provided by a plebiscite."

"I am the earliest outside supporter of Marshal Tito. It is more than a year since in this House I extolled his guerrilla virtues to the world. Some of my best friends, and Major Randolph Churchill, are there with him and his forces now. It is my earnest hope he may prove to be the savior and unifier of his country as he undoubtedly at this time is its undisputed master."

"Recently Bulgaria and Rumania have passed under the control of Soviet military authorities, and Russians and Russian-controlled armies are in direct contact with Yugoslavia. As we feared that there might be misunderstanding and contrary policies between us and the Soviet Government about Yugoslavia, the Foreign Secretary reached at Moscow an understanding with Marshal Stalin by which our two countries pursued a joint policy in those regions after constant discussions. This agreement raised no question of division of territory or spheres of interest after the war. It aimed only at avoidance, during these critical days, of friction between the Great Allies."

"In practice I exchange telegrams on behalf of the British Government personally with Marshal Stalin about difficulties which arise and about what is the best thing to do. We keep President Roosevelt constantly informed."

"In pursuance of our joint policy we encouraged the making of an agreement between the Tito Government which, with Russian assistance, has now installed itself at Belgrade, and the Royal Government of Yugoslavia which is seated in London and recognized by us, and I believe, by all the Powers of the United Nations. Marshal Stalin and the British Government consider that agreement on the whole to be wise."

"We believe that the arrangements of the Tito-Subasich agreement are the best that can be made for the immediate future of Yugoslavia..."

"King Peter II agrees in principle with the arrangement, but he makes certain reservations. The nature and effect of this is, I understand, at present under discussion. I should hesitate to prophesy or promise how all this will turn out, but under all circumstances and having regard to the chaotic conditions arising out of this war, I do not see what else except this agreement could be done by the British Government and the USSR to contribute what they can to bringing about the widest possible measure of agreement among the Yugoslavs and to insure that those issues should not be a cause of friction among the Allies."

"It is a matter of days within which a decision must be reached upon these matters and if we were so unfortunate as not to be able to obtain consent of King Peter, the matter, in fact, would have to go ahead, his assent being presumed."

The King's point of view, as I understood it, was that he was anxious about becoming responsible while he had no power for any severities which might take place in his country before a plebiscite decided whether it was to be a monarchy or a republic. Such scruples must be respected but they cannot necessarily in these times indefinitely prevent the march of events.

At this time the bloody events in Greece were taking their toll in innocent human lives, and Winston Churchill was fighting with his back to the wall not only for his beloved Empire but also for his very political future.

3.

I was in Cairo when Tito's new Minister, a Croat by the name of Milan Martinovich, arrived in the Egyptian capital. Immediately he ordered all Yugoslavs in the Middle East since 1941 to prepare for their return to Yugoslavia. Most of these Yugoslavs are military men who came to the aid of Great Britain in the crucial days of El Alamein. For many months they fought alongside the British and Americans. Now, as reward, they had a choice of going back to Yugoslavia where, as supporters of Mihailovich, they would face Tito's firing squads or internment in British concentration camps in the, Middle East. This, to be sure, would not be the first time that the Allies, bowing to Moscow's wishes, would jail pro-Allied and democratic Yugoslavs.

I first heard of the Yugoslav "refugee" camp at El Shatt, near the Suez Canal from a representative of UNRRA, the United Nations Relief and Rehabilitation Administration. Everyone in Cairo who was interested in refugee relief spoke to me with indignation about this infamous camp. Finally, fortified by a dozen documents and permits from Sir Matthews, the head of the British Middle-Eastern Relief and Rehabilitation Administration, I braved the Egyptian sun, the sands of the Sinai Desert, and the Egyptian railroads, and went out to speak to the Yugoslavs of El Shatt. To visit the camp I had to cover practically the same ground traversed by Moses six thousand years earlier. Now I was able to appreciate why my ancestors were eager to return to the fleshpots of Egypt.

Beyond the Suez Canal a hundred square miles of bare desert were studded with primitive tents housing about 17,000 Yugoslav citizens. Everywhere I saw ragged and starved looking women and children, but there was a surprisingly large number of young men, most of whom wore caps decorated with the Communist red star.

At first young Major John Langman, the British director of the camp, took me for an American bore who came to satisfy his craving for things exotic. When he discovered that I spoke a little Serbo-Croatian, he grew alarmed. He began to hurry me. By this time, however, I had already spoken to many of the inmates of El Shatt and had formed a fairly good picture of the camp.

In May 1944, the United States and Great Britain still recognized the Yugo-slav government of which General Mihailovich was Minister of War, yet the El Shatt Camp was run entirely by Tito. It had what Major Langman called local autonomy. Thus, while the United States and Great Britain were supplying the food and other physical needs of the camp, the political committee actually running El Shatt was appointed directly by Marshal Tito who was in charge of the spiritual education of the 17,000 inmates. No representative of the then legal Yugoslav government could enter the camp.

What disturbed me most during my visit to El Shatt was the question: What were these unfortunates doing in the Sinai Desert? Most of them were Dal-matian peasants and as such not in any greater danger than most of the non-Jewish population of Yugoslavia. With shipping space scarce and with thousands of people whose lives were in immediate danger waiting to be rescued, why were these Yugoslavs first shipped by Tito's boats to Italy and thence by Anglo-American transports to Egypt?

Part of the answer was supplied by Major Langman.

"When Marshal Tito, due to German pressure, was forced to evacuate Dalmatia," he told me, "he was particularly interested in saving the chil-dren so as to be able to bring them up in a democratic spirit. After all, they are the future citizens of Yugoslavia. The women went with the children."

"And what about the young men parading idly in the camp?" I asked. "They could be used much more effectively either in the army or doing some con-structive work."

"Oh, these," replied the Major disdainfully, "they are unreliable elements, Chetniks, who have to be watched. Marshal Tito had the choice of dealing drastically with them or evacuating them. He chose a humanitarian solu-tion."

"Why, then, are they wearing the red star on their caps?"

"They are hypocrites," replied the Major, "hypocrites."

"Why are the British helping Tito keep these people prisoners?" I asked.

The Major was annoyed. I realized that I was no longer welcome at El Shatt. Before parting I spoke to two Catholic priests from Croatia who did all they could under the circumstances to brighten the lives of the inmates. Their last words to me were: "Please help us."

When I returned to Cairo later in November 1 discovered that a new camp, at El Arish, had arisen in the Sinai Desert.

This time the inmates were officers of the Royal Yugoslav Army who had fought alongside the Allies.

"What crime have these people committed?" I asked a British officer. "Why are they confined at El Arish?"

"It is the fault of the new Yugoslav Minister," he replied casually, "a Croat appointed by Tito. He called together several hundred of the Yugoslav officers and ordered them to swear allegiance to Tito. About a hundred complied but the rest refused."

"So you rewarded them for their services to the Allies by placing them at El Arish?"

"What else could we do? You Americans always ask questions but never supply the answers."

Now Tito wants these people in Yugoslavia... "Mihailovich sympathizers," says a dispatch from Cairo, "contend that they dare not return to Yugoslavia for fear of their lives. Thus it would seem that a fairly sizable group of political refugees similar. . . to those who fled Russia after the revolution is in the making. At present there appears to be no internationally recognized authority similar to the League of Nations, which issued special Nansen passports for such persons."[36]

36   New York Times, Feb. 22, 1945.

What will Britain and America, whose rulers at the Yalta Conference so light-heartedly sealed the doom of Yugoslav independence, do to save these heroic men and women from Tito's hangmen?

Yugoslavia alone of the Balkan countries was singled out for special consideration at the Crimea Conference. "We have agreed," said the joint declaration of Roosevelt, Stalin, and Churchill, "to recommend to Marshal Tito and Dr. Subasich that the agreement between them should be put into effect immediately and that a new government should be formed on the basis of the new agreement." Draja Mihailovich, and his thousands of Chetniks were completely forgotten. And then, to add insult to injury, the Big Three also suggested the extension of Tito's hand-tooled "Anti-Fascist" Assembly of National Liberation by including members "of the last Yugoslav *Skupchina* (parliament) who have not compromised themselves by collaboration with the enemy."

By this time all democratic members of the former *Skupchina* were either in exile or in Tito's dungeons, for the trek of the Serbs from the Nazi concentration camps to those of Tito commenced immediately after the Red Army entered Belgrade and installed Tito in power. To implement the Yalta suggestion these men would have to be resurrected or dug out of Tito's prisons.

Even a pro-Tito correspondent like John Chabot Smith has admitted that the Communists of Yugoslavia have been exterminating men and women whose only crime was opposition to Tito's totalitarianism, or merely doubt about his regime. "They are extremists," wrote Mr. Smith. "They are intent on the business of revolution, they liquidate the opposition ruthlessly... . Political commissars keep close watch on everything done by both military and civilian officials. Their spy system is apparently well organized, for people who are seen in the wrong company, or who make unwise remarks in public are promptly punished... Generally speaking, in Partisan-held [Tito] territory, if you are not a Partisan you do not eat – at least you don't eat well."[37]

When Mr. Smith asked one of Tito's lieutenants what the Partisans intended to do about the Yugoslav government after the Germans were driven out, the answer was: "Marshal Tito will decide that when the time comes."

The political pattern of the Partisan government follows that established by Russia in Bulgaria and Rumania: an amalgamation of "converted" fascists and Communists. Two of Tito's closest collaborators are Sulejman Filipovich and Colonel Marko Mesich. Before his "turn" Filipovich was the leader of the fascist *Ustashi* in Bosnia. He has on his hands the blood of many innocent Serbs. At present he is Minister of Supply in Tito's Government, although before his "turn" he was on the list of war criminals compiled by the Yugoslav Government in London. Mesich is a bird of the same feather. In 1941 when Yugoslavia was fighting for its very existence, he deserted and joined the *Ustashi* troops of the quisling Ante Pavelich. For his services on the eastern front against the Russians he was promoted by Ante Pavelich to the rank of lieutenant colonel. After Mesich was captured by the Red Army he had a convenient "change of heart," and today he is one of Tito's closest assistants.

The Yugoslav people, especially the majority of the Serbs, are democratic almost without exception. But the compromise candidate chosen by London and Moscow for Premier of Yugoslavia, after the existing Yugoslav Government had been forced by Churchill to resign, was a Croat named Dr. Ivan Subasich who, significantly enough, was the *Ban* (governor) of Croatia under the pro-Nazi Regent of Yugoslavia, Prince Paul. As Ban, Subasich exercised despotic local power under a pro-fascist central government. There was in Croatia at that time an illegal terrorist organization known as *Seiliachka Zaschita* which was patterned after the Nazi Storm Troopers. This and a similar illegal organization, *Gradjanska Zaschita*, which was confined chiefly to the towns, were legalized by Dr. Subasich in his capacity of *Ban*. Under his protection both terrorist organizations were financed by funds belonging to the State.

But even Subasich was only a stopgap Premier. The immediate purpose of his appointment at that time was to afford Marshal Tito, the future Premier, the political, administrative, and financial support which he needed and could obtain only from Britain and America. This "government," however,

37 John Chabot Smith, "The Cost of Our Jugoslavian Blunder," Saturday Evening Post, Feb. 17, 1945.

could not fulfill its task except in an illusory manner since it was not acceptable to the Serbs who represent a majority in Yugoslavia, nor even to the Croats and Slovenes. It could establish itself in the country only with the help of outside armed forces. Soviet Russia supplied these forces.

The "democracy" in the present Stalin-Tito Yugoslavia was summed up succinctly by Dr. Topalovich, President of the Yugoslav National Committee and of the Social Democratic Party, who recently escaped from his country to Rome:

"All further struggle for democratic liberties of our people ... is useless, since the Allies wish the dictatorship of Tito's Partisans."

"We cannot nor will we fight against our ally – the Red Army – we, who have sacrificed over a million men in our resistance to the Germans and who are in our sentiments so closely bound to the Allied cause..."

"Our Allies should take steps – if only for humanitarian reasons – to save from starvation and complete extermination the army of General Mihailovich, now squeezed between the Red Army and the Germans.... Our political situation is hopeless and can be improved only by a speedy defeat of Germany or by a change in British policy... It would be most desirable and most useful to put General Mihailovich's troops under Allied Command immediately and employ them according to Allied plans."

When the Russians invaded the Balkans, General Mihailovich mobilized several hundred thousand men and offered to assist his Slav brothers. The Russians refused, apparently thinking that their own propaganda about the strength of Tito's Partisans was true. But when the Red Army found itself in a difficult situation in the west valley of the Morava River they gladly accepted the aid of a Chetnik army corps under the command of Colonel Keserovich.

With the aid of the Yugoslavs the Russians were able to capture Kragnievach, the former ammunition center of Yugoslavia, and Krusevach. During the night following the capture of these strategic points, however, the Russians disarmed the Serbian force and imprisoned it. Together with the Serbs they imprisoned an American military mission which had accompanied Colonel Keserovich's corps into action.

Convinced that all further attempts at collaborating with the Russians was hopeless and that Soviet-Tito concentration camps now faced the majority of the Serbs who had already experienced Nazi brutality, Mihailovich ordered his troops to disband. He sought to avoid fighting against an ally even though Tito's Russian backers were bent on his destruction. However, he authorized those wishing to remain with him to withdraw to the west. About 70,000 officers and men of the Yugoslav Army, and 30,000 democratic and liberal intellectuals chose to follow him. In the middle of the bitter Serbian winter they made their trek across the snow-covered mountains together with the Chetnik leader.

The tragic mess into which misguided Allied diplomacy has plunged the Balkans is perhaps summed up in one piece of Homeric irony: Colonel Veltcheff, the Moscow-made Bulgarian Minister of War, ordered the First Bulgarian Army in southern Serbia to join Tito's Partisans and to march with them north of the Morava Valley "to liberate Serbia and to establish liaison with the Red Army." To savor the irony, we should note first, that Veltcheff is an implacable foe of Great Britain, the United States, and democracy in any form; second; that the Bulgarian forces to whom he addressed the order had occupied southern Serbia together with the Germans when Bulgaria was still at war with the Allies though at peace with Russia.

Thus the very troops which had massacred Serbs during four years under Hitlerite orders Bulgarians, Albanians, Croat *Ustashi*, and Italians now began to "liberate Serbia." Under Tito's supreme command and wearing the red star of Bolshevism, these same troops now proceeded to massacre some of the troops of Mihailovich's army who had failed to withdraw to the west fast enough. The weapons they used were in large part made and paid for by Americans and delivered through lend-lease, directly or by way of Russia.

I have heard many eyewitness accounts of Tito's capture of Belgrade. Despite the fantastic number of men that were claimed to be under his command when the Russian troops finally entered the Yugoslav capital, the Partisan commanders had to be transported from Montenegro by British planes. But when it came to butchering defenseless Serbian officers, intellectuals, and just plain peasants who would not pay homage to Moscow's *Gauleiter* of the Balkans, Tito was right on the spot. It was at his insistence that the Anglo-American military missions had been withdrawn from those territories in order to eliminate embarrassing witnesses.

Following the "liberation" of Belgrade, Tito with the aid of the Russian GPU (now NKVD[38]) immediately established a secret police Section for the Defense of the People, also known through "liberated" Yugoslavia as the dreaded *Ozna* and appointed a Serbian quisling priest, Lieutenant Colonel Vlada Zechevitch as its director. Almost at once lists of democratic persons were compiled "war criminals" in Soviet parlance and the bloody purges commenced. To facilitate the purges a curfew was ordered by the Red Army at 8 P.M. (instead of 10 P.M. as it was under the Nazis). After this hour the *Ozna* would systematically visit the homes of "marked" men and women and round them up for execution without trial[39]. The number of men and women thus executed was estimated by some competent observers among the Allied diplomats in Cairo to have totaled 40,000. Many Serbs who escaped execution were deported to Siberia.

Simultaneously, with the aid of *Ozna*, Tito began to indoctrinate the Yugoslav masses. Groups to instruct the young were formed under the United Alliance of Anti-Fascist Youth of Yugoslavia – actually the Young Communist League – and children were organized in pioneer formations similar to the Pioneer groups of Soviet Russia.

True to Communist tradition, propaganda is one of Tito's strongest weapons. Four daily newspapers are now published in Belgrade: *Borba*, official organ of the Communist Party, edited by one of Tito's most ruthless lieutenants, General Djilas; *Glas*, mouthpiece of the National Liberation Front; *Omladina*, of the United Alliance of Anti-Fascist Youth; and *Politika*, which is edited by Vladislav Ribnikar, the National Liberation Front's Minister of Information. In addition, strict censorship has been introduced and criticism of the regime is punished by imprisonment or death.

In an attempt to make himself more popular with the Yugoslav people, Tito places much emphasis on parades, displays, slogans, and posters. Every public place is forced to display large portraits of Tito and Stalin. Through

38   Later KGB (Ed.)

39   In addition, approximately 30 thousand Hungarian civilians were summarily executed in Voivodina. See: Cseres,T.: Serbian Vendetta in Bacska, www.hungary.com/corvinus

loudspeakers supplied by Soviet Russia and installed on street corners in Belgrade, almost as much praise and obsequious adulation is now showered upon the Yugoslav Marshal as upon his Russian superior in the Kremlin.

Terror grips the whole country. In Partisan concentration camps in Serbia the guards still wear their old *Ustashi* uniforms. Although true war criminals and murderers of the defenseless Serbian population, these fascists received immunity when they joined Tito's Partisans.

The full story of Yugoslavia and the struggle of its people for liberation will, I am certain, be told some day. It is as fantastic as it is tragic. In addition to our rescued aviators there were a number of other American officers with Mihailovich when he was fighting for us and with us. They know the truth. They know, too, that many of the communiqués in the American press about Tito's successes were not victories over the Germans but over the poorly armed forces of Mihailovich. Let us hope that eventually these Americans will be in a position to tell the whole truth. In the meantime, the plight of Yugoslavia is desperate.

 Mihailovich appealed to the Allied world through a recent tragic message to his friends in this country on behalf of the dwindling Yugoslav forces of freedom.

"The army and people are naked, barefoot, and hungry. Unless help is given all the Serbs will perish. In what way did the innocent Serbian people sin against God and their Allies that they should be so punished? Is there nowhere a friend who will raise his voice? The Serbians would rather perish than submit to Tito's command or embrace Communism."

Much more, however, is at stake in this vast and grim Yugoslav drama than the fate of the shattered forces of Mihailovich. Democracy throughout Europe is at stake and a just and lasting peace.

In March 1945, abiding by the decisions of the Yalta declaration, Tito took the final logical step: he appointed himself Premier and Minister of National Defense of the Yugoslav "government," with Dr. Ivan in the unenviable position of Foreign Minister. At the same time the Yugoslav State

Commission on "war criminals," in a broadcast over the Moscow radio, declared Draja Mihailovich a "war criminal."[40]

Once more, the triumph of the lie.

40   Despite international protests, Mihailovich was executed in 1946 in Yugoslavia.

Romania

Stephen Bonsal; 1920:

Excerpts from *Suppliers and Supplicants: The Little People at Versailles*, Port Washington, NY: Kennikat Press, Inc., 1946.

BEETLE-BROWED BRATIANU AND THE RUMANIANS

January 10, 1919

Duly announced with a flourish of trumpets over the telephone from Rumanian headquarters, M. Goga came to see me this morning. Fortunately I had heard that a man of this name, the "bard of Transylvania," was expected to join Bratianu [prime minister] and bear testimony to the pure Rumanianism of the people who dwell in that beautiful mountain country where the Telekis and the other Hungarian magnates have lorded it for centuries and carved out for themselves quite sizeable estates which, not unnaturally, they are extremely reluctant to give up.

Goga said what he had to say and he said it beautifully. Transylvania was the cradle of his race. Here on these mountain slopes and in these sunlit valleys the scattered remnants of the Roman legions had taken refuge from the Dacian hordes. He mentioned Varus and Trajan, the Latin leaders, as glibly as we talk about Joffre and Foch. Here these refugees had found safe harbor and prospered while Mother Rome sank into insignificance and decay. Then, alas, into this paradise where the Christian faith and brotherly love held sway there came another horde of invaders, the Moslems under their green banners; and the war for land and religion was waged with varying fortunes for generations.

"At times we fought alone," explained Goga, "at others the Christians of the West aided us – but not unselfishly. In the last campaign, Magyar lords fought at our side, but when the war was won they parceled out our lands and our peasants to suit themselves. This is the history, the sad history of my people," insisted Goga, "and our day of redemption only dawned when Wilson sent his soldiers across the seas and liberated Europe." That was his story, and it was perhaps a fair one of the land of his birth; but of course I fail to do justice to the poetic prose in which it was unfolded.

I told Goga that America had no special Transylvania policy, but that I had no doubt that his aspirations were fully covered by the Wilsonian doctrine of the self-determination of peoples. "We can now take care of ourselves," he went on. "We have rifles and we know how to use them. 'We do want medicines and perhaps a little food. The Germans swept out our storehouses and devastated our farms, and the Russians who came to our aid brought us the plague of typhus. Our need for medicines is great, but Bratianu has already spoken to Mr. Hoover about this and he has promised to do what is possible." With this I thought the interview was at an end, but suddenly the poet darted off on another tangent.

"I came to Paris in a roundabout way," he said, "and with good reason; throughout the war my voice had been raised against them, so when I was selected to represent my province of Greater Rumania at the Conference I had to avoid the lands of the Germans and the Magyars. So, I floated down the Danube and across the Black Sea to Constantinople. There I shipped for France, but not for Marseilles as I had hoped. My ship was bound for Bordeaux and the captain would not deviate from his course. This meant a delay of a week, but what a fortunate delay it was! I now sailed through the Pillars of Hercules, and as I looked our across the boundless Western Ocean a song straight from my heart fell from my lips. It was my salute to America from where our salvation had come. It was an ode of Thanksgiving to the American people, and when it is perfected I shall send it to you."

[The poem never came[1]. Perhaps it was never "perfected." The atmosphere that now prevailed in Paris was not helpful to expressions of gratitude. In

---

1   As Repington noted in his book, "After the War": "Roumanians are not remarkable for keeping promises or appointments." (p. 327)

fact they all went out the window. Years later Goga, the poet-politician, became Prime Minister of Greater Rumania (1937). He made a mess of his difficult job, and his ministry that was distinguished for anti-Semitism soon fell. So Goga, my charming visitor, died, it is said, of a broken heart and was carried back to his beloved hills by a cortege which included all the poets of his land.]

All this was interesting, but I was a hard-driven man and my desk was piled mountain high with prosaic communications that had to be attended to, so perhaps the gesture of impatience which I now permitted myself was pardonable.

March (undated), 1919

One of President Wilson's marked dislikes is his aversion for Bratianu, the beetle-browed prime minister of Rumania with the notorious Byzantine background. Up to the present he has avoided the *tête à tête* with him which the Bucharest leader so ardently desires. He puts him off with messages through House. "Tell him," says the President, "that the frontiers we are tracing are temporary, certainly not final, and that later on, in a calmer moment and informed by longer study, the League of Nations will intervene to adjust provisional settlements which may be found to be imperfect."

Last week, however, the Colonel said to me: "Bratianu insists upon an interview with me and I do not think it wise to put him off any longer. I have every reason to think it will be stormy and I want you to be present. Misu, the Rumanian Ambassador, is coming with him, but I prefer to have you interpret."

The interview was more stormy and the language of the Bucharest "Bull," as he is sometimes called, was even more outrageous than had been anticipated. Little Misu did what he could to soften the words of his chief, and in asides to me was often apologetic, but it is difficult for a mere ambassador to stand up against his chief, a prime minister.

Bratianu's blast began by a violent and yet by no means an untrue account of how after entering the war Rumania had been let down by the "promising" Allies. "Solemn pledges were given us that a great Russian army would come to our aid, and that, as the Germans would be held by intensive operations on the Western Front, the invading army of Mackensen would not be a force larger than we could cope with. Now what happened? The Grand Duke did not move, and on the Western Front the Allies went to sleep. An unholy calm settled down on that sector, and Mackensen drew from there all the divisions he needed to overwhelm our gallant resistance. But mark you, we have learned our lesson; it has cost us the complete devastation of our country; so for its restoration we are demanding naturally something more substantial than verbal pledges. We know now what these are worth."

After excoriating Briand and Lloyd George (as to Clemenceau he was reserved), suddenly the Rumanian scold went after Hoover. "He will not permit us to have loans, or food, except in return for oil-land concessions. Without these we can expect no help, he says. I have been advised that no assistance of any kind will be forthcoming unless special privileges are granted our Jewish minority. And the American Jews, bankers and big businessmen, seem to think that our country is to be turned over to them for exploitation. Their agents in the thin disguise of food organization officials are on hand and they are earmarking industries and concessions which they must have, they say, otherwise no assistance can be expected. Once for all I have come to say that these people may go to Palestine, or to Hell for all I care, but I shall not let them settle down upon my country, devouring locusts that they are!"

This went on for three quarters of an hour. It should in all fairness be admitted Bratianu was in a nervous condition, although not "concerned in liquor," for which he should not perhaps be held responsible. Several times Misu intervened with placating words, but without success. He, however, whispered to me: "His Excellency has had very had news from Rumania in the last few days..." Then, shrinking from the fierce frowns of his chief, he stopped short, and so the details of the bad news were not forthcoming.

Suddenly the Colonel's patience was exhausted and he ended the interview with, "I think you will admit that I have listened to you very patiently. If you furnish me your charges in writing I can assure you that they will be carefully investigated and answered. And now, Mr. Prime Minister, I bid you good day."

Misu was most embarrassed; throughout the tirade of his chief he made deprecatory gestures and now and again he had murmured, ''Yes, but..." Evidently he wished to pour oil on the stormy waters, but all his efforts only tended to infuriate "Bull" Bratianu. Shouting, "I shall file with you a memorandum dealing with the matter, officially," Bratianu bounced out of the room while little Misu slunk after him with an apologetic smile.

After a moment's reflection the Colonel said: "I must ask you to make a record of what has been said. It will furnish a basis of comparison with the Prime Minister's charges when they are put in writing. When, and if, this is done, in justice to Hoover we must make them a matter of official record. I think Bratianu, when comes to himself, will hesitate and that the formal charges will never be filed. In the meantime I must ask you to type out what he has said and give it to me for the confidential file. It must be 'graveyard,' even to our stenographers."

The result was I made almost a night of it. Never expert in typing, I had not tapped on my old-fashioned Blick for months. It was near morning when I concluded the unusual task. My hatred of Bratianu was unbounded. At sight of me little Misu always slunk away. My transcript was placed in the confidential files and as we say in conference circles "the incident is closed."

The memorandum that Bratianu agreed to file never came. Perhaps on second thought he never wrote it. More likely, however, little Misu intercepted it. That is one of the things that a wise ambassador sometimes gets away with. On the following day House advised Hoover in general terms of what the Prime Minister had said. He received it with the most perfect equanimity. "Bratianu is a liar and a horse thief – that's all there is to it." Then as an afterthought. "I hope God will help the Rumanians – I cannot."

[Months later Bratianu indeed had a short day of popularity. When his armies invaded Hungary and flouted the veto of the Supreme War Council, many delegates of countries who would have liked to do the same, had they dared, cheered Bratianu – at least under their breath. And there was something in Bratianu's contention at this moment. "We are looting Hungary, it is true," he said. "But we are only taking back what the Hungarian regiments stole from us when as an important contingent of Mackensen's army they invaded our country.]

Bratianu is undoubtedly the most unpopular of the prime ministers who are assembled here. He is not, however, the only one of the statesmen present who during the war fell between two stools and flirted with the opposing forces, but it would seem that he fell more awkwardly than the others and that his flirtations were the most shameless. And it should be said that his shortcomings are emphasized and perhaps magnified by the diplomatic and social activities of his adroit rival, Take Ionescu, whose prophecies as to the outcome of the war have been justified. He is having a splendid time running around and saying, "I told you so! But Bratianu..."

Much of the correspondence in regard to the entrance of Rumania into the war is still closely guarded in the secret files, but on the facts that are known, Bratianu's policy, whether in power or out, was anything but adroit. It landed his unfortunate country in disasters which many think might have been avoided. At the outbreak his sympathies seem to have been with the Entente, but there was the Hohenzollern king who had to be "managed," and the burly Rumanian statesman had quite a soupçon of the Italian *sacro egoismo* in his composition. Ionescu traveled up and down the country shouting, "Our rôle is that of an unconditional ally of the democracies. We must not drive a bargain. We should and can rely on the appreciation of our allies when the victory is won.

Not so, decidedly not so, Bratianu. He wanted military guarantees and blueprints of territories to be annexed in advance of mobilization. He blew hot and he blew cold, and always at unhappy moments. His timing was always bad. He fascinated the Queen Marie who is now here bringing her undeniable charm to bear upon some of the more susceptible statesmen. As a granddaughter of Queen Victoria, she always thought as an English woman, and Bratianu assured her that she "would come out of the war as Empress of all the Rumanians wherever they were seated."

In the early years of the struggle, when the adherence of Rumania could have been of great assistance to whichever of the powers that secured it, the great talking point and the preferred prize of all the Rumanians was the possession of Transylvania – "The cradle of our race," says the Queen Marie (the daughter of Edward VII's brother and a Russian Grand Duchess). Czernin, who had served as minister in Bucharest and understood Rumanian aspirations fully when he took charge of the Austro-Hungarian foreign office, certainly toyed with the idea of ceding some districts of

Transsylvania to the Rumanians as a bribe – to keep them in line – but the Hungarian Premier Tisza was strongly opposed; the project came to nought, and all thought of it was abandoned when the Central Powers made their break through at Görlitz and captured Warsaw. The result of the shilly-shallying and at times bare-faced bargaining was that Rumania joined her forces with the Western Powers just as Russia began to disappear as an important factor on the Eastern Front. Three months later Field Marshal Mackensen was in Bucharest and in possession of the coveted oil fields.

When his armies were defeated and his country almost completely overrun, in the opinion of the military men of the Supreme War Council, Bratianu's behavior was neither loyal nor intelligent. They assert he capitulated too soon and bargained too promptly with the Germans; they insist that the remnants of the Rumanian armies were in fine fighting trim and had they but stood up they could have held in Rumania many, very many, of the German divisions which were then needed so desperately on the Western Front. So, rightly or wrongly, Bratianu is charged with entering the war too late and of having surrendered too soon, a difficult position from which only a diplomat of great tact could have extricated himself. I however, he plumes himself upon not signing the Treaty of Bucharest. Take Ionescu is on the worst of terms with the Bratianu group now in power, but he represents, as president of the National Council of United Rumania, the will of his people. At least that is his claim. He is a voluble talker and inclined to boast about his four pre-war prophecies all of which came true. "It is a too perfect score," I remind him and shut him off, a proceeding which he accepts with the most perfect good nature. He is strong for the League, however. He calls the Covenant the Fifth Gospel and American participation the hope, the only hope, of the European world.

Undated - probably March 6, 1919

The event of the week, with all its social, political, and economic repercussions, is the expected arrival any day now of the beautiful Queen Marie of Rumania. 'While like almost everyone else she comes a-borrowing, the ceremonial officer has decided that in homage to protocol some important member of our delegation should be at the station to greet her, to see that the red carpet is worthy of royal feet and properly spread. Frazier and I discussed the matter without any particular personal enthusiasm and we decided that a flip of a coin would decide who should perform this diplomatic chore. Gordon Auchincloss, son-in-law and secretary of our Colonel, overheard this conversation, at least in part, and, "getting us wrong," advised the Colonel that in his judgment the most beautiful woman in Europe should not be greeted on her arrival in "gay Paree" by men whose hair was gray or at least on the "graying side." And he offered to go to the station himself.

This remark started quite an uproar in the "family." It was promptly quelled by the Colonel deciding that as the Queen was coming to borrow money for her bankrupt country and food for her unfortunate subjects we might well await her appearance at the Crillon. He was confident she would not fail to put in appearance, and soon.

So the affair was settled by our chief with his usual wisdom, but the remark about the graying hair rankled. Then a copy of the *Temps* and an article which spread over several columns arrived which exalted us and gave sweet revenge. It was written by Mentchikof, the great scientist, biologist, and anthropologist, and the present head of the Pasteur Institute. He said that for some years now (in the midst of the greatest war in history) he had indulged himself in an intensive and extensive study of mammals. One of the discoveries lie had made was that the superior animals of the fauna family, with the passing of the years and the coming of age, turned gray, while the inferior animals "moulted." We placed many copies of this informative article on Auchincloss' desk and others came to him by mail and special messengers.

And was he angry! The joke, at least from our viewpoint, is that while A. is quite young and, as some think, even juvenile, his head is as bare of hair as a billiard ball. He, like other members of the inferior tribes, must have "moulted" years ago. Jests such as these relieve the tension of world-shaking events.

Harry Hill Bandholtz; 1919:

Excepts from *An Undiplomatic Diary – by the American Member of the Inter-Allied Military Mission to Hungary 1919 - 1920*; Columbia University Press, 1933.

CONFIDENTIAL MEMORANDUM

from Mr. Rattigan to Earl Curzon, Followed by a Critique on the Same by General Bandholtz

South-Eastern Europe.   Confidential

Mr. Rattigan to Earl Curzon – [Received October 15.]

Bucharest, October 8, 1919.

My Lord,

The relations between this country and the Allies appear to me to be reaching so serious a stage that I venture to draw the attention of your Lordship to certain aspects of the situation which are perhaps easier to comprehend here than abroad.

I cannot help thinking that an atmosphere has been created by a chain of extraneous circumstances which is obscuring the main issue. It would seem that the first question we should ask ourselves in deciding upon our policy in the Near East is "What are the chief elements of order upon which we can rely to carry out that policy?" Roumania is, in my opinion, the first of such elements, if not the only real one. The fact that the country has for some time past been exploited by a gang of unscrupulous politicians is apt to blind the eyes of the average foreign observer to the real qualities of this people. The mass of the population, and especially the peasant classes, are simple primitive people, with many of the virtues one would expect to find in such conditions as exist here. They are, for example, sober, hard-work-

ing, easily contented, fairly honest, and above all orderly. These character-
istics make Roumania very unfruitful soil for the propagation of the new
communo-socialism. In fact, the peasants are fiercely hostile to the idea of
communism. They are, on the whole, contented with what they have got,
but are determined to retain it, and will oppose with all their any attempt to
pool their small properties. In these circumstances there is little doubt that
Roumania may be relied on to resist any Bolshevist wave which may advance either from the east or west. A glance at the map will show that she
stands a rock in a sea of actual or potential Bolshevism.

If, therefore, it is once admitted that Roumania may be regarded as the most
reliable weapon to our hand for the carrying out of the policy of law and order, based on such ideas as the League of Nations, as opposed to the Bolshevist tendencies the surrounding Slav, and possibly Magyar races, then it
seems to me that we should attempt to do all in our power to conciliate her
and bring her back into the fold from which she in danger of being severed.
She will then inevitably develop to the outpost of Western civilization
against the disruptive tendencies of Bolshevism.

I do not for a moment suggest that Roumania has not brought on herself
much of the treatment with which she has met. Her choice of representatives at the Paris Conference was undoubtedly unfortunate. M. Bratiano is
certainly a patriot, but his character lacks the pliancy necessary for such
work, and he apparently succeeded in exasperating all those with whom he
came in contact by the excessive nature of his claims and the somewhat arrogant and unbending manner in which they were presented. Naturally this
state of things reacted very unfavourably upon the Roumanian case. Moreover, it created an atmosphere of suspicion, in the light of which the actions
Roumania, even when possibly of an innocent character, were looked
upon, not unnaturally, with a grave mistrust.

To take a case in point, presumably no reasonable man would now maintain
that her action in resisting the Hungarian Bolshevists' wanton attack upon
her, defeating it, and pursuing the remnants of the beaten enemy to Budapest, was anything but justifiable. Yet it must be admitted that at first, at any
rate, Conference was inclined to take the view that she was entirely at fault,
and that she was openly flaunting the Allies. Surely nothing could have
been further from the truth. She was in fact accused of disregarding an armistice in which she had taken no part, which had not protected her from

attack, and which the Allies themselves could not have regarded as still in existence by the fact that they had asked for Roumanian co-operation in the event of an Allied advance on Budapest. This is, of course, past history, and I only venture to bring it before your Lordship in illustration of the atmosphere of suspicion to which I have referred above.

From the moment of the Roumanian entry into Hungary proper the question entered on a new phase. Anyone with a knowledge of the Roumanian character could not but be aware of the fact that there would be abuses. As I had the honour to report to your Lordship, I lost no time in endeavouring to impress both on M. Bratiano and the King the vital importance of doing nothing further to shake the confidence of the Allies. I implored them to show all possible moderation in the way of requisitions, &c. I strongly advised M. Bratiano to tell the Conference frankly that, though he accepted the principle of the common property of the Allies in respect to goods taken from the enemy, yet that the critical situation of Roumania obliged him to remove certain quantities of railway material, &c., without waiting for its eventual distribution amongst the Allies. He should at the same time make a full return of all that he had been obliged to take, and ask that it should be set off against the share to be apportioned eventually to Roumania. This M. Bratiano would not agree to do. The real reason for his refusal was that he was well aware of the disfavour with which Roumania was regarded at Paris, and was consequently afraid that any such proposal would be rejected.

Thus the elements of discord and suspicion were sown at the very outset. It must be remembered that there is much of the naughty child in the Roumanian character. Conscious that he is doing wrong, and frightened at the impending punishment, he becomes almost impossible to deal with. In such conditions there is need of the greatest tact to prevent the situation developing along fatal lines. Unfortunately this tact has been throughout conspicuous by its absence. The Allied generals, with all their many qualities, are necessarily inexperienced in diplomacy or statecraft. I venture to state, upon the fullest reaction, that they entered upon their duties in a wrong atmosphere, and that their focus became more and more distorted in the progress of events. They are necessarily dependent to a very large extent for their views on elements frankly inimical the Roumanians. Most of their agents are of course Hungarians. The more the latter perceived that reports hostile to Roumanians were acceptable, the more violent were the reports they made. There was of course sufficient material of a true nature to serve as a basis for these stories. Large numbers the governing classes of Roumania are corrupt, and it was not to be expected that there would not be many abuses. But I cannot help thinking that more could have been done to combat these abuses by a spirit of friendly advice and co-operation than by the methods employed.

I had the honour to recommend in my dispatch No. 168, that, in view of the above circumstances, it might be advisable replace the four Allied Generals by one high civil functionary representing the Conference. This would have the advantage of making the Roumanians understand that the Allies have one single policy. At present it cannot be said that the Allied Generals are entirely "solidaires," and the Roumanians are consequently inclined to try to play off one group against the other. As your Lordship is aware, the French by their attitude here give the Roumanians the impression that are really on their side, but are obliged to yield to Anglo-American pressure. Presumably the same impression is given at Budapest. If one civil representative of the Conference were appointed, and he combined the requisite qualities of tact and firmness, there would be every hope of a speedy and satisfactory solution of the present difficulties. Possibly it might be advisable to appoint a mixed commission, under the presidency of the representative of the Conference, to enquire into the whole question of requisitions. The Roumanian authorities profess themselves ready to place at the disposal of an Allied delegate full information in regard to everything requisitioned or removed by them. They indignantly deny that they are responsible for the starvation of Budapest. On the contrary, in response to the representations made by me on receipt of your telegram No.410, they informed me that they had sent 3,000 wagon loads of cereals to Budapest and two trains of wood fuel to Kecsemet. The 3,000 wagon loads of cereals had been requisitioned from the district between the Theiss and the new Roumanian frontier – a district which, it is alleged, is overflowing with food – and had been promised to the Transylvanians and paid for by them. In spite of the protests of the latter, these cereals had been sent to Budapest. With regard to the wood they informed me with some truth that Bucharest itself is almost completely destitute of wood fuel, but that in spite of this they had handed over the two trainloads in question to the Hungarian authorities.

There appears to be almost a deadlock in regard to certain questions at Budapest. For example, the Roumanian Government claim that they have an absolute right to co-operation in the formation of a Hungarian Government in so far as to ensure that no Government hostile to themselves is installed. Again, with regard to the evacuation of Hungary by their forces, they maintain that what is asked of them is entirely unreasonable. They assert that they themselves are anxious to leave. The Friedrich Government has also expressed a wish for their withdrawal. The Allies, however, they allege, desire them to remain until a Government which is hostile to Roumania is firmly established in the saddle. They maintain that they are most anxious to co-operate loyally with the Allies in settling the Hungarian imbroglio, and that they are ready to extend their support to any Government chosen by the Hungarian people and acceptable to the Allies, provided this Government is calculated to restore order and is not imbued with hostile sentiments towards Roumania. But the Allies can, they say, hardly them to assist a Government which is openly hostile to themselves. With regard to the demand of the Allied Generals the handing over of 10,000 rifles for the use of the Hungarian police force, they say that they had a right to ascertain, before handing over these rifles, what were the numbers of the armed forces in Hungary over and above these 10,000 police troops. To meet the wishes of the Allies they have, however, now waived their objections and delivered the required quantity of rifles.

Whatever the real rights and wrongs of all these questions may be, they would appear capable of adjustment if handled with tact and goodwill on both sides. In Budapest, however, at present these qualities are, as I have said above, conspicuous by their absence. I do not suggest that firmness is not also needed in our relations with the Roumanians. On the contrary, I consider that in dealing with them it is essential to exercise great firmness so as to make them understand that no nonsense will be tolerated. But it should be possible to combine firmness with an attitude of friendliness and goodwill.

In view, therefore, of the considerations which I have ventured to emphasize, I would respectfully suggest that some such solution as that proposed above is necessary, and that the whole question of our policy towards Roumania may be examined from the standpoint of her importance to us as the representative of law and order in this part of the world.

I have, &c.,   F. Rattigan.

Critique by General Bandholtz on Mr. Rattigan's Confidential Memorandum to Earl Curzon

Budapest, Hungary   13th November 1919

There must be something besides mixed metaphor in the Roumanian "atmosphere created by a chain of extraneous circumstances" that obfuscates even strong mentalities. Mr. Rattigan is of the opinion that we should "do all in our power to conciliate" Roumania, but unfortunately he does not go into details as to what further conciliatory offerings should be made, in addition to the great gobs of soft-soap conciliation already thrown at our Ally, and which, to continue mixing metaphors, it has been almost impossible to deliver telegraphically.

Next he accuses M. Bratiano of being a patriot, one who truly loves and serves his fatherland. "Nuff sed." Then in Bratiano's own words, we have a sophistical explanation of the occupation of Budapest, followed by an ingenious defense of the principle of Roumanian seizures, and the condensation of the whole situation into the statement, "It must be remembered that there is much of the naughty child in the Roumanian character. Conscious that he is doing wrong and frightened at the impending punishment, he becomes impossible to deal with." Beautifully euphemistic but decidedly un-John Bull-like. What today would have been the situation in India, Egypt and South Africa if other naughty children had been coddled and cuddled as has been naughty little Roumania with her hands and clothes all daubed with grease from locomotives and machinery stolen from the assets of her Allies, her face smeared with loot jam and her belly distended from gorging on supplies that her Allies will have to replace? What she needed was to have the shingle of common sense vigorously applied to her.

"The Allied Generals, with all their many qualities [fortunately not enumerated and blushes thereby spared] are necessarily inexperienced in diplomacy or statecraft." To which charge, considering the international fame of their accuser, they must plead "guilty" and throw themselves on the mercy of the court. However, when Mr. Rattigan "upon the fullest reflection" locates the Generals' distorted "focus," makes definite statements as to their sources of information, and begins to think, all bets are off, he in effect confesses that he knows as much about the Budapest situation as does an Ygorrot dog-eater about manicuring.

"The Roumanian authorities profess themselves ready to place at the disposal of an Allied delegate full information in regard to everything requisitioned or removed by them. They indignantly deny that they are responsible for the starvation of Budapest. . . . The Allies, however, they allege, desire them to remain until a Government which is hostile to Roumania is firmly established in the saddle," etc., etc., "Can you beat it? 'Nem, nem sabat!'[2]" Verily a personification of Roumanian veracity would make Baron Münchhausen or St. Ananias look like a glorified George Washington.

"It cannot be said that the four Allied Generals are entirely 'solidaires.'" Nevertheless fifty per cent of them, "not mentioning names," have displayed a fine example of solid cohesion. "One high civil functionary," especially one experienced like Mr. Rattigan in diplomacy or statecraft, would have been the solution and he would have had a carnival of effervescence trying to precipitate in himself the closely allied interests of the Allies in the land of Hunyadi János[3].

Passing from the Rattigan solution, which should have been received with paeans of joy, and adopted with alacrity by a brain-fagged Supreme Council, we then come to a well-rounded and fitting climax: "Whatever the real rights and wrongs of all these questions may be, they would appear capable of adjustment if handled with tact and goodwill on both sides. In Budapest, however, at present these qualities are, as I have said above, conspicuous by their absence." The Gospel truth! Every effort humanly possible has been made by an Inter-Allied Military Mission, with the patience of a setting hen on a nest of china eggs, to coax Roumanian Headquarters into carrying out

2   Bandholtz attempts to write in Hungarian: No, it can't be.

3   13th century Hungarian hero of Turkish wars. See footnote 2 on page 89.

the expressed wishes of the Supreme Council or into keeping any of its solemn promises. The goodwill was one-sided with a vengeance.

Judging from the Roumanian occupation of Hungary, our little Latin Allies have the refined loot appetite of a Mississippi River catfish, the chivalrous instincts of a young cuckoo, and the same hankering for truth that a seasick passenger has for pork and beans.

Referring to the first sentence hereof it would seem that the writer of the original monograph on South-Eastern Europe had become a Rattigianu instead of remaining a British chargé d'affaires.

Leon Dennen; 1945:

Excerpts from TROUBLE ZONE – Brewing Point of World War III ?; New York - Chicago: Ziff-Davis Publ. Co., 1945

RUMANIAAFTER THE YALTA CONFERENCE

1.

While the late President Roosevelt was reporting to the United States Congress, on March 1, 1945, on the Yalta Agreement which "guaranteed" the peoples of the liberated and former Axis satellite countries the right to create democratic governments of their own choosing, Rumanian Communists were busy overthrowing by a bloody coup d'état the legal coalition government of General Nicolai Radescu. This small Black Sea nation thus became the first concrete test of the efficacy of the agreements reached at Yalta also, symbolically enough, on the Black Sea.

The *coup d'état* of a minority party, with no popular support in the country other than that derived from the presence of Red Army troops of occupation, against a coalition government at the moment when it was preparing to carry out free and secret elections, as stipulated by the Yalta Agreement, made Mr. Roosevelt's words meaningless even while they were being spoken.

According to an official radio broadcast from Moscow, the Rumanian Communists, led by three well-known agents of the "dissolved" Communist International Lucretiu Patrascanu, Gheorghe Ghergiu-Dej, and Anna Pauker also demanded in an ultimatum to King Michael that Premier Radescu and "the murderers Iuliu Maniu and Savel Radulescu" be at once "arrested and punished" as collaborators of the fascists. Iuliu Maniu is the leader of the National Tsarinist Peasant Party the largest and most democratic political organization in a country which is almost eighty per cent peasant. Savel Radulescu was the head of the Rumanian delegation to the Allied Armistice Commission.

One must know the events that preceded the bloody riots in February to have a clear picture of the present situation in Rumania.

Early in the spring of 1944 a Rumanian peace delegate, pro-British Prince Barbu Stirbey, arrived in Turkey to consult with British and American representatives. As in the case of Bulgaria, Prince Stirbey was left to cool his heels for some days in Ankara. Subsequently he went to Cairo where he submitted Rumania's peace proposals to the Anglo-American authorities. The latter communicated these proposals to the Russians. After consulting with Moscow, the Russian Minister in Cairo flatly declined Rumania's peace offer, and Prince Stirbey returned to Bucharest.

In Rumania, in the meantime, the movement for peace with the Allies, under the leadership of Iuliu Maniu, was growing rapidly. A leader of the largest and most progressive political party and uncompromising in his democratic beliefs, Dr. Maniu has been described by the London Institute of International Affairs as the "only disinterested statesman" in Rumania. Even a pro-Soviet publication like *The Central European Observer* speaks of him as "the uncorrupt and honest Maniu a national symbol for considerable parts of the peasantry." When his present Bolshevik detractors were still fraternizing with the Nazis following the Stalin-Hitler Pact in 1939, Iuliu Maniu, like Nikola Mushanoff in Bulgaria, braving German concentration camps and torture, fought uncompromisingly against the Nazi invaders of his country and also against domestic fascists.

For months following the creation of General Jon Antonescu's pro-Nazi regime, Dr. Maniu had been in correspondence with the Allies. It was no secret to me and other Americans in Istanbul that early in 1944 he had come to an understanding with General Maitland Wilson, then Allied Commander-in-Chief in the Mediterranean, to force Antonescu to ask for an armistice and, in the event of failure, to over-throw the Nazi satellite government by a coup d'état. The only resistance movement existing in Rumania at that time was the Peasant Party's National Guard of Transylvania, which, incidentally, was instrumental in saving the lives of many Jews, as I know from my own refugee rescue work.

In June 1944 Iuliu Maniu, having failed to convince Antonescu to sue for peace, formed an anti-Nazi Democratic Bloc consisting of four political parties. Although Communists never counted more than two thousand in Rumania and their influence was nil, they were invited to join the Bloc. Dr. Maniu used the occasion to issue a secret appeal to the people of Rumania whose echoes reached all the Balkan capitals that were under Nazi rule. "In the name of the country," the appeal read, "the National Democratic Bloc demands that this war cease without further delay; that the alliance with the Axis be severed and the dictatorship at home abolished." It also promised to guarantee the political rights of the Rumanian people "under a regime of liberty and democracy."

Undaunted by the Allied rebuff to Prince Stirbey in Cairo, Iuliu Maniu influenced democratic party leaders to send a new peace emissary to Turkey: Constantin Visoianu, a left-wing democrat who had long been associated with liberal Rumanian Foreign Minister Nicholas Titulescu, and was once Minister to the Hague and to Moscow. M. Visoianu received wider authority than Prince Stirbey, including the full right to negotiate with Soviet Russia.

Upon reaching Turkey, this emissary at once informed the Allies that Rumania was ready to declare war on Germany, and ready also to cede unconditionally the territories of Bessarabia and Northern Bucovina to the Soviet Union. In return Rumania asked to be allowed to re-incorporate the territory of Transylvania occupied by Hungary, and also for the control of the Danube Delta. Again the Russians flatly refused to accept Bucharest's proposals. The only terms they were prepared to give Rumania, they said, was that she pay an indemnity sum to be decided upon by Moscow solely and that the Soviet Army should remain in the country until that unspecified sum was paid in full.

Rumania's cause was hopeless. By the secret terms of the Teheran Agreement she had become an exclusive Soviet "sphere of influence." Winston Churchill publicly urged the Rumanians to "make their terms with Russia." On August 22, 1944, in a brief proclamation to the Rumanian people which we heard in Istanbul at 9:25 in the evening, the King ordered the Rumanian armed forces to cease fire against the Russians. Rumania had accepted their order of unconditional surrender. Soon thereafter the Red Army entered Bucharest. To the surprise of the local inhabitants it was equipped almost entirely with American arms and was moving on American trucks and jeeps.

2.

Like the Bulgarians, the Rumanians greeted the Red Army troops as liberators. Here, too, the joy was short-lived. The Bolsheviks had no intention of playing the role of liberators. They were *conquerors*: the Red Army wanted that clearly understood.

I have heard many eyewitness accounts of the Red Army's entry into Bucharest, but one incident remains vivid in my mind: A little Jewish boy, overjoyed at the Russians presence in Bucharest, was running after a detachment of Red Army troops. The streets were slushy. Unwittingly he splashed some mud on the boots of a Red colonel who was passing by. The colonel ordered the boy to stop, but the latter apparently did not hear him and ran on. The Russian whipped out his gun from the holster, but other children who saw the incident ran over to him and began to wipe the mud off his boots with the sleeves of their coats. The Red colonel was adamant. The little offender had to be brought back. Only after he had knelt in the mud and wiped the muddy boots did the Russian's wrath subside. As soon as the Red Army entered Bucharest it commenced to requisition valuables, homes, automobiles, furniture, dishes, and radio receivers. In the case of radio receivers the Russian order was explicit: "No demand for exemption will be considered."[4] An order was also issued forcing storekeepers to "sell" to the Russians goods for the invasion rubles with which the Red Army men were supplied in abundance. On September 5 the Mayor of Bucharest was able to inform the population that there were large stocks of wheat and flour sufficient for all needs. "Fear of lack of bread," he said, "is therefore not justified." Two weeks later there were few loaves of bread or sacks of flour in all of Bucharest; it had all been requisitioned and shipped to Russia.

Particularly distressing was the behavior of the Red troops. In contrast with their disciplined conduct in many other places, they broke loose in Rumania, looting peaceful citizens and taking their women. The reports of this behavior spread through the Balkans and were repeated everywhere in Istanbul. I was reluctant to believe it until the evidence, in eye-witness stories by refugees reaching Turkey, whose honesty I could not doubt, convinced me.

According to these reports, Red officers looked on unconcernedly and in some cases participated in the spree. The demoralization of the forces grew so serious that Moscow was obliged to employ propaganda devices to stop it. The valiant soldiers were exhorted to shun the "painted sirens of capitalism." The orgy ended only when the Russian troops were withdrawn from Bucharest and stationed in outlying districts. Red soldiers traveling on trains were forbidden to get out at stations en route even if a delay of several hours was involved.

The Rumanian refugees after the Soviet occupation told me harrowing tales of tragedy, suffering, and brutality. Tens of thousands of Rumanians, under one pretext or another, were rounded up and deported to Russia in forced labor battalions. Corroboration of these deportations has come since then in newspaper dispatches from London, Paris, and elsewhere by American writers.

Especially tragic was the situation of the Jewish survivors in Transnistria. Because Moscow regards them as "Russian citizens" and not Rumanians, they were immediately deported to Russia. According to eyewitness ac-

4   Confiscation of radios, to prevent populations from hearing any but the prescribed
Soviet news, is standard Russian procedure, enforced also in Russia itself.

counts which reached me in Tel-Aviv, three thousand Jews, rounded up indiscriminately, had already been deported by the end of November.

3.

Following Rumania's capitulation, the first government was formed by General Constantin Sanatescu, young King Michael's intimate and Lord Chamberlain who induced the King to support the anti-Antonescu coup d'état.

An officer of pronounced pro-French views, General Sanatescu had, at the time he assumed the premiership of the new government, an interesting and varied career behind him. From 1925 until 1928 he was Military Attaché in London and Paris. In 1940 he was entrusted with the difficult task of heading the Rumanian delegation which was sent to Moscow to fix the Russo-Rumanian frontier after Bessarabia had been occupied by the Soviets with the acquiescence and active support of Hitler. There is little doubt that General Sanatescu was expressing the sentiments of all the anti-German Rumanians when he said in an article in the Bucharest *Semnalul* of September 20, 1944:

"To wage war against the Soviet Union is tantamount to committing national suicide... The former rulers of Rumania are criminals for, against the interest of our people, they embroiled us in a war against the Soviet Union which fights for the freedom and independence of all peoples. Our interests demand close and friendly relations with the Soviet Union."

Apparently taking at its face value the statement of Viacheslav Molotov, Soviet Foreign Commissar, that the Soviet Government "does not pursue the aim of acquiring any part of Rumanian territory or altering the existing social order in Rumania," Sanatescu proceeded to form a broad and representative government. Included in it were Iuliu Maniu, Constantin Bratianu of the National Liberal Party – the second largest political organization in Rumania – Constantin Petrescu and Lucretiu Patrascanu, representing the minor Social Democratic and Communist parties respectively.

By this time the Red Army was firmly in control of Rumania. The guiding hand of the new government therefore was no longer Iuliu Maniu, representative of the most popular party, but Lucretiu Patrascanu, leader of the tiny Communist group. Once a lawyer in Czernauti, Patrascanu had joined the Communist Party while still a student in Vienna. Some years later, however, he publicly resigned, and rumor had it that his resignation was only a blind to cover up his work as a GPU agent. Subsequently he spent three years in prison for Communist activities and twelve months under house arrest. He emerged again as a principal Rumanian representative in Moscow during the armistice discussions.

In this case the Russians, to all intents and purposes, negotiated with themselves, since the principal Rumanian delegate had long been subservient to Moscow. Characteristically enough, Patrascanu at once requested and received the portfolio of Minister of Justice which placed him in charge of the Rumanian police and of the special commission to purge "war criminals and other undesirable elements."

The government, consisting of the Democratic Bloc of four parties which overthrew the dictatorship of Jon Antonescu, paved the way for a popular backing of this coup d'état as well as for the armistice terms worked out in Moscow by Patrascanu and Stalin. But with the Red Army where it was and what it was, Iuliu Maniu became an embarrassment to the Rumanian Communist leader, especially since Maniu insisted upon carrying out the promise of the Democratic Bloc to restore full civil liberties to the Rumanian people. Moreover, a government under the majority peasant party of Dr. Maniu would have popular roots and would therefore tend to become independent of Russian support.

In an effort to destroy Iuliu Maniu's influence in the country and to weaken the National Peasant Party, the Rumanian Communist leader like his counterpart Anton Yugoff in Bulgaria therefore made an unholy alliance with the most reactionary and pro-fascist elements in the country, including ex-Premier George Tatarescu who, together with ex-King Carol, was responsible for the establishment of a fascist regime in Rumania.

Shortly before I left Istanbul, Colonel Radu Ionescu, notorious for his torture of Jews and democratic anti-Nazis under the Antonescu regime, a man condemned by all democratic persons as a war criminal, was appointed chief of Rumania's secret police. The appointment was sponsored by ex-Premier Tatarescu with the approval of Stalin's "personal representative," Lucretiu Patrascanu. Liberal journalists who protested the appointment were jailed and their newspapers suspended.

As the representative of an American relief organization I had an opportunity to interview many of the Jewish refugees who went from Rumania to Palestine. In the thirty pages of testimony I took from them there is the story of a Jew about fifty years old who had lost his entire family during the Nazi extermination campaign of Jews in Jassy.

"I have lost my wife, my two sons and a daughter," he told me, "but the Rumanians have given me a present so that I should not forget them." He pointed to an ugly red gash on his right cheek. "This," he said, "is a present from Carlaontz."

Sometime later I learned that this very General Carlaontz, who as commander at Jassy[5] in 1941 was responsible for the massacre of twenty thousand Jews, had been appointed by Patrascanu as Undersecretary of the Interior! It was this pro-fascist general who had issued the famous order forbidding the publication of all accounts and photographs of the massacre of Jews under Antonescu[6]. News from Rumania is now scarce and I have no way of knowing whether Carlaontz and Colonel Radu Ionescu were ever removed from their posts and tried as war criminals. But their appointment in the first place is symptomatic of Soviet policy everywhere in the Balkans.

The manner in which Iuliu Maniu was eventually forced out of the government is described in some detail by the Soviet *Pravda*:

"On October 12 the leaders of the Communist Party and also of the Union of Patriots, The Agricultural Front, and the United Trade Unions [paper organizations created by Lucretiu Patrascanu overnight] met to discuss the formation of a National Democratic Front. The project for this Front was

5   See details in: Matatias Carp: Holocaust in Romania, Simon Publ. 2000.

6   Under the Iliescu regime, during the mid-1990's, Antonescu was commemorated by a number of statues and by naming several avenues after him in Romania.

presented by the Central Committee of the Rumanian Communist Party. Representatives of the National Tsarinist [Maniu's Peasant Party] and of the National Liberal parties were invited to the meeting. Only a representative of the liberals showed up. However, he did not participate in the discussions and left before the conclusion of the meeting..."

On the evening of October 12, Lucretiu Patrascanu . . . informed the leaders of the National Tsarinist and National Liberal Parties that in view of the formation of a National Democratic Front the [original] Democratic Bloc of Four has been dissolved.[7]

At the same time the Soviet news agency, *Tass*, reported a visit of the Communist leaders to King Michael. They in formed him that since Maniu and Bratianu failed to respond to their invitation to join the National Democratic Front, a new government would be formed without them.

General Constantin Sanatescu who was entrusted to form the new government took the hint: neither Iuliu Maniu nor Constantin Bratianu were included in it. In the process of reshuffling the Cabinet the lone Social Democratic representative disappeared altogether. But the Communists, under their new disguise of the National Democratic Party, received seven cabinet posts although they represented a party of only two thousand.

In Turkey I had occasion to discuss the Balkan situation with Burton Y. Berry, our Consul General in Istanbul, who was particularly pleased that my mission included the rescue of democratic and liberal men and women who had been actively engaged in resisting the Nazis. Mr. Berry was genuinely concerned over the fate of those heroic people. But, he added hopefully, "soon the Red Army will occupy the Balkans and the democrats, liberals, and socialists whom you seek to help will probably form the new governments.

Mr. Berry is now United States Minister in Rumania. I wonder what he now thinks.

7   Pravda, Oct. 13, 1944.

Rumania is, of course, an important element in Russia's expansionist plans in the eastern Mediterranean, but much of her present plight can be attributed to her corrupt politicians. There is an old Balkan adage, says Bernard Newman in his admirable book on the Balkans, that you can trust a Rumanian so long as his shirt dangles outside his trousers; that is to say, so long as he remains a peasant. If he turns politician and goes to town, he tucks his shirt inside his trousers – Western-fashion, and then he is no longer the same man.

Baksheesh and corruption have been the great tragedies in Rumania as in the rest of the Balkan countries which suffered under Ottoman rule. Thus, although after World War I Rumania came out with territorial aggrandizement because of her participation on the side of the victorious Allies, World War II found her on the Axis side. Codreanu's Iron Guard, Professor Cuza's Christian Defense League, and other anti-Semitic and fascist groups which since 1933 were employed by ex-King Carol and others as pawns to destroy the pro-democratic National Tsarinist Peasant Party eventually paved the way for Jon Antonescu's Nazi dictatorship. The sins of Rumanian politicians, however, scarcely justify Soviet elimination of democratic leaders, especially when this is done with the help of some of the most notoriously anti-democratic samples of Rumanian political reaction.

American and British diplomats concerned with Balkan affairs told me that Iuliu Maniu and the National Tsarinist Party were the only mainstays of a popular representative government in Rumania. Should anything happen to Maniu, they said, the democratic process in that country would be retarded for years. Now Dr. Maniu is branded by the Communists as a "murderer." We need not be surprised if before long he, too, will be denounced as a "war criminal" like Mihailovich and tried by some "General Carlaontz."

There is indeed little that is mysterious about Soviet policy in eastern or southeastern Europe. Everywhere the pattern is the same and repeats itself with a deadly monotony. Our failure to understand it, however, augurs ill for the future of democracy not only in Europe but in the world. Events move swiftly in the Balkans. The second Rumanian government of General Sanatescu lasted only seven weeks. It fell at a mere hint from the Russian General Vinogradov, head of the "Allied" Armistice Commission in Rumania. The country had been bled white by this time, but the Red General demanded a more "sincere" fulfillment of the Bucharest Government's obligations and commitments.

The fate of the third Rumanian government formed on December 5, 1944, by General Nicolai Radescu merely adds the final touches to the general picture. Radescu is by no stretch of the imagination a person of democratic views although he had been interned in a concentration camp for many months by the pro-Nazi Antonescu regime ostensibly for anti-Nazi views. He was little more than a figurehead, a front for a government that was completely dominated by Lucretiu Patrascanu and the Rumanian Communist Party. Moscow was by now the undisputed master of the country.

According to a clause in the armistice terms, Bucharest agreed that "the printing, importation, and distribution in Rumania of periodicals and non-periodical literature, the presentation of theatrical performances and films, the work of wireless stations, post, telegraph, and telephone shall be carried out in agreement with the Allied [Soviet] High Command." The Red Army was not slow in enforcing this clause. Intellectually and spiritually, Rumania became a no-man's land. When Iuliu Maniu ordered his peasant partisans, the Rumanian National Guard of Transylvania, to disband, the official comment of the Moscow radio was as cynical as it was ominous:

"M. Maniu's declaration is extremely tardy, since even before this order.., the Red Army command had liquidated all bandit groups styling themselves volunteer detachments or volunteer guards."

Neither Washington nor the pro-Soviet crypto-liberals who shed so many tears over General Scobie's effort to disarm the ELAS bands in Greece said a word in protest over the Red Army's action. Rumania was being groomed to become the seventeenth Soviet Republic. The Society for the Improvement of Russo-Rumania Relations spread its branches all over the country. The hungry people were constantly fed with lectures on "Soviet progress." The Russian language became a compulsory subject in all Rumanian schools.

Why then was it necessary for Anna Pauker, a Russian citizen and well-known agent of the Comintern, who before departing for Moscow to complete her training was active in the United States, to stage a bloody coup d'état to overthrow General Radescu's government? Why the attempt on Radescu's life? And why the failure of the Red Army commander in Rumania, who was not slow in disarming Maniu's volunteer detachments, to intervene and terminate the bloody massacre?

In the Greek civil war the core of the dispute – at least on the surface was clear: General Ronald MacKenzie Scobie, a representative of British imperialism, was employing his troops against the "revolutionary" forces of that country. What if EAM, the Greek National Liberation Movement, and its armed auxiliary, ELAS, which originally comprised many of the genuinely democratic men and women of Greece was, following the outbreak of the civil war, completely dominated (especially in Macedonia) by Bulgarian, Albanian, and Yugoslav Communists as well as by members of the dwindling terrorist Macedonian Revolutionary Organization, IMRO? What if these Communist agents employed American lend-lease arms, generously contributed by Marshal Tito? The "liberal" world was shocked. General Scobie was shooting down in cold blood "innocent" Greek revolutionists. Even official Washington shed a tear or two.

But who was killing whom in the civil war in Rumania? The answer is not far to seek. Although completely subservient to the Russians, Premier Radescu, encouraged it seems by British and American diplomacy, summoned enough daring to protest against the forcible recruiting of Rumanian nationals for forced labor in the Ploesti oil fields and in Russia. It was a fatal error. By this act Radescu revealed himself as not the complete puppet that he was expected to be. With the approach of "secret" elections – as stipulated by the Yalta Agreement – the Rumanian Premier could no longer be entrusted with their supervision. Hence Anna Pauker's coup d'état. As in Greece, Moscow formally kept its hands "off".

This game will be played to the bitter end until every vestige of freedom is stamped out in eastern and southeastern Europe. But what good liberal and democrat can oppose the will of the *masses* – as represented by a handful of Communists led by a Comintern agent – to establish a true democratic regime?

It is significant that the coup d'état was staged simultaneously in Bucharest, the Rumanian capital, and in the provincial towns of Brasov, Craiova, and Caracal, agricultural centers and strongholds of Maniu's Peasant Party.

No spontaneous uprising in Russia's favor could conceivably be expected in such places.

No one who wants to live to see a world of peace and human decency will fail to agree with the late President Roosevelt that the United States "shall have to take the responsibility for world collaboration" or "bear the responsibility for another world conflict." No one, too, will doubt the sincerity of his motives when, in discussing the liberated areas in his report to Congress, he stated:

"The three most powerful nations have agreed that the political and economic problems of any area liberated from Nazi conquest, or any former Axis satellite; are a joint responsibility of all three governments. They will join together during the temporary period of instability after hostilities, to help the people of any liberated area, or of any former satellite state, to solve their own problems through firmly established democratic processes. They will endeavor to see to it that interim government, and that the people who carry on the interim government between occupation by Germany and true independence that such an interim government will be as representative as possible of all democratic elements in the population, and that free elections are held as soon as possible thereafter."

But if Rumania was the first concrete test of the efficacy oft the Yalta Agreement it was a dismal failure and a portent of similar failures in other countries. Exploiting the prestige of the British and American representatives in Rumania who were in no position to affect the course of events, the *Tass* news agency reported from Moscow on February 21 that "intervention by the Allied Control Commission obtained the release of leaders of the Craiova Council of the National Democratic Front who were surrounded in the prefecture by Rumanian Army troops." In other words, Anglo-American prestige was used not to help the embattled Rumanian people who fought with their last gasp for freedom but those who with the aid of the Red Army were destroying that freedom. No sooner had Comrade Pauker staged her *coup d'éat* than Lucretiu Patrascanu, the Communist Minister of Justice, demanded "decisive action against the pro-fascist elements in the Government [meaning the representatives of the National Peasant and National Liberal Party but not the seven pro-Communist Ministers] and the dismissal of Radescu." The outcome was a foregone conclusion. Moscow dispatches "predicted" the fall of the Radescu Government,

280

and two days later the unsuspecting American public read in the newspapers that the "Rumanian Premier Resigns His Post."

In an eleventh-hour attempt to preserve the semblance of Rumanian independence, Prince Barbu Stirbey, also a leader of the National Peasant Party,
was entrusted with forming a new government. By this time Andrei
Vishinsky, Russian Vice Commissar of Foreign Affairs, of the Moscow
blood-purge trials fame, had already arrived in the country "for a first hand
study of the situation." Democracy *à la Yalta* scored a complete triumph.
Dr. Petru Groza, Chairman of the newly-formed Peasants Union – a paper
organization formed to destroy Iuliu Maniu's National Peasant Party –
solved, according to Moscow, "the long postponed question of forming a
new Rumanian government of genuinely democratic parties."

It is difficult to predict with any degree of certainty the ultimate course the
Russians will adopt in Rumania and in the other Balkan countries under
their domination. It is doubtful whether Rumania will be annexed outright
by the USSR. The "softening up" process of the democratic elements in the
country has not yet been completed. Moreover, the Rumanian oil fields and
refineries are chiefly owned by British and American companies. They are
now in possession of the Red Army, but the Royal Dutch Shell and the
Standard Oil Companies will undoubtedly put up a stiff struggle for their
properties.

Since the Germans were driven out of Rumania, a large part of the equipment has been removed from the Rumanian to the Russian oil fields. At the
request of Shell and Standard Oil the British and American governments
lodged a protest against this removal with the Soviet Government. Moscow
replied that most of the equipment was German and urgently needed inside
Russia to replace destroyed equipment. Not satisfied with this explanation,
American representatives of the Allied Control Commission who in this
were galvanized into action requested permission to visit the oil fields. This
permission was refused. The Soviet Government promised, however, to
protect Anglo-American financial interests in Rumania. But who will protest the fate of the Rumanian people, including the Jewish survivors? When
it was a question of property rights, London and Washington were moved
to some action, but when it is a question of people's lives and freedom, the
apathy in those capitals remains overwhelming.

The situation of the Jews in Rumania is desperate. As in Bulgaria, anti-Jewish laws have ostensibly been abolished, but no action has been taken to restore Jewish property and normal democratic rights. The Red Army has even refused to restore Jewish institutions, such as schools, homes for the aged, and hospitals. One hundred and fifty thousand Jews who survived Nazi massacres, deportations, and forced labor camps face starvation and death.

A similar situation prevails in Bulgaria. Over the radio and in the press the Government condemns the former fascist regimes for enforcing anti-Jewish laws which are described as cruel and inhuman. It declares that Jews now are free and enjoy "equal rights" with the rest of the citizens. Yet Bulgarian Jews have been forced to disassociate themselves from the Jews in Palestine with whom they have many intimate ties. Under the pressure of Moscow's "Jewish Anti-Fascist Committee" the militant Zionist movement in the Balkan counties has now been branded as "chauvinist and bourgeois." Hebrew language which, as a reaction to Nazi torture, was making rapid progress among the Jews of those counties, has been summarily banned.

The vast majority of the "liberated" Jews in Rumania and Bulgaria would like to leave those countries and go to Palestine. Of this I can testify from personal knowledge. But in addition to restrictions imposed on immigration to Palestine by the British White Paper, the "democratic" governments of Anton Yugoff in Bulgaria and of Lucretiu Patrascanu in Rumania have prohibited all Jewish emigration.

As a denouement to the tragic Rumanian events it is worth recording that while Radescu was forced to seek asylum in the British legation, the fascist George Tatarescu was appointed Vice-Premier and Foreign Minister of the pro-Communist government formed by Moscow.

Macedonia and Albania

Stephen Bonsal; 1890:

Excerpts from: *Heyday in a Vanished World – Adventures of a Foreign Correspondent at the Turn of the Century*; New York: W. W. Norton & Co. Inc. 1937.

[Continued from the chapter on Bulgaria]

For many years the pleas of the Slav peoples of Macedonia that they be given the benefit of clergy had been on file at the Sublime Porte. Now and again they were brought to the attention of the Sultan himself by a good-natured ambassador from western Europe, but they made no headway. Ever since the fateful battle of Kossovo, which established the supremacy of the Turk, the war-waging Christian bishops had been expelled from their sees although from time to time humbler clergy in a clandestine manner had been permitted to shepherd the unfortunate Christian *rayahs*. Even these interlopers were persecuted after 1860 when it was thought, and not without some justification, that their activities were political rather than spiritual.

Then by a master stroke the Sultan split the Christian churches in twain. From the days of the Byzantine Empire the Christians had been under the control of the Greek Patriarch in Constantinople and so it happened that until the middle of the last century, and even down to the Congress of Berlin, the Serbians, the Bulgarians and even the roaming Roumanians of the Peninsula were regarded as Greeks and were so called from the Church to which they were in subjection. But as the spirit of nationalism was awakened in the Balkans, and as the poor *rayahs* learned of the corruption of the Holy Synod and saw how all the ecclesiastical plums were given to Greeks, men often far from worthy, an effort was made to separate the congregations according to race. With characteristic alacrity the Porte saw the opportunity of sowing discord among the Christians and in 1870 by a special *firman* the Sultan established the exarchate, which was given religious control of all the professing Christians of the Bulgar tongue. The outraged

Greek Patriarch of the day denounced the new church as outside the pale and radically schismatic, although its members professed the same doctrines and held to the same dogmas – but there was the difference of the languages in which they prayed and, of course, their political objectives were as far apart as the poles.

And so in 1890 the Sultan threw another apple of discord into the midst of the warring churches. It was announced that, in pursuance of their immemorial practice of religious toleration, the members of the Divan who sat at the Sublime Porte had issued *berats* to two Bulgarian bishops, nominated by the Exarch, who would soon be installed in the Macedonian sees of Üsküb[1] and Ochrida. It would be of little interest to inquire at this late day what the motives were behind this concession. At best it would only shed light upon a state of affairs which has gone forever, but certainly the idea of encouraging Stambouloff in his anti-Russian policy, which could not fail to strengthen the hold of the Turks over the Christian provinces, entered into the calculations of the astute men in Stamboul.

It may be explained that the Turkish word *berat*, at the time so confusing to the world press, has no relation at all to the Italian word *berretta*, a cap

---

1   Skoplje today, capital of Macedonia.

which I believe is conferred by the Holy Father in Rome upon certain of his bishops with whom he is well pleased. The *berat* is simply an ecclesiastical exequatur, passport or permission to carry the comfort of the word and the blessings of the sacraments to a benighted people who, in this instance at least, and for many generations, had been deprived of the benefit of an official clergy. At the last moment, for some reason that never was quite clear, the *berat* for the Bishop of Ochrida was held up, but as it was announced that the other *berat*-bearer was leaving Constantinople in a few days for his dangerous post I determined if possible to be there when he arrived. In those days we had no diplomatic or even consular representative in Bulgaria, and the Turkish agency there refused to recognize my Washington passport. However, Stambouloff and Sir Nicholas O'Connor, the British diplomatic agent in Sofia at the time, were good enough to concoct between them what might be called an Anglo-Bulgarian passport for an American citizen.

However lacking in legal status, it was a formidable looking document and on several occasions it served me and my purpose well.

I took the night train north and on the following morning at Nish, once the capital of Servia, I transferred to a train bound for Salonica on the line which Baron Hirsch constructed and which had only been opened to the sea a few weeks before. My passport sustained a careful examination at the frontier station of Zebeftche and soon I found myself in Macedonia or in Old Serbia, in Greater Bulgaria, or in the *vilayet* of Kossovo – for here geographical terms depend upon the ethnic origin of the speaker. It was an uneventful journey through a gray gaunt country until, in a district of free Albanians, as we came out of the Karadjik tunnel, our train was greeted by a well-sustained volley of musketry fire. All the windows were shattered and the passengers in my car, a Greek merchant and two Jewish peddlers, struggled with me, whom they evidently regarded as an interloper, as to who should lie nearest to the floor.

"The bullets were intended for His Beatitude, the Bishop Theodosios," explained the Maltese conductor of the train. "But what numbskulls they are! Of course he will be on the up-train." Be this as it may, as the smoke cleared away, the not very sharp shooters emerged from behind the rocks and exchanged cordial salutes with our engine driver and his fireman. "They are on very friendly terms," explained the conductor drily, "they exchange presents – the crew gives cartridges and gets Macedonian tobacco, and every now and then obliges by running over a donkey who has seen better days but has to be paid for by the company in piasters." Well, it was quite an unusual railway in many ways.

Three days later I rubbed my eyes which for some moments I thought were victimized by some Biblical mirage. The hills and crags about Usküb were alive with people. Crouching behind boulders or squatting in the innumerable cemeteries that surrounded the shrunken town, that was once the imperial city of Justinian, were gathered the forlorn children who, descended from the martyrs, had survived the generations of persecution. Here with their sick, their crippled, and even with their recent dead I was told, the Christians of the highlands had gathered and were waiting in the shadows which the tall tombs of bygone pashas cast, like arrows over the arid plain, the coming of the holy man who was to mend their fortunes and perchance make whole their crippled bodies. All wore the somber dust-colored garments they have worn since the day of the destruction of the churches, when the empire of Stefan Dushan was dismembered – "while the good Lord was sleeping" as the Macedonian peasants say.

Even in the town the narrow winding streets were thronged with the most venturesome of the mountain folk, but the large Turkish garrison was conspicuous by its absence. Of this surprising circumstance two explanations were current. Some said Edhem Pasha, second in command, had led most of the troops to the Montenegrin frontier where trouble was brewing. Others, and these, the timid and fearful, were the most numerous, whispered that the garrison had been sent out of the way so that there would be no restraining force in case the Albanian *arnauts* who had also assembled in the town should decide to oppose the decree of the great Padishah and make short shrift of the Bishop and his flock who, as they thought, were preparing to defile the holy places by their presence.

One morning shortly after daybreak the long awaited cortège appeared, coming from the railway station. It was headed by a tall cross-bearer immediately followed by the Bishop in gorgeous episcopal garb but riding upon an humble ass. Thousands upon thousands followed, mostly, it seemed to me, the lame, the halting and the blind, as the Bishop led the way to the desecrated and ruined shrine of St. Dimitri where in the darkness of the forgotten ages his predecessor had been stoned to death. Soon the great multitude

286

outpaced the procession and, as the Bishop approached the sacred edifice, a path had to be made for him and his almoner, his chaplains and his theologians. His path was blocked by the sick and the dying who kissed the hem of his garment as he passed. For hours the holy man blessed all who were in the reach of the benediction that he gave with outstretched arms, and upon those who were near him he laid his trembling hands from time to time. In praise of a God, who had at last relented, psalms were sung, and when the darkness came that followed on the long day the people still crowded around their shepherd with hope and confidence in their eyes. All defilement had been washed away from the long deserted church, every stone of the walls that had been thrown down in fury by the Moslem had been blessed and in some measure replaced. Thousands pressed their wan cheeks against the cracked foundations of the long abandoned church and tenderly caressed every standing pillar. To them it was not a picturesque ruin but the Ark of the Covenant of their Lord and Savior, which after so many bitter years of probation they had been found worthy to have and to hold again.

I too was weak from fasting and all the emotions of the day when, the ceremonies of reconsecration being over and as the multitudes were returning to their campfires on the hillside, before supper I stumbled into the Turkish bath over which my friend the barber Omar presided.

"And what do you think of it all?" I asked.

For a moment the good Omar was silent and then, "What do I think? Well I think it is a great misfortune for me that a man has come to town with an income of forty pounds Turkish and that he wears a beard!"

On the following day the thousands of Macedonian Christians who still lingered about the ancient shrine awakened with an indefinable feeling of disappointment and anxiety. To begin with, the advent of the good Bishop had not been signalized by the signs and wonders that, long predicted, had, of course, been confidently expected. For four centuries every plague upon their race, every blight upon their lives and crops had been dismissed by these people of the Macedonian hills and valleys with the confident assurance, "Ah! when we have in our midst again an anointed of the Lord our slavery will end, our misfortunes vanish and on that blessed day the black magic of the magicians and the Moslem wizardry will not prevail against our prayers." And then mad Ivan the town crier strode through the camps, and it was anything but cheerful tidings that he croaked out in his raven voice.

"Myriads of blackbirds are alighting on the field of Kossovo," was the burden of his warning message. "Not so many have been seen there since the evil day when the sky was darkened and King Lazar and the champions of Christendom went down before the Horde. Woe is me! The curse survives even unto the twentieth generation!"

And, of course, the hostile bearing of some of the Turks and of all the Albanians on the preceding day served to depress and further disturb the Christians. On the other hand there was comfort in the thought that both the Vali and the Mudir of the town had been polite and even, to some extent, helpful. The good Theodosios had, as the protocol demanded, called upon them and with much ceremony drunk the three obligatory cups of coffee, and the greetings exchanged had been formal and dignified; however it was now recalled that not a word was spoken to indicate that the officials regarded his presence among the Christian flocks, so long without a shepherd, as anything but a fortuitous incident of the travel season.

About nine o'clock the fears of the anxious people were intensified by the appearance of a messenger from the Mudir accompanied by a horsed troop of irregulars before the hovel where the Bishop had spent the night.

"His Excellency sends his salaams; Your Beatitude is bidden to the Divan." Swifter than the flight of birds these ominous words traveled through the wretched camps that clustered about the shrunken city, and a low wail arose from the anxious people. Some indeed hastened to leave, to secrete themselves in the mountain recesses whence the first ray of hope and salvation that had shone upon their race for four centuries had lured them. But by far the greater number sat about, pitiful pictures of hopeless woe and dejection.

Most of them maintained a helpless silence but not a few were crooning as I passed in their midst. "Mad Ivan has spoken truly and to our blight. Again the blackbirds are winging their flight over the dark field."

In a few minutes Bishop Theodosios, followed by his yellow-haired cross-bearer and by about a score of mountain Slavs, who were too brave or too curious to remain behind, and by myself, entered the courtyard of the *konak* where we were met with unctuous politeness by the Vali and a number of other officials. Behind the Vali, encased in a uniform strung with many decorations, sat Akinet Ayoub the last Field Marshal of the Turkish Empire, who had always shown himself as a fiend incarnate during his long reign in the *vilayet*. His great red face was blank of all expression but in his eyes were reflected the green banners which the Prophet of Mecca had unfurled. In sullen silence the Field Marshal overlooked the scene, ignoring the presence of the Bishop and the Christians who came with him. And only the Vali spoke:

"Men learned in the law, Your Beatitude," he said, "have throughout the night studied the *berat* and the papers you brought, and this study has confirmed in our minds the suspicion of a misunderstanding which was apparent to us yesterday but of which in all hospitality, in the moment of your arrival, it would not have been courteous to speak. But even now the confirmation of our suspicions has come by wire from Stamboul and we must inform you, I need not say with what regret, that the hours of your stay among us, until a more propitious season, are numbered." The last words of the Vali were emphasized by a shrill warning whistle from the railway station, and in conclusion he added, "I have the honor to announce that His Beatitude's train is even now awaiting him."

Much that was said was well beyond the reach of my meager Turkish, but I knew the language of the human heart, and when the wail from the inner courtyard was caught up by the waiting multitude outside I recognized the despairing cries as coming from a people beaten down upon their knees and in poignant, mortal anguish.

For all answer the Bishop made a low obeisance, and followed by his supporters withdrew from the courtyard. His features expressed the humility of a saint but in his upright carriage and sturdy stride there was something militant, something that suggested to me that the thought of resistance to the stern decree was not entirely absent from his mind. In the crowded streets outside the *konak* the reserve that had been evidently imposed by orders from on high had vanished, and as the sad cortège passed, the Albanians, and even the Turks, with the Vali's consent if not by his express command, gave full vent to their hatred.

"Ey! Ey!" they shouted. "His Beatitude is not staying long with us. Can it be that he has shriven clean his flock in so short a time?" "Dog brothers you are! And dog brothers you remain," cried the Albanians, nervously fingering their crooked knives as the slovenly rag-clad Slavs, bowed down under the weight of their years of servitude, stumbled along the rough way, cringing before their arrogant conquerors. "Ey, ey," they moaned. "It is true that the plains of Kossovo are black with the birds of ill-omen." And some whispered one to another, "In the beginning there must have been grievous sin for even in this the thirtieth generation His face is turned from us. How long 0 Lord! How long must we wander in the wilderness?"

As one in a dream the good Bishop walked at the head of the sad procession. He seemed oblivious of the vile words and the menacing gestures of the conquerors. Now and again he would stop for a moment to smile upon and bless his own people, who crouched at his feet and for the last time sought to kiss the hem of his garment. Perhaps a realizing sense of the misfortune that had overtaken his mission, and frustrated it, only came to him as the cortège reached the Church of St. Dimitri, the ruined shrine which only yesterday he had consecrated anew, for the preservation and sanctity of which so many hundreds of martyrs had died in vain. There, as his eyes fell upon the holy ruin which he had vowed to upbuild, a tremor ran through his frame. He turned and cast a searching look upon his cringing flock. And then suddenly, as though in answer to a command which had not been spoken, a tall, stalwart young man, clothed in the shaggy fleece which the shepherds of the highlands wear even in summer, strode out from the wailing multitude.

"Your Beatitude," he shouted. "In God's name, raise here the standard of revolt. Bid us die for you and our faith rather than we should see again the shrine of St. Dimitri become the kennel of the dog brothers."

The yellow-haired cross-bearer and two others stepped to the Bishop's side and raised on high the sacred symbol, but the many were too slow, perhaps too apathetic, and the Turks too quick.

"Seize him, the speaker of treason," shouted a police captain, "seize him in the name of the Padishah." In a moment the *zaptiek* were upon their man. He was beaten, bound and gagged, and no helping hand was raised as they led him away.

An hour later the good Bishop, the vicar of Christ on earth, regarded by all as the messenger from Heaven, was gone with but a silent blessing, all he was allowed to give, to his unhappy flock.

When it was all over I went to the han to talk over the events of the day with Schilka, the Austrian Vice-Consul, and Spadoni, the Maltese telegraph agent. I found that the magnificent Albanian Arnaut, a picturesque, silent figure who had adorned their table for some days, was gone, but not without booty. He had availed himself of the excitement of the Bishop's reception to carry off to the mountains the most beautiful girl of the many born to the Christians of the town. Omar, the gossipy barber, had all the details, and on his way to the Turkish bath to attend a noble patron he stopped in at the *han*.

The last seen of Scander Beg, for such was the illustrious name the Arnaut bore, was his dignified retreat up the mountainside with the girl slung across his shoulder, while his stalwart slave covered the rear with glistening silver pistols in his hands and a crooked knife in his mouth, The girl, the "rose" as Omar called her, screamed and sobbed, "but not overmuch," averred the barber. "I have no doubt that she will live to be consoled. And now," concluded Omar triumphantly, for in politics this barber was not a trimmer, "she will wear the *yashmak*, and none but the eyes of her lord will feast upon the rare beauties of her face and form."

There had been reported to Omar some commotion among the Christians, based entirely upon a misunderstanding of the incident, as he explained; for when it was noised abroad that Scander Beg had sent back to the bereaved father the wedding gift, a ransom of five pounds Turkish, it was admitted by everyone that the kidnaper (!) had behaved with perfect gallantry, like the Albanian gentleman he was.

Three of the brave but foolhardy peasants who had urged the Bishop to resist the Turks and raise the standard of the Cross were kept in close confinement in the vermin- infected prison for a week, and then staggering under their weight of chains and their days of starvation, I saw them walk to the new railway station which all Europe had said would exert such a civilizing influence upon Macedonian conditions, and there embark for Constantinople, where their judges were awaiting them.

On this the day of their departure the narrow lane-like streets of the once-Christian city were empty; none seemingly dared to wish these martyrs of liberty Godspeed upon their calvary. Two of the brave fellows were simple peasant lads, who had acted instinctively and without thought of what the consequence might be. The other was a man of very different caliber, a born agitator and one whose trail in the mountains the Turkish soldiers had been following for weeks. He was, I learned, this stalwart fighter for the Cross, a Serbian of excellent family, who had devoted his life and the considerable fortune which he had heired to the propaganda of the Pan-Slavic doctrines in Macedonia in general and to the re-establishment of the old Serbian Empire in particular. His name was Bozidar Illitch,[2] and the Servians should recall his services in this the day when the dreams he dreamed have at last taken on form and substance.

Some years later another bishop came to the villages along the Vardar. This time he was a Serbian. On close examination the wise men in Stamboul had ascertained that Stefan Dushan who built the cathedral church in Usküb was a Serb, and, of course, the government in Belgrade was more tractable and Prince Ferdinand in Sofia was leaving nothing undone to cultivate friendly relations with Holy Russia. In any event the appointment of a Serb would sow discord among the Slavic tribes and all other Christians of the peninsula, and that was a boon from Heaven for which all good Moslems pray every day in their afternoon prayer![3]

I shall now relate with considerable detail an incident of my Balkan experiences, not particularly noteworthy perhaps, but because it had an influence upon shaping my course and because it reveals the obstacles we met with in presenting the news of the turbulent peninsula to the Western world. I do

2   Undoubtedly a "war" name such as all revolutionists assumed to shield their families from ruthless retaliation.

not think our clients, that is our readers, appreciate the difficulties of such situations as I was called upon to describe, with which my successors in this and other equally perplexing fields of reporting are today also confronted. Facts are slippery as well as stubborn things; and human nature is - well – human nature! As a prelude to my confession I must tell you how shocked I was in the early days of my apprenticeship, when one night in the Union Club in Sofia, as we stood before the bulletin board and read the news of the first Armenian massacres that took place in and around Erivan, I heard H.B., that famous correspondent who had been for twenty years purveying news to the English public, say, "I m sorry so many Armenians were murdered if they were murdered. But I am convinced, if the Turks acted in this way, they had good reason for it."

I was outraged at this callous remark and showed it. To me this Turcophile correspondent was always anathema, but two years later I had descended from (perhaps it would be more correct to say I had been toppled off!) my judicial pinnacle and was becoming as guilty of partisanship as H.B., but the descent brought me frankly and openly into the pro-Christian camp. Everything they did was quite right with me. Fortunate it was that the changes and chances of my profession transferred me at this juncture to another and less complicated field of investigation, and when I was returned to the Balkans I had in a measure regained my equanimity. I at least thought so.

These weighty thoughts are suggested by the memory of my second foray into Macedonia (May 1889) and its consequences for me and the unfortunate people involved. Suddenly out of a clear sky an "atrocity scare" possessed London. Great meetings were held and the indignation of large church congregations was provoked by the burning words of divines who in Exeter Hall described with many bloodcurdling details the sufferings and

---

3   Those who are familiar with the nationalistic rivalries and the church feuds that prevail in this unhappy country, will he surprised at the reverent enthusiasm with which the coming of the Lord's anointed was greeted by the followers of the Patriarch, and of the Exarch, and indeed by all other Christians without distinction of race or ritual. It was indeed "A truce of God." Unfortunately, it was not long before the propaganda of the churches resumed its devastating sway.

the tortures to which the Christian peasantry of Macedonia were subjected. An English Cathedral Canon, who it developed had traveled down the Danube on a freight boat, was quite certain he had seen the mangled and disemboweled bodies of Macedonian peasants hanging from bean poles as he passed. This far-sighted Canon was by no means discountenanced when it was pointed out that his ship had navigated in waters at least three hundred miles distant from the Macedonian highlands.

But while this was doubtless the spark that started the conflagration, from other sources came more circumstantial stories. They came from correspondents who though for very good reasons they had not ventured out from the security of their bases in Salonica or Zemlin (now Zemun), described the villages they had beheld going up in flames and how the villagers, after seeing their women ravished, had been shot down or marched off to exile in Tripoli, a fate that was worse than death. Sharp-eyed Argus in Paris (as we often called the Commodore) ordered me to the scene of these atrocities and with me went – very reluctantly – my interpreter Tryko.

After three weeks of hard riding, during which the Turks neither assisted me nor placed obstacles in my path, I was satisfied that this atrocity yarn was the most fantastic fairy tale that ever came from the Balkans which is saying much. It soon became apparent that many of the villages reported destroyed had never existed. Others we found quite peaceful. The inhabitants were not aware of their extinction or that their countryside had been devastated by fire and sword. Of course I saw many things that made my blood boil, and I said so. It was indeed a sad and moving picture of a weak and long oppressed people who were suffering for their faith and for their racial determination, to both of which they clung so tenaciously.

But I had to report that the indictment fell to the ground, no – not a single count could be substantiated.

I came upon one village where atrocities had indeed been committed, but they had occurred twenty years previous to my visit. They had taken place at the time when the *Bashi-bazouks* had been let loose in the highlands to wreak their vengeance on the villagers who, hearing that the Russians were coming to liberate them, had thought it their duty to help. These unfortunate people lost their property and their lives because they did not appreciate for one moment that, to maintain the balance of power in southeastern

Europe, the concert of Christian Powers would block their emancipation that had been so nearly accomplished.

When my dispatches dealing with this episode were read in the House of Commons by the Under Secretary for Foreign Affairs, and when they were endorsed and confirmed in every detail by the report of Her Majesty's Consul-General in Salonica who was sent to the scene of the alleged atrocities, some weeks after my visit, the matter was dropped. Heartrending as was the state of affairs in the *vilayets* as described by Mr. Blount (the Consul-General) and myself, it was so much less terrible than had been reported by the sensation-mongers that the English public and the English press with a sigh of relief let the matter drop, and the note of protest dealing with general conditions in Macedonia, which might have served at least as a word of warning, and which I asked for, was never sent to the Porte.

Not even in the most hot-headed days of my Turcophobia did I say that the authorities in Constantinople had launched this atrocity scare as a *ballon d'essai* to test out the strength of righteous indignation in western Europe. Yet this may have been the case and they certainly profited by the demonstration of our weakness that followed. Within three months the atrocities which I had disproved were perpetrated, the lands that I had found peaceful and fairly smiling were devastated, and many of the villages I had found intact were ruthlessly wiped out. The news of what was taking place gradually leaked out, but it fell upon the ears of a public that had heard the cry of "Wolf" too often and grown cynical. The unhappy thought possessed me that these crimes would not have been committed but for the clean bill of health I, and others, had given the Turks a few weeks before. As a result my departure from the role of an impartial and fair-minded observer was complete, so when a year later Tashin Pasha, the "gray Eminence" of Sultan Abdul Hamid, wrote and asked the Commodore to remove me from the field of southeastern Europe on the stated ground "that I always held with the Greeks and other Schismatics and would not believe a Turkish official even when he took an oath on the Koran or swore by the beard of the Prophet," I could do no other than admit the truth of the accusation. In reverse, my attitude had become very much like that of the Turcophile H.B. When, as sometimes happened, the Christians got the upper hand and behaved in an unchristian manner I was slow to believe it, and I consoled myself with the thought that after all, at the worst, they were only engaged in evening up a bit the terrible score.

11. THE LAND OF INCORRUPTIBLE VIRGINS

Rather at loose ends, after the Biblical scenes I have sought to describe had been enacted, I lingered on in the now famous town on the Vardar. It was in those days a place that was hard to get to and even harder to get away from, and besides I clung to the belief that the ambassadors of Christendom in Stamboul would react energetically to the snub that the Sultan had administered to them. I thought the good Bishop would come back. I had witnessed his humiliation and naturally I wanted to be present when he was exalted and then, as usual, I fear I was actuated by mixed motives. Before his return (and clearly I would be justified in awaiting it), in the intervening days, I would have an opportunity to make a superficial scamper into Higher Albania, by the back door. If anything sensational exploded elsewhere in the Balkans during my absence I would have a defense. It was high time for me to have a look at Albania; certainly it was my duty to go there although specific instructions to that effect had not come.

It was my good friend Herr von Smucker, the Austro-Hungarian Consul-General, who, while he quite properly disclaimed all responsibility for the venture, by his good offices made it possible. When the plan was first suggested, Tryko, my Bulgarian interpreter from Sofia, a former student of Robert College, declined to accompany me. As he knew but little Turkish and no Albanian, in any event he would have been of but slight assistance. Smucker, however, had with him as *cavasses* or soldier-guards of the Consulate two brothers, handsome young Albanians, who, by some freak of fortune that was most lucky for me, had been educated in a mission school at Durazzo by the Italian Franciscan fathers and spoke Italian well. At that time I could also speak Italian fluently, although mine was certainly not the *lingua Toscana in boca Romana.*

It was decided that we should travel light and only avail ourselves of ponies as far as possible and then foot it. Our first objective and the only one we disclosed was Kossovo Polje, the "dark field of the Blackbirds"[4] where five hundred years before, the Christian Host had been defeated by the Turkish Horde in one of the decisive battles of history. This was in the permitted zone of travel. "When you have concluded this pilgrimage you will return here, but, of course, conforming your movements to circumstances," said von Smucker with a portentous wink.

Our early morning start was marred by an incident which I did not appreciate at its true value until later. After we had drunk the stirrup cup in excellent Tokay wine, the memory of which often tortured me in the thirsty days that were to follow, it became apparent that the *cavass* who had been selected as my guide did not want to serve me and that his brother was very loath to see him go. But with an imperious gesture the Consul silenced all remonstrances and then, – consuls were consuls in those days!– at least in the East, he took the *cavass* who was to remain behind, by the arm, escorted him to the consular jail and locked him up behind formidable iron bars!

In answer to my inquiry he said, "The prisoner and his brother, your guide, both belong to an important highland clan. The prisoner will serve as hostage for your good treatment and safe return. Of course I shall treat him well and when you come back unharmed he will be liberated immediately and, if you like, you can reward him for the inconvenience he will have suffered. It is the custom of the country and we must conform to it and in fact it is the only halfway safe way for you to attempt the journey."

Üsküb, my point of departure, then the headquarters of the Turkish forces in the *vilayet*, and now Serbian again, is the key to Macedonia, and as it commands the Kachanlik Pass between Shar Dagh and the Kara Dagh into Kossovo, it also stands guard over the approaches to Albania from the East. Along this road and through this Pass were herded the "tribute" children, the "sons of the Eagle" who for centuries furnished the backbone of the Turkish armies and the Janissaries of the Sultans. Curiously enough in the end it was these *Yeni-asker* or "new soldiers" who brought about the overthrow of Abdul Hamid, the last independent Ottoman Sultan. It was a case where a guardian of the guards was needed and fortunately was lacking.

4   Kossovo, under the rule of the Sultan was a vilayet or province and comprised the sandjak of Üsküb and the sandjaks or districts of Prisren and Novi Bazaar. This territory I saw something of in a later journey.

Even I, though little versed in military matters, as I looked about me could well understand why Üsküb (Skoplje of the Slavs) has from the dawn of history been a place of strategic importance even before the Roman era when it became the capital of Dardania and the residence of a Pro-Consul. Our first night we spent at the "Sheepfold" of Kumanovo where, in 1912, the German-trained troops of the new régime in Turkey gave way before the impetuous Serbians. In this war the tables were turned completely. At Bregalnica the Serbians wiped out their disastrous defeat by the Bulgarians at Slivnitsa, and at Kumanovo the defeat of Christendom at nearby Kossovo was cancelled, or rather should have been. The victory at Kossovo made southeastern Europe Turkish for centuries, while the defeat of the Turks at Kumanovo did not send them packing to Anatolia and out of Europe altogether, as it should have done.

About noon of the second day we descended into the desolate plain of Kossovo. It sits like a great amphitheater beset on all sides by the frowning Macedonian highlands. It was a predestined battlefield and here on that never to be forgotten day in June 1389, the armies of the Cross and the Crescent met and the fate of the Balkan peninsula was decided for five hundred years. The people we met were mostly Albanians heavily armed and gorgeously attired. They seemed most arrogant and were evidently encroaching on the lands of the obsequious Slavs.

"Soon we will manure the plain with the carcasses of the Christian dogs," said one of them.

I wandered over the dreary fields but how the battle, so tragic in its consequences to Christendom, was fought I got no idea; but how and why it was lost I was to learn when evening came. We had no tents, but a Slav peasant bowed low and asked the mighty Effendi to share his humble hovel, but with good reason I wrapped myself in a blanket and lay outside under the stars. After he had enjoyed the cigarettes I gave him the peasant came and sat beside me and upon his monotonous *gusle* and in a broken voice told the story of how the great Tsar Lazar, who on the fateful day commanded the Christian Host, had chosen the Heavenly Kingdom and let worldly triumph go, how he and his chief men had elected for bliss eternal, leaving the poor *rayaks* to the chains and the servitude they have borne for centuries and still were bearing.

As the ballad filtered through to me it runs,

"Flying came a gray bird, indeed a noble falcon, from the Holy City of Jerusalem. No little sparrow brings he to the Imperial tent but a letter from God's blessed Mother. Sinking upon his knees our Champion received the missive which said, '0! Tsar Lazar! Thou of glorious line. The parting of the ways is near. Between two empires which wilt thou choose? Dost thou desire the Kingdom where God's beloved dwell or dost thou choose the empire of this World? If 'tis the worldly empire that thou lovest most, call thy mighty men to arms, bid them saddle their horses and tighten their girths. Let them gird on their sharp swords and lead them on and then the Turkish horde will be brought low. But if it is the Heavenly Kingdom that thou wouldst choose then have Christ's Bread prepared, for here on this dark plain where the blackbirds moan you and they destruction shall find...''

"' Dear God, what shall I answer? What decide? Upon which Kingdom shall I set my choice? The Empire of this world or the Heavenly Kingdom and the days of joy and Grace. But Dear God! How can I hesitate? The Empire of this earth is a little and a fleeting thing while Thy Kingdom endures for ever and aye.' So the great Tsar Lazar summoned his warriors and kneeling before twelve bishops of saintly mien they received the sacred host and still kneeling they met death at the hands of the infidel horde – and life eternal from God."

From the first my *cavass* was not a gay companion. He was always mumbling to himself or to me something about how precarious was the position of his dear brother whose life was forfeit unless he brought me safely back to the Vardar. But I did not really appreciate how dark was his foreboding until the third night of our wandering away from the permitted zone of Kossovo. A sullen virgin in her strange mannish attire was guarding us. The wolfish watchdogs stood by our sleeping place in ominous silence. The food that I offered the dogs had been refused with growls. It was very cold, and owing to the recent rain our campfire would not burn. I sat up and there, too, was the *cavass*, sitting on his heels and with tears streaming down his cheeks.

"Have you had a bad dream?" I inquired, as sympathetically as I could.

"It was not a dream," he answered. "I have just seen my brother. He tells me he is dead."

Then for the first time I began to appreciate the situation. My own death was an indispensable preliminary to the demise of the greatly-loved brother, and I determined to walk circumspectly, to get through smilingly if I could. I would go to great lengths in my endeavor not to bring another sorrow to the already overflowing cup of my dreary companion and guide.

The fact that from the moment we arrived footsore and weary in one of the mountain villages we were placed under the guardianship of a woman whom the *cavass* always qualified as a *"virgin incorruptible"* requires some explanation, although the only one I can offer may appear to the reader, as it did to me at the time, one that is halting and far from plausible. They were always women no longer young who had put away all thought of love or marriage. They were unveiled, although they might well have been veiled to their advantage, and they wore men's clothes. At times they carried blunderbusses of ancient make and always their belts bristled with crooked knives. They would indicate the place on the village common where we were to camp and they made it quite plain that we were to camp nowhere else. Their countenances were always dour and forbidding – so forbidding indeed that their incorruptible status was immediately accepted and neither I nor my *cavass* made the least effort to undermine it.

These women were the acknowledged mistresses of the wolfish watchdogs that abounded, and the appearance of the dogs was such that I could readily believe as reported that their sires had intermarried with the wolves of the mountain. Obedient to an emphatic gesture from the sinewy hands of their mistresses these wolf-dogs took up their posts of duty. If we moved they moved too. They were stationed to the right and the left of us, in front and behind us, and I must say that they displayed one virtue which I came to appreciate. During our stay in the village which was evidently so unwelcome to all, man as well as beast, they never approached nearer to our anxious persons than ten feet. It was only years after wards that I learned why we were always placed in the custody of these women who once for all had put men out of their lives. It was Essad Pasha, the hero of Scutari, who, as will be disclosed on a later[5] page, gave me the explanation of this arrangement which at the time was so puzzling.

I made a map of our wanderings with a list of the mountain villages and the traces of the goat tracks by which they are reached, but I gave it to Consul Smucker in recognition of his assistance in the foolish venture and the rough copy that I retained has now disappeared. With the reconquest during the World War all the names have been changed, I am assured, so even if my map had survived the wear and tear of time it would not prove helpful today to the wanderer in these parts.

I remember Pristina very well and the clear mountain stream in which I bathed my blistered feet, and also the Greek inn-keeper who was not afraid to serve us with food which after the unchanging diet of goat's milk or goat's cheese was delightful. But the little villages in which we met with such a cold reception were certainly picturesque, and each and every one of them was on a war footing. Over and above the crazy crooked hovels in which the villagers housed, there always arose in a commanding position a *kula* or fortress stronghold. It was built of rough uncemented stones and the walls were loopholed to command the approach from every direction. The fort when the nature of the ground permitted was four-sided, and at each of the corners there was a little tower in which invariably there was a man or woman on the lookout with rifle near at hand. The only entrance to the stronghold was an opening about two by four and about ten feet above the ground.

Through this when the guard was changed the fighting villagers crawled. Sometimes they were aided by a ladder they drew into the fort after them, but more often they would pile a few stones one upon the other which, once inside, they pushed over with a great beam which seemed to be retained at the entrance with this purpose in view.

On a high pole before each *kula* was suspended a grinning horse's skull. Why, I never learned. My *cavass* simply said it was the custom of the country, and this was the only answer I received to many queries which I considered pertinent. Inside, as far as I could judge from the distant view, which was all that I was permitted to obtain, the men and the women of the garri-

5   See page 147.

son took potluck together and they certainly drank a good deal of *raki* before the meal was served. Then they would squat around a huge bowl suspended over a charcoal fire and with their fingers they would draw out what appeared to be morsels of goat's flesh. Only once I saw that the mess was equipped with one great communal wooden spoon.

In the evening, sometimes but not often, these stern and generally silent sentinels of the mountain villages would break out into weird music. The only instrument I saw in use was one that resembled the Serbian *gusle* but with two strings only from which stiff fingers coaxed pathetic mournful notes. Several times late in the evening the sentinels in the towers broke out into monotonous song. What the words were and what they portended I never made out. Invariably my *cavass* would say, "He is simply recalling his family tree – so that he may not forget it." But I cling to the interpretation of the German professor who maintains that these were the songs that the Pelasgians sang in the days when Homer was assembling his great song book.

In the villages our relations with the fair sex, as I have made quite plain, were of the most distant character, in fact they were practically non-existent save with the stern-visaged, heavily armed virgins, who invariably stood guard over our bivouac. But sometimes on the mountain goat paths we met rather beautiful girls all unveiled, although truth to tell they were generally a little too stalwart for my taste. As a rule they were carrying great sacks of charcoal from their lofty nests to be exchanged in the valleys for flour.

My journey was nearly ended before we came into even remote contact with the blood feuds for which this turbulent country is famed. Outside Prizren we were overtaken by a violent thunderstorm and decided to stop for the night at a little village which lay right across our path. If I cherished the least hope that in the circumstances some sort of shelter might be offered the drenched travelers I was soon disillusioned. Only the usual guard was furnished, and the unpleasant dogs. I was depressed by the weather conditions and the innumerable sepulchres that here abounded. They were quite as numerous as the one-sided stone hovels where the living were lodged, and certainly they did not strike a cheerful note. About our smoky fire, however, we later heard a tale of the custom of the country and what is called the "law of the mountains," which indicated that even at that day the toll of life as a result of the vendetta was very high.

This was by way of being a Christian village and on the Sabbath before our arrival, in the little square plot of ground which served the community as an open air church, the solemn mass had been said. The visiting priest from one of the coast parishes had just concluded his benediction when suddenly a shot rang out and a man fell dead. It was explained that as service ended one of the worshipers looked about him and unfortunately caught sight of a man whose family, as the saying is, owed his family a "life," and of course as in duty bound he shot him dead in his tracks. The affair might have passed off without the massacre which followed but for the fact that the man who fired the first shot, who did not live more than a few seconds to enjoy his victory, and his victim, were both united to many in the congregation by the closest blood ties, and the inevitable result was a pitched battle. The priest by all accounts behaved very gallantly, rushing here and there over the improvised battlefield, now imploring the wild men to desist and now lifting on high the Host, seeking to terrify them. Before reason prevailed, or more probably when the call of the blood was satisfied, there lay in the place of worship eleven dead, two of whom were women, and this was not approved and indeed deeply regretted as now inevitably some of the males would have to carry the charcoal down into the valley...

In the morning, at dawn, as our incorruptible virgin of the guard snuffled and the watchdogs withdrew snarling, we, in leaving the village, had to cross the grass plot where the savage scene had been enacted. Here on this consecrated-desecrated patch of ground where the villagers had gathered to beg forgiveness of their sins, prisoners of tradition, they had run amok, and in the performance of an inescapable duty had taken part in mass murders. Gingerly, in and out among the eleven grave mounds, some of them still be-spattered with blood, we slowly picked our way. But once out of sight we moved more quickly. That was a rude village; we were glad to leave it behind and for good.

After many long days, each followed by its even longer night, we got back to the valley of the Vardar somehow. Long before we saw it we heard the roar of the mountain water as it rushed through its rocky bed toward the sea. The moment the welcome sound fell upon his ear my *cavass* was transformed. "Our lucky star has been in the ascendant," he shouted, and though footsore and weary I did not gainsay him. An acquaintance of his bobbed up out of the bush and on the moment the *cavass* abandoned his limping pony to the care of his friend and dashed off down the rocky road. Every now and then he would turn handsprings and then his *fusta* skirts would billow out in the breeze like so many balloon jibs.

Half an hour later I hobbled into the consular compound and surprised Smucker with the keys in his hand standing before the little prison, and saw the affectionate brothers embracing, as best they could, through the dungeon bars.

"Ah," said Smucker, "There you are! Now I will let him out," and a moment later the sorely tried brothers were enjoying a fraternal embrace. The kindly Consul led me to the Turkish bath which he pre-empted for the evening, one of his diplomatic privileges. For an hour I revelled in the steaming atmosphere and the hot water. Then he produced some river-cooled Pilsner, we had supper and I felt much better; indeed in a few minutes I was bragging about the trip and saying how I would not have abandoned it for many pounds Turkish.

To celebrate my return to what with some exaggeration we chose to call civilization, Smucker wanted to make a night of it, and sent for the lean dark-skinned Gypsy dancing girls, but I soon limped off to my room at the *han*. At first and indeed for long I could not sleep. At the foot of the bed stood the incorruptible virgin in man's attire with her ancient musket and her sash bristling with crooked knives, and all about me lowered the band of unapproachable wolf-dogs who would not come near and yet would not go away. Then the friendly Omar came and by the light of a lantern cut off my long locks. Confidentially he remarked that while most of the "sons of the Eagle" professed a noble faith after all, under the skin, they too were but so many "dog brothers." When at last I fell asleep I slept for eighteen hours on end.

It had been a foolish business and wholly unprofitable, how unprofitable it had been I was only to learn the following day when I began to move about and face my situation, when on my blistered feet again I went to our "treasury," under a brick in the floor. There I found that most of the money was gone, but there was an explanatory note from Tryko, my Bulgarian interpreter. He wrote that his life was in danger from the despicable Serbian propagandists and so he had gone away and had been so free as to take the funds that were necessary for his escape, "as he knew I would like him to do." He said nothing about my wonderful Albanian shirts with which he had outfitted himself for the journey and of which I was very proud and at the moment in sore need.

It would be most unfair if in closing this incident I should leave Tryko under the implication of a charge of cowardice. He was far from timorous, and on several occasions in journeys with me he had demonstrated his courage, but here in Üsküb, in this hotbed of racial animosities and religious feuds, he had recognized that discretion was the better part of valor and so took his departure in the somewhat indelicate way I have described. Of course his position was far more precarious than mine. In the circumstances by which we were surrounded the interpreter is held responsible rather than the dolt to whom the information is translated. Of course I was regarded as outlandish, a freak of no particular importance, and probably idiotic, but there was no reason why the agitators and the propagandists should not cozen up to me. But if their information failed to stick, only Tryko was to blame.

Tryko was not indifferent to the situation into which he was born but the lessons he had learned at Robert College had not developed a broad philosophy. His views were those he had imbibed with his mother's milk; the Turks were dog-brothers, the Serbians were pig-brothers and the Greeks? Well, I shall not put on paper what he thought of the Greeks! On the other hand, he was confident of the future, there was no justification for desperate measures, at least not as far as he was concerned. In God's own time and according to His will some day the Exarch would be reading prayers according to the ritual of Saint Cyril and Saint Method in the Church of Holy Wisdom so long defiled by the Mohammedans. In the meantime he wanted to amass wealth, though with me it was uphill work. However, there was consolation in the thought that he was learning American newspaper methods that would prepare him to launch a great paper in the Balkans, just like the *New York Herald*, some day. His slogan was "the Balkans for the Bulgarians" – but as far as he could see there was no reason for hurry. Yet in spite of his aloofness from the current agitation, and his non-political devotion to the daughter of the Maltese station-master during my absence, the Albanians and the Serbians had combined against him and Tryko was doubtless wise to sneak away from Üsküb between two suns.

At the time, outsiders, and particularly those who occupied official positions, led very precarious existences along the Vardar; notable among these was the Serbian Consul-General, a very cultivated man who in addition to his official duties was writing what he regarded as the definitive history of his heroic people. I often called upon him and he frequently pointed out to me the mistakes that the great von Ranke had made in his standard history. This official, whose name escapes me, was by no means a coward, but for twelve months now he had not left the narrow precincts of the consular compound. He had advised the Belgrade government of the attitude of the people and the course he had thought it wise to pursue, and Belgrade had approved. It was enjoined upon him to avoid all public appearances and to leave nothing undone to escape assassination. At that time Serbia wished to avoid war or any incident that might bring it about.

Well, what did this fatiguing and undoubtedly dangerous Journey profit me? I fear very little; I at least had the satisfaction of doing a thing that for months I had wanted to do and that, of course, was something. As many pointed out on my crestfallen return, the pilgrimage to High Albania was doomed to failure from the very beginning. I was under the patronage of the Austro-Hungarian consulate and under the guidance of the Consul's *cavass*. I was consequently identified with their politics and racial plans, and the idea that I was a collector of rare plants which so delighted Smucker that on setting out he thrust a trowel in my hand, hoodwinked no one. But it can be said I had no alternative. I had to go in this way or not at all, and so I went and in retrospect I enjoyed the experience. I learned to like the Albanians even though they used me despitefully. In fact I came to like them better than some of the other Balkan peoples who perhaps when judged by Western standards are more worthy of esteem.

It was interesting, even for me, a rank outsider, and far from the family circle, to listen to the sing-song pedigrees of these strange Pelasgian people. Most of them ran back to Adam but even the parvenus knew by whom they were begotten, or at least thought they did, back to the Homeric days. And these were not bought and paid for pedigrees produced by a professional genealogist. These were the names of stalwart heroes handed on through the generations, that had been learned by heart. It was the tale of a proud line that extended from the dawn of history to the present day. It was a family creed clung to from the cradle to the grave, as long as there was life in their bodies. They were, and I have no doubt still are, a serious and a silent folk, as well they might be. At this time, by conservative figures, at least seventy-five per cent of the men died violent deaths and the casualties among the women who became involved in blood feuds reached a not inconsiderable figure.

Many of the things that happened to me during this ill-advised journey were inexplicable at the time, but years later at the Paris Peace Conference Essad Pasha, who represented some of the Albanian wild tribes at the great pow-wow, made them plain to me.

"Why were the virgins, the incorruptible ones, always detailed to watch over us? Was that not a man-sized job?"

"Yes and no. You see the village Elders expected, and not without reason, that, resenting your intrusion, you might be attacked. Certainly your behavior justified suspicion. Now it would have been the duty of the guard to defend you, as well as to see that you did not escape. If a man had been killed in your defense that would have been a serious matter, but if a Virgin had fallen in the performance of her duty a cause of *jak* or vendetta would not lie. The incident could have been arranged without starting a blood feud of the kind that so often entails the loss of scores of lives."

"But why were all the doors closed in our faces? Did they fear we brought smallpox with us?"

"Not at all, the villagers acted in strict accordance with the 'law of the mountain.' Had you been admitted into a household and then been slain as an intruder by other angry villagers, the head of the house and indeed all his kinsfolk would have been compelled to declare a blood feud against the murderers and that would have been very annoying. You see our laws of hospitality are very exacting. They are our birthright and above all our obligation. Many a man has died with his boots on because he ignored them. I am sorry you were not received in a more hospitable manner. If you had had a line from me things would have been very different, but in the circumstances you were lucky." And I have no doubt we were...

Three months later it fell to my lot, under instructions from the Commodore in Paris, to spend six weeks with Edhem Pasha and his so-called mobile army in the hills and valleys of Macedonia. In Üsküb we heard that the expulsion of the Bishop had exasperated the Christian Slavs of the *vilayet*, and it was also asserted that Turkish patrols had been attacked, and in these circumstances the Vali had ordered Edhem, as a preventive measure, to traverse the disturbed districts with his troops and overawe the malcontents. There was no demur from the authorities when I announced my intention of joining the expedition, although, of course, the Pasha must have been well aware of the thought behind my instructions. The Pro-Macedonia Committees in Paris and London had announced that the purpose of the expedition was to destroy the Christian villages and put the unfortunate inhabitants to the sword.

When I joined Edhem he was encamped with his force on a broad open space down the valley of the Vardar about twenty-five miles below Üsküb. Apparently the Pasha welcomed my coming and he made me as comfortable as he could. He had with him what he called two infantry brigades and a small detachment of cavalry, all told about five thousand men. The rifles of the infantry were of many makes, and the distribution of ammunition was a difficult problem. The mounted men all carried smart Spencer carbines and they were the best trained and the most energetic men in the little army. The infantry were the strangest assortment of soldiers that I have ever seen assembled under war banners – not even excluding from the comparison some Moorish and Chinese armies I was to march with in later years.

In getting together this heterogeneous force, the recruiting sergeants had, as the saying goes, evidently "robbed both the cradle and the grave." Even after making due allowance for the hardships they had sustained, it was apparent that many of the so-called *redifs* were well over sixty, while of the youngsters more than fifty per cent were but half-grown. As far as I could learn, none of them came from Thrace. They had all been brought from Anatolia across the Straits. At this time conscription in the Turkish army, barring a happy conjunction of most unusual circumstances, was a life sentence, and well aware that they would never see their distant homes again its victims were a very depressed lot, as indeed have been most of the drafted soldiers I have accompanied in my long career as a camp-follower. Once in the Turkish army, the only way of escape was by stopping an enemy's bullet. The Young Turks when they came into power in 1908 changed all this, and a three- to five-year term of service was ordered, but as the Old Turks remarked after the crushing defeats of 1912 this did not improve the *morale* of their forces!

I can only find praise for my treatment by Edhem Pasha, into whose family I was catapulted by circumstances over which he apparently could exercise no control. Orders had come from Constantinople to accord me every facility, and he carried them out with good temper and grace. He was quite different from any Turk I have ever known and I have always regarded him as a "sport" in the Ottoman tribe. Indeed many and curious were the stories that circulated in the bazaars as to his origin, and the one that appealed to me as the most probable ran as follows. During one of the innumerable Cretan insurrections a Turkish detachment stormed a mountain village, and after setting fire to the hovels and putting to the sword all its Christian inhabitants as was the orthodox custom, was marching away to the next devoted hamlet when the soldiers were amazed by the appearance on the scene of a smiling child crawling toward them from a still smouldering ruin. The child was too young even to walk. In one of those moments of compassion, that overtakes even the most cruel and hard-bitten, the soldiers adopted the waif, and this firebrand from the burning pile became in a way the regimental pet and mascot. When the campaign was over, the orphan was carried to Stamboul where he attracted the attention of, and was adopted into, a family of high official rank. Through their kindness and influence he received an excellent education and later was given a commission in the army. Step by step he won his way, but at the time I was thrown in with Edhem the only indication of his future power and renown was the magnificent war tent in which he lived.

In front of his gorgeous headquarters, wherever camp was pitched, two great spears were driven in the ground and from each of them was suspended a horse tail. I had an idea that this was an indication of the general's army rank, that he was then a Pasha of Two Tails although, of course, he climbed much higher and I believe sported as many as seven tails in later years. When the Ottoman Turks came out of Asia and overran southeastern Europe they came as mounted men and it would have been natural for them to have indicated military rank by the equine symbol, but I am bound to admit that, while I often made discreet inquiries, I was never given a frank explanation of the horse tails which were, however, always in evidence in any camp that I visited.

While Edhem Pasha, unless for reasons of his own he concealed it from me, had no knowledge of French or English, he could read German well, and at the time of my visit he was greatly interested in a book on tactics and strategy by Verdy du Vernois, a famous Prussian General with a very French name. Over this we often mulled in the evenings, and while my German was more fluent than his, he, the trained soldier, always got at the gist of the military problem which the writer sought to explain, more quickly and above all more understandingly than I did.

I must admit that these days with what the Turks called the Peace Restoring Army of Macedonia were very trying to my patience, to my nerves and to my sense of smell. Not that the little army of Edhem Pasha was more unfragrant than that of the Christian or the Confucian, the Shinto, the Moslem or the back-sliding Buddhistic hosts with which I have consorted in Europe, Asia and Africa. I would not give that impression, as that was far from being the case. No! the powerful smell of an army, pungent and penetrating, rises superior to race and creed and is always nauseating. All armies smell alike and what they smell like can only be described by a word that our wise censors are in perfect agreement in saying is not fit to print.

During the days of waiting, while information was being collected and news was being sifted by the Staff, none of which was worthy of being placed on our Broadway bulletin board, I used to get away from camp whenever I could and indeed I continued to do so, for the reason above-mentioned, even when the Pasha through one of his aides asked me to restrain my restless feet and stay closer to headquarters. When it was quite apparent that no important movements were contemplated, I would often take my horse to where the grass seemed fresher, less weedy, and then once out of sight of headquarters, I would wander down the river to dells and dingles where the atmosphere was sweet with flowers, where the alpine waters made music as they rushed through a narrow gorge. And there was still another attraction to what had become my favorite retreat. Here the river bank was dotted with tumuli. They were of ancient mud brick and evidently of great antiquity. In one of Charles Diehl's delightful as well as learned books I came across a reference which led me to conclude that before he started on his career of world conquest, Alexander, the greatest adventurer the world has ever seen, had campaigned along the Vardar. These mounds might well mark the resting places of some of his soldiers who fell in the first skirmishes. Here indeed appropriate sacrifices may have been made to their manes and on this very spot, with Alexander himself presiding, what M. Diehl calls the *carrousel sacré* may have been celebrated.

At last the army began to move. Leaving about five hundred men at the base camp on the Vardar, and also two very ancient cannon of Venetian origin and dating well back in the eighteenth century, we sallied out into what for me at least was the unknown. An excellent and sure-footed horse was assigned to me, and also a cheerful orderly whose Turkish, if Turkish it was, did not harmonize with the wayfaring dialect I was fast picking up. Our food arrangements were casual and sketchy but we had plenty of Turkish coffee and excellent Macedonian tobacco, and so as far as creature comforts were concerned I have been much worse off in climes and with armies reputed to be more civilized. In long snake-like columns we wriggled through the passes and visited scores of mountain villages. It was apparent that, warned of our approach, most of the inhabitants and all the women had sought safe refuge elsewhere, but we were always welcomed by a delegation of old men trembling and perspiring in the furs they wore even in mid-summer and always offering, often on bended knee, a sheep or a goat for the table of the Generalissimo.

Owing to the prevalence of smallpox none of the men were quartered in the villages. At the end of the day's march the soldiers would drop exhausted in their tracks, and camp for the night in the open where they had fallen. After a short rest they would begin to move about, start small charcoal fires for the coffee they ground and cooked very carefully and also very slowly, and anything else they may have been so fortunate as to "rustle" on the road. I was with the column for three weeks and never witnessed a distribution of rations or anything that indicated the presence of a commissary. The Pasha lodged in his magnificent tent and I shared with four staff officers a nearby tent that was much less regal. Neither my food nor my quarters were anything to boast about, but they were luxurious in comparison with the fare of the soldiers. In wind and all weathers, wrapped in dirty ragged blankets, they lay throughout the night until the bugle gave the signal that another marching day had dawned.

In this way and without any adventures worthy of record we wandered about for a week in this gray treeless country, and then to my surprise we found ourselves back at the base camp. Several times the column had been fired upon as it wound its way along the goat tracks. Two men were crushed by a great boulder human hands had set in motion, but we had no other casualties and the strenuous efforts that were made to catch these bushwhackers did not, as far as I could see, lead to the shedding of blood. Edhem was of the opinion that the rumors of unrest and of a probable uprising were greatly exaggerated, and he so reported to the Vali. But after an idle day in camp to rest the footsore and the weary, in belated recognition of the extent of the territory he was expected to overawe, the Pasha changed his tactics. He announced that half the force was to remain in the base camp while the other half, divided into patrols of one hundred and fifty men each, was to zigzag throughout those less accessible sections which the larger force had not visited.

I will not disguise the fact that I was extremely suspicious as to the motive behind this change of plan. Quite unduly, no doubt, I flattered myself that it was due to my presence with the army. It was a plan to escape my surveillance and, of course, I would leave nothing undone to defeat it. As three or four columns were sent out at the same time I could only accompany one of them, but which one? - there was the rub. Which was the column that had been told off to do the particularly dirty work that I was now confident was being planned?

The Pasha said I could go with the column that I preferred, and I thought to keep him on pins and needles by not indicating my choice until instructions had been given and the column I had chosen was well under way. In the course of the following weeks I participated in four expeditions, and until the last one they were as uneventful as the grand march of the main force had been. But the last one was different. We were halted at a junction of goat tracks and quite a discussion ensued as to the path we should take. Suddenly a volley came from what I had regarded as a deserted sheepfold of stone on the hillside, and three saddles were emptied. The young officer ordered an attack and it was made courageously, but three more men fell and the sheepfold was never reached. Our dead had ghastly wounds inflicted doubtless by old-fashioned rifles loaded with slugs; one of the wounded indeed had a side of his face blown off. The young officer said in answer to my unspoken inquiry, *"Komitadjis"* – "revolutionists" – and then called the attacking party back. The dead he left in their tracks but the wounded he brought off out of the line of fire and soon we were jogging back to the distant base camp which we reached with our disturbing report long after midnight.

On the following morning for at least five minutes the Pasha seemed to have lost the equanimity which I had regarded as his most marked charac-

teristic – but he soon regained it. He was, I could see, enraged that his report assuring the pacification of the country should have been so quickly
contradicted by developments. He made haste to retrieve the situation but,
like the good soldier he was, he made haste slowly. Three days elapsed; all
the other patrols were back, having met with no opposition, and then a detachment of one thousand men was selected from among the most
able-bodied for the campaign of retaliation which was planned. In the evening the mounted men went on their way with the purpose, I think, of holding and closing all the possible avenues of escape. The following morning
the infantry column was to start for the district that was now devoted to destruction, and the Pasha said he would not have the slightest objection to
my joining it.

But did I want to go? I knew perfectly well what was in store for the people
of the unfortunate villages and I knew that the punishment of bushwhack-
ing which would be meted out to them would be in strict accordance with
the laws of civilized warfare, so called. The village nearest the sheepfold
from which the deadly volley had come would be destroyed and its inhabitants put to the sword. If I went along would I prove a restraining influence?
I could hardly flatter myself that this would be the case. I had reached no
decision when the matter was taken out of my hands by a disagreeable experience, the like of which I had never suffered before. As I lay down for
the night I developed or perhaps only then became conscious that I was running a high fever, had a splitting headache, and that my bones hurt as
though they were being crushed upon a rack of medieval torture. From
what I have read of the thousands who suffered in this way from the intensive local malaria of the Vardar valley, as the army of Salonica pushed its
way inland from Salonica in 1918, I conclude that I too, doubtless was laid
low by a violent attack of malaria. Be this as it may I was certainly laid low.
The only medicine that remained in my traveling case was quinine and I
helped myself to large doses. All next day I lay on my cot stunned and certainly powerless to move – but the quinine bottle lay close at hand and I ate
up the pills and on the morning of the second day after the attack began I
could sit up. I was without fever for the time being but weak and giddy...

The Pasha insisted that I return to Üsküb and said that, as the campaign was
over and the little army would be distributed as garrisons at strategic points,
he himself returning to Constantinople, I would miss nothing that was of
importance and, with great kindness, he offered to send me to Üsküb in one

of the two army litters available. As I had seen the litters engaged for some days now in carrying smallpox patients over the hill to the pest house I asserted that I could mount my horse and by a sturdy effort did so. While I was saying goodbye to the Pasha the Commander of the punitive column came in and gave what I am sure was a frank account of how it had fared with him and his expedition. The villagers had gone away before his arrival and as the cavalry who were to intercept them on their probable flight had been unsuccessful up to that time, he concluded they had doubtless taken refuge in caves. The *komitadjis* had put up a stout defense of their stone sheepfold but after bringing down ten of the Turkish soldiers they had all been killed.

"All?" inquired the Pasha.

"Yes, all" and then he added, "There were only five of them."

"And then?" asked Edhem.

"Then," continued the officer, "we built a gallows and hanged their bodies from it – in front of the church which we set on fire."

"You did well," commented the Pasha, and I went on my way.

Certainly there was not the slightest indication of window dressing on the part of the Pasha in the way in which he handled this terrible incident...

We left the base camp about two o'clock. I was in charge of a young lieutenant who had studied under von der Goltz Pasha, the German military adviser of the Sultan, and spoke his language fluently. He had with him ten mounted men and before sunset we were through the dark defiles where danger might have lurked. I must confess, however, that the only danger I apprehended was that of falling off my horse. As a matter of fact when I dismounted at Üsküb I fell sprawling, and was so weak I had to be carried into the Turkish *han*. As my escort trotted back toward the mountains where unenviable fates were doubtless in store for them, the young officer shouted, *"Auf Wiedersehn"* and the soldiers muttered softly, *"Ade Hadji."* My good friend Smucker, the Austrian Consul, appeared shortly and placed his great store of quinine at my disposal. In three days I began to hobble about, but some weeks elapsed before I could claim to have regained my normal good health. In my later Balkan experiences I had to visit Üsküb on several occasions, but fortunately I was always able to give the lower valley of the Vardar a wide berth.

In later years I was to see Edhem Pasha frequently but, as I was at the time involved in the preparations for our own war in Cuba, I did not accompany him in his campaign in Thessaly in which, after the victories of Pharsala and Domokos, he crushed the Greek army, imposed a war indemnity of four million Turkish pounds, and was given the title of *Ghazi* or Conqueror by the grateful Sultan.

Henry Pozzi; 1935:

Excerpts from *Black Hand over Europe*; 1935 op. cit.

III. THE BULGARIAN SCENE: II. The Macedonian Question

In the heart of the Balkan peninsula, stretching from Lake Orchrida, which washes the Albanian frontiers, to Drima on the Aegean Sea; from Salonika to Mount Shar north of Skopje, lies Macedonia, a beautiful country nearly three times as large as Belgium and inhabited by two and a half million people who possess the same language, the same culture, and with few exceptions, the same religion. Of this people, seventy per cent, are pure Bulgars.

Behind this country lie twenty centuries of tumultuous and tragic history, Rome, the Barbarians, the Crusades, Venice, the Ottoman, Alexander and the Empire of the Old World. On of the most powerful efforts for liberty of the Turks; always crushed, always regenerated, up to the victory of the Balkan Allies in 1912. A first distribution of Macedonian lands between Belgrade and Athens after the first Bulgar defeat in 1913. A second in 1918 after the World War and the second Bulgar defeat.

Today, a heavier servitude than the old one rests upon Macedonia, because the new master are stronger than the Turks, and more violent, and Europe, this time, supports and approves them. Five to six hundred thousand Mace-

donians (an entire people) have sought refuge in Bulgaria since the of their
country by Greece and Serbia.

Those who were able to leave have left, since the peace of July 1913, and
since the Armistice of October 1918, rather than suffer foreign domination.
All the intellectuals, all the teachers, all those whom their antecedents or
their relations rendered undesirable or suspect, have been expelled since
the installation of the conquerors. Thousands more, before the frontiers
closed, fled and abandoned all their property, often leaving behind them all
or a part of their family.

Of the same blood, the same language, the same traditions as the Bulgars,
they have been received by them as brothers.

Finally, the Greek authorities expelled thousands of Macedonian families
en bloc after the disaster of Smyrna, in order to install the Hellenic population of Asia Minor on their lands and in their homes, which they had confiscated without indemnity. The outcasts of Macedonia were shepherded by
the Bulgarian Government, with the aid of the League of Nations, towards
Bourgas, on the Black Sea and towards Dobroudja.

There they transformed what was before only broken stones and swamps
into a flourishing country. Nothing distinguishes these Bulgars of Macedonia from the Bulgars of Bulgaria in the midst of whom they live. They are
neighbors in the same villages, a number of them have won high social positions, some have become ministers, even Presidents of the Bulgarian
Council.

Yet all have remained Macedonian. They look incessantly towards their beloved Fatherland, towards the obscure hamlets, the little white-and-rose
cities of the frontier. There they were born and there most of them lived for
so long that, if the barriers were removed tomorrow, every one of them
would return to his native land.

"But your fields, the lands which the Government of Sofia have given to
you and which your children and you have worked for fifteen years," I
asked a Macedonian labourer near Belica, "would you abandon them?"

"My lands?" he replied. "They are over yonder in Macedonia. They are waiting for me. I hope to live long enough to return and sit on the stone bench which my father had placed under the apricot-trees before the door. He, also, is waiting for me."

Five hundred thousand Macedonians in Bulgaria, where they are at home, where they have married, where they have nothing to fear from anyone, still think and speak as this old peasant of Belica.

Fifteen hundred thousand Macedonians, in the annexed land under Greek or Serbian domination, live and have their children in the hope of this return, and in the expectation of it.

What a tremendous pressure is here! What a colossal weight of desire waiting only for the right moment to take shape in action.

Soon after the annexation, attempts were made to "Hellenise" or "Serbianise" the Macedonians who remained in their country, and when they attempted their first gestures of revolt, they had the breath knocked out of them by the crushing violence of their new masters. The gendarmes, the prison, the certainty that they had no chance of help from anyone, has taught them in the past fifteen years to walk straight along the road indicated to them. They have become docile, respectful, obedient. They have learned to smile through their tears.

I have seen them, and the memory of the decay into which these free men have fallen makes my blood boil still.

The Macedonians in Bulgaria are waiting also. But they are free, and for fifteen years they have pursued an obstinate dream that they will liberate their lost brothers. All the resources they have are consecrated to this task. There is not one among them, wherever the hazard of exile has placed him, who does not belong to a society, an association, a group of some sort destined to keep up among its members, and especially among the youth, the sentiment of national solidarity and the cult of a native land momentarily lost.

These organizations have their form in associations of Macedonian women; student associations; organizations for the assistance of old people, orphans, sick; associations for propaganda abroad; all form a network that lets nothing pass between its meshes.

Not a Macedonian in Bulgaria! Not a Macedonian in foreign countries! That is the national slogan. And the apex of this organization is a handful of men working in broad daylight with legal methods and means; the Macedonian National Committee, which commands its energies, centralizes its resources, and directs its activities.

In the shadow, beside the National Committee, but absolutely distinct from it, absolutely foreign to its work and actions, is another group of men, directed by other chiefs of the ORIM. We shall meet with it again.

The Macedonian question has existed for half a century. The desire for Macedonian liberty has become a burning obsession. This determination for liberty cost the Turks their possessions in Europe. Initial cause of the two Balkan wars, it was in order to liberate Macedonia that Bulgaria prepared the coalition in 1912, and it was in order to seize her from the victorious Bulgars, that the Serbs and the Greeks, in turn, joined against her in 1913. Macedonia was indirectly, but certainly, at the origin of the World War. A hot spot, indeed!

Since the peace of 1918 the question of Macedonia has become like a worm in the brain of Yugoslavia. To pretend to reduce the Macedonian question, as the propagandists of Belgrade try, to the proportion of an absurd struggle between a great modern state and a few handfuls of bandits, is an absurdity.

A latent insurrection which has lasted fifteen years and which will surely excite a new European conflagration unless things change drastically, merits more than two or three thousand lines of trite nonsense in certain recent news stories.

Whence comes the danger?

From the Macedonians themselves? From legal organizations such as the National Committee, or extra-legal as the ORIM?

Not at all!

The peril comes from the fact that the Serbs have annexed, thanks to France's support, territories and populations which they have declared Serb when they were, and intended to remain, Bulgarian. They have been able to subject them, but they have not been able to assimilate them, and Macedonia, always ready for the insurrection, weighs upon Serbian politics like a ball and chain.

In order to free themselves from this impediment, the Pan-Serb directors of Belgrade have decided to use the activity of the Macedonian nationalist organizations as an excuse for attacking Bulgaria. The Pan-Serbs have calculated in this way that they would kill two birds with one stone, and that they would compel the Macedonians to renounce all hope of liberation by destroying their support in Bulgaria. By destroying Bulgarian independence, also, they would reach Salonika and the Aegean.

Pan-Serbism has been working with all its force for several years to carry out this design. The violent campaign conducted by the Pan-Serb Press Bureau in France within the last few years, by means of books and newspapers, and by faked documents has had no other object than to prepare French opinion for a Bulgaro-Yugoslav conflict.

History has shown them the need for this. In June 1914, assured of the support of Russia (whose Pan-Slav party, directed by Sazonov, pushed them to action), the Pan-Serbs risked their all. French public opinion accepted the denials of the Serb Government that it had organized the double assassination at Sarajevo. It was because of the Serbs, and in order to defend their rights, that France went to war.

Today, since the publication of the debates which ended in the condemnation of the assassins of the Austrian Archduke, it is no longer possible to deny that these men acted at the formal instigation of certain Serbian officials. The Provision of money, arms, forged passports, and guides for crossing the frontier as far as in order to ascertain the most favorable spot for the attack, the act of Gavrilo Princip and the Tchabrinovitch, has all been shown to be the work of men depending directly on the Government of Belgrade.

France must not be duped by another Sarajevo staged to save the Yugoslav dictatorship.

....

During my visit to Bulgaria I took the opportunity of visiting Dr. Stanicheff, the President of the Macedonian National Committee.

I have rarely encountered a more engaging personality than this "revolutionary." Little over fifty years of age, tall, with steel-grey hair, clear of eye, a long, fine face lengthened still more by a pointed beard, he has incarnated the determined strength of his people. I saw him last on a fine morning of August 1932, at the Committee, in Alexandra the First Street in Sofia, a few steps from the National Bank.

The great Macedonian organization has chosen for its headquarters an old bourgeois house with a ramshackle facade occupied on the ground floor by a *coiffeur de dames*. It is a peaceful street where lovers, because of the near-by garden, have their rendezvous. Nearly opposite, at the corner of the street leading towards the Central Post Office and the Opera, is the most important pavement shoe-shine rank in Sofia. I have often thought that they were the men whom a young colleague of mine must have taken for the sentinels who, he alleged, were posted around the National Committee. From a distance, the shining brushes which they carry at the belt might, indeed, give the illusion of hand-grenades or Browning pistols.

This place has been described as a mysterious and terrible fortress, with cellars encumbered with bombs and infernal machines, rooms barricaded and transformed into laboratories, manned by a garrison armed to the teeth, and always on the watch. This description, written in between two glasses of *slivovitza* on a cafe table and published last year in great Parisian journal, made thousands of honest men shudder!

Yet in reality, what does one find: not even a doorman at the street door; no one on the stairs; not the shadow of a doorman in the lobby at the end of which, in a little side room, sits a simple smiling old man, scribbling addresses and keeping ledgers. Nothing which might prevent the first comer, should it suit his fancy, from entering the office of the president and shooting him down like a rabbit.

Dr. Stanicheff greeted me cordially and asked my business. My answer was a follows: "I have come to the Balkans to investigate by myself, in my own

320

manner, where and how I please. I do not want to be a machine for registering the voices of those whose opinions I like. I want to be a photographer who chooses his viewpoint and his personages for himself. I want to operate the camera and develop the negatives myself. I have NO other mission than to 'photograph' things and people at the right angle and under a good light, and to present them to the public without retouching."

My host with a sign of his head showed his appreciation of my attitude.

"The Macedonian question," I asked. "Will you explain to me as if I knew nothing about it. I have read all the books that your friends have written about it. All the replies from Belgrade and Athens, also. If I have made an opinion, I want to forget. Give me yours."

I still hear the laughter of Dr. Stanicheff:

"My opinion?" he said. "It is the opinion of a man with a Serbian price on his head? But you know it in advance! It is very simple. There is no Macedonian problem!"

I startled. Everyone from one end to the other of the Balkans has given me the same answer! "There is no Macedonian question" was just what Dr. Radovanovitch said to me in Belgrade not eight days before.

Dr. Stanicheff continued. "The word 'problem' stands for a very doubtful, controversial thing. Whereas the Macedonian question is clearness itself. To men of good faith it possesses the accuracy of a geometrical or algebraic theorem.

"The vast majority of Macedonians are Bulgars, at least in the proportion of four to one. They are Bulgars by origin, by custom, and by language. And all the geographers, all the philologists, be they German, Russian, English, French or Swiss, are all of the same opinion. Not fifty years ago all the Serb specialists said so too.

"The celebrated orientalist and historian, Louis Leger, professor at the College of France, whom the savants of the entire world recognized as their master in all Slav questions, wrote in 1917 in *Le Panslavisme et l'Interet francais*: 'Macedonia is almost entirely peopled with Bulgars in spite of the affirmations to the contrary of the Serbs and the Greeks whose pretensions cannot prevail against the precise declarations of independent ethnologists, such as Lejean, Kiepert, Rittich, Grigorovitch, Helferding and MacKenzie. It was only when Serbia lost Bosnia and Herzegovina by the treaty of Berlin that certain statesmen had the idea of seeking a compensation on the Macedonian side and claiming the existence of Serbs in this country, which is solely peopled with Bulgars."

"M. Ludovic Naudeau, former war correspondent of the *Journal* in the Balkans, declared on 7th February, 1927, to the *Comite National d'etudes sociales et politiques de Paris*: 'Before the War, when one traveled about Macedonia, one encountered Bulgars, and not Serbs. Now Macedonia today has been baptised Serb.'"

"It is not necessary to be a great savant in order to substantiate our claims. We do not need to rummage in archives, to compare phonetics and to follow the migrations of races across the ages. It suffices to see, one beside the other, a Bulgar from Bulgaria and a Macedonian from Geuvgueli, from Veles or from Skopje. Try it yourself."

"The Serbs say the Macedonians are Serbs, Serbs torn from Serbia by the Ottoman conquest, five centuries ago," I told him.

"The Serbs said that to you, did they? Naturally! The unfortunate part of it is that they waited to make this magnificent discovery until they had need of pretext to justify their political designs on Macedonia, and that up to then there was not a single Serb to deny the exclusively Bulgarian character of Macedonia."

"Today, thanks to your Frenchmen who won the War for them, the Serbs have achieved their ends. They are installed in Macedonia. And they have made haste to declare solemnly, peremptorily, to the world that all the population of Macedonia are purely and undisputably Serb. As for the five hundred thousand Macedonians refuged in Bulgaria since 1913, the Serbian statistics soon reduced them to a few tens of thousands of Bulgar immigrants returned to their country of origin."

"Why this lie, which is so clumsy that it has become an insult even to those who use it? Thousands of Europeans of all nationalities who have come to

Bulgaria in the past fifteen years have been able to verify with their own eyes the presence of Macedonian refugees and to give an account of their numbers."

"Why the Serbs find themselves bound to deny the evidence, you know as well as I. They have done it to avoid the application in Macedonia of the stipulations of the treaty of Saint-Germain which organized the protection of ethnic minorities in the annexed territories. In order to accomplish this it was necessary to make the Great Powers admit that the Macedonians were not Bulgars (to whom the special statutes of the treaty were applicable) but Serbs subject to all the laws of Serbia. It was also necessary, consequently, to deny the existence of the immense Macedonian emigration into Bulgaria."

"The move has succeeded perfectly, thanks to the support lent by certain of your statesmen to the men of Belgrade. Not one of the Macedonian requests for frontier revision has ever been examined by the League of Nations. When they arrive at Geneva Belgrade says: 'No!' France supports her, all the friends of France say 'Amen!' and the trick is done."

"For the League of Nations there are no Macedonians; hence there can be no Macedonian question! And today fifty thousand Serb soldiers, gendarmes and irregulars, fourteen years after the so-called return of Macedonia to her pretended country, occupy our country and impose upon her a regime which you will be able to judge when you have seen it."

"They told you at Belgrade that the violence and the abuses which we denounce exist only in our imagination and that Serbian Macedonia lies satisfied and happy under the administration of Belgrade? Naturally! Well, since you count on leaving shortly for Macedonia you will be able to judge for yourself – at least to the extent which they will permit you to do so. Over there you will see who lies, we or Belgrade. Don't try to be discreet with me. For us you will never be too outspoken. In the battle which we are waging alone, against all, for the liberty and the life of our people, there is one weapon which we never employ: the lie."

"When you come back from over there, on the condition, however, that you have been able to see behind the curtain, you will think as I do! There you will see a horror that exceeds all imagination. You will find a whole people crushed without pity, tortured cruelly, assassinated by the most abominable means."

"Let us forget about that, my dear Doctor," I interrupted him. "The Serbs have replied to all of the accusations made against them by your friends by categorically denying them. You pretend that they lie. They declare that it is you and your friends who lie. Well, I shall see for myself! Let us come back for a little while ago. How do you expect Belgrade, after fourteen years of uninterrupted Serb occupation, to consent, with a good will and without being constrained by force, to give up Macedonia? The independence of Macedonia? The hypothesis of the Dantzig corridor to Germany."

"I know it!" agreed Dr. Stanicheff. "Today it is impossible. Too many interests are leagued against right, our right. To give satisfaction to Macedonia would be to open the door to a general revision of all the peace treaties. Unless France, without whom they cannot live, compels them to do so, they will never consent. So we must learn to wait. We know that a day will come when our legitimate aspirations will be satisfied. We shall be patient. We have waited for such a long time that we can wait still longer."

"But what do we demand today? Only that the Government of Belgrade gives to our miserable annexed compatriots, loyally and without reservations, all the rights and all the liberties which they agreed to give them by the treaty of Saint-Germain. That, in other words, it stops treating them like outlaws. Nothing more!"

"If Belgrade did that, loyally and without reservations, if property, honor, and individual liberty were guaranteed in Macedonia as they are in all civilized countries, all conflict between Yugoslavia and us would cease. Our refugees would return to their old homesteads. They would agree to be Yugoslav subjects – which does not mean Serbs!"

"And Belgrade knows all this very well. They know we are ready to admit Macedonia as a sister nation with Croatia, Serbia, and Slovenia, all going to form a Yugoslav Federation in which all its members would have equal rights – with a common army, common diplomacy, public finance and Parliament. This Federation, these United States of the Balkans, would form that Union of all the Southern Slavs of which the Serbs dream."

"And the ORIM, my dear Doctor?" I asked. "What are you going to do with the ORIM in all these fine projects?"

"What program and what intentions do you attribute to the ?" he asked in reply. "The men who direct the ORIM think as do those who direct the National Committee. Many times they have publicly declared that they were ready to lay down their arms if Belgrade would cease to maltreat the annexed Macedonians and give them the legal guarantees and the liberties to which they have a right. The ORIM added, however, that until then they would continue the struggle."

"Unfortunately, I admit, we are still a long way from this solution of justice and good sense! The Serb administration is nowhere near abandoning the methods of violence which have raised all the Macedonians up against her. She will not modify her methods. She will even aggravate them and, besides, look what is happening in Croatia."

"Doctor," I said, "confess that your organization does all it can to exasperate the Serbs. Three months ago at Nisch two bombs killed or crippled twenty people. A month ago at Chtip a gendarmerie was burned; not fifteen days ago the train I was on was dynamited in the station at Geuvgueli."

Dr. Stanicheff looked straight into my eyes.

"If you knew me better," he said, "you would know how horrible such violence is to me. But there are cases where violence is just, where violence becomes a sacred duty. They reproach our revolutionary organizations for reprisals against the Serb administrators and police, their terrorist attacks in annexed Macedonia, but they say nothing of their deeds which have inspired our attacks."

"Tell me how your public opinion would have received the following facts if they had taken place in Alsace-Lorraine during the German occupation? I cite them to you among a thousand others – and I could cite worse..."

"At Souchitza, which is a hamlet between Skopje and Veles, four women, Raina Nalzev, Miyana Paneva, Victoria Andreeva and Vassa Mitreva, who refused to reveal where their husbands had fled, were whipped until they bled by Serb gendarmes who then poured petrol on their armpits and loins and set them on fire.

"At the village of Debrevo, a young girl of sixteen, Kostadine Miladin Tatcheva, was declared guilty of having hummed a Bulgarian song. She was stripped naked, strapped to a bench, given sixty blows of a club on her back, and then was violated by the chief of the detachment and his six men.

"At Katchanik, the peasant Eftine Athanassof, suspected of having sheltered agents of the ORIM, was clubbed to death with rifle-stocks after having been crucified by the irregulars of the Serb White Hand. His neighbor in agony, Manassi Antoff, had thorns buried under the nails of his hands and feet by his executioners.

"At Yastermnik, by the order in the presence of the Chief of the State Police, Jika Lazitch (the man who is today Minister of the Interior of Yugoslavia) three peasants, Kostadin Demianoff, Ivan Angeloff and Georgui Stoicheff, and three peasant women Llinka Ivantcheva, Mita Dimitrieva and Mirsa Valinove, all of whom were denounced for having given refuge to revolutionists, were whipped to death before all the village. The women were first outraged in a dreadful fashion.[6]

"These abominations," went on Dr. Stanicheff, "against which nothing protects our unfortunate compatriots, make it impossible to find a peaceful solution in Macedonia.

"Since the Serbs have occupied her, Macedonia has become a hell. Hundreds of homes and farms, entire villages, under the pretext of punishing their inhabitants because of their alleged sympathies for revolutionary organisations, have been burned by gendarmes or Serb irregulars. All our cemeteries have been profaned, all the monuments to our dead have been destroyed, all the riches of our churches, of our libraries, of our monasteries have been stolen. Innumerable women and young girls have been sullied; countless Macedonians have been tortured, beaten, imprisoned and put to death without trial. Our priests have been insulted, and our teachers too: our children have no longer the right to bear their names unless it has a Serb termination. An entire people has been deprived of the right to think, to speak or to pray, other than as their masters wish. They can no longer come and go, even from village to village, without permission; they can no longer go

out in the evening after certain hours, they are crushed by taxes have no
justice, have no recourse against the pleasure or the crimes of administrators and police to whom they are subjected.

"That is the Macedonian question, sir. The agony of a martyred people who
yet do not wish to die.

"Imagine a man who has succeeded in finding a refuge in Bulgaria after
weeks of hiding himself in the mountains, and who learns that his wife has
served as a plaything, before all the terrified neighbors, for the police come
to search her home. Imagine the feelings of the father whose daughter has
been treated as a prostitute. Imagine the feelings of a brother whose dishonored sister has drowned herself in despair. Do you dare call their vengeance
assassination?

"The Carnegie Commission, which included besides the Belgian Minister
Vandervelde, two Frenchmen, M. d'Estournelles de Constant and M. Justin
Godart, published a report on the Macedonian atrocities that is more over-
whelming than any of our accusations."

6   I have since verified these things for myself. I saw the scars of the two victims at
        Souchitza, and heard with my own ears from the mouths of three witnesses (whose
        names and addresses I had obtained from a responsible source) the story of this
        abominable thing.
        The truth of the atrocities of Dobrevo and Yastremnik has been certified to me by a
        diplomatic representative of France. T have held in my own hands the reports of our
        two agents who related them. One of these reports ends with the following words: Such
        facts, which would stir public opinion to horror if they were known, justify,
        unfortunately, all the reports of the Macedonian revolutionists and are absolutely
        without excuse. They maintain sentiments of hatred and a desire for revenge in the
        population which only await the occasion to manifest themselves.
        "A country which employs a Lazitch," said the French diplomat whose testimony I have
        mentioned, "dishonours herself. This minister is a man of blood...I have seen him at
        work!"
        I, too. I was at Belgrade, in July 1932, dining at the Excelsior Restaurant behind the
        royal palace, with my old friend Dragomir Stefanovitch, former charge d'affaires of
        Serbia at Paris during the War.

"I defy you, sir, to find a single copy of their report. Belgrade has somehow succeeded in making them vanish."

....

We talked until the office closed. I left Dr. Stanicheff at the corner of the avenue Marie Louise. My eyes followed him as he made off among the crowd jostling each other on the burning sidewalk. He walked with head held high and with a rapid step, as unmindful of the sweltering sun as of the assassins who were perhaps waiting for him at his door, as they waited for his friend Dimitri Mihailoff in June 1932; and as they waited for Simeon Evtimoff – one of the most noble and most upright young Europeans.

The Macedonian question is not solved by a long, long chalk.

III. The "ORIM"

ORIM. What innumerable legends surround it! "Organisation of bandits," say the Serbs.

"Union for a sacred aim of liberation of a people atrociously oppressed," say the Macedonians."

"The heroic personification of a greater idea," wrote Stjepan Radic on 19th June, 1928, the eve of his assassination at Belgrade."

Lazitch came to sit down next to us. Stefanovitch who knew him introduced us. I noticed his intelligent, hard eyes and brutal jaws. His nails were black, but he talked well. He had just returned from Macedonia where he had been organizing the State Police. I noticed one thing particularly, all the while he was animatedly telling us risque stories about women, he did not stop picking little flies from the table cloth which he would hold for a moment struggling between his fingers. Then, without stopping his flow of talk, gently, one by one, he tore off their wings, and with the end of his cigarette, tapping lightly, unhurriedly, he forced them to crawl by burning their abdomens.

"With the Macedonian women also," he said to us, "in order to render them amorous, when they are insensible, we place hot irons on a good spot."

What is this ORIM – this Macedonian Revolutionary Organisation?

Let us go back forty years.

In 1893 Serbia and Bulgaria were still very small. The Red Sultan pressed his yoke upon the lands of Macedonia which extend from Orchrida in Albania to Adrianople in Thrace; from Mount Char, which is south of Nisch, to Salonika at the mouth of the Vardar.

Three Macedonians, the oldest of whom was not thirty years of age: Dane Groveff, a teacher, Dr. Tatcheff, a young doctor and a professor, Pere Tocheff, gathered one winter evening at the village of Ressene, near Bitolj, to decide that the hour had come to put an end to it. Macedonia had suffered enough. If she were organized, if she were armed, if she had chieftains, the Turks would be thrown out.

Alone, these three were going to organize her and arm her. They swore on sacred ikons to consecrate their lives to their task.

Their program, from which the ORIM has not deviated one iota in forty years, was: Prepare the Macedonian populations for armed combat against the oppressor; obtain security for the people and guarantees of order and justice in the administration.

Less than three months afterwards hundreds of Macedonians, young and old, had taken the oath of the ORIM. Rich and poor, great poets such as Christo Matoff, university men like Gouchtanoff, doctors of law like Todor Saeff, professors of science, merchants, bankers, officials, doctors, celebrated officers like Boris Draganoff, and also obscure peasants, poor mountain shepherds, artisans and village teachers, all had taken the oath which bound them for ever to incessant propaganda, to supreme devotion, without pity for traitors, without excuse for the cowardly.

They were subjected to an iron discipline. Courage, integrity, purity of morals defense of the oppressed and the weak, total abnegation – they must always set the example! Any failure on the part of members of the ORIM punished as mercilessly as she strikes the enemies of the country.

Soon they were a thousand, ten thousand, twenty thousand – all Macedonia!

Any Macedonian, whatever his official nationality, whether Bulgarian, Roumanian or Albanian, provided he were Christian and morally above reproach, could be a member of the organization. It was sub-divided into groups of ten members, each one of whom obeyed a chief or voivode elected by secret vote. All the groups of a locality constituted the local organization, directed by an elected committee. The local committee was subordinate to a central committee, which was placed under the absolute authority of the chief, chosen from among its members to be the supreme voivide of the ORIM.

Immediately the ORIM set to work. In the solitudes of the mountains old soldiers trained volunteers. Soon the first shots echoed in the defiles, the first fires were lighted, the first bombs exploded in the garrisons, the stations and the official buildings. The Venitza affair in 1896; Valandovo in 1897; Enidje-Vardar in 1990; devastation and terror sown in Salonika the following year, then at Seres, then at Skopje, then at Veles. They fought every day, everywhere, from one end to the other of Macedonia.

The Macedonian falcon was soaring!

On 2nd August, 1903, fires lighted on the mountain peaks from Kostom to Orchrida, signaled the 30,000 volunteers of the ORIM that the hour had sounded to chase the Turks. All Macedonia rose *en bloc*.

The struggle was fearful; and when at last the ORIM, outnumbered, crushed, had to admit defeat, the slaughter was unimaginable. Seven thousand heads fell, 5,000 prisoners were impaled, hanged, or burned alive; 3,000 children were mutilated or eviscerated, all the women and young girls in the regions of the insurrection were violated.

But Europe was affected. The Great Powers demanded autonomy for the martyred provinces and liberty, thanks to the ORIM, began to dawn over Macedonia.

But the long-awaited sun did not appear. The Young Turks had just replaced Abdul-Hamid. Hardly installed in power, they tried to settle for good their accounts with Macedonia. The massacre recommenced. The resistance of the ORIM recommenced also. Four years of struggle followed, without mercy on one side or the other; ambushes, terrorist attacks, mass executions and insurrections without cease. Conquered in their turn by the Balkan allies, the Turks left in 1912. The volunteers of the ORIM had their large part in the victory. They had guided, informed, supported the Serbo-Bulgarian armies. They had fallen by thousands on the battlefield. They had been sacrificed in vain.

Macedonia, abandoned by the Turks, was dismembered by the conquerors who had turned against their Bulgarian ally after the Ottoman defeat. The Great War ended the disaster. The heart of Macedonia, Chtip, Skopje, Bitolj, Veles, Ochrida, Guevgueli, became Serb. The rest, Xanthi, Seres, Salonika, Florina was Greek. A little corner was left to Bulgaria.

And while 500,000 Macedonians, an entire people, fled the domination of the Greeks and the Serbs, still more merciless even than that of the Turks, the ORIM resumed the struggle, but this time against Belgrade and Athens.

To the hangings of prisoners, the massacres of suspects, to the fearful persecutions of the people, they replied with the execution of hangmen and judges; rendering violence for violence, they matched the administrative terror by guerilla warfare, and by their infernal machines.

In the last fourteen years, hundreds of Serbs stations, trains, gendarmeries, public buildings, warehouses, and munition depots have been burnt or dynamited in annexed Macedonia. The ORIM has not disarmed.

Installed in Bulgaria, where it can count on the absolute support of all Macedonian exiles, the ORIM negotiates with the enemies of Yugoslavia, concludes alliances with the revolutionary organizations of Croatia and of Slovenia, perfects her means of action, and awaits patiently the hour of the great interior crisis of Yugoslavia which, by war or revolution, will permit the liberation of Macedonia.

She has her representatives in all the great European capitals, her diplomatic delegates, and her secret codes.

Her chief is Ivan Mikhailoff, whom the bullet of a traitor eight years ago made the successor of the great Todor Alexandroff. He is the adversary Belgrade dreads most. By the sharpness of his political sense, by his inflexible will, by the devoted fanaticism which he inspires, he has made of the ORIM, as for all men of Macedonian blood, the very incarnation of his country.

A legend persistently broadcast by the Pan-Serb propagandists declares that Ivan ("Vrantche" as his faithful call him) lives surrounded by armed guards, never sleeps twice under the same roof, never shows himself in public for fear of the reprisals of those whose parents or friends he has assassinated. This legend I heard defended at Sofia even, at the Union Club, and in diplomatic circles by men from whom one had the right to expect authentic information.

Appendix

Since Bonsal described his visit to Hungary under "Hungarian Divertissement" [on page 105] to show the cultural divide between Balkan Serbia and Central European Hungary, it is fitting to include the following to describe Hungary after World War 1.

Repington; 1923:

Excerpt from *After the War: London – Paris – Rome – Athens – Prague – Vienna – Budapest – Bucharest – Berlin – Sofia – Coblenz – New York – Washington; A Diary* by Lt, Col. Charles à Court Repington, Boston-New York: Houghton Mifflin, 1922.

7. THE SORROWS OF HUNGARY

Budapest, Friday, April 15, 1921. The Danube is a nobler river than the Moldau, but Budapest has a strong resemblance to Prague, with its heights and palaces on one bank and the lower part of the town on the other. Went up our Legation. Hohler has been and still is seriously ill with 'flu and bronchitis. Saw Athelstan-Johnson, the First Secretary, and looked over the Legation — I beg its pardon the Headquarters of the British High Commission[1] which has a beautiful view over the river from the heights close to the old cathedral. Very comparable with Sir Clerk's view from his terrace over Prague, but the Legation here is much smaller. A charming place of an old-word type with arched and vaulted roofs and an inner court.

1   The Treaty of Trianon had not been ratified at the time.

Left a card and note on Count Albert Apponyi who is away. Lunched with A.-J. in his house and we discussed European politics. He thinks that the old nobles party here is losing ground, and that the various countries round hate each other too much to combine. He would approve of the final break-up of Austria, part going to Czechs and Serbs and part to Germany and Hungary. I said that I did not see the continued existence of Czecho-Slovakia on these terms and that Italy would not like Germany on her borders.

He told me that Lord Bertie's correspondence[2] was lodged at Welbeck[3] in two strong boxes and that it would not be published for fifty years. I asked if it included the private letters written to the Foreign Office and were they not very Rabelaisian? Yes, he said they were. Bertie had copies of them all, for he was a bureaucrat and had kept everything. I grumbled because we should never see these gems. A.-J. said that they were a most faithful and accurate representation of Bertie's time in Paris during the war.

Went on to see Brigadier-General Gorton, my old friend of past Intelligence days, now at the head of our Military Mission here. The French press seems to be quite off the rails in belittling the Little Entente and in boosting a Karl Kingdom here and in Austria. I am amazed that they seem quite off the Czechs. The Frenchmen ought to travel a bit and they would see how the land lay. I saw Mr. Barber of our Commercial Branch, Mr. Humphreys being away, and am to come in and gain a little trade wisdom from him to-morrow. Went to the opera with the Gortons at 6 P.M. A good house and a competent orchestra. "The Evening Star," by Meyerbeer. I have never heard it before. Very well done. Went on afterwards to dine at about 9.15 with the Gortons and General Bellini, the Italian Military Commissioner, and his

2   Ambassador Sir Francis Bertie was known for his unsubtle language. In January 1907, for example, he wrote: "The Germans aim to push us into the sea and steal our clothes".

3   Mansion in Nottinghamshire, now military college.

wife. I asked the Italian General whether Italy's natural frontier on the Alps appeared to him worth the passing over of the Tyrol to Germany, as seemed to me likely to happen eventually. He thought it was worth even having Germany on the border for Italy to gain the natural frontier. Doubt whether Sforza will agree with this opinion. Am afraid that our own people at home are too much immersed in their Martha-like worries to understand where all this affair is leading. The abandonment of Austria is the beginning of a great future disturbance which will entail the ruin of the Benès scheme and of Czecho-Slovakia, and the eventual spread of German dominion over not only Austria, but Hungary, which is hard beset by Roumanians and Jugo-Slavs not to seek refuge in a German, or in fact in any combination which is against the Roumanians.

Saturday, April 16, 1921. A Hungarian Cabinet crisis which followed the Karl *Putsch* has resulted in the replacement of Dr. Gratz from the F.O[4]. here and his replacement by Count Banffy, Count Stefan Bethlen, aged about forty-eight, becomes Minister- präsident, or P.M. I am told one effect of recent losses of territory by Hungary has to leave about fifty per cent of the present population Protestant with some affinity to the Wee Frees. This counts for the visit of the American and English Unitarians to Transylvania last autumn. The Magyars had shrieked about their treatment by the Roumanians. The parsons after a three months' tour gave the Roumanians a dressing-down, and said that it was like placing Mexicans over two million Americans. Had an innings with Barber about trade and commerce. He gave me interesting and relevant facts. I never realised before Hungary was now only one-third her former size and population; had lost all her mines, iron ore, forests, half of coal, headwaters, etc., and was reduced to the status of a large farm. Albert Apponyi recommends a waiting policy, sure that the peace is untenable, but also that no basis exists yet for modification. In fact — *pensons-y toujours!* Quite sound. Colonel Alfred Stead is specialising here in films, oil, river transport, banks, and other speculations, have a suspicion that the clauses about Danube navigation are the most sensible

4   Foreign Office

things in the Peace Treaties. They are the only things not demonstratively cursed by everybody. I must look into them. I am told that the Hungarians secretly do a night's drill a week. They can place 70,000 men in the field, but of course one cannot neglect their old war-trained veterans whom Gorton puts at 800,000 men. Pesth very full of officers in uniform. Not quite the old aristocratic-looking lot. Expect they are all pretty hard hit. Ministers here get the equivalent of thirty-six pounds a year.

Motored with Gorton up to the golf course on the Downs behind Buda. Fine air and views and a perfect mass of wild flowers of all sorts. The Gortons dined with me. He told me that the Archduke Joseph stayed on here all through the Bela Kun Bolshevist régime and called himself Joseph Anschut from the name of his country house. Joseph a regular Magyar and speaks the lingo. He is forty-eight. He means to call himself Lorraine instead of Habsburg as he is entitled to do by his descent from Maria Theresa. It would evade the proscription of the Habsburg, but Gorton tells him that the Allies might see through the plan. He is a tiptop shot and a fine sportsman. The Hungarian Habsburgs seem to have been little in touch with F. J.'s crowd. When F. J.[5] came here he stayed with the Andrássys, etc. When Karl came here to be crowned he scarcely left his railway train. G. says that the reverence of the people is not for an individual, but for the sacred crown of St. Stephen. Last night at the opera the Archduchess occupied the Royal Box. Met the American Military Attaché Enslen and his wife. Nice people. One thing I must say for Francis Joseph. He was the greatest builder of towns in modern history. History will admit it if we do not.

Sunday, April 17, 1921. Wrote on Austria; then lunched with Mr. Davidson, of the *Chronicle,* and Mr. Dicker, of the *Chicago Daily News.* They have been about in this part of the world all the winter and were interesting. We are all agreed that the opening-up of all frontiers of the old Dual Monarchy is the only economic salvation for Austria and the Succession States. We walked down to St. Margaret's Island and had tea there.

5   Repington refers to Emperor-King Francis Joseph. [Ed.]

Athelstan-Johnson dined with me in the evening and we had a good chat and wrangle over Central European affairs. A capable man with strong and decided views.

Ex-Kaiser Karl is still King of Hungary and has never abdicated in this capacity. The Government is still the "Royal Hungarian Government" and uses the Royal Crown on its official paper which I have examined in order to make sure. The Governor Admiral Horthy[6] is a kind of Protector. In fact he is Regent. All who swore allegiance to Karl and the sacred crown of St. Stephen still adhere to him. If they did not – and some were away – they consider themselves free agents. The mass of the people are Monarchists, but do not want the King back just yet. Quite a number would like to elect a King. Joseph is much liked, but they say that there are other reasons why not many like to plunge in that direction. Albrecht is talked as a substitute. He is very rich, whereas poor Karl is said to be very broke. Still I would back Karl from belief the *"moriamur pro rege nostro"* 1741 sentiment of a loyal peasant people, and because one cannot get over the fact that he has been crowned. Why are my friends in Vienna, Mensdorff apart, backing Joseph? Why does not Austria like or wish for Karl? Is it from jealousy of Hungary? Perhaps it is all of scant practical import because all feel that the matter is not urgent. There is a King to be had if the people want one, but Karl is not a great figure, and he has done little to make Austria stand up for him, while in Hungary many think that there is a period like our Commonwealth to be got over before a Restoration. There is so much else to be done first! All the same the Hungarians seem to be so deeply incensed against Roumania, which now bullies two million Magyars in Transylvania, that they will join any combination against her which promises success, and they might want a King then.

I don't much care for all the reports here against Roumania. She is said to be rotten, everybody bribed, no governing personnel fit to run her new territory, railway hopeless for military and commercial uses, etc., and alto-

<hr>

6   See details in Adm. Nicholas Horthy: Memoirs, ISBN 0-9665734-3-9.

gether a very sorry story of graft, incompetence, and peculation. Not good when Germany must have such a grudge against her and the Hungarians are always ready for any mischief on her borders.

It is also very enlightening to study here the new map of Hungary and to size up her losses under the Trianon Treaty. Especially to note that all the headwaters of her rivers are cut off from her to the north and east and the foresters in the north unable now to float down their logs to Budapest. One peasant of Tlemcen was asked how he got on under the Czechs. He said that when the Vag ran to Prague upstream instead of to Budapest, it might be all right. Population, mines, forests, salt, iron, the grain of the Banat, and much more all taken away. A peace of justice? How can the Magyars think it?

Monday, April 18, 1921. The *Corriere* correspondent here came to talk. Lunched with Captain Thomas Domaille in charge here of the Danube Navigation Company, run by Furness's house in London, chiefly by Sir F. Lewis, and by Cox's Bank through Eric Hambro. The Fleet consists of the D.D.O.G. (Austrian) and M.F.T.R. (Hungarian) fleets on the river, of which fifty per cent were annexed by Roumania and Serbia, who say that Paris can decide what they like about the ships, but they are not going to give them back. The fifty per cent remaining, now the Company's, include fifty-six steamers, sixty-eight tugs, seven hundred barges, and eleven motor barges with a total personnel of some six thousand people. D. is keen about taking over and improving the Mannheim-Regensburg Canal. This is little used now, and only three feet deep, but a million would make it fit to take the D.N. Company's barges, and they could then ascend the Rhine and pass by the Canal to the Danube and deliver a ton of steel at Budapest at twenty-seven shillings a ton. The other way costs forty-five shillings a ton up from Galatz alone. It is energetic of England to have got hold of the Company, but I doubt that it more than barely pays its way yet. The Regensburg scheme offers great possibilities. A great fault in the International control of the Danube is that one set of men look after the actual navigation, and another after dams and agriculture. It is a fault because everything done to the banks, etc., affects navigation, rate of current, fall of water, and so on. The Danube is a five-knot stream; the Rhine, they affirm, only one to one and one-half knots.[7] So it is much easier to ascend or tug up the Rhine than the Danube. I doubt whether the Danube Commission in Paris is much good. The riparian States play tricks as they please.

Spent the afternoon in studying agricultural facts statistics. Much hampered by want of figures since Peace; all statistics are for the old Hungary. The Alföld, the great Hungarian basin or lowlands, has lost all timber by the recent partition; i.e., about six and a million hectares out of seven and a half; much of its livestock and its fodder, twenty-four per cent of its horned cattle, thirty per cent of its sheep, and forty per cent of horses, half of its coal supplies, and 128,000,000 out 144,000,000 of tons of its iron ore. All its salt supplies gone, all its gold, silver, lead, copper, zinc, quicksilver, antimony, cobalt, nickel, and aluminum mines, and natural gas. The splitting-up of a hydrographically united economic whole is especially fatal to Hungary. The problem of water power will now be difficult of solution, irrigation most precarious. The sources of energy and reservoirs should be, and now are not, in the same hands as the territory to be watered. The new arrangement is handing over the Assuan Dam to the dervishes. The Vág (Waag), Tisza, and Maros can only carry their timber the timberless Lowlands, and are not allowed to do so now. The tobacco factories and sugar refineries in the mountains will also languish, as their raw materials come from Lowlands. The appeal of the Hungarian Geographic Society to the world is, to my mind, one of the strong arguments against the recent so-called settlement. But what settlement, here or elsewhere, was ever made but by force?

The chief agricultural products of Hungary are wheat, rye, oats, and spring barley. Potatoes are widely grown, and clover and lucerne among the fodder plants. Wheat is the chief product of the Alföld. Maize is a big crop. So is sugar beet. That remarkable publication, the *Magyarország Gazdasági Térképekben*, or *Hungary in Economics Maps* (1920), shows in a series of maps in the most striking manner the loss to Hungary by the settlement in every class of crop and industry. It is painful reading. I wonder if the victors at Paris will allocate those forty million saplings to the afforestation of the barren tracts that the Hungarians used to do. What will happen to the Forestry School[8] at Selmeczbánya? I wonder how the extensive irrigation sys-

7   Quite incorrect. The Rhine stream between Mainz and Coblenz is at eight knots an hour.

tem will get on when it has been broken into by the new boundaries. But the more one looks round one in this part of the world, the more one wonders and at last one ceases to wonder, for one's capacity for wonder becomes exhausted. Don't know whether the world has been made safe for democracy, but am sure that democracy has shown itself unsafe for the Austro-Hungarian world.

I have seen figures which show that large estates under the intensive farming system, compared with the small estates, often produce double the crops. Deep steam ploughing in the autumn, frequent hoeing, good manuring, a proper rotation of crops, adequate capital (sometimes), and efficient management are the main causes. Many of these large estates will soon pass into the hands of the small farmers under the Agricultural Reform Act, so it is unsafe to speculate on the results.

Nemesis is evidently reaching the selfish Succession States too. I hear on all sides that they are losing by their protectionist tariffs.

Two good stories at dinner to-night. One, the receipt of a letter by the Hungarian Government from the League of Nations requesting them to establish a sanitary cordon on the Polish frontier to prevent the spread of typhus. The fact that there is no such frontier is not yet known at Geneva. The other, an F.O.[9] letter refusing to send petrol to Budapest, but saying that a lorry would be sent out via Trieste and that it could travel backwards and forwards from Budapest to Bucharest for supplies which, they believed, were available there. A rough calculation showed that the journey to Bucharest and back was one thousand miles or nearly as far as from Budapest to London. I wished that Henry Labouchere had been alive and in diplomacy here to answer that letter. He would have made the F.O. squirm.

8   College of Mining and Forestry. Today it is the University of Sopron. – Ed.

9   British Foreign Office.– Ed.

Tuesday, April 19, 1921. Went off to the Parliament hear Count Stefan Bethlen announce the new Government's policy. A huge and uncommonly late Gothic pile, the central part with a dome too narrow at the base, and most well-arranged inside. Had a front seat in the diplomatic box. Three tiers of public galleries, quite full except behind the Presidential Chair where there is only one tier all round the house. I should say some two thousand of the public could find places. The horseshoe system of talking-shop with tribune and president's desk. The Ministers sat in the front row of the horseshoe facing the tribune. Good light and air. Bethlen was speaking when I arrived and he spoke for about an hour. His wife, an attractive lady, in a gallery on my left. B. rather like Lord Lansdowne twenty years ago. He spoke clearly, his notes in his left hand, and using the other for gestures mainly up and down as if he were hammering in nails. A strong Calvinist, without the agile flexibility of Teleki, and wanting in the sense of humour. Captain Rapaics, the High Commission liaison officer, translated for me when there were important points in the speech. The chief things seemed to be that the whole Parliament was in unison, that it would take three years to carry out legislation already proposed, that the question of a King was not yet safe to discuss, and so forth, ending up with a quotation from Lord Salisbury about strong and weak nations.

I saw the P.M. in his private room after his speech, and afterwards saw Count Andrássy, Count Albert Apponyi, Mr. Szabo[10], the head of the Small Holders' Party, prince Windischgrätz, Count Pallavicini, Mr. de Bárczy, and several others, and had good talks with them all. I liked the look of the members. They resemble what our House of Commons used to be twenty-five years ago. I asked them how it was they managed to get such a nice lot of members out of universal suffrage, and they said that formerly Budapest had sent its carpet-baggers round to be elected, but that Bela Kun's Bolshevist rule had so disgusted the people that they had all elected their own natural chiefs locally. I liked Bethlen. He is going to give me a paper for publication with his views. We had a brief talk of affairs. Szabo

10   Istvan Nagyatadi-Szabo. – Ed.

farms thirty-five acres. He does not talk any language but Hungarian, though I believe he reads French. We had a little talk through de Barczy, who has the curious post of sort of permanent secretary to Prime Ministers, and is a sort of Chief Whip as well. A young man, alert, and capable. Szabo is a good peasant type, squarely built, medium height. Wearing high boots to the knee, crinkly at the top. He controls the largest party in the house, namely, the Small Holders' Party, which has some eighty-six members. We had some talk of the agricultural and irrigational consequences of the Peace Treaty. He is Minister of Agriculture. He is popular, though Pallavicini grumbles that he is a trifle Bolshie.

Count Julius Andrassy is getting on in years now, but these Magyars wear well, and both he and Count Albert Apponyi, who is seventy-five, are very spare, hale, and hearty. Andrassy is an interesting figure. He told me how he had always loved and admired England, and how deeply disappointed he and others had been that England had deserted her old principles and had put her name to such an act of injustice as the Trianon Treaty. Hungary had never hated England all through the war; since the Peace her sentiments had changed, but it was not the England that Hungary used to know that had made the Peace. Windischgrätz told me that it was his grandfather who had made the famous remark that "no one counts below the rank of a baron." It seems to be the other way about now.

Bethlen was well received by all the House. They seem a very united Parliament. I am found fault with when I call them Conservative. I can believe that they often get too excited and interruptious. The House was built for a larger body than the present members. They used to be 413 and now are little over 200. The number of empty benches is a perpetual reminder of Hungary's loss. The House of Magnates still exists to the north of the Parliament House, but is not in being. Feeling is more or less liberal when not quite democratic, I am told, and the continuance of a House of Lords is regarded as an anachronism. But a Second House or Senate is to be created, probably on a basis of county representation. Many are for proportional representation in order to secure the middle classes adequate voice in affairs. The Houses suspended the sitting for about a quarter of an hour when Bethlen sat down, and then I had a talk with him on the general results of the Treaty, but he was soon called back to the House. I did not see Kovács who is said to be the brain of the Farmers' Party. All these figures might easily be duplicated by members of our House of Commons. They all talk

English except the peasants. The Magyars have marched with the times, but it is odd to find a Windischgrätz an advanced radical! Generally speaking, the oldest noble families are losing ground somewhat, and it is the Bethlens and the Telekis who are coming to the front. A critical, interested, and very attentive House. Ditto the public in the galleries. Lunched with the Gortons; the Greek Minister and his English wife; the Roumanian Military Attaché and First Secretary; Mr. Athelstan-Johnson; Mr. Robinson, the English Consul here; the American Military Attaché and his wife, and a Spanish diplomatist. A nice garden on a terrace at the back of the house looking over the river.

I was amused to hear that the Roumanian Minister had not got a house yet, and that the Military Attaché had only a room some 2x2 metres for a bedroom and office. They had purchased a house, but the tenant refused to turn out, and it is most difficult to put one out under the present laws. The Magyars detest the Roumanians on account of their looting during the occupation following the Béla Kun régime. They rejoiced at their arrival, but the Roumanians really came in order to treat Hungary as they had been treated by Germany. They are accused of having stolen everything moveable—plate, pictures, carpets, linen, furniture, even down to the cloth off billiard tables. They took the best thoroughbreds and let them die in the train for want of food. They took twelve hundred locomotives and left the Hungarians only four hundred. In my hotel Bela Kun had done five million crowns' worth of damage. The Roumanians did seven millions worth. They took literally everything, and the rooms are still without telephones as a result of their brigandage. This, of course, is all the Hungarian account of what happened. The other side of the story must be heard in Roumania.

The Roumanian Military Attaché, by name Margaretezen, or some such, tells me that he is followed by three agents and cannot go anywhere without his movements being reported. He gives the Magyars a bigger force than most people, and two hundred and fifty guns. He thinks that the country is stiff with rifles, and declares that German equipments keep on flowing in. He does not believe that when the Reparations people come here they will discover much, for the watch-posts stop travellers everywhere and communicate with their friends when anything has to be concealed. The American thinks that this is all exaggerated, but admits 600,000 men capable of being mobilised if arms, guns, and equipment are here for them. I saw Hohler after lunch. A pretty sick man still and was only in an armchair for an hour or two before returning to bed. He is fully of opinion that great injustice has been done to the Magyars under the Treaty, and we had a good talk over it all. He gave me a note to the Finance Minister Hegedüs. A capable representative, and I wish I could have found him fit and well.

Went on later to the F.O. and saw Count Banffy, the new Foreign Minister, who was very courteous and interesting. I told him that I found a difficulty in describing what the Government here was, for there was nothing quite like it anywhere else. Whitaker's description of it as a Republic seemed incorrect when they called themselves a Royal Hungarian Government, but I was not sure whether to describe it as a Monarchy in suspense, or what. Banffy said that the meaning of the Crown of St. Stephen to the Magyars could not be understood except by Magyars. Every single Magyar was a member of this Crown, and regarded it as the sanction of his personal rights and liberty. The Golden Bull was only a few years after Runnymede, and the development of Hungarian life and political thought, except for the one hundred and fifty years of Turkish domination, had followed English lines. English constitutional history was well known here and our political precedents were frequently quoted in Parliament when they had none of their own.

It was true that Károlyi had declared a Republic in 1918, but in March, 1919, the Bolshevist reign of Béla Kun had begun, and to this succeeded a Governor, now Admiral Horthy, who was much what Cromwell was in England in his day. The feeling of the whole country was undoubtedly monarchical, but it was realised that considerations relating to foreign policy made it highly inconvenient to raise the question now. Why had not Karl understood this? I asked. He said that the facts were not yet all fully known, but that the whole history of this affair would eventually be set down. No one knew of his coming. Perhaps he had expected support in various matters. In any case B. said, that every Hungarian had done his duty and that the Government had given Europe proofs of its good-will and of its desire not to disturb the Peace.

He said that if Benès opened his campaign for freeing the customs within the old Empire, Hungary would be with him, but that Hungary's great difficulty was the millions of Magyars annexed to the neighbouring countries, and the incessant complaints of ill-usage which they brought back with them. Scarcely a day passed without the return of refugees with these stories, and the result was that opinion in Hungary was so incensed that it would be difficult to make Parliament accept any economic agreement that did not take into full account the interests of these unfortunate Magyar minorities. Who looked after them now? – I asked, and why was it left to Scottish and American Unitarians to represent the hardships of these people? The Allies had forced the Treaty on Hungary, and it seemed to me their duty to control the execution of it. Yes, said B., but after the ratification he presumed it would be the League of Nations. This question of the four million Hungarians in the neighbouring States evidently gave him great concern and will affect his foreign policy very much. I told him that I thought Benès was ready for accommodation. Without it I doubt that Bánffy can go far. The Magyars are a chivalrous, warm-hearted people who will always support their unfortunate fellow-countrymen.

We had a talk about the other effects of the Treaty and B. confirmed all my opinions of it. I also gather that. Sir George Clerk's intervention here was most happy when all was in disarray. Clerk told them they were not divided on any essential matters and that they should have a coalition Government and get on at once. They seem to have followed the advice exactly, and it all worked out, though not fully till the Socialists were put out and the present lot came in.

I talked for an hour with Bánffy on these and other matters, and went on to see Count Albert Apponyi with whom I stayed till nearly eight discussing the general situation. He tells me that he is an independent and has not joined any party. He is Karlist. He watches events. He says that the main result of the war has been to change completely the mentality and outlook of all people. The masses, who fought the war, and expended so much blood, courage, and fortitude, now look for compensation to a larger share in the Government, and Apponyi is prepared to support them. They have lost faith in the old leading circles who brought about all their sorrows. He was biting about the ignorance of the Peacemakers of all the conditions of Eastern Europe. They had to be shown the positions of the largest towns. He, with Teleki, Bethlen, Hegedüs, etc., were in Paris. He had found that they were given no opportunity of explaining their views, so had written to the Big Four, and finally was allowed to explain the situation on the express understanding that there should be no discussion. He spoke in French and then in English. Lloyd George seemed struck by his remark that particular blocks of Magyars had been violently and unnecessarily detached from Hungary, although they were physically in contact with her. L. G. had passed a note to Clemenceau and afterwards had asked for further explanation and had brought out his ethnographical map. He had heard from an English friend that L. G. had trounced his staff for the treatment of the Hungarians, but unfortunately nothing had been changed. The injustice remained. A. thought that the Treaty could not stand, but they had intention of doing anything to upset Europe. It is pathetic how all these Magyars confide in the legendary justice England and in her power to put matters right. I tell them all that the mass of our people were too much preoccupied with affairs more vital to them to worry about little Hungary, and that I felt sure that few outside the official classes knew of the measure meted out to her and what all implied.

Wednesday, April 20, 1921. Hegedüs, the Minister Finance, is the financial magician of Hungary and either be described hereafter as a genius or a lunatic, I do know which. I went to see him this morning on introduction. I found a deputation with him demanding higher salaries. He told them that he had doubled their purchasing power by raising the crown from 2200 to 1000 for the pound sterling and that this was his system and would do no more. A man of devouring energy, rapid thought, and torrential speech. He has, in fact, raised crown as he says, and hopes to raise it to 500. This is our English comparison; actually these foreigners' standard value is usually the Swiss franc, and the crown is compared with the number of centimes that it is worth in the Swiss money, but it is all one. He has stopped the printing paper notes, and contemplates the destruction of masses of them still in circulation. He is dead against foreign loans. He is the apostle of self-help. How does he work?

He regards every taxpayer as a congenital liar and so shuns valuations and income-tax returns. He thinks direct taxes useless because so much is paid in kind for work done, and the values cannot then be appraised. He does not like inquisitions and knows that Hungary is not accustomed to them. He goes to work a different way. He increases the indirect taxes, and incidentally mentioned a new tax on cigarettes which would bring in several millions. He taxes the war profiteer by taxing him double amounts on all increases since 1914. He takes for the Government a first mortgage of twenty per cent on all houses. Here the value has to be stated, but if the value of a house is understated he may buy it, and sell it again. He calls upon all companies of whatever kind to increase their share capital by fifteen per cent. He takes these new shares and sells them back to the companies if they want them, and if not, then in the open market, or keeps them and his mortgages as securities to use for any purpose. This avoids all question of prying into capital and profits. He takes twenty per cent of all moneys on deposit in the banks. He proposes to take two, three, or four years' annual rent from all estates except the large ones as a capital levy on them, and if he cannot discover the amount of the rent he judges by the nearest farm from which figures are available. From large estates he takes twenty per cent of the land and sells it to peasants and small farmers, thus making an agrarian law of his own; and from all these sources he reduces his deficit, which he found when he came in, of twelve milliards[11] by seven milliards, and proposes to cover the remaining five milliards deficit by an internal loan. He has a foreign debt which he places at 130 milliards, and thinks that as he is the debtor of France and England these countries will give him time, say ten years, as France has already undertaken to do, to pay the debt. Before that time he hopes to have re-established Hungary's financial stability and to have brought back the crown nearly to the pre-war parity. The payment of foreign debt will not then cost the country what it would cost to pay it now.

He thought the Treaty, when he first read it, not bad but good, because it was so bad that it could not endure. Had it been better it would have been worse. He has passed twelve out of some twenty-one Bills which complete his programme, and if he gets through his capital levy and agrarian schemes he thinks that the whole programme will be completed. It is coming up to-day. Much depends on what he is asked to do about reparations. He hopes that his efforts to restore Hungary's credit without appeals for help may be taken into consideration, and that a fair amount of Hungary's debt may allocated to the Succession States which have annexed the territories and populations. He is against what he calls the morphinisation of a country by foreign loans. He tries to copy English finance, and by copying England and America in stopping the printing of notes he hopes to advance in time to their standards in exchange. He is most ardently in favour of free

---

11   billions

trade in the Succession States and says that England ought to help as she can sell nothing to them at the present rates of exchange. He is furious with Roumania for allowing no letters to go from Hungary to Magyars now in Transylvania, and says that his relatives and friends are constantly returning, as they find themselves unable to endure Roumanian rule from its cruelties, exactions, and corruption. He says that the Hungarians are the only race in Europe who are neither Slavs, Germans, nor Latins, and would hope that we should extend our protection to them. He amused me by saying that the first thing he looked at in the morning was not the state of the exchange, but the meteorological reports. The recent slight rain, he said, meant milliards to him. We had forty-two days of drought before it came.

Whatever the result of all these schemes may be, it must certainly be admitted that Hungary is facing her difficulties bravely and helping herself. It is only to be hoped that the reparation people when they come here will not be such a great expense to this little country as they have been elsewhere, or try to exact payments from a people who are trying to avoid appeals to Europe. The best reparation is to allow Hungary to recover economically and then trade.

Alfred Stead came in late and told me much about his efforts to galvanise British trade into life again. He too is doing something and is one of the few Englishmen really working here. He gave me his views about the future of the Danube. Dined with the Greek Minister and his wife.

An interesting visit and am sorry that it is so short, as there is much more that I should like to have seen and done here. The real obstacle to progress in this part of the world is the racial rivalry of all these people, who are all embittered by the war, while the vanquished are still more embittered by the Peace and by the loss of so many of their people by the transfers of territory. All the same I find that Austria and Hungary are ready in principle for free trade and I think it was a pity that free trade within the old Empire was not enforced at the Peace. I expect that I shall find more objections to sensible economics in Roumania, Jugo-Slavia, and perhaps Bulgaria than I find in Prague, Vienna, and Budapest. I think that we should reconsider our attitude to Hungary. It seems to me that Hungary, Jugo-Slavia, and the Czechs are the strong people in these parts, and I doubt from all accounts whether Roumania will prove any serious barrier against Bolshevism if a barrier be needed. Hungary, I think, will, and all except Jugo-Slavia are horribly afraid of her. Her martial reputation has survived defeat. Altogether Central Europe is full of fascinating problems, but one must keep a more or less open mind till one has visited Bucharest, Sofia, and Belgrade. Then one can conclude.

Thursday, April 21,1921, As there was no direct train to Vienna to-day, I made a virtue of necessity, started dawn, and made a long detour through Hungary round Lake Balaton and so to Vienna by 7 P.M. Very glad have seen this country and to have gained this bird's view of Hungary's wealth. The crops looking better the few days of light rain. A general air of content. The black soil looks amazingly rich. Flocks of sheep, large droves of pigs, plenty of horses and cattle, extensive vineyards, much beekeeping, and any amount of farmyard fowls. The houses well-built and looked comfortable. Usually single-storied, brick and tile. Balaton of length and fair breadth. Hardly any coal on the railway: the stations had piles of wood. Went to the Imperial again, and managed to get dressed in time to dine with Sir William Goode at the Bristol, where I found a party of a dozen men, largely Americans, including General Churchill, U.S.A., Walker D. Hines, just back from looking into the division of enemy Danubian shipping, American Chargé d'Affaires, and a few Austrians, like Police President Schober and the clever doctor who has done so much for the Vienna children.